1972

STUDIES IN THE
FRENCH RENAISSANCE

TITLE-PAGE OF JEAN DU RUEIL'S *DE NATURA STIRPIUM*

STUDIES IN THE FRENCH RENAISSANCE

BY

ARTHUR TILLEY, M.A.
FELLOW OF KING'S COLLEGE, CAMBRIDGE

BARNES & NOBLE, Inc.
NEW YORK
PUBLISHERS & BOOKSELLERS SINCE 1873

First published, 1922.
Reprinted, 1968 by Barnes & Noble, Inc.
By permission of the
Cambridge University Press

L. C. Catalog Card Number: 68-20698

Printed in the United States of America

PREFACE

ALL except two of the papers contained in this volume have appeared before in some form or another. But all have been revised, added to, and in some cases largely rewritten. The result is that nearly half the volume consists of new matter.

The first paper, "The University of Caen," was originally printed in a volume entitled *Fasciculus Joanni Willis Clark dicatus*, in which many friends of the late J. W. Clark united to express their sense of his lifelong devotion to the cause of knowledge and the service of the University. My own contribution seemed a fitting tribute from an *alumnus* of Henry VI's twin foundations of Eton and King's College, and I was pleased to find that one of the Rectors of the University of Caen was in many respects a prototype of our friend. He was not only Registrary of his University, but he was distinguished for his devotion to its interests; he gave freely of his books to its library; and he wrote a play for the students, in which he took the chief part.

The paper on "The Prose Romances of Chivalry" appeared in French in the *Revue du seizième Siècle* for 1919; besides translating it I have carefully revised it. "Rabelais and Geographical Discovery" was contributed to the *Modern Language Review* from 1906 to 1910. "Rabelais and Henri II" is practically new, only six pages having appeared before—in French, in the *Revue du seizième Siècle* (1907 and 1916). The first part of "Rabelais and the Fifth Book," which relates to the *Ile Sonante*, was published in the *Modern Language Review* for 1906–7; in the second part I have examined the rest of the book. It is for others to determine how far I have solved the long-disputed question of Rabelais's authorship.

The account of "Humanism under Francis I" is an expanded and practically rewritten version of an article in the *English Historical Review* (1900). Even now it does not pretend to be more than a sketch of a small part of a very large subject—the history of French Humanism—which still awaits its historian. Such a history was once contemplated by M. Pierre de Nolhac, but was abandoned by him under the pressure of other work. It was also contemplated by René Sturel, the author of *Jacques Amyot, traducteur des Vies parallèles de Plutarque* (1909), and he might have carried it to a successful conclusion had he not, in the words of M. de Nolhac, "given his life for his country, after honouring her by his writings." He was mortally wounded in the first month of the war and died soon afterwards in a German ambulance. "With him vanished great hopes." Another able worker in the same field is M. Louis Delaruelle, the historian of Budé, and it is with pleasure that I note his return to the subject with an article on the study of Greek at Paris (1514–30), which has recently appeared in the *Revue du seizième Siècle*. It came too late for me to profit by it, except that I have adopted the French form of the name of Ruellius which he found in the archives.

The paper on "Galliot Du Pré," which originally appeared in *The Library*, has been revised and recast, and the list of books published by him has been augmented by from thirty to forty titles. "Dorat and the Pléiade" is mainly concerned with Dorat's work as a scholar and textual critic. M. de Nolhac's fine volume on *Ronsard et l'Humanisme*, in two chapters of which he deals with the same subject, also came to my notice too late for me to do more than refer to it in a supplementary note. Of the next two papers, both of which are entirely new, the first is concerned with Rabelais and Montaigne, and the second with Montaigne alone. The last paper of all was published in the *English Historical Review* as far back as 1899. I have revised it in the light of later research, without however making any important changes in it.

I must express my thanks to the subscribers to the volume published in honour of J. W. Clark, to the *Société des études rabelaisiennes*, to the Syndics of the Cambridge University Press, to Messrs Longmans and Co., and to Sir J. Y. MacAlister, the proprietor of *The Library*, for their courtesy in permitting me to republish the papers above referred to.

A. T.

June 24, 1922.

CONTENTS

LIST OF PLATES

The following is a transcription of the manuscript
addition as finally corrected by Montaigne. Note the
differences in the ink and the writing.

Les paisans simples sont honestes gens, et honestes gens les
philosophes ou selon nostre temps des natures fortes et cleres
enrichies d'une large instruction de sciances utilles. Les
mestis qui ont desdeigné le premier siege de l'ignorance des
lettres et n'ont peu iouindre lautre (le cul entre deux selles)
desquels ie suis, et tant d'autres, sont dangereux, ineptes, im-
portuns: ceus icy troblēt le monde. Pourtant de ma part ie
me recule tant que ie puis dans le premier & naturel siege,
dou ie me suis pour neant essaie de partir. La poësie populere
et purement naturelle a des naïfvetez et graces par ou elle se
compare a la principale beaute de la poësie parfaicte selon
l'art: comme il se uoit es uillanelles de gascouigne, et aux
chançons qu'on nous raporte des nations qui n'ont conois-
sance d'aucune sciance ny mesmes d'escriture. La poësie
mediocre qui s'arrete entre deus est dedeignee, sans honur et
sans pris.

The editor of the *Édition Municipale* has made use
of the text of 1595 to restore the letters ploughed
away by the binder.

I

THE UNIVERSITY OF CAEN AND THE RENAISSANCE

THE twin colleges of Eton and King's were not Henry VI's first experiment as a Founder. Nine years earlier, when he was still a child, his uncle, John Duke of Bedford, had founded in his name the University of Caen. In the Charter, granted at Rouen, January 31, 1431 (N.S.), he is made to say that "there being no Faculty (*studium*) of Civil Law in any of his French provinces, he thereby established and founded a *studium generale* for Canon and Civil Law in his town of Caen, a town convenient, peaceful, and secure, adorned with famous monasteries, colleges, convents, and other ecclesiastical foundations, situated on a fertile soil, and near the sea, and so of convenient access for both students and merchants from nearly every quarter of the earth[1]." The foundation of the new University was keenly resented by the University of Paris, but the English government paid no heed to its remonstrances. On the contrary, they added new faculties, Arts and Theology in 1437, Medicine in 1438. On May 29, 1439, the foundation was confirmed by a Bull of Eugenius IV, in which the Bishop of Bayeux was designated as Chancellor. Just before this, on May 26, the King had issued from his palace of Kensington letters-patent containing the statutes for his new University, and on October 20 of the same year it was solemnly inaugurated with an imposing ceremonial in the Church of Saint-Pierre. In the following January a Rector was appointed in the person of Michael Tregury, a former

[1] A. de Bourmont, *La fondation de l'Université de Caen* in *Bulletin de la Société des Antiquaires de Normandie*, XII (1884), 293 ff. *Pièces justificatives*, I. See also for the history of the University, L'Abbé de La Rue, *Essais historiques sur la ville de Caen*, 2 vols., Caen, 1820; H. Rashdall, *The Universities of Europe in the Middle Ages*, II. pt i. 194–198, Oxford, 1895; H. Prentout, *Renovatio ac Reformatio in Universitate Cadomensi*, Caen, 1901.

Fellow of Exeter (1422–1427) and a future Archbishop of Dublin (1449–1471). He held office till October—the regular term of office was for six months—when he was succeeded by Jean Lenfant, a man of some note, and one of the chief supporters of the English rule in Normandy.

The most famous of these early Rectors was Thomas Basin, Dean of the Faculty of Canon Law, who at the time of the siege of Caen by the French (June 1450) held the rich and important bishopric of Lisieux. It was mainly through his influence that the town capitulated on favourable terms. He rallied to Charles VII, who placed great confidence in him, but, having incurred the displeasure of the Dauphin, the future Louis XI, he had to submit to many indignities during his reign and was finally compelled to resign his see. His chief work is a Latin history of the reigns of Charles VII and Louis XI[1], which contains much valuable first-hand information, but which, owing to the writer's natural bias against Louis XI, must be used with caution. Basin also assisted in the rehabilitation of Joan of Arc and at the request of Charles VII wrote a memoir on her behalf.

Among the other more important officials of the University was the *scriba* or secretary, who performed many of the duties of the Cambridge Registrary. He also had charge of the catalogue of the University library, and assisted the Rector in his inspection of the books. The minor officials included six bedels, one for each of the five Faculties, and one for the special service of the Rector, two booksellers (*librarii*), two parchmenters, two illuminators, two bookbinders, a bell-ringer (*pulsator*), and seven messengers, who carried on the postal service in the seven dioceses into which Normandy was divided.

The new University had no local habitation of its own, but the Founder assigned to the two original Faculties of Civil and Canon Law part of a house in the street which is still called the Rue des Cordeliers, and later the other three Faculties were installed in the remaining part. The house was the property of the Duke of Orleans, whose widow, mother

---

[1] Edited by Quicherat for the *Société de l'histoire de France*.

of the future Louis XII, gave it to the University in 1477[1], when it became known as *Les Grandes Écoles*. The University itself, as distinguished from the Faculties, had to be content with the hospitality of the neighbouring Franciscan convent, where its Congregations were generally held and where its archives were deposited.

The students were obliged to lodge in the University quarter. The rent of their lodgings was assessed, not by taxors, as at Cambridge and in most Universities, but by a Syndicate composed of the Rector, a representative of each Faculty, the Vicomte de Caen, and two or three "notables" of the town. This was also the practice at Orleans. As in other Universities there were Colleges with bursaries or scholarships for poor students, but only three of these can be said to have flourished. The oldest and least important was the College of Le Cloutier, founded in 1452 by Roger Le Cloutier for a Principal and two scholars. The College of Arts was founded by that Faculty in 1460, and installed in a house which the Faculty had purchased immediately opposite the *Grandes Écoles*. The College of Du Bois in the Rue Saint-Sauveur was founded in 1491 by Jean de Gouvis. Fifty years earlier (1442) Pierre Cauchon, Bishop of Beauvais, of infamous memory, had left a sum of money for the support of two scholars at Caen or elsewhere. But the will had been disputed by his heirs, and it was not till 1491 that Gouvis, who was one of Cauchon's executors, definitely founded the College, with provision for a Principal and six scholars. It seems probable, as Bourmont suggests, that Cauchon's legacy was in the nature of an expiation, and that the name of the College perpetuated that of Nicolas Du Bois, Dean of Rouen and Master of a *pédagogie*, whose house Gouvis bought for the local habitation of his scholars. It was natural that he should have shrunk from associating his College with the Bishop who had been the chief instrument in the fate of Joan of Arc, and against whom the populace had manifested their hatred by disinterring his remains and flinging them into the sewers.

The College of Du Mont, when the Jesuits captured it in

---

[1] H. Prentout, *La vie de l'Étudiant à Caen au XVI*[e] *siècle*, Caen, 1905.

1609, had only existed as a College for fifteen years. Huet, the learned Bishop of Avranches, claims, indeed, in his *Antiquités de Caen*, that it was of much older foundation, but it has been clearly shown that its earlier condition was only that of a *pédagogie*, which owed its name to its being rented from the abbot and monks of Mont-Saint-Michel[1].

The subjects of study at Caen were the same as in other mediaeval Universities. Aristotle as elsewhere occupied the chief place. Beside the famous *Summulae* of Petrus Hispanus we find in use those of Albertus Magnus and Buridan, that Paris professor of philosophy, whose name has been preserved, not by his learned treatises, but by the strange tradition, which inspired the lines in Villon's *Ballade*:

> Semblablement, ou est la royne
> Qui commanda que Buridan
> Fust jette en ung sac en Seine?

and which suggested the name of Dumas's hero in *La Tour de Nesle*. As in other Universities too, Disputations were the constant occupation of the student and the only method of examination. In the Faculty of Arts, for instance, the whole of Lent was consecrated to these exercises.

This mediaeval system of education retreated but slowly before the incoming tide of the Renaissance. We know what a stubborn resistance the University of Paris offered to the new studies, and that it was not till 1530, when the Royal Professors were appointed, that the first breach can be said to have been made in her defences. Caen, as was natural, was even slower than Paris to leave the old ways. The reform imposed upon the University by the *Parlement* of Rouen in 1521 only affected the superior Faculties, and was concerned rather with the conduct and manners of the students than with their education[2]. But if the University as a whole was unfavourable to the new studies they met with a readier reception in the Colleges. Thanks to Léopold Delisle's admirable record of the books printed and published at Caen from 1480

---

[1] See La Rue, I. 235 ff.
[2] H. Prentout, *Une réforme parlementaire à l'Université de Caen* in *Bull. Soc. Ant. Norm.* XXII. pp. 241 ff., Caen, 1902.

to 1550[1] we can in some measure trace the progress of the new movement. For, as Delisle points out, a noticeable feature of the printing and bookselling trade at Caen during the first half of the sixteenth century is its close connexion with the University. A very large proportion of the books are school-books.

It was at once a school-book and a classical book which inaugurated the printing press at Caen,—an edition of the *Epistles* of Horace with blank spaces for manuscript notes between the lines[2]. Of the printers, Jacques Durandas and Gilles Quijoue, nothing more is known, and no other book was printed at Caen till the year 1509. Meanwhile the Caen publishers, Pierre Regnault (1492–1519) and Robert Macé (1498–1506), provided their clients with books printed at Rouen or Paris. The only other classical work which appeared before the close of the fifteenth century was an edition of Ovid's *Metamorphoses* (1496), with a commentary revised by Jean Gouvain, a doctor in theology of the University[3]. Even during the first two decades of the sixteenth century the number of classical works issued at Caen was very small, consisting of Ovid's *Liber de remedio amoris*, another edition of Horace's *Epistles*, Terence, two editions of Virgil's *Eclogues*, and one of his complete works. Of the two editions of the *Eclogues* one was printed at Caen by Laurent Hostingue, who had set up a press there in 1508 at the instigation of the publisher Michel Angier. To these must be added Boethius's *De consolatione*, five editions of which were published at Caen during the first decade of the nineteenth century, two being printed there.

It must not be supposed that the record of books published at Caen includes all the classical texts that were read in the

---

[1] *Bull. Soc. Ant. Norm.* XXIII and XXIV; and see *Essai sur l'imprimerie et la librairie de Caen*, Caen, 1891.

[2] There are three known copies, one in the Bibliothèque Nationale, Paris, one in the collection bequeathed to the town of Paris by the brothers Dutuit, and one in the Rylands library at Manchester. Dr J. H. Clapham, Fellow of King's College, who kindly examined the latter copy for me, tells me that it has interlineatory notes in faint handwriting on the first 36 leaves but none on the remaining 40.

[3] For the preface see Delisle, *op. cit.* II. 4.

University. Many were doubtless imported from Rouen and Paris. Besides the texts themselves we find the Caen publishers producing other humanist school-books, such as grammars, dictionaries, phrase-books, and other aids to composition, a large proportion of them being edited by professors of the University. We have an abridged edition of Despauterius under the title of *Contextus grammaticae artis*, and two smaller treatises, *Ars versificatoris* and *De introductione artis grammatice*, by his blind countryman Petrus de Ponte of Bruges (*c.* 1475–after 1539), who lectured at Paris from about 1505, and who in one of his works attacks Despauterius with much acerbity. The well-known grammar of Nicolas Perotti, the first large Latin grammar of the Renaissance, which Erasmus in his *De ratione studendi* praises as the most complete of his day, was published about 1510 by Michel Angier in conjunction with Jean Macé of Rennes, with whom he had a joint establishment at Rouen. The same publishers, with Richard Macé for a third partner, brought out an abridged edition of Valla's *Elegantiae* by Guy Jouennaux (Guido Juvenalis) of Le Mans. A larger work of the same character, the *Elegantiarum precepta* of the Sienese humanist, Agostino Dati, was edited with copious commentaries by Josse Clichtove and Josse Badius Ascensius, to which was added the popular treatise of Sulpizio di Veroli, *De epistolis componendis*. Dati's work was rendered into Latin verse by Robert Buisson (Dumus) of Lisieux, and the same professor published with Michel Angier a grammar (*Epythomata grammatice*) for beginners. Together with Nicolas Cadier, who edited Terence, and Pierre Des Prés, he was a versifier of some skill and taste, though his verses are not free from false quantities. The contribution of Guillaume Le Moine, of Villedieu in Lower Normandy (the birthplace of the famous author of the *Doctrinale*), to the cause of rising humanism was a small Latin-French dictionary, which went through three editions, all published at Caen about the year 1530, and gained for the author the honour of being mentioned by La Croix Du Maine in his *Bibliothèque*.

A favourite text-book at this time for students of Latin

was the *Contra poetas impudice loquentes* or *Contra impudice scribentes* of Baptista Mantuanus, the "good old Mantuan." An edition of it was printed by Laurent Hostingue for Michel Angier. No edition of his equally popular Eclogues appears in Delisle's record, and his verse is only represented by religious poems, including parts of his long poems on the Virgin Mary and the chief Virgin Martyrs.

Side by side with the new school-books there still flourished the time-honoured ones over which Gargantua pored under Thubal Holofernes and Maître Jobelin Bridé, the *Grecismus*, the *Doctrinale*, *Donatus*, various works by Joannes de Garlandia, the *Compotus* of Anianus, and the eight moral treatises in prose and verse which were known collectively as the *Auctores octo*, Cato, Aesopus, the *Parabolae* of Alanus, *Facetus*, *Floretus*, *Theodulus*, *De contemptu mundi*, and *Tobias*[1]. Nor was the collection of sermons, entitled *Dormi secure*, which Gargantua had read to him on festivals, forgotten by the Caen publishers[2].

A higher type of humanistic literature than school-books is represented by the *De triplici vita* of Marsiglio Ficino, the Florentine Platonist, and by the *Adagia* of Erasmus. An edition of the latter, without place of publication, but almost certainly published at Caen, contains an epitaph in Latin verse on Jean Goubey, Syndic of the University, who is memorable as the only Caen professor of this period of whom it is recorded that he gave public lectures in Greek. He is

[1] *Thobias* (as it is invariably spelt in the old editions) was printed separately less often than the other *Auctores octo* and in consequence seems to be less well known. It is a poem in Latin elegiacs on the story of Tobit and his son written in the twelfth century by Matthieu de Vendôme, the author of various Latin poems, who has often been confused with the far more famous Matthieu de Vendôme who acted as regent of the kingdom on two occasions in the thirteenth century (*Hist. Litt.* xv. 420 ff.). According to the *Histoire Littéraire Thobias* was printed at Lyons by Jean du Pré in 1489, but nothing is known of this edition, and the only authenticated one printed in the fifteenth century is a Haarlem one of about the same date. It was printed twice at Caen, with a commentary, during the period 1500–1520. The last separate edition of it is that of Bremen, 1642.

[2] See Rabelais, *Gargantua*, xiv, where most of these books are mentioned as playing a part in Gargantua's education, and *Rabelais*, selected by W. F. Smith (Cambridge, 1920), who in an appendix describes fully the text-books of the old learning.

described in the epitaph, the date of which is about 1529, as *Nestoreis annis*. Charles de Bourgueville, Sieur de Bras, the historian of Normandy, who was a student of the College of Du Bois from 1517 to 1519, attended his lectures[1].

On the whole then, it appears that the new studies made but slow progress, even in the Colleges. Thus in the year 1530 we find David Jore, who held office as Rector in the following year, inveighing in eloquent terms against the unlearned condition of his University ten years back. *Quanta barbarie, Deum immortalem, nostra Cadomensis academia squalebat! Emoriar si quid latinum expostulabatur.* Even in 1530 things had not much improved. "Good literature" [he means, of course, classical literature] "flourishes in Britain and Germany, but with us a Latin scholar is far to seek. The fault lies with our nobles, whose sole care is to give their sons the best masters for the training of dogs and horses[2]."

Five years, however, before this Jeremiad was uttered there died at Coutances in his seventy-fifth year a Caen professor of real distinction and wide repute as a humanist. This was Guillaume de La Mare[3] (1451–1525), who, having migrated from Caen to Paris on account of the plague, completed his studies and took his degree in the latter University. Then returning to Caen he gave several years to the study of law and the humanities, and at the same time made himself a name as a writer of Latin prose and verse. But at the age of forty-one he sought a more remunerative career, and for ten years acted as secretary successively to Robert Briçonnet, Archbishop of Reims and Chancellor of France, to his successor in the Chancellorship, Guy de Rochefort, who was a liberal patron of the new learning, and to Guillaume Briçonnet, the grasping and ambitious Cardinal of Saint-Malo. He returned to Caen in 1503 or 1504, and, having taken his degrees

---

[1] *Les recherches et antiquités de la province de Neustrie, à présent duché de Normandie...et spécialement de la ville et université de Caen*, Caen, 1588; Rouen, 1833.

[2] Delisle, *op. cit.* II. 52.

[3] He gives a brief sketch of his life in the preface to his *Chimera*. See also Trithemius, *De script. eccl.* Add. 1, and Ch. Fierville, *Étude sur la vie et les œuvres de G. de La Mare* in *Mém. de l'Académie de Caen*, 1892, pp. 42 ff.

in Canon and Civil Law, had the honour of being chosen Rector of the University in March 1506.

In 1511 he was appointed Canon and Treasurer of the Cathedral of Coutances, and two years later he was chosen to pronounce the funeral oration of Geoffroy Hubert, the late bishop, whose body had just been transported to the Cathedral. Later in the year 1513 he sent it to the press with nine other orations and with a selection from his correspondence. The book appeared in the following June[1]. The letters and a volume of occasional poems which he had published under the title of *Sylvae*[2] in the previous year (1513) give us a fairly complete list of the leading French humanists at this period. It includes Robert Gaguin, Jacques Lefèvre d'Étaples, Fausto Andrelini, Josse Badius, Paolo Emilio, and three Paris professors, Gilles de Delft, Charles Fernand and his brother Jean[3]. Only the first, it may be noticed, was a Frenchman by birth, for Étaples at the date of Lefèvre's birth belonged to Burgundy. Patrons are represented by the Cardinal d'Amboise, Guy de Rochefort, and Charles Guillard, a president of the Paris *Parlement*.

Just before the publication of the *Sylvae* there appeared from the same press a poem by La Mare of a satirical character entitled *Tripertitus in Chimeram conflictus*, and divided into three books, *Superbia, Libido, Avaritia*[4]. The same moral and satirical tendency appears in a short prose work made up of citations from Greek and Latin authors which La Mare published in the preceding year (1512) with the title of *De tribus fugiendis, ventre, pluma et venere, libelli tres*[5]. He also wrote a paraphrase of Musaeus[6] in hexameters. La Mare's reputation as a writer of Latin prose and verse was not undeserved. It is true that neither his syntax nor his prosody is impeccable; but he writes like a man who has something to say,

---

[1] *Epistolae et orationes*, Paris, Regnault, 1514.
[2] *Sylvarum libri quatuor*, Paris, Badius Ascensius, 1513.
[3] See L. Delaruelle, *Guillaume Budé*, 1907, pp. 17, 18.
[4] Paris, Badius Ascensius, 1513. The La Vallière catalogue II, No. 2635, mentions an edition without place or date, but with a dedication by the author dated from Caen University, Christmas Day, 1510.
[5] Paris, H. Stephanus, 1512; Paris, S. Colinaeus, 1521.
[6] Paris, Badius Ascensius, 1514.

and he says it with ease and vigour. His satirical poem especially shows considerable power both of thought and expression, and his verse generally has that quality which is the salt of all poetry, in whatever language it is written, namely movement.

La Mare's immediate predecessor in the Rectorship was Pierre de L'Esnauderie, who held the office of *scriba* to the University, which, as we have seen, combined the duties of secretary and registrary. He was also registrar of the Court of Privileges[1]. He was distinguished for his loyalty to the University and his devotion to its interests. Sometimes indeed these carried him too far, as, for instance, when during his Rectorate he proposed that the Charter and Statutes of Henry VI should be burnt, in order to obliterate the connexion between the University and this country. However, the registrary triumphed over the patriot, and by a happy inconsistency he made a copy of the obnoxious documents for his *Matrologium*, which he presented to the University in 1515. Five years later he gave all his books, about eighty in number, to the University library. His writings include two Latin treatises, one of which is entitled *Opusculum de doctoribus et privilegiis eorum*, a prose work in French, *La louenge de mariage et recueil des histoires des bonnes vertueuses et illustres femmes*, in which he tells the story of a girl in his parish who at the age of fourteen could hold her own in Latin grammar against all the male students who came to dispute with her[2], and a farce or morality-play, entitled *Les Pattes Ouaintes* (*The greased palms*). This latter was written in 1493, when the University was engaged in an embittered dispute with the Crown concerning a tax which, with the consent of Charles VIII, the Pope had imposed on the French Church. It was played on Shrove Tuesday by the students, L'Esnauderie himself taking the part of Pattes Ouaintes and being made up to resemble Girard Bureau, lieutenant to the bailiff of Caen, who was one of the officials charged with the collection of the tax. Another opponent of the University, the Bishop of Châlons, figures in

---

[1] Delisle, *op. cit.* II. cxiv.
[2] Delisle, *op. cit.* II. xcvi.

the play under the picturesque name of Ribonribaine, and the University itself appears as *La Mère*[1].

These farces, which in later years were exchanged for classical plays, remained an interesting feature of Caen University life till the middle of the sixteenth century. Of somewhat later date was the *Puy du Palinod*, or annual poetical contest in honour of the Immaculate Conception of the Virgin Mary, founded in 1527. A similar contest had been held at Rouen since 1486, and there were Puys at Evreux and Dieppe, and in various towns of Picardy. The contests at Caen were managed by a *Confrérie*, to which all members of the University might belong on payment of a fee. The President for the year bore the grandiloquent title of *Premier prince du Palinod*. On the first day of the festival the competitors recited their poems, which took the form of *Ballades*, *Chants royaux*, *Rondeaux*, or Latin epigrams, and were all in honour of the Immaculate Conception. On the second day the judges were appointed, and within three days they had to make their report. The prizes were then distributed, one prize being awarded for each class of composition. The successful pieces were printed, the expense being defrayed out of the fines paid by officials who failed to attend the Annual Congregations of June 28 and October 10[2]. In 1550 the contests were abandoned, but they were re-established in 1558, and before long, owing to the remarkable literary talent displayed at Caen during the last quarter of the sixteenth century and the first half of the seventeenth, they attained considerable celebrity. Among the prize-winners were Bertaut, Malherbe, Sarasin, and Segrais.

[1] H. Prentout, *La vie de l'Étudiant à Caen au XVIe siècle*, Caen, 1905, pp. 43–50.

[2] La Rue, *op. cit.* II. 154–160; Delisle, *op. cit.* II. 99.

II

THE PROSE ROMANCES OF CHIVALRY

THE great majority of the prose romances of chivalry were written during the second half of the fifteenth century. But the oldest are much earlier than this. At the beginning of the thirteenth century men began to make prose versions of the Arthurian romances, and from 1215 to 1230 *Lancelot*, the *Saint-Graal*, *Merlin*, *Perceval*, and *Tristan*, after one or two re-shapings, took the form which the printing-press later made definitive. These prose versions were produced under the same influence as the poems which they represented, that of the courtly love to which we owe the lyrical poetry of the *trouvères* and the first part of the *Roman de la Rose* (*circ.* 1225). To the same period belongs the prose rendering of the *Roman de Thèbes*, the starting-point of which was a compilation written between 1223 and 1230, and printed in the sixteenth century under the title of *Edipus*. The second half of the thirteenth century is represented only by *Alexandre le Grand*, a translation of the *Historia de Praeliis*, which owed its success largely to that of the celebrated poetical romance, the *Roman d'Alexandre*.

Five romances out of those which were afterwards printed were written in the fourteenth century—*Les quatre fils Aymon*, *Giron le Courtois*, *Meliadus*, *Bérinus*, and *Mélusine*. The last-named romance, which was written by Jean d'Arras for John, Duc de Berri, dates from 1387 to 1393; *Giron le Courtois* and *Meliadus*, which represent respectively the second and the first part of the poem of *Palamède*, are assigned, one to the first half and the other to the second half of the century. The date of the composition of *Bérinus* has not been determined with precision, but seeing that it contains Greek and Oriental elements, it may be conjectured that it belongs to the first quarter of the century, that is to say, to a period when projects for a new Crusade were still in the air. Finally, *Les quatre fils Aymon*, also called *Rénaud de Montauban*, the oldest prose representative of the *chansons de geste*, dates from the end of the century, either from those years of perpetual festivity which preceded the madness of Charles VI, or a little later, from the period of the truce with England.

The first half of the fifteenth century, during which the kingdom was rent by civil and foreign warfare, was little favourable either to literature or to the leisure necessary for the reading of long romances. It was only about 1450, the year in which the English were driven out of Normandy, that the transformation into prose of the romances of chivalry received a fresh impetus. *Pierre de Provence* was put into prose in 1453, and *Huon de Bordeaux* in 1458; *Galien rhétoré* is of about the same date. The place where this class of literature flourished most was the Court of Burgundy under Philip the Good. We owe *Jason et Médée* (about 1450) and the *Recueil des histoires de Troye* (1464) to Raoul Le Fèvre the Duke's almoner. *Perceforest*, that encyclopedia of chivalry, was refashioned about 1450 by his librarian and copyist, Daniel Aubert, who also translated or more probably wrote the romance of the *Trois fils de Roi* (1463). Another of the Duke's copyists, Jean Wauquelin, made prose versions of *Girard de Roussillon* (1447) and *La belle Hélène* (1448).

By the end of the fifteenth century nearly all the romances of chivalry which found their way into print, had been turned into prose. I only know of three prose versions which date from the sixteenth century: *Richard sans Peur* (about 1535), *Flores et Blanchefleur* (about 1550), and *Guillaume de Palerme* (about 1550). *Turpin* (1527), *Mabrian* (1525 or 1526), and *Meurvin* (1540) are original works.

In his interesting paper *Les Adaptations en prose des chansons de geste*[1], the late Émile Besch pointed out that the printed prose romances bear the impress of a spirit which is partly *bourgeois* and partly clerical. Seeing that the majority of those which are derived from the *chansons de geste* or the

---

[1] *Revue du seizième siècle*, III (1915), 155 ff.

romans d'aventures were compiled during the second half of
the fifteenth century, the *bourgeois* colouring is not surprising.
For during that period the influence of the *bourgeoisie* steadily
increased. One of the keystones of Louis XI's policy was the
creation of an aristocratic *bourgeoisie* to serve as a counter-
weight to the power of the feudal lords. Thanks to their growing prosperity, the newly enriched *bourgeois* bought the lands
of the ruined nobles, built châteaux and hôtels, and became
patrons of artists and men of letters. Thus it came to pass
that their practical and positive spirit communicated itself to
the prose romances and helped to determine their character.

The first prose romance to be printed was probably *Pierre
de Provence*, the *princeps* of which, from the press of
Bartholomé Buyer at Lyons, is assigned by Mlle Pellechet to
the year 1472. Next come the two works of Raoul Le Fèvre,
the *Recueil des histoires de Troye* and *Jason et Médée*, both
without place or date of publication, but now recognised as
printed at Bruges by Colard Mansion, and either in 1477
(according to the most recent authority, Mr Gordon Duff), or
about that year (Hain-Copinger, Blades, Proctor). It must be
added that the *Recueil* is certainly earlier than *Jason et Médée*,
and that it is just possible that a Lyons edition of the latter
from the press of Philippi and Reinhard, who printed from
1477 to 1482, is earlier than the Bruges one.

Three romances bear the date of 1478: *Mélusine*, the printing of which, by Steinschaber of Geneva, was finished in
August; *Fierabras*, which came from the same press on
November 28; and *Baudoin de Flandres*, printed at Lyons by
Buyer. A little later come *Ponthus et la belle Sidoine*, printed
with the same type as *Mélusine* and *Fierabras*, the *Destruction
de Jérusalem* and *Apollin de Tyr*, both printed at Geneva
about 1480, and *Les quatre fils Aymon*, attributed to a Lyons
press and assigned to the years 1480–1485. In 1484, according
to Proctor, Pierre Schenck printed *Clamadès* at Vienne; at
Lyons *Valentin et Orson* was printed by Maillet in 1489,
Robert le Diable by Mareschal and Chaussard in 1496, and
Bertrand Du Guesclin by an unknown printer after 1480.

Passing from the south to the north we find Jean le Bourgeois inaugurating the Arthurian romances at Rouen with *Lancelot* in 1488 and *Tristan* in 1489, the latter in partnership with Jean du Pré. The same Jean du Pré, in partnership with Pierre Gerard at Abbeville, after printing the *Somme rurale* of Boutillier and the magnificent edition of St Augustine's *Cité de Dieu* in 1486, crowned his enterprise in that town with the *princeps* of *Les Neuf Preux* in 1487.

Curiously enough, Paris did not take any share in the printing of the prose romances of chivalry till the last decade of the fifteenth century, and down to 1500 the sole publisher of them was Verard. His publications were *Clériadus* (1495), *Ogier le Danois* (between 1492 and 1499), and *Galien rhétoré* (1500). In 1500 he had a rival in Michel Le Noir, who issued *Les prouesses d'Hercule*. There remain to be noted *Paris et Vienne*, printed at Antwerp by Gerard Leeu in 1487, and *Olivier de Castile* and *Artus de Bretaigne*, printed in 1482 and 1493 respectively by presses which have not yet been identified.

Thus by the end of the fifteenth century twenty-four prose romances of chivalry had been printed, some of them several times.

Twelve followed during the years 1501–1514; twenty-seven date from the reign of Francis I; and four—*Gérard d'Euphrate* (1549), *Geoffroy à la grand dent* (1540), *Guillaume de Palerme* (1552), and *Flores et Blanchefleur*—were printed in the reign of Henry II.

Both at Paris and at Lyons there were booksellers who specialised in these romances. At Paris, it was chiefly the two establishments which bore as respective signs the *Shield of France* and the *Image of St Nicholas*. Both were situated in the Rue Neuve-Notre-Dame. The successive owners of the *Shield of France* were Jean Trepperel and his widow, Jean Jehannot, Alain Lotrian, and Nicolas Chrestien; of the *Image of St Nicholas* Jean de Saint-Denys and his widow, Pierre Sergent (all three associated with Jean Longis), Jean Bonfons, who married Sergent's daughter, and his son Nicolas. At Lyons the two booksellers and printers who published the most romances of chivalry were Claude Nourry (1499–1532 and Olivier Arnoullet. As everyone knows, it was Nourry who printed, in 1532, first, *Les grandes et inestimables Cronicques*, the burlesque romance of chivalry which owed its great success to Rabelais's revision, and then *Pantagruel*.

Judging from the number of times that the various romances were printed, the most popular of all was *Les quatre fils Aymon*, which by the close of the reign of Francis I had been printed at least eighteen times, the first five editions coming from Lyons presses. Next comes *Fierabras* of which I have counted fifteen editions down to 1536, eight printed at Lyons and three only at Paris. From 1501 its title was *Conqueste du grand roy Charlemagne des Espagnes et les vaillances des douze pairs de France, Et aussi celles de Fierabras.* The third place is taken by *Pierre de Provence*, which was printed twelve times in the same period, four times at Lyons, twice at Paris, and twice at Rouen. It furnished Marot with the subject-matter for his First Epistle, *La belle Maguelonne à son ami Pierre de Provence.* For the fourth place there are two competitors, *Mélusine* and *Artus de Bretaigne*, each with ten editions from 1478 to 1550. Then come, more or less together, but all with fewer than ten editions, *Baudouin de Flandres, Galien rhétoré, Valentin et Orson, Ponthus et la belle Sidoine, Ogier le Danois, Robert le Diable*, and *Huon de Bordeaux*, the last being printed relatively late, viz. in 1513.

But we must not accept the number of editions which have come down to us as an infallible test of their relative popularity. Seeing that some of the editions are represented by a single copy, there are very possibly others which have disappeared altogether. For instance, we know that *Huon de Bordeaux*, the impressions of which (including an undated Rouen edition, and one from the Paris press of Jean Bonfons, who printed from 1547 to 1568) do not exceed six, was very popular, largely on account of the part played in it by magic. It is cited by Montaigne (*Essais*, I. 25) with *Lancelot* and *Amadis* as a type of "these nonsensical books which amuse children," and it figures with *Robert le Diable, Fierabras* and other books of "high growth" (*haute fustaye*) in the Prologue of *Pantagruel*.

We may compare with the testimony of the printed editions the names of the heroes of romances who appear in Rabelais's picture of the infernal regions (*Pant.* II. xxx). Here are Fierabras, Valentine and Orson, Giglan and Gauvain[1], Geoffrey with the great tooth (a son of Mélusine), Godfrey of Boulogne, Jason, Arthur of Britain, Perceforest, Ogier the Dane, Galien *restauré*, the four sons of Aymon, Mélusine, and Matabrune. In the *ballade* prefixed by Charles de Bourdigné in his *Légende de Pierre Faifeu*, which was printed at Angers in the same year (1532) as *Pantagruel*, mention is made of Artus, Lancelot, Merlin, Tristan, Robert le Diable, Fierabras, Orson, and Ponthus. Lastly, Noël du Fail in his *Contes et discours d'Entrapel* says that in the time of "the great King, Francis," you would find on the dresser in the sitting-room of a country gentleman a French Bible, the *Calendrier des Bergers*, the *Légende dorée*, the *Roman de la Rose, Les quatre fils Aymon, Ogier le Danois*, and *Mélusine*.

When the *Bibliothèque bleue* came to an end in 1863, it still numbered amongst its chap-books, *Valentin et Orson, Les quatre fils Aymon, Huon de Bordeaux, Galien*, and *Robert le Diable*, besides two which in their original form were comparatively late to appear in print, *La belle Hélène* (1528) and *Richard sans peur* (c. 1535).

The passages in Rabelais cited above, and others which refer to particular romances, have been carefully recorded and commented on by M. Plattard in his *Œuvre de Rabelais*[2]. He notes reminiscences of *Ogier le Danois, Fierabras*, and *Valentin et Orson*, and a reference to the tomb of Geoffrey with the great tooth at Maillezais (*Pant.* chap. v). It was natural, he points out, that Rabelais should take a special interest in the legend of Geoffrey and his mother, Mélusine, connected as it was with the château of Lusignan, which Mélusine inhabited, and with the abbey of Maillezais, which Geoffrey burnt.

---

[1] *Giglan fils de Gauvain* was first printed by C. Nourry. The romance entitled *Gauvain* was not printed till 1540.

[2] Pp. 1–10.

Rabelais seems also to have had a special affection for *Les quatre fils Aymon*, which was printed three times by Nourry (in 1506, in 1526, and in 1531) and once by his successor, Pierre de Sainte-Lucie (in 1539). It was perhaps under the influence of Nourry that Rabelais, after editing *Les grandes et inestimables Cronicques*, a burlesque of the Arthurian romances, turned to the romances founded on the *chansons de geste* for the framework of *Pantagruel*[1].

The only prose romance belonging to the Arthurian cycle which was at all popular in the true sense of the term was *Artus de Bretaigne* or *Le petit Artus*, which is attached to the cycle by a purely artificial link, the hero being merely a descendant of Lancelot. The true Arthurian romances never left their stately and sumptuous folios for the less expensive *format* of a quarto or an octavo. Thus they were bought only by great lords and ladies or by rich *bourgeois*. Those which had the greatest vogue were *Lancelot*, *Merlin*, and *Tristan*. *Lancelot* was printed six times and the other two five each. *Lancelot* fully deserves its pre-eminence; it is one of the literary masterpieces of the Middle Ages; whether, as its latest interpreter, M. Ferdinand Lot, believes, it is in all its four parts the work of a single individual, must be left to experts to determine. Of the other romances of the Round Table I find three editions of *Giron le Courtois*, two of the *Saint-Graal*, *Meliadus*, and *Perceforest*, and only one of *Perceval le Gallois*. The last four were all late to appear in print, the *Saint-Graal* in 1516, *Meliadus* and *Perceforest* in 1528, and *Perceval* in 1530.

During the second half of the reign of Francis I (1536–1547) only two romances were added to those already in print, and in 1540 the old French romances encountered a serious rival in the translation by Herberay des Essarts of the first book of the Spanish *Amadis de Gaula*. It met with immediate favour and, followed by seven more books, soon eclipsed the French romances in popularity, at least with aristocratic readers. The French sources, however, had not

---

[1] See W. F. Smith, *Rabelais in his writings*, Cambridge, 1918, pp. 20–21.

quite run dry; as we have seen, four romances were printed for the first time during the reign of Henri II, but the author (who professes to be merely the translator) of *Gérard d'Euphrate* (1549) says that he was encouraged to publish it by the success of *Amadis*. When François de la Noue, the stout Huguenot soldier, writing in his Spanish prison (1580–1585), inveighs against the pernicious influence of the *Amadis* books, he refers to "the old romances of which we still see fragments here and there, that is to say, *Lancelot du Lac, Perceforest, Tristan, Giron le Courtois*[1]."

The four columns of the following tables give (1) the title of the romance; (2) the place and date of its first appearance in print; (3) the date of its composition; (4) its source. In columns 3 and 4 I have merely given the results of investigations by competent authorities. For the date of impression, besides inspecting personally several of the works, I have controlled the statements of Brunet and of Scott de Martinville (the author of the *Essai de classification des romans de chevalerie* (1870) which appeared under Didot's name[2]) by the more recent typographical researches of Proctor, Picot, Mlle. Pellechet, Renouard, and others[3].

I. ROMANCES DERIVED FROM *CHANSONS DE GESTE*

Beufves d'Anthonnes	1502. Paris, M. Le Noir	14th cent.	Fashioned from the poem of *Bovon de Hanstone* (13th cent.).
Conqueste de Trébisonde	[1511–1512.] Paris, Veuve Trepperel	15th cent. (end)	An original work forming a sequel to *Les Quatre fils Aymon*; it relates an episode in the life of Renaud de Montauban.
Doolin de Mayence	1501. Paris, Verard	,,	Fashioned from two *chansons de geste*: I. *Les enfances Doon de Mayence*; II. *Doon de Mayence*.

[1] *Discours politiques et militaires*, VI.

[2] See the introduction, p. xvi. Scott also helped Brunet with the revision of the last edition of his *Manuel*.

[3] R. Proctor, *An Index to the early printed books in the British Museum*, 3 vols. with supplements, 1898–1902; M. Pellechet, *Catalogue général des incunables des bibliothèques publiques de France*, 3 vols. published, 1897–1909; É. Picot, *Catalogue des livres composant la bibliothèque de feu M. le baron James de Rothschild*, 3 vols. 1887–1893; Ph. Renouard, *Imprimeurs parisiens...depuis l'introduction de l'imprimerie à Paris* (1470) *jusqu'à la fin du XVIe siècle*, 1898.

ROMANCES DERIVED FROM *CHANSONS DE GESTE* (*cont.*)

Fierabras	1478. Geneva [Steinschaber]	*circ.* 1475	Compiled from I. A prose version of a poem with the same title; II. *Chronique de Turpin*; III. *Miroir historial.* G. Paris, *Hist. poétique de Charlemagne*, pp. 27–29; H. L. D. Ward, *Catalogue of Romances in the manuscript department of the British Museum* (3 vols. published), 1883–1910, I. 615–619.
Galien rhétoré	1500. Paris, Verard	*circ.* 1450	A prose version of the poem of *Galien*. Galien is a son of Olivier. L. Gautier, *Les épopées françaises*, 2nd ed. III. 315–345; G. Paris, *Hist. litt.* XXVIII. 221–239.
Gérard d'Euphrate	1549. Paris, Sertenas	15th cent.	Claims to be translated from a Walloon poem, but beyond doubt an original work. The hero=Gérard de Fratte, one of the many sons of Doon[1]. G. Paris, *Hist. poétique de Charlemagne*, p. 325, n.[2].
Girard de Roussillon	1520. Paris, Le Noir[2]	1447	An abridgement of a prose version by Jean Wauquelin of a fourteenth century poem. P. Meyer, *Gérard de Roussillon*, 1884.
Guérin de Montglave	[1502–1511.] Paris, J. Trepperel	14th or 15th cent.	Another prose version of *Galien*, preceded by an expanded version of the poem of *Gérard de Vienne*. G. Paris, *Hist. litt.* XXVIII. 221–239, and *Romania*, XII. 1–13.
Jourdain de Blaves	1520. Paris, Le Noir	,,	A prose version of the *chanson de geste* with the same title.

[1] Genealogical tree of the descendants of Doon:

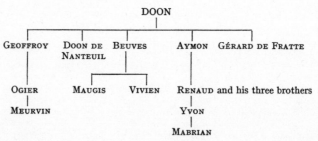

[2] It is possible that the edition printed at Lyons by O. Arnoullet (1517–1558) is earlier than that of Le Noir.

ROMANCES DERIVED FROM *CHANSONS DE GESTE* (*cont.*)

Mabrian	1525 or 1526. Paris, G. Du Pré[1].	14th or 15th cent.	An original work forming a sequel to *Maugis d'Aigremont*.
Maugis d'Aigremont	1527. Paris, J. Trepperel[2]	,,	A prose version of the *chanson de geste* with the same title. Maugis = Ariosto's Malagigi.
Meurvin	1540. Paris, Longis and Sergent	,,	An original work.
Milles et Amys	[1500–1503.] Paris, Verard	,,	A prose version of the poem of *Amis et Amile* (12th cent.). Gautier, I. 463–473; Ward, pp. 674–680.
Morgant le Géant	1519. Paris, Petit, Chaudière, and Le Noir	16th cent.	An imitation of the *Morgante maggiore* of Pulci.
Ogier le Danois	[1492–1499.] Paris, Verard	14th cent. (2nd half)	Fashioned from the *chanson* of the same name. Ward, pp. 604–610.
Quatre fils Aymon	[*circ.* 1480–1485.] Lyons	14th cent. (end)	A prose version of the *chanson* of *Renaud de Montauban* (12th century). F. Castets, *Recherches sur les rapports des chansons de gestes et de l'épopée chevaleresque italienne*, 1887.
Turpin	1527. Paris, R. Chaudière	1527	Made by order of François I after the *Chronique de Turpin*.
Bertrand du Guesclin	[After 1480, Lyons?]	1387	Compiled from a poem written soon after the death of Du Guesclin by a Breton *trouvère* named Cuvelier (ed. E. Charrière, 2 vols. 1839, *Doc. inédits*).
Baudoin de Flandres	1478. Lyons, B. Buyer	15th cent.	Prose version of a lost fourteenth century poem.
Godefroi de Bouillon	1504. Paris, J. Petit[3]	15th cent. (end)	The work of Pierre Desrey, part being translated from the *Speculum historiale* of Vincent de Beauvais.

II. ROMANCES DERIVED FROM *ROMANS D'ANTIQUITÉ*

Alexandre le Grand	1506. Paris, Le Noir	13th cent.	Translated from the *Historia de praeliis*. P. Meyer, *Alexandre le Grand dans la littérature française au moyen âge*, 2 vols. 1886.
Apollin, roi de Tyr	[*circ.* 1480.] Geneva, Garbin	15th cent. (?)	Translated from a Latin version of a Greek novel. Ward, I. 161–170; Douce, *Illustrations to Shakespeare*, II. 135–144.

[1] Probably 1526, as the privilege is dated November 5, 1525.
[2] This edition is older than that of Lotrian, s.d. (see H. Harrisse, *Bibliotheca Colombiniana*, p. li, n.[3]), but Michel Le Noir had previously published *Guérin de Montglave* and *Maugis d'Aigremont* together in a single volume (Paris, 1518).
[3] The prologue of Desrey is dated 1499, which presumes an older edition than that of 1504.

ROMANCES DERIVED FROM *ROMANS D'ANTIQUITÉ* (*cont.*)

Destruction de Jérusa-salem or *Vespasien*	[*circ.* 1478.] Geneva	15th cent.	Represents a poem of the thirteenth century, the Latin original of which is lost. P. Meyer, *Bull. soc. des anc. textes franç.* (1875), pp. 52–55; *Hist. litt.* XXII. 412–416; Ward, I. 176–180.
Édipus	[1532–1547.] Paris, Sergent	1223–1230	A rendering in prose of the *Roman de Thèbes*. L. Constans, *Le roman de Thèbes*, 2 vols. 1890, II. cxiv–cxlv.
Florimont	1528. Paris, J. Longis	15th cent.	Based on a poem written by Aimon de Varenne in 1188. The hero is supposed to be the grandfather of Alexander. G. Paris, *Littérature française au moyen âge*, p. 83.
Hector de Troye	[1517–1558.] Lyons, Arnoullet	,,	An extract from the *Recueil des histoires de Troye.*
Jason et Médée	[1477, Bruges, C. Mansion[1].]	*circ.* 1450	Written by Raoul Le Fèvre before the *Recueil.*
Judas Machabée	1514. Paris, Bonnemère	16th cent.	Translated by Charles de Saint-Gelais from the Latin text of the Apocrypha.
Recueil des histoires de Troye	[1477. Bruges, C. Mansion[2].]	1464	Translated by Raoul Le Fèvre from the Latin version made by Guido Colonna in 1287 of the *Roman de Troie* of Benoist de Sainte-More (1175–1185).
Neuf preux, les	1487. Abbeville, J. du Pré and P. Gérard	15th cent.	The nine knights are: Hector, Alexander, J. Caesar, Joshua, David, Judas Maccabeus, Arthur, Charlemagne, Godefroy de Bouillon.
Prouesses d'Hercule, les	1500. Paris, Le Noir	,,	An extract from the *Recueil.*
Trois grands, les	?	?	Alexander, Pompéius, Charlemagne.

III. ROMANCES DERIVED FROM THE ARTHURIAN ROMANCES

Artus de Bretaigne	1493.	15th cent.	Or *Le petit Artus.* It has little connexion with the cycle of the Round Table; Artus, son of John, Duke of Brittany, is a descendant of Lancelot.
Cleriadus et Meliadice	1495. Paris, Verard[3]	,,	Meliadice is a descendant of King Arthur. Ward, I. 383.
Gauvain	1540. Strasburg	15th cent. (?)	

[1] E. Gordon Duff, *Fifteenth century English books*, 1917, no. 244. This edition (Bibl. nat.; Eton College) is probably earlier than the Lyons edition printed by Philippi and Reinhard, who printed from 1477 to 1482.

[2] E. Gordon Duff, *op. cit.* no. 243.

[3] Only one copy is known (Yemeniz-Didot).

Romances derived from the Arthurian Romances (*cont.*)

Giglan, fils de Gauvain, et Geoffroy de Mayence	[1499–1532.] Lyons, C. Nourry	15th cent.	Compiled by Frère Claude Platin from the poem of *Guinglain* or *Le bel inconnu* (13th cent.) and the Provençal poem of *Jaufré*. G. Paris, *Hist. litt.* xxx. 196–197.
Giron le Courtois	[1500–1503.] Paris, Verard	14th cent. (1st half)	Represents the 2nd part of the poem of *Palamède* as abridged by Rusticien de Pise (*circ.* 1270). Ward, i. 369–371.
Lancelot du Lac	1488. Rouen, J. Le Bourgeois and J. Du Pré	*circ.* 1220	In four parts: (1) *Histoire du Saint-Graal*; (2) *Lancelot*; (3) *Queste du Saint-Graal*; (4) *Mort Arthur*. Ward, i. 345–356; *Merlin*, ed. G. Paris and J. Ulrich, 2 vols. 1886 (*Soc. des anc. textes franç.*), i. lix; G. Paris, *Romania*, xii. 459–534; F. Lot, *Étude sur le Lancelot en prose*, 1918.
Meliadus de Leonnoys	1528. Paris, G. Du Pré	14th cent. (2nd half)	Represents the first half of *Palamède*. Ward, i. 364–369.
Merlin	1498. Paris, Verard	*circ.* 1230	Compiled from the *Merlin* of R. de Boron, with additions to link it with *Lancelot du Lac*. *Merlin*, i. xxiv.
Perceforest	1528. Paris, G. Du Pré	*circ.* 1450	Refashioned by Daniel Aubert, librarian to Philip the Good, from a prose romance of the fourteenth century. Ward, i. 377–381.
Perceval le Gallois	1530. Paris, G. Du Pré	*circ.* 1230	A prose version of the poem of Chrétien de Troyes with continuations by Gaucher de Dourdan and by Menessier (see the preface).
Saint-Graal	1516. Paris, J. Petit, G. Du Pré, and M. Le Noir	*circ.* 1230	Compiled from the *Joseph d'Arimathée* or *Le petit Saint-Graal* of the pseudo R. de Boron.
Tristan, fils de Meliadus	1489. Rouen, J. Le Bourgeois	1215–1230	A vast compilation, probably based in part on a lost poem of Chrétien de Troyes. E. Loseth, *Le roman en prose de Tristan*, 1892.
Ysaie le Triste	[1522 or 1523.] Paris, G. Du Pré	15th cent. (towards the end)	Ysaie is the son of Tristan and Yseult de Cornouailles.

IV. ROMANCES DERIVED FROM THE *ROMANS D'AVENTURES*

Belle Hélène, la	1528. Lyons, Arnoullet	1448	Compiled by Jean Wauquelin from the poem of the same name.
Bérinus	[1521 or 1522.] Paris, J. Janot	14th cent.	"Réduit de langage inconnu," but probably an original work. It contains Greek and Oriental elements.
Clamadès	[1484.] Vienne, P. Schenck	15th cent.	Compiled by Philippe Camus from the poem of *Cléomadès*.
Conqueste de Grèce, la	1528. Paris, G. Du Pré	„	"Faicte...par Philippe Madien," from the lost work of Perrinet Du Pin.
Florent et Lyon	[1528–1546.] Paris, Lotrian	„	A prose compilation from the poem of *Florent et Octavien*.
Flores et Blanchefleur	1554. Paris, Fézandat	*circ.* 1550	Translated by Jacques Vincent from a romance in Spanish prose which represents the twelfth century poem of *Floire et Blanchefleur*.
Geoffroy à la grand dent	1549. Lyons, Arnoullet[1]	?	Sequel to *Mélusine*.
Gérard de Nevers	1520. Paris, Hémon Le Fèvre	15th cent.	Prose version of the *Roman de la Violette* (13th century).
Guérin Mesquin	1530. Lyons, Arnoullet	15th cent. (end)	Translated from the Italian poem of *Guerino meschino*.
Guillaume de Palerme	1552. Lyons, Arnoullet	15th cent.	Compiled by Pierre Durand from the poem of the same name. *G. de Palerme*, ed. Michelant (*Soc. des anc. textes franç.*).
Guy de Warwick	1525. Paris, F. Regnault	15th cent.	Made at second hand from a *roman d'aventures* with the same title. Ward, i. 471–491; *Hist. litt.* XXII. 841–851.
Huon de Bordeaux	1513. Paris, M. Le Noir	1454	A prose version with additions of a fourteenth century poem. *Huon de Bordeaux*, ed. S. L. Lee, *Early English Text Society*, 1882.
Mélusine	1478. Geneva, Steinschaber	1387–1393	Written by Jean d'Arras (probably first in Latin) by order of John, Duc de Berri. Ed. Ch. Brunet, 1858. See L. Desaivre, *La Légende de Mélusine*, Niort, 1885.
Olivier de Castile	1482. ? ?	15th cent.	Translated from the Latin by Pierre Camus.
Paris et Vienne	1487. Antwerp, G. Leeu	„	Professes to be a translation by Pierre de La Seppade, from a Provençal work.

[1] First edition with a date, but that of Jean Bonfons (undated), who began to print in 1547, may be earlier.

ROMANCES DERIVED FROM THE *ROMANS D'AVENTURES* (*cont.*)

Pierre de Provence	[1472–1478. Lyons, B. Buyer[1].]	1453	"Mise en cette langage par un redacteur inconnu, qui peut être Ph. Camus" (É. Picot). But it is still a question whether the work from which the prose romance was compiled was in prose or verse, in Latin or Provençal (see Marot, *Œuvres*, ed. Guiffrey, III. 5, n.[2]).
Ponthus et la belle Sidoine	[*circ.* 1478.] Geneva	15th cent. (1st half)	Compiled from the French version of the English poem of *Horn*. Ward, I. 469–470; *Hist. litt.* p. xxii.
Richard sans peur	[*circ.* 1535.] Paris, A. Lotrian and D. Janot	*circ.* 1535	"Translaté," by Gilles Corrozet, "de vieille rime en prose," that is to say, from a fifteenth century poem which was printed at the beginning of the sixteenth century.
Robert le Diable	1496. Lyons, Mareschal et Chaussard	end of the 15th cent.	A compilation from a thirteenth century poem of the same name. K. Breul, *Sir Gowther*, Oppeln, 1886.
Syperis de Vinevaulx	[1531 or 1532.] Paris, veuve de J. Saint-Denys	15th or 16th cent.	Abridged from a prose compilation from a fifteenth century poem. Syperis or Ciperis = Chilperic. *Hist. litt.* XXVI. 19–40.
Theseus de Cologne	1534. Paris, Longis and Sertenas	*circ.* 1483	A compilation from a thirteenth century poem of the same name, probably written by D. Aubert. G. Paris, *Hist. poétique de Charlemagne*, p. 96.
Trois fils de roi	1501. Lyons, J. de Vingle	1463	The three sons are Philip of France, Humphrey of England, and David of Scotland.
Valentin et Orson	1489. Lyons, Maillet	15th cent.	Burlesque of *Cléomadès*, said to have been made for Charles VIII. Ward, I. 849.

[1] Essling-Yemeniz-Didot-Crawford (the only perfect copy).

III

RABELAIS AND GEOGRAPHICAL DISCOVERY

I

The Novus Orbis of Simon Grynaeus

IN his fascinating book *Les Navigations de Pantagruel*[1] M. Abel Lefranc has made it abundantly clear that Rabelais followed with a lively interest the great geographical discoveries of his day, and that certain portions of *Pantagruel* which have hitherto been regarded as pure fantasy rest on a foundation of solid fact. But can we pursue the subject a little further? Can we trace the actual authorities which Rabelais used for his geographical descriptions? Can we, as has been done with regard to other elements of his great medley, put our finger upon the very passages which he had before him?

In the earliest days of maritime discovery the results of the voyages were briefly recorded in the despatches of Venetian ambassadors at the courts of Spain and Portugal, or by the correspondents of Venetian or Florentine banking-houses. A little later they formed the subject of special letters or short pamphlets, which were rapidly multiplied by copies and sometimes printed. In one or two instances the record was made by the discoverer himself, as by Columbus and Vespucci. It was not, however, till 1507 that the first collection of voyages, the prototype of all succeeding collections, made its appearance. It was entitled *Paesi novamente retrovati e Novo Mondo da Alberico Vesputio Florentino intitulato*, and was printed at Vicenza[2]. The editor was

---

[1] Paris, 1905.
[2] Published in facsimile, *Vespucci reprints, texts and studies*, IV. Princeton, N.J.

Fracanzio da Montalboddo, a native of Monte-Alboddo in the march of Ancona, and professor of literature at Vicenza from 1502 to 1505[1]. It is divided into six books, which are composed as follows:

I. Voyage of Ca da Mostó (chapters 1–47).

II. (1) Voyage of Pedro da Cintra to Senegal, written by Ca da Mosto at the dictation of Pedro's secretary (chapters 48–50).

(2) First Voyage of Vasco da Gama, recounted in a letter by Girolamo Sernigi, a Florentine residing at Lisbon when the expedition returned[2] (chapters 51–62).

(3) Voyage of Pedro Alvarez Cabral, written by his pilot in Portuguese and translated by Giovanni Matteo Cretico, secretary to Domenico Pisani, Venetian ambassador to Spain, but employed on a special mission to the Portuguese Court at the time of Cabral's return[3] (chapters 63–70). This was the voyage in the course of which Cabral discovered Brazil.

III. Voyage of Cabral continued (chapters 71–83).

IV. A reprint of *Libretto de tutta la navigazione de re di Spagna de le isole et terreni novamente trovati*. Venice, 1504. (The only known copy is in St Mark's Library at Venice.) The anonymous writer of this narrative is now known to be Angelo Trevisan, fellow-secretary with Cretico to Domenico Pisani. He took the substance of it, as he acknowledges, from Peter Martyr's then unpublished First Decade[4]. It contains accounts of the following voyages:

(1) First three voyages of Columbus (chapters 84–108).

(2) Voyage of Pedro Alonso Niño[5] (chapters 109–111).

(3) Voyage of Vicente Yañez Pinzon (chapters 112, 113).

V. Third voyage of Vespucci, described in a letter to Lorenzo di Pierfrancesco de' Medici (grandson of Cosimo's brother). A re-translation into Venetian dialect from Fra

---

[1] See *Raccolta di documenti e studi pubblicata dalla Commissione Colombiana*, pt III. vol. II. pp. 209–211; H. Harrisse, *Bibliotheca Americana Vetustissima*, pp. 96–99; É. Picot, *Cat. Rothschild*, II. 426–429.

[2] See E. G. Ravenstein, *A Journal of the First Voyage of Vasco da Gama* (Hakluyt Society), 1898.

[3] *Comm. Colomb.* pt III. vol. I. p. 83.

[4] *Comm. Colomb.* pt III. vol. II. p. 171.

[5] Here called by his nickname, Negro.

Giocondo's Latin version of the original Italian (chapters 114–124).

VI. (1) Letter from Cretico to the Doge Leonardo Loredan giving an account, similar to that contained in Books II and III, of Cabral's voyage[1] (chapter 125).

(2) Letter from some merchants in Spain to their correspondents in Florence and Venice describing a treaty between the King of Portugal and the Zamorin of Calicut (chapter 126).

(3) Letter from Pietro Pasqualigo (Pisani's colleague in the special mission to Portugal, and his successor as ambassador to Spain) to his brothers relating the recent arrival at Lisbon of one of Cortereal's caravels from Labrador (chapter 127). This was the voyage from which Cortereal himself never returned.

(4) Letter from Giovanni Francesco Affaitadi (here called Francesco de la Saita), a merchant residing at Lisbon, to Pasqualigo, concerning the expedition of João da Nova, the discoverer of St Helena (he is not mentioned by name), to the Malabar coast (chapter 128).

(5) An account of Calicut, Carangore, and other places on the west coast of India, from the report of a Nestorian priest, named Joseph, who had come to Portugal with Cabral (chapters 129–142).

The *Paesi novamente retrovati* had a great success. Fresh editions were published at Milan in 1508[2], 1512, and 1519, and at Venice in 1517 and 1521. It was translated into German and French, and of the French translation entitled *Le Nouveau Monde et Navigations faites par Emeric de Vespuce Florentin*[3] there were six editions. More important for our present purpose is the Latin translation, made by Michelangelo Madriganni, Abbot of a Cistercian monastery near Milan, and afterwards bishop of Avellino in the kingdom of Naples. It was printed at Milan in 1508 under the title of *Itinerarium Portugallensium e Lusitania in Indiam et inde in Occidentem*

---

[1] *Comm. Colomb.* pt III. vol. I. p. 43.
[2] This is far superior to the original edition from a typographical point of view.
[3] The privilege is dated January 1, 1517 (N. S.); *Vespucci reprints*, VII.

et demum in Aquilonem. It is full of mistakes, especially in the matter of dates.

The popularity of the *Paesi novamente retrovati*, with the prominence given to Vespucci's name on its title-page, no doubt greatly contributed to the adoption of the proposal made by Martin Waldseemüller in his *Cosmographiae Introductio* (of which several editions were printed at Saint-Dié in Lorraine in a few months) and embodied by him in the globe and map which he published in the same year (1507), that the New World (meaning thereby the northern part of South America) should be called after Vespucci. Moreover the Latin version of Vespucci's letter to Lorenzo de' Medici had obtained a far wider circulation than any other narrative of recent geographical discovery. Under the title of *Mundus Novus* it had been printed fourteen times during the years 1503–1505—in Italy, in France (five times) and in Germany[1]— and it had been translated into French and German and back into Italian[2].

The next great collection of voyages is the Latin one generally known as the *Novus Orbis* of Simon Grynaeus. It was published at Basle in 1532, the full title being *Novus orbis regionum ac insularum veteribus incognitarum una cum tabella cosmographica et aliquot aliis consimilis argumenti libellis quorum omnium catalogus sequenti pagina patebit.* The real compiler and editor of the work was a German antiquary named Johann Huttich, Grynaeus merely contributing a preface. Sebastian Münster, the well-known Hebrew scholar and mathematician, contributed an introduction. The first part of the book is a reproduction of Madriganni's Latin version of the *Paesi novamente retrovati*, the mistakes of which it perpetuates. Then follow ten new pieces, all of which, except the second, had already appeared in print. They are as follows:

1. A Latin version of Vespucci's letter to Piero Soderini, Gonfalonier of Florence, giving an account of his four voyages

---

[1] Only two of these editions are dated. See É. Picot in *Cat. Rothschild*, II. 423, for a discussion of the question as to whether it was originally printed at Paris or Venice.

[2] It has been translated into English by Professor G. T. Northup (*Vespucci reprints*, v).

(first printed in 1507 as an appendix to Waldseemüller's *Cosmographiae Introductio*)[1].

2. A letter from King Manuel of Portugal to Leo X relating the conquest of Malacca and the relief of Goa by Albuquerque[2].

3. Madriganni's Latin translation of the *Itinerario* of Ludovico di Varthema, here called Ludovicus Romanus patritius. The original work was printed at Rome in 1510, and the Latin version at Milan in 1511. The Italian edition was reprinted at Venice in 1517, 1518, 1520 and 1522, and at Milan in 1519 and 1523.

4. A description of the Holy Land by a German Dominican of the thirteenth century, named Brocardus, who spent ten years in the monastery at Mount Sion. It was first printed at Lubeck in 1475 as part of the *Rudimentum Noviciorum*[3], and separately at Venice in 1519.

5. A Latin version of the travels of Marco Polo. According to Yule it is a translation at fifth hand and utterly worthless as a text. It certainly differs considerably from the fourteenth century Latin version, made from the original French through an Italian translation by Fra Pipino. This was first printed by Gerard Leeu at Gouda in 1483 or 1484[4].

6. A Latin version of the travels of Hayton the Armenian (Hetoum, Prince of Gorigos), edited by Menrad Molther and first printed at Hagenau in 1529. Hayton's narrative, like Marco Polo's, was originally written in French at his dictation by Nicolas Falcon, who afterwards translated it into Latin.

---

[1] The original letter is most closely represented by a Florentine impression entitled *Lettera di Americo Vespucci delle isole novamente trovate in quatro suoi viaggi* (*Vespucci reprints,* ii). The Latin translation was made through a French version from an Italian original, the translator altering the heading of the letter so as to make it appear that it was addressed to René, Duke of Lorraine, instead of to Soderini. See for the whole question Prof. Northup's introduction to his translation of the letter (*Vespucci reprints,* iv).

[2] I can find no trace of this having appeared in print before. It is included in the *Chronicon Citizense* of Paul Lange, a German Benedictine who died about 1536, but this remained in manuscript till it was printed by Pistorius in his *Scriptores Germanici* in 1583.

[3] The well-known *Mer des histoires* is a translation of this.

[4] Not at Antwerp in 1485, as is commonly stated. See R. Proctor, *Index to the early printed books in the British Museum.* There are three copies in the British Museum and one in the University Library, Cambridge.

It was this Latin version which Molther edited. He has corrupted Falcon's name to Salconi. In the same year there was published at Paris under the title of *L'histoire merveilleuse*, etc., a French translation of Falcon's version made in the fourteenth century by Jean Le Long of Ypres. There were also incorrect reproductions of the original French narrative under the title of *Les fleurs des histoires de la terre Dorient*[1].

7. A description of Russia by Matthias of Miechow, a Polish physician, first printed at Cracow in 1517 under the title of *Tractatus de duabus Sarmatiis Asiana et Europiana et de contentis in eis*.

8. Another description of Russia by Paolo Giovio based on the information of an ambassador from Basil the Great to Pope Clement VII, first printed at Rome in 1525 under the title of *Pauli Iovii Novocomensis libellus de legatione Basilii magni, principis Moschoviae ad Clementem VII. Pont. Max.*

9. An abridgement of Peter Martyr's Fourth Decade by the author, first printed at Basle in 1521 under the title of *De nuper sub D. Carolo repertis insulis simulque incolarum moribus R. Petri Martyris Enchiridion.*

10. An account of the antiquities of Prussia by Erasmus Stella, a physician of Leipsic, first printed at Basle in 1510 under the title of *De Borussiae antiquitatibus libri II*. Stella died in 1521. His name probably refers to his father's trade of saddler and wheelwright (Stellmacher)[2].

The *Novus Orbis* appeared in March 1532, and in the following October the well-known Paris publisher and bookseller, Galliot Du Pré, issued a reprint of it. In 1537 another edition was published at Basle[3]. It included an additional treatise, the account of Magellan's Voyage by Maximilian Transylvanus, contained in a letter to his father, the Archbishop of Salzburg. This was first printed at Cologne in 1523.

I have described the *Novus Orbis* thus in detail, because it was a book which Rabelais undoubtedly used. It will be well to make this evident at once by putting side by side his

---

[1] See *Histoire littéraire*, xxv. 479.
[2] See Zedler, *Universal Lexicon*.
[3] Grolier's copy of this edition is in the University Library, Cambridge.

account of Pantagruel's first voyage and a passage from
Sebastian Münster's preface:

Primum itaque cum Hispani in
Indiam traiecturi sint, petunt
Portum sanctum, Mederam, et
septem *Canarias insulas,* quae
olim Fortunatae dictae sunt...
Hinc navigatur ad *Caput album,*
portum continentis Africae...Re-
licto Capite albo et insulis ad-
iacentibus...venitur ad regnum
*Senegae...*Haud longe ab ora
huius fluminis est *Caput viride...*
Relicto Capite viridi ductore Aus-
tro pervenitur ad ostium *fluvii
Gambrae...*Hinc navigantibus of-
fertur caput *Sagres,* ac deinde
transito *regno Meli* pervenitur ad
caput Bonae spei, quod corrupte
et Hispanice *De bona sperantza*
quidam appellant...Nam hinc
navis sensim redit versus aequa-
torem, ubi scilicet est *regnum
Melindae.*

Ils...prindrent la haulte mer,
et en briefs jours, passans par
porto sancto et par Medere, firent
scalle es isles de Canarre.

De la partans passerent par
Cap blanco, par Senege, par Cap
virido,

par Gambre, par Sagres, par
Melli,

par le Cap de bona sperantza, et
firent scalle au royaulme de
Melinde.

It will be noticed that Rabelais adheres very closely to his
authority, using the strange form *Cap virido* and spelling
sperantza in exactly the same way. He continues his narrative
as follows:

De la partans, feirent voille au vent de la transmontane, passans
par Meden, par Uti, par Udem, par Gelasim, par les isles des Phees,
et jouxte le royaulme de Achorie, finalement arrivent au port de
Utopie.

Here we seem to have left real countries for the land of pure
fantasy, and the names of Achorie and Utopie are obviously
borrowed from Sir Thomas More. But M. Lefranc's conjecture that in Meden, Uti, and Udem, three Greek words which
signify "nothing," we have a play upon the places Medina and
Aden is almost certainly right, for on turning the page of the
Novus Orbis Rabelais would have come upon a summary of
Ludovico di Varthema's journey, in which Medina and Aden
are mentioned in two consecutive lines. It is a bolder conjecture that Gelasim stands for Ceylon, but I think there is

a great deal to be said for it, though I should rather regard "Gelasim" as an anagram (with the addition of the initial letter) of Seilam, the form which the name of Ceylon assumes in the Latin version of Marco Polo in the *Novus Orbis*[1].

It is even possible that, as M. Lefranc suggests, "the islands of the Fairies" may vaguely represent the wonderful islands beyond Taprobana (Sumatra) which Albuquerque's conquest of Malacca had opened up to the Portuguese—Ternate with its cloves, Banda with its nutmegs, Borneo and Java with their cinnamon, of all of which Rabelais might have read in Varthema's narrative[2]. He might have read too the abridged French translation of Pigafetta's narrative of Magellan's voyage (dedicated to Louise of Savoy), which Simon de Colines printed at Paris in 1526 or soon afterwards[3].

In the next chapter (xxv) it is just possible that the encounter with the six hundred and sixty knights may have been suggested to Rabelais by Vespucci's narrative of the fight with the natives off the island of Giants (Curaçoa).

In the last chapter Rabelais promises his readers a continuation of the story. "You shall see," he says, "how Panurge was married...and how Pantagruel...*passa les mons Caspies, comment il naviga par la mer Athlantique et deffit les Caniballes, et conquesta les isles de Perlas.*" Here again he is almost certainly following the *Novus Orbis*, for in the account of Columbus's voyages there is a chapter, *De Canibalorum moribus*[4], and another, *Quomodo Admirans adivit Canibalorum insulas*[5], that is to say, the Caribbean islands. For by a misunderstanding which the habits of the natives amply justified the Caribs were at first called Cannibals. A little further on in the *Novus Orbis* we read of the voyage of Pedro Alonso Niño to the Islands of Pearls, and how "he returned home laden with pearles" and "how he fought with the Cannibals." By the Pearl islands is meant Margarita, which,

---

[1] Lib. III. c. xxii (*Novus Orbis*, p. 353).

[2] See Varthema, Lib. VI. cc. xxiv–xxx (*Novus Orbis*, pp. 235 ff.).

[3] *Le voyage et navigation faict par les Espaignolz es Isles des Mollucques* (printed at the sign of the *Soleil d'Or* and therefore not before 1526. There is no printer's device).

[4] c. lxxxviii (p. 81).   [5] c. xcii (p. 83).

with a few much smaller islands, lay off Venezuela, and was celebrated for its pearls in all the marts of Europe[1].

Rabelais then continues, *Comment il espousa la fille du roy de Inde nommé Presthan*. M. Lefranc infers from this in conjunction with the whole passage that it was intended that Pantagruel like Columbus and many explorers after him should sail for the East by the West, and so reach Cathay and India. This is a brilliant suggestion, and it is only the mention of the Caspian mountains that makes one hesitate to adopt it. In any case it is interesting to find Rabelais placing the mythical kingdom of Prester John in India, in accordance with Marco Polo, Mandeville, and other mediaeval travellers[2]. For at the close of the fifteenth century it was generally located in Abyssinia. This is the position assigned to it in the account of Vasco da Gama's first voyage, in Varthema's *Itinerary*, and especially in the letter of King Manuel, who says that Albuquerque had a scheme for draining the Nile into the Red Sea with the assistance of Prester John. In spite, however, of this combination of authority in the *Novus Orbis*, Rabelais adheres to the mediaeval tradition. In this he agrees with the interlude of *The Four Elements*, written about 1515, in which *Experience* is represented as saying:

> This quarter is India minor,
> And this quarter India major,
> The land of Prester John.

So too in one of the legends inscribed on "Sebastian Cabot's" Map of 1544 we read of a mighty king in Central Africa "whom some call Prester John," but "this is not Prester John, because Prester John had his Empire in Eastern and Southern India until Genghis Khan, first king of the Tartars, defeated and overcame him in a very cruel battle in which he died[3]."

The defeat of Prester John by Genghis Khan is recorded

---

[1] Readers of *Westward Ho* will remember how Amyas Leigh and his companions took the pearls at Margarita from the Spaniards. Curiously enough Kingsley in this very chapter refers to Panurge's behaviour in the storm.

[2] It appears in Central Asia in Martin Behaim's globe of 1491, which is based for these parts on Marco Polo.

[3] C. R. Beazley, *John and Sebastian Cabot*, p. 233.

by Marco Polo who adds that Genghis Khan married Prester John's daughter. But Marco Polo describes Prester John correctly as a Tartar prince, and it is Sir John Mandeville who first speaks of him as the Emperor of India. He also says that the great Cham married his daughter[1]. This makes it probable that Rabelais got his information from Mandeville, to whom he refers as *Monteville* in the prologue to *Pantagruel*[2].

If Rabelais seriously entertained the idea of writing a continuation of his story which should include the account of a long sea-voyage, he was diverted from his intention for many years. It was not till the autumn of 1545 when he was writing the final chapters of the Third Book that he returned to it again. There are, however, in *Gargantua* occasional references to the New World and other matters of geographical interest. Thus in chapter xxxi he speaks of "those who dwell beyond the Canary Islands and Isabella," the latter being the city which Columbus founded in Hispaniola or St Domingo. Again in chapter lvi we are told that every year seven ships were brought to the Abbey of Thelema "laden with gold ingots, raw silk, pearls, and precious stones from the islands of Pearls and the Cannibal islands."

Rabelais is also indebted to the narratives of travellers for some of his descriptions of animals, and we find instances of direct borrowing from the *Novus Orbis* in the account of the Island of Satin in the Fifth Book (chapter xxix). Thus the description of the elephants is taken partly from Ca da Mosto and partly from Varthema.

Ils ont le museau long de deux coudées, et le nommons proboscide, avec lequel ils puisent eau pour boire, prennent palmes, prunes, toutes sortes de mangeaille, s'en deffendent et offendent comme d'une main: et au combat jettent les gens haut en l'air, et à la chute les font crever de rire.

Hominem nisi laesus non laedit; et ubi laedit, manu hominem comprehensum iacit in sublime ultra arcus iactum: ea dicitur manus elephanti, quam alii promuscidem appellant...manum habent in inferiore maxilla, quam exserunt et retrahunt pro libitu, hac cibum capiunt et hauriunt potum omnem.

CA DA MOSTO, *c.* xxix.

---

[1] Mandeville, c. xxx.
[2] See L. Sainéan in *Rev. des études rab.* IX (1911), 265–275.

Ils ont moult belles et grandes oreilles de la forme d'un van[1]. Ils ont joinctures et articulations es jambes: ceux qui ont escrit le contraire, n'en veirent jamais qu'en peinture: entre leurs dents ils ont deux grandes cornes...et sont en la mandibule superieure, non inferieure.

Verum sunt plures qui existimant in cruribus elephantes non habere internodia, plicareque ob id nequire tibias: quod profecto a vero plurimum abest. Habent iuncturas ut caetera animalia, sed in ima prope parte crurum...Bini dentes qui prominent collocantur in superiore maxilla: auriculas quaquaversum gemini palmi magnitudine habent.

VARTHEMA, IV. *c*. X.

Rabelais's unicorn is not, as I had first supposed, a compound of Marco Polo's rhinoceros and a mysterious one-horned animal which Varthema saw in the temple of Mecca, but comes straight from Pliny[2].

In the next chapter (xxx) we are introduced to "a little hunch-backed, misshapen and monstrous old man," who was called Hearsay; and round him were "a number of men and women listening attentively,...and among them one held a Map of the World and was explaining it to them compendiously in little aphorisms....There I saw Herodotus [here follow the names of various ancient writers on geography]; moreover:

Albert le Jacobin grand, Pierre Testemoing, Pape Pye second, Volaterran, Paulle Jovio, Le vaillant homme Cadacuist, Tevault, Jacques Cartier, Hayton Arménien, Marc Paule Venetien, Lodovic Romain, Petes Aliares,

and I know not how many other modern historians, hidden behind a piece of tapestry, stealthily writing fine stuff, and all by Hearsay."

I have given the names according to the reading of the manuscript in the Bibliothèque Nationale. Alter Testemoing to Tesmoing, Cadacuist to Cadamosto, Tevault to Tenault, and Petes to Petrus, and connect *le vaillant homme* with Jovio instead of with Cadamosto, and the result is a better text than that of the printed editions, which read Charton for Hayton, and omit Cadamosto and Tenault altogether. The order in which the names are put is not altogether fortuitous. They are arranged in two divisions, first, five writers who were

[1] This sentence is omitted in the printed texts.
[2] *N.H.* VIII. 21. 31. W. F. Smith pointed this out to me.

not travellers, then seven travellers who have left records of their travels. Possibly Petrus Aliares, the Latin form of the name of Pedro Alvarez Cabral, one of the two discoverers of Brazil, is put last because he wrote no account of his voyage. But it is more probable that Rabelais was misled by the heading in the *Novus Orbis* before chapter cxxv, which runs *Rerum memorabilium Calechut quae non sunt absimiles illis quas Petrus Aliares secundo et altero tractatu scripsit*, referring to his pilot's narrative in the second and third books of the *Paesi novamente retrovati*.

Seven of the twelve are represented in the *Novus Orbis*, namely Peter Martyr, Paolo Giovio, Ca da Mosto, Hayton the Armenian, Marco Polo, Ludovico di Varthema, and Cabral, and the form which three of the names assume in Rabelais's text, namely Paulle Jovio, Lodovic Romain, and Petrus Aliares, points to his acquaintance with them through the Latin.

Paolo Giovio is represented only by a single short treatise, but Rabelais was possibly acquainted with his *Descriptio Britanniae Scotiae Hiberniae et Orchadum*, printed at Venice in 1548, with a special privilege for publication in France, though I can find no trace of his having used it. There is a short sketch of the history of maritime discovery at the end of book xxxiv of his *Historiarum sui temporis libri xlv*, which was published at Florence in 1550.

Similarly, there is nothing of Peter Martyr but a summary of his Fourth Decade. Soon after the publication of the *Novus Orbis* Simon de Colines issued a volume entitled *Extrait ou recueil des isles nouvellement trouvées en la grand mer Oceane ...item trois narrations*, etc., which contains (1) a summary of the first three *Decades* of Peter Martyr; (2) an account of the conquest of Cuba, taken from his *Enchiridion*; (3) and (4) abridged translations of Cortés's Second and Third letters to Charles V[1].

---

[1] Printed January 12, 1533 (N. S.). See É. Picot in *Cat. Rothschild*, II. 435 ff. M. Chinard in his interesting volume *L'Exotisme américain dans la Littérature française au XVIe siècle*, 1911, would have us see both in Pietro Martire and Marco Polo sources of some of Rabelais's descriptions, particularly of the Abbey of Thelema and the temple of the Bottle; but with the best will in the world I cannot detect any indebtedness.

Of the five who are not represented in the *Novus Orbis* Albertus Magnus has a place probably by virtue of his *Liber cosmographicus de natura locorum* (first printed in 1514 both at Vienna and Strassburg), and possibly also of his *De Animalibus*, and Pope Pius II (Aeneas Sylvius) as the author of *Cosmographiae libri II*[1], a very popular work, of which there is a Paris edition, edited by Geofroy Tory for Henri Estienne I, of 1509, and another of 1534 with the title of *Asiae Europaeque elegantissima descriptio*[2]. By Volaterran is meant Raffaelle Maffei of Volterra, whose *Commentariorum urbanorum libri xxxviii* was first printed at Rome in 1506 and went through many editions. There are Paris ones of 1510, 1511, and 1526. It is a sort of encyclopaedia, compiled with little critical power, of which the first twelve books deal with geography, the last chapter being devoted to *loca nuper reperta*.

Tenault is Jean Thenaud, guardian of the Franciscan convent at Angoulême, who in 1511 was sent by Louise of Savoy on a mission to the Holy Land and who after his return wrote in 1512 an account of his travels. It was printed at Paris between 1525 and 1530 under the title of *Le voyage et itin[er]aire de oultre mer*[3]. Rabelais cites him in *Gargantua* (chapter xvi) as an authority for the fact that "a little truck has to be fastened behind the sheep of Syria to bear up their tails, so long and heavy are they[4]." He gets from him too the *cocodrilles* of the Nile (v. xi) and the *Catadupes* or falls of the same river (IV. xxxiv), and the term *calloier*, which he applies to himself on the title-page of the first edition of the Third Book (*Calloier des Isles Hieres*), and which occurs frequently in Thenaud to signify a Greek monk or patriarch. So also the word *seraph*, the name of an Egyptian gold coin, which is found on nearly every page of Thenaud, is used by Rabelais, though he may have got it from another source[5].

---

[1] It was first printed at Venice in 1477.

[2] By Claude Chevallon and Galliot du Pré.

[3] Edited by Ch. Scheffer in the *Recueil de Voyages*, Paris, 1884.

[4] This is also mentioned by Herodotus, III. 113 (of the sheep of Arabia), and by Leo Africanus in his *Description of Africa*, first printed by Ramusio in 1550. See Rawlinson's notes to the passage in Herodotus; also Aelian, x. 10; Yule, *Marco Polo*, I. 100 n.

[5] See for these borrowings from Thenaud L. Sainéan in *Rev. des études rab.* VIII (1910), 350 ff., and VII. 464 ff.

A name that we miss among the writers after Hearsay, and who deserves a place more than any of those mentioned, is that of Mandeville or Monteville. The so-called "travels" of this French impostor (*ob.* 1372), who wrote under the name of an English knight, were very popular in Rabelais's day. Several editions were published at Lyons from 1480 to 1490, and another by Barnabe Chaussard about 1500[1]; and there is a Paris edition by Philippe Le Noir (after 1516).

II

Jacques Cartier

The expeditions made from France to the new world during the first two decades of the sixteenth century were private adventures undertaken in the interests of commerce. The chief port of departure was Honfleur, which was for the French mariners, says M. de La Roncière, what Seville was to the Spanish *conquistadores*[2]. But in 1523 there was an expedition on a larger scale and under the patronage of the King of France. It was financed by a syndicate of Italian silk-merchants living at Lyons, whose trade had been ruined by the Portuguese discoveries in the East Indies, and who were thirsting to find a shorter route to the wonderful spice-islands. The leader was a Florentine gentleman, named Giovanni Verrazzano, who sailed with four vessels from Le Havre[3] in June or July 1523 with the intention of reaching Cathay by Russia and the North-east passage. But meeting with a violent storm in the northern seas he lost two ships and was driven back to the French coast. Having refitted, he now sailed down the coast of Spain and then with one vessel only, *La Dauphine*, manned by fifty men, struck

---

[1] University Library, Cambridge, SSS. 60. 21, formerly in the Yemeniz collection (Copinger, no. 3829).

[2] See for these early expeditions, especially for that of the *Espoir* (under Captain Gonneville, 1503–1505), Ch. de La Roncière, *Histoire de la Marine française*, III (1906), 129–140.

[3] This is a practically certain inference from the known fact that the preparations for the voyage were made at Rouen, where Verrazzano lived.

westward from a small island near Madeira across the Ocean (January 17, 1524). After a voyage of twenty-five days he touched land at Florida, and explored the coast northwards till he reached Newfoundland, whence, provisions running short, he returned to Dieppe at the beginning of July, having failed to find a passage to Cathay, but having given the name of New France to the whole coast between Florida and Cape Breton.

In the early summer of 1526 he followed the same route, but again failed to reach Cathay by the west. Finally, in 1528, he made a third attempt, changing his route to that followed so successfully by Magellan. But while making a land reconnaissance in the Rio de la Plata he fell into an ambush of savages and was roasted and eaten before the eyes of his companions who had remained on board the ships. "Such," says Ramusio, "was the unfortunate end of this valorous gentleman[1]."

It was the weakness of Francis I that he was for ever being diverted from the many excellent projects which he formed. The development of French commerce and maritime enterprise owed far less to the French King than to a private individual, who for a quarter of a century organised, sustained, and directed, almost single-handed, the colonial campaign of France against her Spanish and Portuguese rivals. This was Jean Ango, a wealthy shipowner of Dieppe, who held numerous high administrative offices, and whose manor at Varengeville, four miles from Dieppe, still exists, turned into a farmhouse. The loggia with its round arches supported on massive columns, the picturesque tower, the dovecot, and the medallions are still eloquent of that blending of the old with the new, of Gothic with Renaissance, which was characteristic of the reign of Francis I. The influence of the Italian

---

[1] *Raccolta di navigazioni e viaggi*, 3 vols., Venice, 1550–1559, III. 417. Thus the first volume of Ramusio's great collection of voyages appeared in Rabelais's lifetime. I have taken the account of Verrazzano from La Roncière, *op. cit.* pp. 255–267. Verrazzano wrote an account of his first voyage to Francis I, but it is very vague, and the best evidence for the three voyages are the maps of his brother Girolamo (1529) and of the Genoese cartographer, Vesconte di Maggiolo (1527), who accompanied him on his second expedition (see below, p. 56).

Renaissance was made still further evident by the discovery of a fresco, six feet long, dated 1544, and supposed to be of the Florentine school[1].

This manor and the hôtel at Dieppe were visited by many of the Florentine exiles, who had established themselves at Dieppe or Rouen—bankers, shipowners, merchants, artists, corsairs, pilots—and thus became important centres for the diffusion of the Italian Renaissance. It was Ango who financed the second expedition of Verrazzano, it was Ango who sent Jean Parmentier to Sumatra in 1529, it was Ango who organised a new voyage by the route followed by Magellan and nearly secured the services of one of Magellan's pilots (1531), it was Ango who tried to give France a colonial empire in Brazil and who, when Brion-Chabot, the High Admiral, betrayed his country for a bribe (1531), sustained alone by his energy and his money the unequal struggle against the Portuguese for the liberty of the seas[2].

Among those who profited by the King's temporary change of policy was the Breton pilot, Jacques Cartier, the discoverer of Canada. I have no intention of repeating here at length the narrative of this discovery. It is sufficient for my purpose to note that he set sail from Saint-Malo on April 20, 1534, touched Newfoundland at Cape Bonavista, sailed through the strait of Belle Isle between Newfoundland and Labrador, visited the Magdalen Islands, reached Chaleur Bay between New Brunswick and the province of Quebec, coasted northwards as far as Gaspé, where he planted a cross from which hung a shield with the legend *Vive le Roy de France* (July 24), rounded the island of Anticosti, and retracing his course through the strait of Belle Isle reached Saint-Malo on the 5th of September.

For this voyage Cartier had received a subvention of 6000 *livres* from the royal treasury. Though he had failed to discover a passage to the West, his experiences seemed encouraging, and less than two months after his return he was commissioned by the High Admiral on behalf of the King to

---

[1] See *Bibl. de l'École des Chartes*, XIX (1858), 10–12.
[2] He died in 1551 ruined by his patriotic efforts.

fit out a fresh expedition on a larger scale. On May 19, 1535, he put to sea again with three ships provisioned for fifteen months and sailed straight for the island of Anticosti. When he got near the mouth of the St Lawrence, he was told by two Indians whom he had captured in the preceding year and had brought back with him that this was "the way and beginning of the great river and way to Canada, which went always narrowing clear to Canada; and that one found the water fresh in the said river, which goes so far that never man might have been up to the end that they had heard." They also affirmed that there was no other passage. Cartier then turned northwards and coasted for some distance along the shores of Labrador, trying to find a passage. But passage there was none. So on the faith of what the Indians had told him he turned again westwards, and made his way up the St Lawrence to Stadacone (Quebec) and to Hochelaga (Montreal), which he reached on October 2. From the mountain near the town, to which he gave the name of Mont-Royal, he saw the vast prospect of fair land, "level and tillable" and in the middle the broad river flowing towards the south-west as far as the eye could see. This was the limit of his journey. Returning down the river he wintered at Saint-Croix near Quebec. On May 6 of the following year he started on his homeward journey, and after leaving the mouth of the St Lawrence steered south-east for the Magdalen Islands, passed between Cape Breton Island and Newfoundland, came to Cape Race the southern point of Newfoundland on June 16, and reached Saint-Malo on July 6. He brought with him Donnacona the "lord of Canada" and other Huron chiefs, whom he had treacherously kidnapped.

It was an inopportune moment. A new war with Charles V had broken out, and in the following August the Emperor invaded Provence. The issue of letters-patent forbidding all attacks on Portuguese ships (August 26, 1536) was probably prompted by a desire to conciliate Portugal in this hour of need. The treaty of Nice (June 1538) brought peace once more, and for two years the rival monarchs were outwardly close friends. In 1540 Admiral Chabot was at last brought to trial for his bribery and corruption, and the King, no longer thwarted by his intrigues, returned to his project of colonising the newly found land of Canada. On October 17, 1540, he commissioned Cartier to organise a fresh expedition and made him "captain-general and master pilot of the ships." But over him he appointed as "lieutenant-general, chief leader, and captain of the enterprise," Jean-François de La Rocque, Seigneur de Roberval (January 15, 1541). Cartier was soon ready, but Roberval took some time collecting colonists and procuring artillery. So Cartier sailed alone with five ships on May 23, 1541, reached in a couple of months the harbour of St Croix near Quebec, and selected for a settlement a spot about four leagues further up the river, to which he gave the name of Charlesbourg Royal, after the second son of Francis I. Having secured his base he set out with two boats for Hochelaga and from there made his way partly in boats and partly on foot to the second rapid, that of Carillon on the Ottawa river. Here he learnt that there was only one more rapid to pass before arriving at the kingdom of Saguenay. But having come to the end of his provisions he determined to return to his fort and to delay further exploration till the spring. However, when the spring came, the constant hostility of the Indians compelled him to abandon the fort and return to France. Arriving at the harbour of St John in Newfoundland in June, he found Roberval's ships riding there at anchor. For Roberval had at last set sail with his colonists from La Rochelle, having secured the services of the most experienced pilot in France, the celebrated Jean Alfonse of Saintonge (April 1542). Disobeying Roberval's orders to return to the St Lawrence, Cartier slipped his cables in the night and sailed for Saint-Malo, while Roberval proceeded to Charlesbourg Royal and began his proposed settlement. After a winter of terrible experiences he set out in the spring to explore the Saguenay. Here, however, the record of his voyage stops short. All we know is that in June 1543 Cartier was sent to bring him home and that both had returned by the following February.

The initiative which Francis I had taken in the exploration

and colonisation of Canada had stimulated his subjects to a corresponding activity. From 1541 to 1545 fishing-ships from various Norman and Breton ports sailed for Canada every year. In May 1541 a Spanish spy reported to his government that in addition to Cartier's expedition ships were being fitted out or had already sailed from Dieppe, Harfleur, and Honfleur, from Morlaix, Quimper, and Croisic[1]. But in 1545 the interest in Canada began to slacken. Though the third war against the Emperor had been ended by the treaty of Crépy in the preceding September, France was now at war with England, and Jean Ango was devoting all his energies and money to the maintenance of the royal navy. However, in the early part of the year the moment seemed still propitious for the publication of an account of Cartier's discoveries, and on February 28 a privilege was granted to Ponce Roffet and his brother-in-law Antoine Le Clerc for the publication of a book entitled *Brief recit et succincte narration, de la navigation faicte es ysles de Canada, Hochelaga et Saguenay, et autres, avec particulieres meurs, langaige, et cerimonies des habitans d'icelles: fort delectable a veoir*[2]. It is a simple and modest narrative, occupying only forty-eight leaves, of Cartier's second voyage. Probably a printed account of the first voyage appeared about the same time, but no copy of it now exists. Indeed, when Raphael Du Petit Val published an account of this voyage at Rouen in 1598, he had to translate it from a *langue étrangère*. This was the Italian version which Ramusio had included in the third volume of his great collection of voyages (Venice, 1556), and which was probably translated from a printed text. Some forty years ago a MS. which bears evident traces of being Cartier's original account was discovered in the Bibliothèque Nationale, and edited in 1867 by H. Michelant and A. Ramé under the title of *Relation originale du voyage de Jacques Cartier au Canada*. Cartier's

---

[1] J. P. Baxter, *A Memoir of Jacques Cartier*, New York, 1906, pp. 348 ff.; H. Harrisse, *Découverte et évolution cartographique de Terre Neuve et des pays circonvoisins*, Paris and London, 1900, p. 175.

[2] The only known copy is in the British Museum. Tross discovered a second, but it was lost with the ship which was taking it to America. See H. Harrisse, *Bibliotheca Americana vetustissima*, for a facsimile of the title-page.

third voyage and that of Roberval are represented only by fragmentary narratives in Hakluyt's *Voyages*[1].

Thus when in the summer or early autumn of 1545 Rabelais reverted to the idea which he had foreshadowed at the close of the Second Book of making a long sea-voyage the framework of his narrative, the interest of Frenchmen in maritime adventure had been sensibly quickened. We read in chapter xlix of the Third Book that Pantagruel, having agreed to accompany Panurge on a voyage to the "Oracle of the Bottle," assembled his followers at the port of Thalasse near Saint-Malo, and there made the necessary preparations[2]. The Third Book was published early in 1546, and in the summer of 1547 Rabelais, who had made a hurried flight to Metz immediately after its publication, began his Fourth Book with an account of the voyage. With the date of 1548, but probably in November 1547, appeared ten chapters with the fragment of an eleventh. In June 1548 we find Rabelais at Rome with Jean Du Bellay. He returned to France in November 1549, and obtained a fresh privilege on August 6, 1550. But the complete Fourth Book did not appear till January 1552 and internal evidence points to the fact that much of it was written during the interval between the privilege and publication.

In the first chapter we read that Pantagruel put to sea at the Port of Thalasse, and that he was accompanied by "Xenomanes, the great traveller and traverser of perilous ways, who had been sent for by Panurge and had arrived certain days before." This is followed in the complete edition of 1552 by the statement that "Xenomanes had left with Gargantua, and marked out in his great and universal Hydrography the route which they were to take in their visit to the Oracle of the Holy Bottle Bacbuc." Later on in the same chapter we learn that the course of the ships was set by the

---

[1] For the first voyage Mr Baxter translates the *Relation originale*, for the second a MS. (No. 5589, one of three) in the Bibliothèque Nationale, as he found several errors and omissions in the *Brief recit*, including the omission of two whole chapters (xi and xii). He adds the fragments from Hakluyt.

[2] The privilege for the Third Book is dated September 19, 1545; the concluding chapters were probably written not long before this.

principal pilot, and in the 1552 edition we are told that the pilot's name was Jamet Brayer. In his *Navigations de Pantagruel* M. Lefranc, developing an idea first suggested by M. Margry in his *Navigations françaises*, has adduced several excellent reasons for identifying Jamet Brayer with Jacques Cartier, and Xenomanes with Jean Fonteneau, commonly called Jean Alfonse of Saintonge, who accompanied Roberval to Canada as his pilot.

The arguments in favour of identifying Xenomanes with Jean Alfonse are the following. We are told in III. xlix that Xenomanes "had some small holding of the domain of Salmigondin in mesne-fee," and all the commentators are agreed that Salmigondin stands for Saintonge. We also know that Jean Alfonse before he sailed on his last voyage, on the return from which he was attacked by the Spaniards and mortally wounded in the very port of La Rochelle(1544), had written a *Cosmographie* and that it eventually came into the hands of the poet Mellin de Saint-Gelais, who secured it for the Royal Library. Rabelais, who was a friend of Saint-Gelais's, may well have heard of this circumstance[1]. Moreover, the part played by Xenomanes in the voyage, and the air of authority with which he gives advice and explanation is in complete keeping with the reputation of Jean Alfonse as the most experienced French pilot of his day, who had sailed the seas, as he tells us in his *Cosmographie*, for forty-eight years, and had explored the coasts of America from the Straits of Magellan in the south to Davis Strait in the north[2].

More recently M. Sainéan has demonstrated, fully and conclusively, that the *Cosmographie* is almost entirely an impudent plagiarism of the *Suma de geographia* of Fernandez de Enciro, published at Seville in 1519. It is, in fact, except for the last forty pages, a literal version of the Spanish work—and a version which is disfigured by gross blunders, especially in geographical and historical names[3]. Thus the *Cosmographie*

---

[1] For Rabelais's relations with Saint-Gelais see J. Plattard, *Rev. des études rab.* IX (1911), 90 ff.

[2] See M. Georges Musset's introduction to his edition of the *Cosmographie* in the *Recueil de Voyages*, vol. XX. 1904.

[3] *Rev. des études rab.* X (1912), 19–67.

emerges from M. Sainéan's hands stripped of its borrowed plumes and devoid of all scientific or literary value.

But because Jean Alfonse was a shameless plagiarist and a man of no culture his identification with Xenomanes is not necessarily demolished. The important point is that Jean Alfonse was the most experienced French navigator of his day. That was enough for Rabelais. As for the objection raised by M. Sainéan that the *Cosmographie* was not an *Hydrographie* which Rabelais interprets in the *Briefve déclaration* as a "marine chart," it has never been suggested that Rabelais had seen the work. All that is claimed is that he may have heard from Saint-Gelais that the latter had secured for the Royal Library a work which Jean Alfonse had left in manuscript.

The identification of Jamet Brayer with Jacques Cartier is more doubtful. M. Lefranc points out that Cartier, like Jean Alfonse, had the requisite experience for acting as pilot to Pantagruel on this particular route. He also lays stress on a statement made by one Jacques Doremet, who in a little volume on the antiquities of Saint-Malo, prints the following marginal note opposite a passage dealing with Cartier's discoveries: "Rabelais vint apprendre de ce Cartier les termes de la marine et du pilotage à Saint-Malo pour en chamarrer ses bouffonnesques Lucianismes et impies épicurismes." Doremet's book was not printed till 1628, and the writer was not born till from fifteen to twenty years after Rabelais's death. The statement therefore rests on tradition only, and without further support cannot be said to have much authority. But there are certain indications in Rabelais's book of a personal acquaintance with Saint-Malo, where Cartier lived till his death in 1557. In iv. lxvi Panurge, who is generally the mouthpiece of Rabelais's reminiscences, says that he had seen the islands of Sark and Herm between Brittany and England, from which we may reasonably infer that Rabelais visited them from Saint-Malo. Again in iii. xxiv Panurge suggests that they should make a voyage to the Ogygian islands which "are not far from the harbour of Saint Malo." Lastly we find scattered up and down Rabelais's book various reminiscences of Brittany, showing that he was acquainted with the country generally. The fact that no name is given to the pilot in the 1548 edition of the Fourth Book leads M. Lefranc to suppose that it was not till after this date that Rabelais became intimate with Cartier[1]. If so, the intimacy cannot have begun till after Rabelais's return from Rome in November 1549.

Since writing Les Navigations de Pantagruel M. Lefranc has discovered that Jamet Brayer was the name of a real individual—a merchant who trafficked on the Loire and who was allied with Rabelais's family by marriage[2]. But, though Rabelais has given his pilot the name of his relative, he may still be thinking of Jacques Cartier. There is no longer, however, any reason to suppose that Rabelais was not acquainted with Cartier till after his return from Rome.

But the question whether Jamet Brayer is Jacques Cartier or not is unimportant in comparison with the undoubted fact that the influence of Cartier's voyages is plainly to be traced in Rabelais's narrative. In chapter xxx of the Fifth Book Cartier is mentioned without any disguise among the travellers whom Pantagruel and his company encountered in the country of Satin, and in the Fourth Book there are several reminiscences of his first and second voyage. Pantagruel sets sail, as Cartier did, from Saint-Malo. On the fourth day (according to the primitive edition), which was June 12, he meets with a merchant-vessel returning home, and learns that they are Frenchmen from Saintonge and that they came from Lantern-land. This agrees with the account of Cartier's first voyage, where we read that on June 12, off Labrador, "we perceived a great ship which was from La Rochelle, which had passed the night seeking the harbour of Brest." For Lantern-land, though it stands for other places as well, certainly stands for La Rochelle, where there was a Tower of the Lantern, besides two towers in the harbour.

[1] Les Navigations de Pantagruel, pp. 270–1.
[2] Rev. des études rab. IV (1906), 183.

In the partial edition of the Fourth Book, the first land at which the travellers touch is the Island of Ennasin (Noseless ones) or Alliances. "The men and women," we are told, "are like the red-faced Poitevins, except that they all...have their nose in the shape of an ace of clubs;...and all the people were kindred and related to one another[1]." M. Lefranc very ingeniously sees in this people a double reminiscence of Red Indians and Eskimos, the red skin pointing to the former and the abnormally flat nose to the latter. In his account of his first voyage Cartier, speaking of the inhabitants of Blanc Sablon on the coast of Labrador, says that "they paint themselves with certain tawny colours." These, Mr Baxter thinks, belonged to the tribe of the Beothics who inhabited Newfoundland in Cartier's day, but have since been utterly exterminated. They were probably, he adds, the same people whom John Cabot described as painting themselves with red ochre, and three of whom he brought to England[2]. As for the trait recorded by Rabelais, that "all the people were related to one another," it exactly represents the condition of an Indian totem clan. There is, however, nothing either about this peculiarity or about Eskimos in the accounts of Cartier's voyages, so that if Rabelais is here recording actual experiences he must have got his information from oral sources—either from Cartier or, if he had not made Cartier's acquaintance when he wrote this chapter, from Jean Alfonse. For Jean Alfonse's home was at La Rochelle, and there seems good ground for suggesting that Rabelais had met him there in the Fontenay-le-Comte days, and he may have met him again during the interval between his return from Canada in February 1544 and his departure on his last voyage in July of that year.

From the Island of Ennasin the travellers sail to the Island of Cheli[3], and M. Lefranc suggests that there may be

---

[1] IV. ix (iv of 1548 edition).

[2] See also for the Beothics, Sir J. G. Millais, *Newfoundland and its untrodden ways*, 1907, pp. 17–30. He cites Richard Whitbourne (*A discourse and discovery of Newfoundland*, 1622, reprinted 1870) who made many voyages to Newfoundland from 1582 to 1618, and he gives a portrait of Mary March, a Beothic, who died in 1809.

[3] IV. x (v of 1548 edition).

"some relation between King Panigon's reception of the travellers and that of the Canadian chiefs who fill so large a place in the narrative of Cartier's second voyage." I am prepared to go a step further, and to identify "the good King Panigon" with Donnacona, the "Agonhanna" or lord of Canada. For in the complete edition of the Fourth Book he is called "King Saint Panigon," and in a curious passage in chapter xxv of the Fifth Book, which only occurs in the MS. of the Bibliothèque Nationale, we are told that "Panigon in his last days had retired to a hermitage in this Island" (the Island of Odes) "and lived in great sanctity and the true Catholic Faith." Now this forcibly reminds one of the fate of Donnacona, who was treacherously captured by Cartier's orders, carried off to France, and baptized at Saint-Malo, and who died in "the true Catholic Faith" just before Cartier started on his third voyage in 1540[1]. This resemblance between Donnacona and Panigon leads one the more readily to accept M. Lefranc's suggestion, and to see in Rabelais's words, "Panigon voulut qu'elle [the queen] et toute sa suite baissassent Pantagruel et ses gens. Telle estoit la courtoisie et coustume du pays," another reminiscence of Cartier's second voyage, in the narrative of which we read that Donnacona "pria notre cappitaine luy bailler les bras pour les baiser et accoller qui est leur mode de faire chère en ladicte terre[2]." The expression "faire chère" probably suggested to Rabelais the contempt which Brother John expressed for these ceremonies compared with the more substantial cheer of king Panigon's kitchen.

There is also, if I am not mistaken, another reminiscence of the Indians whom Cartier carried off to France. In iv. xlii we are told that the Queen of the Chitterlings in pursuance of the treaty with Pantagruel sent to Gargantua seventy-eight thousand royal Chitterlings "under the conduct of the young

---

[1] Hakluyt, VIII. 263 and 145 (Discourse of Christopher Carleill). André Thevet, who calls him *Donacova Aguauna*, gives the same account of him in *Les Singularités de la France Antarctique*, c. lxxvii (P. Villey, *Les Sources d'idées au XVIe siècle*).

[2] Rabelais has doubtless also in his mind Erasmus's account of the similar custom in England.

Niphleseth, Infanta of the island. The noble Gargantua sent
them as a present to the great King of Paris; but from change
of air and also for want of mustard,...they nearly all died."
But "the young Niphleseth was preserved and honourably
treated; afterwards she was married in a high and wealthy
position, and had several fine children, for which God be
praised." Does not this too recall the fate of Cartier's Indians,
all of whom died with the exception of one little girl of ten
years old[1]?

M. Plattard notes another possible reminiscence of Cartier.
At Hochelaga the Breton pilot gave the natives "paternosters
of tin and *knives*"; similarly, Pantagruel presented Niphleseth
with "a pretty little knife of Le Perche make (*pargois*)[2]."

After leaving the Island of Cheli Pantagruel came to that
of Procuration, "which is a country all blurred and blotted.
I could make nothing of it. There we saw Pettifoggers and
Catchpoles—folk with their hair on. They invited us neither
to eat nor drink[3]." Here again there seems to be a reminiscence of Cartier's first voyage. Between Chaleur Bay and
Gaspé Bay they met with "thick fogs and obscurity," and of
the people whom they encountered on the shore of Gaspé Bay,
we are told that "they are the poorest folk that there may
be in the world," and that "they have their heads shorn close
all about except a tuft on the top of the head which they tie
like a horse's tail[4]."

The 1548 edition of the Fourth Book ends abruptly with
the fragment of a chapter which tells of the arrival of Panta-
gruel and his companions after the storm at the Island of the
Macreons. It looks as if Rabelais was still under the influence
of Cartier's voyages when he wrote it. The analogy which
M. Lefranc points out between Rabelais's description of the
spirit-haunted Island of the Macreons and that which André
Thevet gives in his *Cosmographie Universelle* of the imaginary
Island of Demons is very striking and interesting. For, as
M. Lefranc says, in several maps of the sixteenth century an

---

[1] Hakluyt, *loc. cit.*
[2] *Rev. des études rab.* VI (1908), 281.
[3] IV. xii (vi of partial edition).
[4] Baxter, pp. 108, 109.

Isle of Demons figures off the coast of Labrador[1], and its legend may well have been familiar to Rabelais. At the beginning of the seventeenth century we find the similar name of the Isle of Devils applied to the Bermudas. It is the name which they bear in the two accounts of the shipwreck of the *Sea Adventure*, by Silvester Jourdan and William Strachey respectively, which Shakespeare probably read before he wrote the *Tempest*[2].

Nearly all the foregoing instances have been taken from the partial edition of the Fourth Book, which Rabelais published in 1548. In the rest of the book, as it appeared in the complete edition of 1552, except for the Island of the Macreons, there are only slight traces of Cartier's influence. Canada indeed is mentioned by name, the Island of Medamothi, the account of which forms the second chapter of the 1552 edition, being compared with it for size; but I very much doubt whether, as M. Lefranc suggests, Medamothi stands for Newfoundland. For while Medamothi is described as a single island, Newfoundland is represented in nearly all the maps which appeared about the time of Cartier's narratives, and which were based for these parts on his discoveries, as a group of islands, varying from nine in the Harleian Map to three in Descelier's Map of 1550[3]. I think also that M. Lefranc exaggerates the realism in Rabelais's description of the *tarande* which Pantagruel bought from a Scythian merchant of the country of the Gelones (Siberia). It is true that the presence of such a merchant in the neighbourhood of Newfoundland agrees with the idea, which Cartier and Jean Alfonse had both formed, that Canada was "an end of Asia," but the description of the *tarande* is practically identical with that of the *Scytharum tarandrus* given by Pliny, and I doubt

[1] In the map of "Sebastian Cabot" (1544) it is placed near the Strait of Belle Isle. In Michael Lok's map (1582) it occupies much the same position. In the map from Peter Martyr's *De orbe novo*, published at Paris and dedicated to Hakluyt (1587), it is put several degrees further north.

[2] Jourdan's narrative is entitled *A Discovery of the Bermudas otherwise called the Isle of Divils*, 1610.

[3] It appears as a single island in the *portolan* of Giovanni Benedetti of Siena 1543 (Harrisse, *Découverte*, pp. 223–4 and frontispiece, from the collection of Mr H. Yates Thompson), and as two islands—which is very near the mark—in a sketch of Jean Alfonse (*ib.* p. 225).

whether Rabelais knew that it fairly well represents a real animal, the reindeer.

There is yet another possible reminiscence of Cartier's voyages in the Fourth Book. May not the vocabulary of the language of the natives which appears at the end of the first and second voyages[1] have suggested to Rabelais the *Briefve declaration d'aucunes dictions plus obscures* which he appended to the Fourth Book?

In the episode of the Ringing Island which opens the Fifth Book, M. Lefranc finds another reminiscence. He suggests that the idea of an island inhabited by birds who were once men is inspired by Cartier's first voyage. There we read of three Islands of Birds; first, the Funk Islands to the East of Newfoundland, which were so full of *Apponatz* (great auks), *Godez* (guillemots or razorbills, or possibly both), and *Margaulx* (solan geese) "that it seemed as if they had been stowed there[2]"; secondly, Greenly Island off the coast of Labrador, which was inhabited by guillemots and puffins; thirdly, the Bird Rocks near the Magdalen Isles in the Gulf of St Lawrence, which were "as full of birds as a field of grass," and which Cartier named Isles des Margaulx. Now the termination of Margaulx is identical with that adopted by Rabelais for the *clergaulx, monagaulx* etc. of his Ringing Island. This may be a mere coincidence, but I am inclined to regard it as lending support to M. Lefranc's suggestion. Further support is to be found in the mention in chapter iii of Robert Valbringue, whom all the commentators agree to be Roberval. I may also note that this theory that the framework for the satire of the Ringing Island was suggested to Rabelais by Cartier's voyages agrees with the view which I hold on other grounds, namely, that the episode

---

[1] There is a similar vocabulary at the end of the French abridgement of Pigafetta's narrative of Magellan's voyages.

[2] *Arrimez*. Du Petit Val has *semés*, a translation of Ramusio's *seminati* (see Baxter, p. 77). For the Great Auk or Garefowl cp. R. Whitbourne, *op. cit.*: "These Penguins are as bigge as geese and flye not, for they have but a little short wing, and they multiplie so infinitely upon a certain flat Iland, that men drive them from thence upon a boord into their boats by hundreds at a time; as if God had made the innocency of so poore a creature to become such an admirable instrument for the sustentation of man."

was written in 1546[1]. At the same time I still hold to the
opinion that the main source of inspiration is the legend of
St Brandan, in which an Island of Birds, who were formerly
men, plays a prominent part[2]. Indeed one source may easily
have suggested the other. For had Rabelais looked at a contemporary map, as, for instance, the great map made by
Pierre Desceliers at Arques near Dieppe in 1546[3], he would
have seen the Isle aux Margaulx in the Gulf of St Lawrence,
and the Isle of St Brandan almost due east of Cape Race.

III

The Short Way to Cathay

Throughout what may be called the golden age of geographical discovery the aim of every maritime explorer,
whether he sailed from Bristol, or Dieppe, or Lisbon, or
Seville, was to find a short way to Cathay. This was the object
alike of Columbus and John Cabot, of Magellan and Gomes,
of Verrazzano and Cartier. In the earlier days, when imagination was strong and knowledge vague, Cathay stood for the
fabled home of the earthly Paradise. But when knowledge
became more precise and Cathay was identified with China,
though the more visionary spirits might still cherish dreams
of terrestrial bliss, practical men were chiefly concerned to
find a short route to the rich Spice Islands, a route which
would save them the long voyage round the Cape of Good
Hope. One such route was made known to Western Europe
in 1522, when the survivors of Magellan's expedition returned
to Seville with the news of the discovery of the straits which
perpetuate Magellan's name. But it was believed that there
were other routes, either by the North-West or the North-

---

[1] See below, p. 98.
[2] See my *François Rabelais*, p. 252.
[3] Known as *La Mappemonde de Henri II*. See below, p. 64. St Brandan's
Isle appears in the maps of Sebastian Cabot and Michael Lok, and in the
Paris map dedicated to Hakluyt. Professor Egerton in the *Cambridge
Modern History* (IV. 746) notes that in 1631 a grant of the island was
gravely requested and as gravely made.

East, or by a northern passage through America corresponding to that discovered by Magellan in the South. It was the
latter belief which found most favour in Spain. The great
Conquistador, Hernán Cortés, says in his Fourth Letter to
Charles V[1], which was despatched on October 15, 1524, that
he proposed to explore the coast from Panuco to the coast of
Florida, and from there, towards the north, as far as the
Bacallaos[2]. "For it is believed absolutely that there is a
strait on that coast which leads to the South Sea." But before
the arrival of this letter Estevão Gomes, the Portuguese pilot
in the service of Charles V who had so basely deserted
Magellan, had already sailed from Coruña in search of the
passage to Cathay in the direction indicated by Cortés. He
returned in November 1525 having explored the American
coast from Nova Scotia to Florida, but without having found
a passage[3]. On the other hand the historian, Fernández de
Oviedo, who for many years held important posts in the
Spanish Indies, and who at this time was living in Hispaniola
(San Domingo), wrote in his *Sumario* (printed at Toledo in
1526) in 1525 that "if there be any such strait we that inhabit
those parts do think that the same should be rather of land
than of water[4]."

In the year previous to the voyage of Gomes a similar
exploration with the primary object of finding a passage to
Cathay had, as we have seen, been made by Verrazzano on
behalf of the King of France, and in most of the maps of this
period, except those made at Seville, the land between Florida
and Bacalhaos is called Francesca or Nova Gallia. The results
of the voyage are said to have been first recorded in a map
which the explorer himself presented to Henry VIII, between
his return in 1524 and the year 1526. Hakluyt speaks of it in

[1] *Letters of Cortes*, translated and edited by F. A. MacNutt, 2 vols., New
York, 1908, II. 207.

[2] *A los Bacallaos*; at this time Bacalhaos (Portuguese for codfish) or, as
it was also called, the "New Land," vaguely designated the region of Canada,
Newfoundland and Labrador. It was not till after Cartier's first voyage
that Newfoundland was known to be an island.

[3] P. Martyr, *De novo orbe*, dec. VI. c. x (end); H. Harrisse, *Découverte*,
pp. 87, 88, and *The Discovery of North America*, 1892, pp. 229 ff.

[4] Eden's translation in *The first three English books on America*, ed. Arber,
Birmingham, 1885.

the following terms: "A mighty large old map in parchment, made, as it should seem, by Verrazzanus, traced along the coast from Florida to Cape Breton, with many Italian names, which layeth out the sea, making a little neck of land in 40 degrees of latitude, much like the straight neck or isthmus of Darien. It sheweth also a short and easy passage by the North-West[1]." This map is now lost[2], but it is generally regarded as the prototype of those made by Vesconte di Maggiolo at Genoa in 1527 (now in the Ambrosian Library at Milan)[3] and by Girolamo Verrazzano the explorer's brother in 1529 (now in the library of the Propaganda at Rome). A new feature of both these maps is that a little isthmus is shown to the East of "Terra Florida[4]," between that country and "Francesca," and there is a statement on Verrazzano's map that it is only six miles across. In Maggiolo's, but not in Verrazzano's, a strait is also shown across Honduras with the legend *Streito dubitoso*. The isthmus also appears in a series of portolans made by Battista Agnese, a Genoese cartographer who worked at Venice from 1536 to 1564. In one of these, unsigned, but dated 1536 (now at Dresden), and in four undated ones a punctuated route is even indicated with the legend *El viazo de Fransa*. Starting from a port of Normandy (doubtless Dieppe), it crosses the Atlantic, passes over the supposed isthmus, traverses the Pacific, and ends at Cathay[5]. The influence of Verrazzano is also shown in the maps which accompany Münster's Ptolemy of 1540 and 1545 (both printed at Basle), and the various editions of his *Cosmography*. In Map No. 1, *Typus orbis universalis*, a passage is marked at the sixtieth degree of longitude between Francesca and Bacalh(a)os, with the legend *per hoc fretum iter patet ad Molucas*[6]. To the same Verrazzanian family belong the copper globe of

---

[1] Harrisse, *Découverte*, p. 94, n. 1.

[2] In his dedicatory epistle to Sir P. Sidney, Hakluyt says that it was in the custody of Master Lok and Lok's map of 1582 is evidently based on it in part.

[3] Harrisse, *Discovery*, p. 553; Winsor, *History of North America*, IV. 39.

[4] Harrisse, *Discovery*, pp. 553 and 216 ff. (with a reproduction), and see for both maps L. Hugues, *Comm. Colomb.* pt V. vol. II. p. 240 f.

[5] Harrisse, *Discovery*, 626 ff.; Winsor, IV. 40.

[6] For Münster's maps see Harrisse, *Discovery*, 607 ff.

Euphrosynus Ulpius (1542) now in the possession of the New York Historical Society[1] and the globe of Bailly dated 1530, the earliest extant map of demonstrably French origin[2].

Both the English and the Portuguese thought that the passage was to be found more to the north, somewhere in the direction of Labrador, or even nearer to the Pole. In 1527 a London merchant, named Robert Thorne, who had lived for a long time at Seville, expressed his views in two letters, written from that city, and addressed respectively to Henry VIII and to Dr Edward Lee, our ambassador to the Emperor[3]. It seemed to this optimist an easy matter to reach the Pole. For only about *two or three leagues* on either side of the Pole would there be any danger, and then you "may decline to what part you list, either by the North-East route, or by the North-West, in the backe side of the new found land."

Meanwhile an important school of cartography was being formed in France at Dieppe. It was from the Dieppe pilots, with whom Verrazzano and his brother, living as they did at Rouen, were in close communication, that the makers of all the Verrazzanian maps, whether Frenchmen, or Germans, or Italians, got much of their information. From about 1536 onwards several remarkable specimens of the cartographic art were produced at Dieppe by Nicolas Deslien, Pierre Desceliers, and others. They represent a new type of map, in which the discoveries of Jacques Cartier for the first time take their place. Cartier too had set out to find a short way to Cathay, and had failed to find a passage in the direction of Labrador. But while he was exploring the St Lawrence, a new solution of the problem presented itself to him. "We have understood," he says, "of the lord Donnacona and others...that beyond the said Saguenay [the district, not the river] the said stream [the St Lawrence] floweth into two or three great lakes, and that then one finds a fresh-water sea, of which there is no mention of having seen the end, as they have heard from those of the Saguenay; for they have told us

[1] Winsor, IV. 32.
[2] Harrisse, *op. cit.* 147. The inscription *Robertus de Bailly* may denote either the maker of the map or the person who ordered it.
[3] Hakluyt, II. 159 ff.

they have not been there[1]." Similarly Jean Alfonse, who, as we have seen, accompanied Roberval to Canada in 1542, says: "The entrance of Saguenay is at 48⅓ degrees of longitude…and it seemeth to be as it were an arm of the sea, wherefore I think that this sea goes to the Pacific or in fact to the Sea of Cathay[2]." This expresses the same vague information which was given to Cartier, for the latter had been told that one way into the interior was by the river Saguenay, but that owing to the shallowness and general innavigability of the stream it presented great difficulties.

In spite of the hearsay character of the Indian chiefs' information this new theory of the passage found great favour in France, and held the field for nearly a century and a half. To find a way to China was one of the two great objects which Champlain had ever present before his eyes. The name of La Chine which La Salle gave to the royal grant of land just across the great rapids which still bear the name, about eight or nine miles from Montreal, testify to the same ambition. When he heard of the river Ohio he thought that it would prove to flow into the Pacific, and it was not till 1682 when he reached the mouth of the Mississippi, into which the Ohio falls, and found that it flowed into the Gulf of Mexico, that the dream was finally shattered.

Such briefly was the state of knowledge and speculation with regard to a passage by water through North America, to the Pacific Ocean and the continent of Asia when Rabelais began to write his Fourth Book in the summer of 1546. I will now cite the remarkable words in which he describes the departure of Pantagruel's fleet on its voyage of exploration:

In good time they set sail to the Greek [north-east] wind as it got up, to which point the chief pilot had shaped their course, and set the needles of all their compasses. For his advice, and also that of Xenomanes was—seeing that the oracle of the Holy Bottle was near Cathay in Upper India—not to take the ordinary route of the Portuguese, who, sailing through the torrid zone and the Cape of Bonasperanza at the south point of Africa, beyond the equinoctial line, and losing the sight and guidance of the arctic pole, make an enor-

[1] J. P. Baxter, *Jacques Cartier*, 1906, p. 189; Hakluyt, VIII. 246.
[2] *Cosmographie*, ed. G. Musset, p. 459. Hakluyt's translation is not quite accurate.

mously long voyage; but to follow as near as possible the parallel of
the aforesaid India, and to turn round the said pole to the Westward,
so that winding under the North they might be in the same latitude
as the port of Olone without coming nearer to the pole, for fear of
coming into and being shut up in the glacial Sea. And following this
regular circuit by the same parallel they might have it on their right
as they sailed Eastward, as on their departure it was on the left.
Now this turned out to their incredible advantage; for without shipwreck, without danger or loss of men, in great calm they made the
voyage to Upper India in less than four months, which the Portuguese could scarcely do in three years, with dangers innumerable.

This is from the text of the partial edition of 1548. In the
complete edition of 1552 Rabelais, besides giving the name of
the pilot as Jamet Brayer, substituted *canonique destour* for
regulier destour, but this makes no difference in the meaning.
W. F. Smith is surely wrong in translating *l'eussent à dextre
vers le Levant, qui au departement leurs estoit à senestre*, by
"they might have the eastward on their right, which at
their departure was on their left." For this rendering takes
no account of the *le* before *eussent*, which must refer to the
"parallel." On the outward voyage Pantagruel and his companions would have this imaginary parallel on their left, for
they would sail to the north of it; consequently on their return
by the same route they would have it on their right[1]. Here it
may be noticed that the latitude of Olonne (to give it its
modern spelling) is 46° 34′, while what was known in Rabelais's
day as Upper India lies roughly between latitudes 45° and
50°. Further, more or less on the same parallel will be found
Cape Race, the southernmost point of Newfoundland (46° 40′),
and Quebec (46° 24′).

The travellers "set sail," we are told, "to the N.E. wind,"
which must be taken to imply that after clearing the northern-
most point of Brittany, they steered in a south-westerly
direction till they reached the latitude of Olonne. For three
days "they neither sighted land nor saw anything new"
(c. ii). On the fourth day (according to the text of 1548) as
they were "beginning by degrees to wind round (*tournoyer*)
the Pole, going further from the Equinoctial" (c. ii = v of
1556 ed.) "they met a merchant-vessel returning from

[1] Cp. Lefranc, pp. 322, 323.

Lantern-land." This gave rise to the remarkable encounter between Panurge and the sheep-dealer, and on the next day but one, "the west wind continuing to blow in conjunction with a little of the south-west" they came to a triangular island greatly resembling Sicily in form and situation (c. iv = ix of 1552 ed.). On leaving this island the S.W. wind was still blowing, and about sundown they disembarked on another island, that of Cheli (c. v = x of 1552 ed.). On the following day they visited the country of Procuration and passed the islands of Tohu and Bohu (cc. vi, vii = cc. xii, xvi, xvii of 1552 ed.). Soon after this they encountered a terrible storm, and when it had abated, they landed at the port of the island of the Macræons. At this point the 1548 edition abruptly ends, but in the complete edition of 1552 we are told that this island was "formerly subject to the ruler of Brittany." On leaving the island they sailed with a gentle and delicious wind called Aguyon, which Rabelais in the *Briefve declaration* explains to be a Breton and Norman name for a sea breeze resembling the west wind on land. This surely implies that Aguyon was a westerly wind. After this there is nothing to indicate the direction of the voyagers until we come to the episode of the frozen words, when it appears from the pilot's explanation of the phenomenon that they had reached the confines of the glacial sea (c. lvi). Finally we learn that after they had been becalmed the wind began to blow from the W.N.W.

There is just one other point in the account of the voyage that calls for notice. At the very close of the Fifth Book (in a passage which occurs in the manuscript but not in the printed text, but which is surely by Rabelais) the priestess Bacbuc after presenting Pantagruel and his friends with three bottles filled with water, tells them that the rarefaction of the water by heat will produce air, and that by means of this air the ships will be carried direct, without touching land if they please, to the port of Olonne. But why to Olonne instead of to St Malo, the port from which they had sailed? For the same reason no doubt that Olonne is mentioned at the outset of the voyage, because it was on the same parallel as the Oracle of the Bottle.

Such are, so to speak, the geographical data of Pantagruel's voyage. The following question now arises: What route had Rabelais in mind when he wrote the words at the close of the first chapter of the Fourth Book which I have quoted above? Did he from the beginning contemplate a voyage by the North-West passage? Or was he thinking of a passage further to the south by way of the St Lawrence? If these words stood alone, if we had no other indications of the direction taken by the voyagers, I should unhesitatingly choose the latter alternative. For, firstly, from the time of Cartier the idea of a passage by the St Lawrence was, as we have seen, the prevailing one in France, and, secondly, the account of Cartier's voyages, as I hope I have shown, had a decided influence upon Rabelais's narrative. But other indications in the narrative, the mention of south-westerly winds— in Rabelais's day the coast of Labrador was supposed to trend to the north-east—and of the approach to the confines of the glacial sea, are in favour of the view which has been so admirably explained and illustrated by M. Lefranc, namely that Pantagruel is represented by Rabelais as reaching the continent of Asia by what is known as the North-West passage.

In my book on Rabelais I suggested that, when he wrote the first chapter of the Fourth Book at Metz in 1546, he was thinking of the supposed passage by way of the St Lawrence, but that later he adopted the idea of a voyage by the North-West passage. I further suggested that this change was due to Cartier's failure to find a passage in the direction of the St Lawrence. I now see that this latter hypothesis is clearly untenable. So far as we can gather, both Cartier and Jean Alfonse returned with the conviction that the passage to Cathay, though they had been unable to find it, was to be sought rather in the neighbourhood of the St Lawrence and the Saguenay than in the direction of Labrador.

There are some difficulties too in the way of my first hypothesis. In chapter i he says that the chief pilot and Xenomanes advised them to keep in the same latitude as the port of Olonne, *without coming nearer to the Pole*. But in chapter v

(ed. 1552) he tells us that they were beginning by degrees to
wind round the Pole, *going further from the Equinoctial*. This
looks as if when he wrote this last passage he had begun to
change his mind. I hope to show in my next paper that in
all probability the incomplete Fourth Book which appeared in 1548 was written in two sections, the first, consisting of chapters i, v–xvi (ed. 1552), at Metz, and the second,
consisting of chapters xvii–xxiv, and a part of xxv, at Paris
in 1547. Thus according to this division of the chapters the
idea of a North-West passage had already suggested itself to
Rabelais at Metz.

Hitherto I have confined myself mainly to a consideration
of Rabelais's literary sources for geographical matters. But
one may suppose that he also consulted maps, and, if so,
what maps?

First, one naturally thinks of the maps which accompany
the *Novus Orbis*. Now in some of the copies of the Basle
editions of 1532 and 1537, the former of which was certainly
used by Rabelais, there is a map which is generally attributed
to Sebastian Münster, chiefly, if not wholly, on the ground
that he wrote the geographical summary which serves as an
introduction to the volume. But the map bears no resemblance
to his undoubted work in the Ptolemy of 1540 and 1545. It
belongs to an early type in which North America is only
represented by two islands, Cuba and Terra Corterealis, and
in fact closely resembles Schöner's globe of 1515. As it is
only found in some of the copies of the *Novus Orbis*, it is very
probable that it does not really belong to it, but was sometimes bound up with it[1]. Rabelais certainly did not use it.
Nor did he use the map which Oronce Finé made in 1531,
and which is found in most copies of the Paris 1532 edition
of the *Novus Orbis*. This belongs to a type prevalent in Germany between 1523 and 1538, in which America is joined to
Asia[2].

A very popular map was the one made by the great Gerard

[1] It is reproduced in Nordenskiöld's *Facsimile Atlas to the early study of
Cartography*, Stockholm, 1889, plate XLII. It is in neither of the two copies
in the Cambridge University Library.
[2] Nordenskiöld, plate XLI (2).

Mercator at Louvain, in 1538, in which he reverted to the older and correct view of the separation of America from Asia, making a *fretum arcticum* between the *baccalearum regio* and the Arctic lands[1]. But with the exception of this indication of a passage, there is nothing in the map to suggest that it was known to Rabelais.

Then there are the maps already referred to which Sebastian Münster published at Basle in his Ptolemy of 1540 and 1545 and his *Cosmographia* of 1541, 1550, etc., of which those which concern us are *Typus orbis universalis* (I) and *Novae insulae* (xvii). In these too America is separated from Asia, and in No. I a passage is marked between "Francesca" and "Terra Nova sive de Bacalh(a)os," with the legend, *per hoc fretum iter patet ad Molucas*. Newfoundland appears as one small island, with the name of Corterati. On the continent of Asia *India superior* is marked between 60° and 70°, that is to say, on the same latitude as the passage. In the map of the *Novae insulae* we find the following legends: *Parias abundat auro et margaritis, Canibali' Regio Gigantum, 7 insulae Margueritarum*. All this is more or less in conformity with Rabelais's ideas about the New World, and M. Lefranc has rightly included these two maps among the illustrations to his book[2].

Finally we come to the maps of the Dieppe school, three of which, at least, were in existence when Rabelais began to write his Fourth Book, namely, (1) a map in the Harleian collection of the British Museum[3], (2) a map made by Nicolas Deslien in 1541, now in the Royal Library at Dresden, and (3) a "boke

[1] Nordenskiöld, plate XLIII. In 1541 Mercator made a globe which is now in the royal library at Brussels. The gores for it have been reproduced at Brussels, 1875.

[2] p. 32, and at the end of the book.

[3] Add. MSS. 5413. The official date is 1536, on the ground that the arms of the Dauphin show an open crown, and that the crown was closed in that year. Was this the case? Prof. Beazley assigns it to 1536–1540. It must certainly have been made after Cartier's return from his second voyage in July 1536. M. Harrisse says it must be later than his third voyage from which he returned in October 1542, but it gives no information which goes beyond the results of the second voyage, except the name San Malo. It is reproduced in facsimile in *Bibliotheca Lindesiana*, Collections and Notes, No. 4, 1898. In the introductory notice C. H. Coote says that it is unquestionably the work of Pierre Desceliers.

of Idrography" or portolan, made by John Rotz (Jean Roze), a citizen of Dieppe, in 1542 for Henry VIII[1]. A fourth map of the same school was made by Pierre Desceliers in the very year, 1546, that Rabelais began his account of Pantagruel's voyage. This is the so-called "Map of Henri II[2]." All these maps give the results of Cartier's discoveries, but there is no proof that Rabelais was acquainted with any of them. None of them indicate any passage by way of the St Lawrence. Indeed in the Harleian map the course of the St Lawrence, after being traced for some distance beyond *Le premier sault* and the junction of another river, which is apparently meant for the Ottawa, is abruptly barred by a large undiscovered tract of country. The only one which shows any indication that it may possibly have inspired some parts of Rabelais's narrative is the "Map of Henri II." On this we find marked not only a Terre des Bretons and the island of Cape Breton, but to the south-east of this in latitude 46° an island called Isle du breton, which perhaps may have suggested to Rabelais his Isle des Macréons. For that island, as we have seen, is said to have been formerly subject to the *dominateur de Bretaigne*[3]. Then, as I have pointed out[4], we find in the Gulf of St Lawrence the Isle aux Margaulx, which recalls the *clergaulx*, etc., of the Ringing Island, and almost due east of Cape Race the Isle of St Brandan. South-east of the Isle du breton between latitudes 37° and 41° numerous islands are marked, and south of the Bermudas is an island called La Catholique, which is vaguely suggestive of the famous Isle des Papimanes. Among the pictures which diversify the surface of this interesting map two are especially noteworthy. One is a small full-length figure with the legend "M. de Roberval," and the other represents the harpooning of a

---

[1] Brit. Mus. O. R. Lib. 20 E ix (see esp. leaf 24); Harrisse, *Découverte*, pp. 201, 220. For the Dieppe maps see *ib.* pp. 149 ff.

[2] Reproduced by Jomard, who then owned it, in *Monuments de la géographie*, Paris, 1858–1862, and in *Bibl. Lind.* It is now in the Rylands Library, Manchester, having been sold to Mrs Rylands by Lord Crawford. Coote deciphered on it in faint writing the words, "Faicte a Arques par Pierre Desceliers presb[r]. 1546." For the section relating to Canada see Plate I.

[3] Some commentators take Bretaigne to mean Britain; this seems unlikely.

[4] See above, p. 54.

PLATE I

Section of the so-called " Map of Henri II " (1546)

whale. I give these comparisons for what they are worth, which is not perhaps much. For not one of them points to the map conclusively as the source of Rabelais's inspiration. But, taken as a whole, they are suggestive, and it must be remembered that even supposing that Rabelais had studied the map, we must not expect too close a resemblance. He was, after all, not a scientific geographer, but a writer of romance, bound only by his own imagination.

In any case there is nothing that I have been able to find in this or any other map which throws light on Rabelais's views as to the short way to Cathay. The only conclusion to which the whole evidence seems to point is that his first idea was to conduct his travellers by way of the St Lawrence, and that for some reason or other he abandoned this for a more northerly route, that of the North-West passage. When Captain Roald Amundsen accomplished his remarkable voyage from the Atlantic to the Pacific, he realised the dream of nearly five centuries. But it was not a "*short* way to the East by the West," for it took three years to accomplish.

IV

RABELAIS AND HENRI II

WHEN Francis I died on the 31st of March 1547, Rabelais
was at Metz, whither, anticipating the censure which the
Sorbonne passed on his Third Book, he had fled early in
1546, and where he had obtained a post as physician to the
public hospital. We know from an entry in the town accounts
that he was paid his salary up to Midsummer 1547, and probably at that date he returned to France. For a passage in the
Sciomachie seems to point to his presence in Paris on July 10
of that year. It runs as follows: "We have seen similar news
[*i.e.* news transmitted with apparently supernatural rapidity]
at Lyons of the battle of Pavia, in the person of the late
Seigneur de Rochefort, and recently at Paris on the day when
the Seigneur de Jarnac and the Seigneur de Chastaigeraye
fought their duel [at Saint-Germain]." The question is whether
"we" is used in a personal sense, either as equivalent to "I"
or at least as including the writer, or whether, as M. Plattard
in his excellent edition of the 1548 text of the Fourth Book[1]
maintains, it merely implies the men of Rabelais's generation
as opposed to the ancient historians to whom he has just
referred. The majority of opinion[2], however, is against
M. Plattard.

The next date in Rabelais's life—and this time it is a
certain one—is June 18, 1548, on which day he signed a
receipt for the value of a bill of exchange drawn at Paris on a
Roman banker. He describes himself as physician to Cardinal
Du Bellay, who had been sent by Henri II on a special mission
to Rome. When did Rabelais leave France? The old view,
based on (1) the publication of the incomplete Fourth Book
with the imprint of 1548, (2) the mention of *nouveaux Henricus*

---

[1] *Le Quart Livre de Pantagruel*, 1910.
[2] Recently L. Romier, *Notes critiques et documents sur le dernier voyage
de Rabelais en Italie, Rev. des études rab.* X (1912), 120 ff., and H. Clouzot,
Rev. du XVIe siècle, VI (1919), 276.

in chapter iii = vi of the 1552 edition, was that he set out in the spring of 1548—at the earliest in the second half of February.

But this view has been upset by M. Romier[1], who points out that *a priori* it is far more likely that Rabelais travelled to Rome in the company of his patron and his suite than that he was sent for by the Cardinal and travelled alone. Now Du Bellay took leave of the King and the Court at Reims on July 27, 1547, after the ceremony of the King's consecration, and set out for Rome by the route usually taken in time of peace with the Emperor—Lyons, the Alps, Turin, Placentia, Ferrara, etc. On the 11th of September he was at Ferrara, where he spent several days; on the 15th he reached Bologna, and on the 27th he entered Rome. But if Rabelais travelled with him, what about the publication of his book in 1548? and then there is the difficulty of the *nouveaux Henricus*.

Of this latter difficulty M. Romier easily disposes. "The *nouveaux Henricus*," says M. Plattard, following Heulhard, "were struck by virtue of an ordinance of January 31, 1548." But the date as given by Cartier, *La Numismatique de Rabelais* (*Rev. de Numismatique*, XII. 347), and Le Blanc, *Traité hist. des monnoies de France*, p. 331, is old style so that the ordinance can have nothing to do with Rabelais's *nouveaux Henricus*. On the other hand, we learn from Le Blanc that double crowns called *Henris* were struck at the very beginning of the new king's reign. M. Romier, therefore, conjectures that Rabelais originally wrote *Franciscus* (for the famous episode of Panerge and the sheep-dealer must have been written in June or July 1546), but altered it to *nouveaux Henricus* before he handed his manuscript to the printer.

There remains the date of publication—1548. But books were post-dated in Rabelais's day as well as in ours, and M. Romier conjectures that the incomplete Fourth Book really appeared at the opening of the Lyons fair, November 3, 1547, at the same time as Rabelais's Almanac for 1548. This conjecture is based on the important conclusions drawn by

[1] *Op. cit.* pp. 113 ff.

M. Abel Lefranc from the publication of *Pantagruel* as to the relations which existed in the sixteenth century between the great fairs and the publication of books. It must have been early in September[1] that Cardinal Du Bellay passed through Lyons, so that, whether Rabelais joined him there or at an earlier stage of his journey, he must have arranged for the publication of his little book at the approaching fair not later than that date. There are very few printer's errors except in proper names and in the technical terms of navigation; but the mistakes in these make it certain that Rabelais did not himself see the book through the press.

M. Romier's contention may be supported by another consideration. Rabelais may have returned to France and continued the writing of his book under the idea that with the new reign the severe measures against heresy which had marked the last seven years of the old one would be mitigated. If so, he was speedily undeceived. Henri II was more orthodox and more sincere in his religion than his father, and the three persons who had the most influence on him, the Constable de Montmorency, the Cardinal of Lorraine, and Diane de Poitiers, if they differed widely in other respects, were at least united in a common desire to repress Protestantism. Accordingly, on October 8, 1547, a second criminal court of the Paris *Parlement*, which became known as *La Chambre Ardente*, was specially created for the trial of heretics. It began its work in the following December, and, sitting continuously till January 1550, passed at least five hundred sentences[2]. It is true that its jurisdiction extended over only a fourth part of the kingdom, but the provincial *Parlements* of Rouen, Toulouse, and Aix were hardly less active. It is, therefore, highly improbable that after the 8th of October Rabelais should have taken steps to publish a work which contained, as M. Romier points out, not only much that is irreverent, especially in the Prologue, but at least two passages (chapter x) which he thought it prudent to suppress in the revised edition

---

[1] In 1537 he took from fifteen to seventeen days to get to Rome from Lyons. In 1547, as he was out of health, he probably travelled more slowly.
[2] N. Weiss, *La chambre ardente*.

of 1552 (chapters xxii and xxiii)[1]. It may be said that Rabelais, who was leaving France under the protection of Cardinal Du Bellay, did not run any risk, but at this juncture would any publisher have given Rabelais anything for his book? For probably, as M. Romier suggests, Rabelais published his book in this incomplete form because he was in want of money. As it was, the publisher and printer, who was certainly Pierre de Tours, the successor of Juste at Lyons, only gave the place of publication, but suppressed his own name.

M. Romier's view therefore rests on two converging probabilities; but it may be disproved by showing that any part of the incomplete Fourth Book was written after the first week of September 1547. Let us then examine its structure. There is an allusion in chapter ii (= chapter v of 1552 edition) to the proposed meeting of the Council of Trent for its sixth session on July 29, 1546. This date was fixed at the fifth session, which was held on June 16, but on July 18 the meeting was postponed. The chapter, therefore, must have been written before Rabelais had heard of the postponement, that is to say, in June or July 1546. But the book opens with the statement that Pantagruel put to sea on June 9, and this is possibly an indication that he began writing the book on that day of the year 1546—that is to say, when he was at Metz.

Now it has been pointed out both by W. F. Smith and by M. Plattard that there are very few references to classical authors or books of any kind in this instalment of the Fourth Book. This is true of the first six chapters (= i, v–xii, xvi of the complete edition), in which Ovid's *Fasti*, Pliny, Gellius, Erasmus's *Adagia* and *Apophthegmata*, Merlin Cocaye, and the narratives of Cartier's voyages form the sum total of Rabelais's library. But for the remaining chapters, vii–xi (= xvii–xxv of the 1552 edition) the list must be increased by the addition of Valerius Maximus, Suetonius, Aristotle, *De Mundo* (translated into Latin by Budé), Virgil, Sallust, Livy, and a contemporary work, *Le Disciple de Pantagruel*.

The natural inference is that the first six chapters were written at Metz, where Rabelais had few books at his com-

---

[1] Romier, *op. cit.* p. 130.

mand, and the remainder after his return to France in the summer of 1547. There is no allusion, however, in chapters vii–xi to any event later than the first week of September. M. Romier's view, therefore, is not negatived by any internal evidence[1].

The date of the composition of the rest of the Fourth Book is a far more complicated one. I will begin by stating M. Romier's view. He thinks that not enough importance has been attached to the chronological data given in Rabelais's letter to Cardinal de Châtillon. He lays stress on Rabelais's statements that, in consequence of the calumny of certain Cannibals, "plus n'estois deliberé en escrire un iota," and that as a result of the privilege and protection granted him by Henri II "je mectz la plume au vent." From these he infers that Rabelais laid down his pen in 1546 and did not take it up again till the summer of 1551, after his third interview with Odet de Châtillon.

But we have seen that Rabelais was still writing his book in the summer of 1547, and surely his words do not imply all that M. Romier supposes. Rabelais says that he was so angered and disheartened that he had determined to write no more, but he does not say that he had kept to his determination. Then he speaks of the "privilege and particular protection against the calumniators which Henri II had granted to the Cardinal on his behalf," referring no doubt to the official privilege granted by the King at Saint-Germain in the presence of the Cardinal on August 6, 1550.

But having obtained this privilege why should Rabelais

---

[1] His statement (p. 139) that the partial edition was completed before the end of 1546 seems a hasty one; nor can I agree with him in thinking that it was begun in 1544. His argument (p. 125) is that the alteration of "about *twelve* years" to "about *twenty* years" which Rabelais made in chapter v (=xi of 1552 edition) indicates an interval of eight years between the original writing of the passage and the revision. But this is too literal an interpretation. In the first place Rabelais could not have written the passage before he had finished the Third Book. Secondly, from the date of his visit to Florence, which was almost certainly in April 1534 (see V. L. Bourrilly, *Lettres écrites d'Italie par François Rabelais*, 1910, pp. 8–9) to June or July 1546 is just "about twelve years." As for the alteration made before publication in 1552, twenty must be regarded only as a round number.

have waited nearly a year before taking up his pen? Moreover would the privilege have been granted, if all that Rabelais had written of his new book at this time was the already published instalment? Certainly the usual practice was not to grant a privilege until a book was nearly completed. There were, no doubt, exceptions, but, even supposing that Cardinal de Châtillon, as the nephew of Montmorency, had considerable interest with the King, would a privilege on these conditions have been granted by so orthodox a monarch to a writer so little orthodox as Rabelais?

The only way to arrive at any sort of conclusion is to consider the date of composition chapter by chapter, or at least episode by episode.

In his *Histoire de la Littérature française classique*[1] Brunetière pointed out that Rabelais's satire on the Court of Rome and on Bishop Homenaz in particular closely reflects the policy of Henri II, and in my book on Rabelais, adopting this suggestion, I said "that it is extremely tempting to draw the inference that the chapters relating to Bishop Homenaz and the Island of the Papimanes were added in 1551[2]." Now the anti-Vatican policy of the French court may be said to have begun to develop in December 1550, when Ottavio Farnese, Lord of Parma, finding that his uncle, Pope Julius III, could not protect him against the hostilities of the Imperial forces, or persuade the Emperor to restore to him Piacenza, applied for aid to Henri II. But the situation did not become acute till July 1551, when diplomatic relations between France and the Vatican were broken off, and the Pope issued a brief attacking the French King in violent language (July 26)[3]. On August 4 Henri II summoned the Papal nuncio, bade him leave the Court and made a bitter attack on the Pope. The rupture was now complete.

Already before this the Sorbonne had enunciated the proposition that neither the French King nor the Gallican Church owed any obedience to the Pope, and at a meeting of the

---

[1] p. 120.　　　　[2] *François Rabelais*, p. 112.
[3] See the account of the crisis in M. Romier's admirable *Les Origines politiques des Guerres de Religion*, 2 vols. 1913, I. 220–296.

Privy Council, held on the 4th or 5th of August, one of the Councillors actually proposed that the Gallican Church should renounce its allegiance to the Pope. It was only the tears of the Cardinal of Lorraine and his remark, "Sire, I appeal to your Majesty's conscience," which moved the King to reject the proposal[1].

But though an actual schism was averted the King was still full of wrath against the Pope, and on September 3 he issued a "Declaration forbidding money to be sent to Rome for expediting the conferring of benefices," in which we may see the direct inspiration of Rabelais's chapter, *Comment par la vertu des Decretales est l'or subtilement tiré de France en Rome*[2]. On the following day, however, the Pope wrote a conciliatory letter to the King, who answered it on October 5 in similar terms. Before the end of November diplomatic relations were resumed.

It will be generally agreed that the episode of the Papimanes is the result of Rabelais's desire to stand well with the King and thus be assured of his protection in the event of any unpleasantness on the part of the Sorbonne or the *Parlement*. But M. Romier goes much further than this. He sees in all the additions made to the Fourth Book in the edition of 1552 a "veritable pamphlet against the Pope and the Roman Curia," and concludes that they were all written between the spring of 1551 after Rabelais's interview with Cardinal de Châtillon at Saint-Maur and the delivery of his manuscript to the printer in the autumn of the same year[3].

But many of the additional chapters have nothing to do with Rome, and there are several others, *e.g.* the attack upon Lent, with its pendant, the episode of the Isle Farouche, which may have occurred to Rabelais independently of the Gallican crisis. Let us therefore examine the different episodes in detail and see how far we can determine the date of their composition.

The episode of the Isle des Papefigues was clearly conceived at the same time as that of the Isle des Papimanes

---

[1] Romier, *op. cit.* I. 258.   [2] *Ib.* II. 269.
[3] *Rev. des études rab.* X (1908), 140.

and therefore may be assigned with it to the period of the greatest tension between France and the Vatican, that is to say, to July–September 1551.

The completion of the episode of the Macreons (chapters xxv–xxviii) is doubtless the earliest of the additions, and was probably written soon after Rabelais's return to France in November 1549 or at any rate when he first took up his pen again. I agree with M. Romier that he wrote little at Rome—not so much because Cardinal Du Bellay's continued ill-health left him little leisure, as because it was apparently not his habit to occupy himself with his book when he was absent from France in the service of the Cardinal or his brother.

The episode of the Island of Ruach (chapters xliii and xliv) has no connexion with what goes immediately before or after. The only possible indication of date is the reference to the death of the giant Bringuenarilles of the Island of Tohu, which has already been mentioned in chapter xvii. It might be inferred from this that it is one of the earlier additions.

The episode of the frozen words, which shows that the travellers had reached the confines of the Glacial Sea (chapters lv, lvi) gives us no clue as to the date of its composition.

On the other hand, the last five chapters, which include the approach to the Island of Chaneph (Hypocrisy), the episode of the calm, and the sighting of the Island of Ganabin, where they did not land, furnish a tempting indication of date in the reference to the surprise of the English garrison at Inchkeith (the Isle of Horses), on June 20, 1549, which Friar John says took place "this morning." This surely implies that when Rabelais was writing this passage he thought of Pantagruel's voyage as happening in the year 1549, though originally he put it in 1546. We might go on to infer that these five chapters were written soon after Rabelais's return to France, and in all probability before March 1550, when peace was made between France and England, for the two last chapters are clearly a hit at our country. But in chapter lxix there is a reference to "nos gras concilipetes de Chesil" which seems to point to a later date. The Council of Trent had not met since June 2, 1547—at Bologna—and on September 17, 1549, it had been prorogued. On November 13, 1550, the new Pope, Julius III, promulgated a bull summoning the Council to meet at Trent on May 1, 1551, but before this, in August 1550, Henri II had expressed to the Papal nuncio his dissatisfaction with the Pope's intentions and his unwillingness that the French bishops should take any further part in the discussions. Would Rabelais have referred to the Council unless it was a topic of actual interest, and could it have been such a topic before July or August 1550, when the resumption of its sittings began to be discussed in France? If M. Romier can explain the reference of Inchkeith, I would willingly follow him in proposing for these chapters even so late a date as the latter half of 1551, but they contain no allusion to the Gallican crisis and they may equally well have been written a year earlier.

The episode of Messere Gaster (chapters lvii–lxii) is, as W. F. Smith has pointed out, probably in part an attack on the gluttony and hypocrisy of the Roman Cardinals and priests. It is therefore quite possible to regard it as inspired to some extent by the Gallican crisis. On the other hand, it may have suggested itself independently to Rabelais as the result of his observations at Rome in the household of Cardinal Du Bellay.

The three episodes of the Island of Tapinois (Sly-land), over which reigned Quaresmeprenant, of the monstrous Physestère or whale, and of the Isle Farouche inhabited by the Chitterlings (chapters xxix–xlii) form a continuous narrative, and therefore in all probability must be of the same date. The last sentence of chapter xxxii, which there is no reason to suppose was added later, helps us to determine that date; for "les demoniacles Calvins, imposteurs de Geneve; les enraigés Putherbes," is evidently Rabelais's retort to the attacks on him by Gabriel de Puits-Herbault in 1549 and by Calvin in 1550. Now Calvin's *De scandalis*, in which the attack was made, was published at Geneva in September or October 1550[1], so that it could not have come to

---

[1] The dedicatory epistle is dated July 10, 1550 (Calvin's birthday), and

Rabelais's knowledge before the latter month at the earliest. We may therefore assign the passage and with it the whole three episodes to some time between October 1550 and the autumn of 1551, when the Fourth Book was completed. Like the last five chapters and like the episode of Messere Gaster, they may have been inspired by the Gallican crisis or they may have preceded it. It should be noted that the name Tapinois or Sly-land is closely akin to that of Chaneph or Hypocrisy, the island inhabited by Hypocrites, Paternosterers, Bigots, and Hermits.

Finally, we come to the chapters which were interpolated in the edition of 1548, that is to say, the episode of the Island of Medamothi (chapters ii–iv), and the additions to the episode of the Catchpoles (the greater part of chapter xii, xiii–xv, and the opening paragraph of xvi). These additions include an anecdote about François Villon, which Gaston Paris thinks may be true in substance, but which M. Champion regards as founded on mere tradition[1].

Chapter ii opens in almost identically the same words as the *Isle Sonante*, "Cestuy jour, et les deux subsequens ne leurs apparut terre ne chose aultre nouvelle. Car aultres foys avoient aré ceste routte." The explanation of this, I suggest, is that Rabelais, having decided not to include the episode of the Ringing Island in the Fourth Book, utilised the opening sentences, first for chapter ii of the incomplete book, and later for the new chapters, ii and v, of the complete edition.

A tantalising clue is offered to us in the second paragraph of chapter ii, in which we are told that Pantagruel learnt that the ruler of the land was King Philophanes, but that he was absent at that time at the marriage of his brother Philotheamon with the Infanta of the kingdom of Engys (ἔγγυς = neighbouring). In the *Briefve declaration* Rabelais interprets Philophanes as "fond of seeing and being seen," and Philotheamon as "fond of seeing." M. Lefranc finds in this an allusion to the marriage of Henri II with Catherine de'

in a letter dated August 19 of the same year he speaks of the work as nearing completion (? =publication).

[1] Gaston Paris, *François Villon*, pp. 73–74; P. Champion, *François Villon*, 2 vols. 1913, II. 250–255.

Medici in 1533, his elder brother, the then Dauphin, being spoken of as "the King of that land," because the name of New France had been given by Verrazzano to the coast between Florida and Cape Breton[1]. This idea is put forward by M. Lefranc with his usual persuasiveness, but the date seems fatal to it. Rabelais, for all his desire to ingratiate himself with Henri II, would hardly have connected with the voyage of Pantagruel an event which happened at least thirteen years earlier. The only marriage of note which took place during the years 1546–1551 was that of François de Guise with Anne d'Este (1548).

M. Clouzot seems to me to be nearer the mark in identifying Medamothi with Jean Du Bellay's château of Saint-Maur-les-Fossés[2]. He finds support for this view in the mention of "maistre Charles Charmois, peintre du roy Megiste," otherwise Charles Carmoy who worked at Fontainebleau from 1537 to 1550 and is qualified, in 1547 and 1548, as painter to the Cardinal Du Bellay[3]. He was entrusted in 1549 by Philibert de L'Orme with the decoration of the chapel at Vincennes, and in a document dated October 6, 1551, he is designated as painter to Diane de Poitiers[4]. We are told that Friar John bought two "rare and precious pictures" by this artist, one of which was the portrait of a valet looking for his master, and the same picture is again referred to in a passage which occurs in the MS. of the Fifth Book (end of chapter xxvi), but not in the printed text. M. Clouzot supposes that Carmoy was employed at Saint-Maur under De L'Orme. This is highly probable, but his further supposition that the two pictures by Carmoy mentioned by Rabelais, the *grand tableau* of Philomela and Procne, the tapestry of the deeds of Achilles, the three "unicorns" and the *tarande*, all formed part of the Cardinal's collections is much more conjectural.

The Cardinal left Rome after the conclave of Julius III on July 19, 1550, and was detained by illness at Scarperia in the Apennines till the end of the month. By September he must have reached Paris and probably he resided for a time

---

[1] *Les Navigations de Pantagruel*, pp. 287 ff.
[2] *Rev. des études rab.* IX (1911), 456 ff.
[3] *Ib.* VIII (1910), 113 ff.   [4] Maurice Roy, *ib.* IX (1911), 77 ff.

in his unfinished palace of Saint-Maur. He was certainly there in the spring of 1551, completing his convalescence[1]. Did he spend the winter there, or did he carry out the intention which he announced in a letter written on August 15, 1550, of wintering at his see of Le Mans[2]? Wherever he was, it is a likely conjecture that his physician, Rabelais, was with him, and a reference to Philibert de L'Orme in chapter lxi of the Fourth Book furnishes a presumption that the episode of Messere Gaster at any rate was written in that "paradise of salubrity," the château of Saint-Maur. It is also possible that Rabelais may have gone there almost immediately after his return to France in November 1549.

M. Clouzot sees in the mention of the "great and solemn fairs of the place" a reference to the important fair of Saint-Maur, which opened on the 23rd of June, and that of the absence of the lord of the island by the fact that Cardinal Du Bellay was still at Rome on that day of the year 1550[3]. But he was also at Rome in June 1548 and 1549.

With regard to Rabelais's conception of the date of Pantagruel's voyage we are met by two perplexing passages which occur in the episodes of the Isle de Tapinois and the Isle Farouche. Thus, while in chapter xxix Xenomanes is represented as saying that "he passed by Tapinois *six* years ago," in chapter xxxv he says that it was about *four* years ago. At first sight it would seem possible to explain this discrepancy, not as a mere slip, but by the fact that Rabelais wrote one chapter two years before the other. But the two episodes are so intimately connected that it is almost impossible to regard them as having been written at different times.

Now it was in April of the year 1542 that Jean Alfonse (? = Xenomanes) set sail with Roberval from La Rochelle, and on the 8th of June that he reached Newfoundland. In the following September he returned to France with two of Roberval's ships under orders to bring back a new convoy and fresh provisions for the colony of Charlesbourg Royal[4].

[1] L. Romier, *ib.* x. 139.
[2] H. Clouzot, *ib.* IX. 457.
[3] *Ib.* p. 459.
[4] La Roncière, *op. cit.* pp. 324 and 327; and see above, p. 43.

In the event, however, it was Cartier and not Jean Alfonse who acted as pilot to the relief expedition. Thus Jean Alfonse's last visit to the New World ended in September 1542, and, if Xenomanes stands for Jean Alfonse, "about four years ago" would imply that Rabelais in chapter xxxv still conceives of Pantagruel's expedition as taking place in 1546. But in chapter xxix Xenomanes refers to his last visit to Tapinois as taking place *six* years ago, and this, unless it is a pure slip, would put Pantagruel's voyage in 1548. But the identification of Xenomanes with Jean Alfonse is not universally accepted, and when Rabelais was writing the last chapter of the book he shows by his reference to the affair at Inchkeith that he regarded the voyage as taking place in 1549. Evidently his conception of the date was a variable one, as indeed was natural for an imaginary event, the narration of which occupied him for more than five years.

But to return to M. Romier's view, that all the additions to the Fourth Book were written between the spring and the autumn of 1551, my analysis of them chapter by chapter, or rather episode by episode, suggests that only chapters xlv–liv and probably chapter ii can be assigned with any confidence to that period; that chapters xxv–xxviii and xliii, xliv are as early as 1550; that chapters xxix–xlii may have been written at any time between October 1550 and the autumn of 1551; that chapters lxiii–lxvii belong either to 1550 or 1551, and more probably to the earlier year; that there is nothing to indicate the date of chapters lv, lvi and lvii–lxii except that the latter chapters, which contain the episode of Messere Gaster, may have been inspired by the Gallican crisis and were therefore written between July and October 1551.

But though one may not be prepared to accept M. Romier's thesis in its entirety, it is clear that Rabelais made important additions to his Fourth Book in furtherance of Henri II's anti-Vatican policy. How far this was inspired by his own undoubted dislike of the Roman Curia, and how far it was an attempt to win the King's favour as a protection against the Sorbonne, it is impossible to say. But there can be no doubt that Rabelais endeavoured to make his new book acceptable to the King by introducing passages of delicate flattery. He refers to him twice as *le roi megiste* (greatest king) and once, in a passage interpolated in chapter v, as King Obebé, a Hebrew word which signifies "lover."

Again, when he tells us in chapter ii that Pantagruel bought the Life and Deeds of Achilles in 78 pieces of tapestry, he is certainly paying a compliment to the *atelier* for tapestry which Henri II founded in the Hospital of the Trinity at Paris. But the most interesting instance of this kind of compliment is an interpolation which Rabelais made in the first chapter. The passage ran originally, "le nombre des navires feut tel que vous ay exposé ou tiers livre," but in the edition of 1552 we have this addition: "*en conserve des Triremes, Ramberges, Gallions et Liburnicques nombre pareil.*" By *Triremes* we must understand galleys, and by *Liburnicques* light cruisers[1]. The *Gallion*, or preferably *Galion*, was properly speaking a vessel of war which resembled a merchant-ship in having sails, and a galley in being furnished with oars as well as sails and in being longer than a merchantman or round ship. Its tonnage varied from 60 to 1000 tons. In popular language, however, the name of *gallion* was given to any vessel of war, even to galleys[2].

But of the four classes of vessel mentioned by Rabelais the most interesting is the *Ramberge*. For the *Ramberge* played an important part in the comprehensive programme of naval construction which Henri II announced in the first year of his reign (September 13, 1547), and which he carried out with great energy. In March 1549 five large ships of war, built by the celebrated geographer and sailor, Jean de Clamorgan, left the Norman dockyards[3]. In October of the same year the French King wrote to the King of Navarre: "I hope to provide for the construction and equipment of twenty *roberges* in addition to the ships of war which I possess already[4]."

[1] Ch. de La Roncière, *Histoire de la marine française*, II. 461–2.
[2] La Roncière, *op. cit.* II. 470; Jal, *Dictionnaire nautique*.
[3] La Roncière, *op. cit.* III. 455.
[4] Champollion-Figeac, *Mélanges historiques*, III. 59 (cited by La Roncière, III. 457).

The *roberges* were to be ready by the spring of 1550, and were to be constructed at Dieppe, Rouen, Brest, Saint-Malo, and Bordeaux[1]. These *roberges* or *ramberges* (also written *remberges*) took their name from the English *rowbarges*, which in the naval engagement off the Isle of Wight in 1545 had so greatly galled the French fleet by the superiority of their fire[2] (Plate II). They were long in proportion to their beam and extremely handy. The French *roberges* were very much larger than the English ones, varying from 80 to 100 tons as against an uniform displacement of 20 tons[3].

The merchant-ships which carried Pantagruel and his friends were twelve in number; the escort therefore consisted of twelve galleys, twelve rowbarges, twelve *galions*, and twelve cruisers, or forty-eight vessels in all. This may be compared with the actual fleet of Henri II, which in about 1550 consisted of forty galleys, twenty rowbarges, eight great ships and three *galions*. Naturally after Pantagruel's fleet had set sail we hear nothing more of the escort. The ships of war would have been out of place in the arctic seas. Moreover, Rabelais had no more use for them. He had brought them in solely for the sake of paying a compliment to the King, on his naval policy, just as he had brought in the tapestry to compliment him on his encouragement of art.

Rabelais's last bid for his royal master's favour was made in the Prologue. With great ingenuity he introduced into the story of the Countryman and his Axe a rapid summary of recent political events. Indeed, so rapid is the summary that it has baffled the commentators, and some of his allusions have not yet received a satisfactory explication. I will discuss them one by one. It will be remembered that Jupiter is supposed to be speaking.

1. "We have ended the quarrel of Presthan, King of the Persians, and Sultan Solyman, Emperor of Constantinople."

There is no difficulty here. In two campaigns, of 1548 and 1549, Soliman the Magnificent had defeated the Persians and

---

[1] La Roncière, *op. cit.* III. 457–8.
[2] See Du Bellay, *Mémoires*, bk X (edd. Bourrilly and Vindry, IV. 290).
[3] Sir J. S. Corbett, *Drake and the Tudor Navy*, 1899, I. 37.

PLATE II

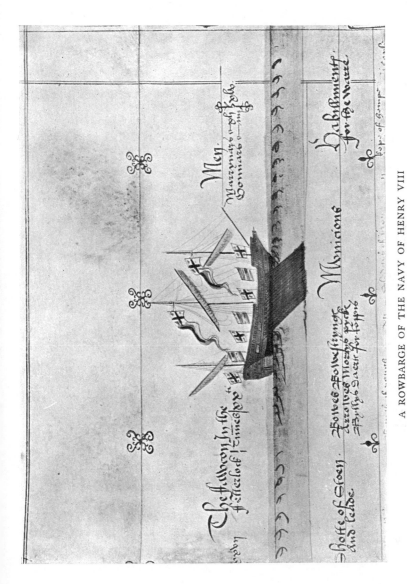

A ROWBARGE OF THE NAVY OF HENRY VIII

From Anthony's Third Roll in the Pepysian Library, Magdalene College, Cambridge

taken from them thirty-two towns. But the quarrel, which had lasted twenty-two years, was not yet "ended." When the Fourth Book appeared in January 1552 the news had just arrived in Europe that the Sophy had retaken Erzeroum. It was not till May 1555 that a more or less definitive peace was concluded.

2. "We have closed the passage between the Tartars and the Muscovites."

This is generally supposed to refer to the capture of Kazan, but this event did not take place till 1552. Possibly Rabelais was thinking of the foundation of Sviyashk, about 19 miles to the west of Kazan. "In 1551," says Soloviev in his History of Russia, "was founded the fortress of Sviyashk, whence the Russians began to lay waste the frontiers of Kazan." In 1548 Ivan the Terrible had resolved to subdue the Tartars and since that year he had undertaken several expeditions against them[1]. It may be objected that the foundation of Sviyashk was anything but a "closing of the passage," but Rabelais cannot be expected to have understood the real significance of the step.

3. "We have answered the Cheriph's petition."

This is rather obscure, but obviously the Sherif of Morocco is meant. At this time there was more or less of an *entente cordiale* between the Sherif and France. On March 15, 1550, Simon Renard, Charles V's ambassador at Paris, writes to his master that "the Shareef might undertake some fresh move against Spain[2]." On September 10 of the same year Sir John Mason, our ambassador at Paris, writes to the Council of Edward VI that "the Sherif had attempted to surprise Oran, but being chased by Don Bernardine de Mendoza had gone to Argel (Algiers) to see if he could succeed better there[3]." On December 13, 1550, D'Aramon writes from Constantinople to Henri II that "V. M. tient practique avec le Shérif de Maroque[4]."

---

[1] I owe this information about Russian affairs to the kindness of Mr A. P. Goudy, University Lecturer in Russian.
[2] *Calendar of State Papers, Spanish*, x. 46, and cp. a letter of May 24, 1550.
[3] *State Papers, Foreign, Edward VI*, p. 55.
[4] Ribier, *Lettres et Mémoires d'Estat*, ii. 193.

4. "We have done the same to that of Guolgots Rays."

The commentators all agree in recognising in Guolgots Rays the Turkish pirate Dragut Rais[1]. It is possible, as some suppose, that Rabelais has purposely altered his name to one suggestive of Golgotha, but it may be noted that Jean de Morvilliers, the French ambassador at Venice, calls him successively Gargout, Gorgout, and Drogout[2]. In a dispatch of March 12, 1550, Morvilliers announces the capture of Africa (see below) by him.

5. "The affair of Parma is dispatched; so also is that of Maydenbourg (Magdeburg), of Mirandola, and of Africa."

On November 3, 1551, Magdeburg, after a siege which had lasted more than a year, capitulated, and six days later Maurice of Saxony entered the town. He represented his success as a triumph for the Imperial arms, but for a long time he had been carrying on secret negotiations with the King of France, and Magdeburg was to serve him as a base for his operations.

The case of Parma and La Mirandola presents greater difficulty. On April 20, 1552, Pope Julius III gave orders to Ferrante Gonzaga to cease hostilities in the Duchy of Parma, the County of Mirandola, and on April 29 he signed an armistice between the Holy See and France[3]. But this was after the publication of the Fourth Book. Perhaps Rabelais had in mind the arrival of the Papal legate on November 28, 1551[4], or he may have had information of the King's intention to negotiate with Julius III. "On December 10," says M. Romier, "Henri II wrote to the Cardinal of Tournon and bade him be in readiness to start for Rome."

Africa was the name given by the Christians to the town of Mahédia or Mehédia—a name which attests its importance[5]. It was re-captured by Andrea Doria, the Admiral of Charles V,

---

[1] See Brantôme, *Œuvres*, ed. Lalasne, II. 48–58; S. Lane-Poole, *The Barbary corsairs*, 1840, c. xii.

[2] E. Charrière, *Négociations de France dans le Levant*, II. 94–98.

[3] L. Romier, *Les origines politiques des guerres de religion*, I. 289–290.

[4] *Ib.* p. 285.

[5] V. Guérin, *Voyage archéologique dans la régence de Tunis*, I. 131–144; C. Tissot, *Géographie de la province romaine d'Afrique*, II. 176–178; Cagnat and Saladin, *Voyage en Tunisie*, pp. 41–45 (with an illustration).

on September 8, 1550. Rabelais is wrong in identifying it with the ancient Aphrodisium, which was situated about 30 miles to the north of Sousse and about five miles from the sea. The ruins which mark its site are now called Henchir-Sidi-Khalifa, but formerly Henchir-Phradise, Phradise being probably a corruption of Aphrodisium[1]. The only ancient author who mentions the place is Ptolemy (III. 3. 1).

6. "Tripoli has changed its master through carelessness."

The Sultan Soliman was greatly annoyed at the capture of Africa, and no sooner had he returned from his expedition against the Sophy than he began to make preparations for war on the Emperor. On August 14, 1551, he possessed himself of Tripoli, which was held by the Knights of St John. It was said that D'Aramon, the French ambassador at Constantinople, who had just visited the Ottoman fleet, had advised the Governor to surrender the town. There was an outcry that the King of France had betrayed Christianity to the infidel, and much moved by this accusation Henri II demanded an explanation from his ambassador. D'Aramon gave it, and on November 17, 1551, he was completely exonerated by the Grand Master and the Council of the Knights of St John[2]. But the scandal did not die down. Rabelais, therefore, makes a point of declaring that the surrender of Tripoli was due to the carelessness of its defenders.

It will be noticed that the only event mentioned in Rabelais's summary which had nothing to do with French policy is the "quarrel" between the Russians and the Tartars. All the other events, except the capture of Africa by Charles V, were winning strokes in the political game. Soliman was the French King's ally and Dragut Rais was a vassal of Soliman. There was an understanding both with the Sherif of Morocco and with Maurice of Saxony, who was preparing to betray the Emperor.

Soon after Rabelais had put the finishing touches to his Prologue the Fourth Book appeared, the printing being

---

[1] Guérin, *op. cit.* I. 313–315; Tissot, *op. cit.* II. 163.
[2] Ribier, *op. cit.* pp. 309–310; Charrière, *op. cit.* II. 154–162; Romier, *op. cit.* I. 270.

finished on January 28, 1552. Alas! all Rabelais's pre-
cautions, his rejection of compromising episodes, his pro-
testations that there was not a word of heresy in the whole
book, his attempts to win the King's favour, availed him
nothing. The book was at once pounced upon and censured
by the Sorbonne, and the *Parlement* of Paris prohibited its
sale pending the King's pleasure (March 1, 1552). Henri II
was on the eve of invading Lorraine; he occupied Toul on
April 13, and Metz on April 28. Rabelais accordingly introduced into his Prologue the epithets "great, victorious, and
triumphant," before the King's name, and reprinted it with
this change. But this last stroke of flattery was no more
successful than the preceding ones. A revised edition of the
Fourth Book appeared in the same year, 1552, but without
name of publisher or place of publication[1].

Rabelais must at last have realised that Henri II was a
much more difficult person to placate than the late King.
He took no personal interest in literature, and his orthodoxy,
unlike his father's, was sincere, unbending, and intolerant.
Moreover, as I have said, however much Diane de Poitiers,
the Constable de Montmorency, and the Cardinal of Lorraine
might differ in other matters, they were at one on the subject
of state-religion.

---

[1] *Reueu et corrir; pour la seconde edition*, 1552. The Prologue contains
the words *gran' victorieux et triumphant*. It was probably printed by
Fezandat, the printer of the first edition. There is a copy in the British
Museum.

V

RABELAIS AND THE FIFTH BOOK

I

THE publication by the *Société des études rabelaisiennes* of a reprint of the *Isle Sonante*, admirably edited by MM. Abel Lefranc and Jacques Boulenger from the unique copy in the possession of a private owner, has enabled students for the first time to make a careful study of the text of this first instalment of the Fifth Book of *Pantagruel*. It will be recollected that the *Isle Sonante* appeared in 1562 (between eight and ten years after Rabelais's death) without either the publisher's name or the place of publication, and that it professed to be the continuation of Pantagruel's voyage written by Rabelais himself. It was followed in 1564 by the publication of the complete Fifth Book, which also professed to be Rabelais's work. Further, there is a manuscript of the whole book in the Bibliothèque Nationale; it is written in a sixteenth century hand which is certainly not Rabelais's. Previous to the reprint of the *Isle Sonante*, it might have been supposed —in fact, I did so suppose—that this MS. represented the oldest form of the text. But M. Boulenger in his excellent introduction to the reprint has made it clear that it really represents a stage intermediate between the *Isle Sonante* and the text of 1564.

Before proceeding to a detailed examination of the *Isle Sonante* it will be well to point out with the help of M. Boulenger's guidance the characteristics of the three texts.

ISLE SONANTE

1. The punctuation is very faulty, with the result that in many places the text becomes absolute nonsense.

2. "The text," says M. Boulenger, "is disfigured with printer's errors." This is true, but it should be added that the great majority of the errors are in proper names, or in technical

terms, or in words taken from Latin or Greek. Mistakes in ordinary words are not very numerous, though when they occur they are extremely stupid. The most glaring are *rouchee* for *conchié* (chapter v), *manifreque* for *magnifique* (chapter v), *trimballe element* for *triballement* (chapter vii), *mouoir* for *manoir* (chapter x), *tharus* for *thaons* (chapter xii), *ains* for *ame* (chapter xiii), *relonie* for *colonie* (chapter xvi). All of these are of course due to inability to decipher the manuscript.

3. There are certain incoherences in the language. For instance, *Il est, dist Epistemon Auriste en preterit plus que parfait des Grecs et des Latins en temps garré et bigarré receu* (chap. i), which gives no sense as it stands, and which is scarcely intelligible, even when it has been corrected into *Aorist yssu en Preterit tres imparfait* (MS.), or *Aorist yssu de preterit* (1564). M. Boulenger gives another instance from the first paragraph of chap. iv: *Ils...nous viennent de l'autre monde part d'une contrée...part d'une autre.... De ces deux contrées auons aboutées. Ces clerczgaulx ici nous viennent laissans pere et mere.* There is clearly something wrong here. Accordingly in the MS. the last part is altered to: *De ces deux contrées tous les ans a boutees* (in flocks) *ces clergaulx icy nous viennent* etc., and this is followed by the 1564 text with the addition of an accent to the *a*. The substitution of *tous les ans* for *auons* is not very convincing, and it seems more likely that the simple correction of *aboutées* into *à boutées* should be adopted. In this case it would merely be an instance of a printer's error.

M. Boulenger infers from these characteristics of the printed text that the manuscript from which it was printed was carelessly punctuated, badly written, and not finally revised; in fact, a rough copy. And he adduces an even stronger proof of this conclusion in the following passage from chap. xi: *...attendant que la dedans tombe la fouldre du ciel et en cendre les reduise comme autres Cytanes pro. et Ther...*, where the true reading, as we learn from the MS. and the 1564 text, is *Tytanes profanes et theomaches* (MS. *theomathes*)[1]. Clearly, as

---

[1] In this and two or three other places M. Boulenger kindly supplied me with the reading of the MS. as given in Montaiglon's edition, which I do not possess, and of which there is no copy in the British Museum.

M. Boulenger says, *pro. et Ther*[o] are not abbreviations introduced by the printer. He must have found them in the manuscript. While agreeing with M. Boulenger's view that the
manuscript represented by the *Isle Sonante* is a rough copy,
I do not believe that the printer had the original draft before
him. It seems to me that the corrupt condition of the printed
text is most reasonably accounted for by the supposition that
it was made from a careless copy of the original draft. Indeed,
I take it that M. Boulenger's theory is not meant to exclude
this hypothesis. It will be convenient for future reference if
I call the original draft A and the hypothetical copy B.

But we may draw another inference from the condition of
the printed text. Whoever the author was, he did not see his
work through the press. The misprints are too numerous and
of too gross a character to make it conceivable that he can
have revised the proofs, even in those days of careless proof-
reading. If the *Isle Sonante* is the work of a forger, that
forger must have been prevented either by death or by some
other cause from seeing it through the press. For it is difficult
to believe that anyone who had taken the trouble to produce
the forgery, either with or without the assistance of fragments
left by Rabelais, should have been at no pains to ensure its
being printed with comparative accuracy. We are left to the
conclusion that the *Isle Sonante* must have been written either
by Rabelais, or by a forger who died before it was printed or
who for some other reason was unable to supervise the printing.

The MS. of the Bibliothèque Nationale

1. It reproduces some intelligent and evidently sound corrections of the text.

2. It leaves blanks in some places where the *Isle Sonante*
has evidently made a guess.

3. It omits whole lines through carelessness.

4. It sometimes transcribes proper names incorrectly.

As the writing, according to experts, is of the end of the
sixteenth century, the MS. cannot be the original draft of the
revised or second stage of the text. It must be a copy made
by a faithful but unlearned and unintelligent scribe. I will

call the missing original of this revised text C. The revision was evidently the work, not of the author of the *Isle Sonante,* but of a later editor.

THE TEXT OF 1564

This represents a third stage of the text, the editor of which, while availing himself of many of the corrections of the MS., introduces fresh ones. He resorts freely to conjecture and otherwise treats the text with considerable licence. He even interpolates a few passages. Many of his conjectures are demonstrably wrong. The text was presumably printed from a revised copy of C, which I will call D. The following diagram will make clear my view of the relationship between our three texts:

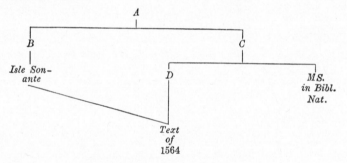

I will now proceed to consider the contents of the *Isle Sonante* in detail. It consists of five episodes:

> *Isle Sonante* proper (chapters i–viii).
> *Isle de Ferremens* (chapter ix).
> *Isle de Cassade* (chapter x).
> The *Chats fourrés* (chapters xi–xv).
> *Isle des Apedeftes* (chapter xvi).

ISLE SONANTE

Chapter I

There is a notable difference of reading at the very outset between our three texts, but I will defer the consideration of this till later.

Jergueau, Medon. MS.: *Jargueau, Mandes* (Mantes). 1564: *Tours, Gergeau, Nantes.* Jargeau is a little town on the Loire above Orleans, from which it is distant twelve miles. It is celebrated in history as the place where the Earl of Suffolk was besieged by the French under the Maid of Orleans and after ten days forced to surrender. The mention of it suggests the authorship of Rabelais, as he was well acquainted with Orleans and its neighbourhood, while there is no apparent reason for its being selected by a forger. On the other hand, a forger might have pitched upon Medon (Meudon), though one does not see why it should have been altered to either Mantes (in Normandy) or Nantes, places with which, as far as we know, Rabelais had no connexion.

au tour du sepulchre en l'isle de Lipare, autour des Arolides. The MS. has rightly corrected this into *l'une des Aeolides.* *Autour* is doubtless a repetition of the previous *au tour*, and may be the slip either of the original author or of a copyist.

tremblement. MS.: *treballement.* 1564: *triballement.*

natif de Glatigny. So MS. 1564: *Glenay.* Glatigny is the name of a château of the Du Bellay family. Glenay, according to Des Marets and Rathery, is a village near Chinon, but I cannot find it on the map.

Il est, dit Epistemon Auriste en preterit etc. I have already referred to this passage, in which there is some evident confusion, suggestive rather of a careless copy than a rough draft.

Beuuons tousiours. Beuuons is evidently a mistake and is rightly corrected in the MS. to *ieunons*, which the sense demands.

Note the inversion in *autrement receuz ne serions.*

W. F. Smith notes several reminiscences of the *Adagia* in this chapter, and two of Servius[1].

Chapter II

les transformations de Proque, Itis, Alcione, Alcithoe, Antigone, Thibeus et autres, en oyseaulx. Before *Proque*, which is of course a mistake for *Progne*, the MS. has *Nyctimene*, which the printer of the *Isle Sonante* doubtless omitted. For *Alcione*

1 See *Rev. des études rab.* VI (1908), 215 ff., and IV (1906), 349 ff.

the MS. substitutes *Alcmene*, an unfortunate correction; it also omits *Alcithoe*, who was changed by Dionysus into a bat, and rightly corrects *Thibeus* into *Tereus*. These metamorphoses are taken some from Servius and some from Ovid.

At the very end of the chapter, the editor of the 1564 text has added a couple of lines which have been alleged by some critics as disproving Rabelais's authorship of the whole Fifth Book, but there is no trace of them either in the *Isle Sonante* or in the MS.

Chapter III

We are here told that it is about 2760 moons since two Popejays were produced. Now, as W. F. Smith has suggested, this must be taken to refer, not to the beginning of the Great Schism in 1378, but to the appointment of an antipope in 1328. Reckoning the moon as 28 days, as he does, this brings us to 1540 or 1541, but taking it as equal to $29\frac{1}{2}$ days it brings us to 1551[1].

Ils auoient en aduertissement par Robert vbalbrun qui par la nagueres estoit passé, comment du pais d'aphrique bien tost y deuoit aduoller une sexte espece lesquels ils nommoient Caputragaulx. For *Robert vbalbrun* (*vb* is obviously a printer's substitute for *W*) the MS. has *Rembert Wabring* and the 1564 text *Robert Valbringue*, but *Walbrun* or *Valbrun* is right. According to Le Duchat the person meant is Jean-François de la Roque, sieur de Roberval, on whom the high-sounding title of Viceroy of Canada was conferred by Francis I, and who "passed that way" on his voyage to Canada in 1542 and on his return in 1543. This is doubtless correct, and, taken in conjunction with Rabelais's debt to Jacques Cartier and the probable identification of Xenomanes with Jean Alfonse of Saintonge[1], points strongly to Rabelais's authorship.

The text of 1564 has made nonsense of the passage by reading *en revenant* for *comment*. On the other hand, it rightly corrects *Caputragaulx* into *Capucingaux*. But this reference to the Order of Capuchins presents considerable difficulties. Seeing that it was founded, or rather received the Papal

---

[1] For W. F. Smith's views on Book v see *Rev. des études rab.* IV (1906), 235 ff., and *Rabelais in his writings*, Cambridge, 1918, pp. 99 ff.

confirmation, in 1528, why is Roberval represented as saying in
1542 or 1543 that "the Capuchinjays were soon to fly thither
from Africa"? As regards the connexion with Africa, I have
no explanation to suggest, but the rest of the sentence may
be an allusion to the fact that the Capuchins, who in consequence of the Protestant heresies of Bernardino de Ochino,
the General of their Order, had been forbidden to preach in
1543, had the privilege restored to them in 1545.

The chapter concludes with a free rendering of the Greek
proverb ἀεὶ φέρει τι Λιβύη καινόν, of which we have a more
literal translation in *Gargantua*, chapter xvi. See Erasmus,
Adagia, III. 7. 10.

Chapter IV

The whole of this chapter seems to me to bear the stamp
of Rabelais. The style throughout is his, and the conception
of the two countries called "Breadless-day" and "Too-many-
of-them," which supply the Clerjays, is worthy of him at his
best. But these are matters of individual opinion; it is more
to the point to note details which suggest Rabelais's authorship. For example, the numerous words coined from Greek
origin: *apotrophées, linostolies, charisteres, catarates, scythropes*
—of most of which the printer of the *Isle Sonante* has naturally made havoc—and the equally numerous references to
ancient religions—to the Vestal Virgins, to Pythagoras, to
Isis, to Oromasis and Ahrimanes—suggest an author of considerable learning[1]. The mention of the island of Bouchard in
the Vienne near Chinon might be due to a skilful forger, but
when one reads of "the mothers who cannot endure their
children in their houses for nine years, but put a shirt over
their dress and cut a few hairs on the top of their heads,"
one is forcibly reminded of Rabelais, of whom his biographer
Le Roy says that he was made a monk "when he scarcely
attained his tenth year." For he came from the country of
"Too-many-of-them," and his father's property—for the
most part in land—was not sufficient to provide for him, as

[1] W. F. Smith pointed out to me that Plutarch's *De Iside et Osiride*,
from which the words coined from the Greek come, was a favourite with
Rabelais.

well as for his two brothers and his sister. Further, we have a very characteristic inversion in *Lesquels ont cerché pour a mort ignominieusement mettre*, and a reminiscence of Virgil's *malesuada fames* in *patir malesuade famine*, the correction of the MS. for *partir mallesuade de faim*. It may be also noted that at the end of the first sentence several words, *je voudrois bien entendre d'ond vous naissent ces clergaux* (1564), which are necessary to the sense, are omitted in the *Isle Sonante*.

la fleur de tripolion ou tenation. MS.: *tripolion ou*. 1564: *tripoleon ou teucrion*. A reference to the *Hypnerotomachia*, chapter xviii (eight lines from the end), shows that the true reading is *tripolion ou teucrion*. Pliny, *N.H.* XXI. 7. 21, refers to the change in colour but calls the plant *polion*, adding that some call it *teuthrion*. Our sea-aster is *Aster tripolium*, but *teucrium* is the botanical name for our wood-germander.

Chapter V

The readings of the *Isle Sonante*, *un diametre*, instead of *deux diametres*, and *une ligne perpendiculaire droicte*, instead of *une ligne perpendiculaire tombante soubz une ligne droicte*, are, M. Boulenger points out, indications that it is printed from an unrevised draft. The second mistake, however, may be due to an omission on the printer's part. Further on we have not only a Rabelaisian inversion in *nous feist par les Alapthes* (read *Aliptes*) *oindre*, but additional evidence of an unrevised draft. For the sense requires *faire* instead of *feist*, a correction which has been made in the 1564 text.

Chapter VI

Atlas et tous les Verones is the characteristic reading of the *Isle Sonante* for *Aeolus et tous les Veioves*. A little further on the three texts differ in an instructive fashion: *De Touraine tant et tant de bien annuellement nous en vient qu'en sommes tous resiouis. Nous dist vn jour par cy passant que....* MS.: *De Touraine...nous vient que* [blank] *nous dist un jour par cy passant que....* 1564: *De Touraine...nous viennent que nous fut dit un jour par gens du lieu par cy passans que....* As M. Boulenger points out, it is evident that the printer of the

Isle Sonante, not being able to decipher the word, evidently a proper name, has made a random guess, which leaves *dist* without a subject. On the other hand, the scribe of the MS. has conscientiously left a blank, while the 1564 editor, who had no scruples about adhering to the text, has got out of the difficulty by altering the sentence.

Ces grosses cloches que voyez pendantes aux tours de leur caiges. This reading of both the *Isle Sonante* and the MS. has been altered by the 1564 editor to *pendues autour*, but as the author doubtless has in his mind the *campaniles* which are still so marked a feature of Rome, the older reading is correct.

The concluding words of the chapter, *O gens heureux o Semidieux, pleust au Ciel qu'il ni aduint ainsi*, are an inaccurate quotation from a well-known epigram by Victor Brodeau. The inaccuracy is more suggestive of Rabelais than of an imitator, and on the whole it may be said of this chapter that the imitator, if imitator he be, must have been not only a man of genius, but a singularly skilful forger.

The reference to the halcyons is from Servius on *Georg.* I. 399 (*dilectae Thetidi alcyones*)[1], and Plin. x. 32. 47.

Chapter VII

This contains the famous apologue of the Charger and the Ass. It seems to me to be told in Rabelais's best manner, and this impression of Rabelais's authorship is confirmed by various details. For instance, we have some remarkable inversions in *ton petit pas avecques moy venir* and *Par la figue, respondit l'asne, laquelle un de noz ancestres mangeant mourut Philemon de rire*. And nothing can be more characteristic of Rabelais's humour than the dignified rebuke which the charger administers to the ass for addressing him as *Monsieur le Cheval* instead of *Monsieur le Roussin.* "*Il y a bien monsieur le Roussin pour toy Baudet.*"

Certain differences between the three texts are deserving of notice.

Apres auoir bien repeu. MS. and 1564: *Avoir bien beu et bien repeu.* The ellipse of *après* is a remarkable peculiarity of

---

[1] W. F. Smith in *Rev. des études rab.* IV. 365.

Rabelais's syntax. It does not occur in the first two books, but becomes common in the third. It is rarely used by writers later than Rabelais (see Huguet, *Études sur le Syntaxe de Rabelais*, pp. 358 ff., A. Lefranc, *Les Navigations de Pantagruel*, p. 190, and the glossary of Marty-Laveaux's edition, pp. 42, 43). Probably the copyist of the *Isle Sonante*, ignorant of this peculiarity, introduced the *apres* here.

non cibus, sed charitas. MS.: *non cibus charitas.* 1564: *non zelus sed charitas.* See Erasmus, *Coll.* ('Ιχθυοφαγία) for the distinction between *zelus* and *caritas* (W. F. S.).

le palefrenier du seigneur de Harenganois. MS.: *le pallefrenier du Seigneur* [blank]. 1564: *le pallefrenier d'un gentilhomme.*

a l'oree d'un buissonnet. So the MS., but the 1564 text has *a l'ombre*, which is correct; the words are the first line of a popular chanson. Rabelais no doubt wrote *a l'oree*.

un tronçon de chere lie. 1564: *un tronçon de bonne chere.* There is no reason for altering *lie*, which is from Lat. *laeta*. La Fontaine has *galante de chère lie* and Balzac (*La Messe de l'Athée*) *tronçon de chère lie*, as here.

erner. 1564: *esrener.* Both these are older forms of the modern *éreinter*.

plutost que ne sont cuicts (sic) *asperges.* From Erasmus, *Adag.* III. 7. 5.

Chapter VIII

The "two little Cardinjays" by whom Popejay is accompanied remind one of the "two little Cardinals," grandsons of Paul III, of whom Rabelais speaks in one of his letters from Rome to the Bishop of Maillezais. They had both been made cardinals by their grandfather in 1534, when they were barely sixteen. Paul III died in 1550, so that, if he is the Popejay of this chapter, it must have been written before that date; it is possible, however, that the writer had no particular Pope in his mind.

Comme sagement nota Michel de Malisconne. 1564: *Michael de Matiscones.* MS.: *Michael de Matisconis.* The MS. is doubtless right and the reference is probably to some bishop of

Maçon. It may be remembered that Charles Hemard, Bishop of Maçon, was French ambassador at Rome when Rabelais was there in 1535–36. No previous occupant of the see bore the Christian name of Michael.

Par moyen autre bien chanter vous feray. Note the inversion. *frapper par la mittre.* MS.: *le mylé.* 1564: *ferir par la moitie.* With the substitution of *mitre* for *mittre* the *Isle Sonante* is surely right.

frappé serois tu et meurtry: tous roys et princes du monde for *frappe, feris, tue et meurtris tous roys* etc. is characteristic of the nonsense which the *Isle Sonante* sometimes produces. For the idea cp. Erasmus, *Coll. (Exequiae Seraphicae).*

Le quatriesme iour. So the MS. This is clearly right, though the 1564 edition has altered it to *troisiesme.*

In the next sentence we find another instructive difference between the three texts. *Lequel il print plus a gre que ne feist Ataxerxes le verre d'eau froide que lui presenta un paisant en Scythie.* So the *Isle Sonante*; but for *Scythie* the MS. leaves a blank, while the 1564 editor stops short after *un paisant.* Now if we turn to Plutarch, *Apophth. Reg. et Imp.* 172 B, we read that during one of Artaxerxes Mnemon's journeys a labouring man having no present to give him took up some water from the river in his two hands and offered it to him. But there is no mention of Scythia, nor, so far as our information goes, did Artaxerxes ever visit that country. Apparently our author is citing from memory, for neither Plutarch nor Erasmus, *Apophth. (Artaxerxes,* 25) speaks of a *glass* of water; but did he write *en Scythie,* and, if so, why did the editor of the text of which the MS. is a copy, leave a blank, and the 1564 editor omit the words altogether? Probably *Scythie* was a guess on the part of the printer of the *Isle Sonante,* and neither the editor of the revised text nor the 1564 editor could supply the right word.

Having now examined the chapters which form the episode of the *Isle Sonante,* it will be well to pause to take stock of the results. The following features are all more or less in favour of Rabelais's authorship.

1. The incorrectness of the printing, showing the absence of any supervision on the part of the author.

2. The indications that the author had not finally revised his manuscript.

3. The reference to Roberval.

4. The numerous illustrations and references derived from classical antiquity, and in particular, the references to Plutarch, Servius, and Erasmus.

5. The use of bold inversions.

6. The frequent references to Touraine and especially to the neighbourhood of Chinon.

Of course not a single one of these features is conclusive in Rabelais's favour. The author may have been a man of considerable learning, he may have taken or simulated interest in French voyages of discovery, he may have introduced references to Rabelais's country with intent to deceive, he may have imitated his use of inversion, and finally he may have died or disappeared before he had seen his work through the press or been able to revise it. But the cumulative weight of the evidence certainly points to Rabelais having had at least a share in the work.

Can we then accept the view which commended itself to the cautious and experienced judgment of Marty-Laveaux, that Rabelais's authentic fragments have been worked up by a later editor? But this does not account for the corrupt condition of the text of the *Isle Sonante*, except on the supposition that the editor had died or disappeared before he had completed his task. Absence from France might indeed have prevented him from seeing his work through the press, but if he was not in France, how did he become possessed of Rabelais's manuscripts? And why did he send his work to the printer in the form of a rough draft?

On the whole, then, the theory that Rabelais is the author of the whole of the *Isle Sonante* certainly presents the fewest difficulties.

Let us now return to the puzzling difference between our three texts at the beginning of chapter i.

Cestuy iour et les deux aultres subsequens ne leur apparut terre ou autre chose nouvelle; car autrefois auoyent erré (arré = "ploughed") ceste couste. Au quatrieme iour commençans tournoier le Pole, nous esloignans de l'equinoctial nous apperceumes terre: et nous fut dict par nostre Pilote que c'estoit l'isle des Triphes, entendismes un son de loing venant.... MS.: Estant montes sur mer et navigans par plusieurs iours avec bon vent entendismes un son etc. 1564: Continuant nostre routte nauigasmes par trois iours sans rien descouurir, au quatriesme aperceusmes terre, et nous fut dit par nostre pillot, que c'estoit l'Isle Sonnante, et entendismes un bruit de loing venant.

It should be further remarked that in the *Isle Sonante* there is no heading to this chapter, while the MS. has *Comment avec le bon Pantagruel montant sur mer fismes scalle en l'isle Sonnante.*

Of these various texts that of 1564 is evidently due to the invention of the editor. That of the *Isle Sonante,* as far as the word *equinoctial,* is almost identical with the opening words of chapter ii of the incomplete Fourth Book of 1548, the only differences being the introduction of *aultres* after *deux,* the substitution of *autre chose* for *chose autre, erré* for *arré,* and *couste* for *routte,* and the omission of *peu à peu* before *nous esloignans.* Now when Rabelais revised and added to these opening chapters of the Fourth Book he split up this passage, putting *Cestuy...route* at the beginning of his new chapter ii, and the rest (with the change of *quatrieme* into *cinquieme*) at the beginning of his new chapter v. Did, then, the copyist of the *Isle Sonante* borrow the passage from the edition of 1548 or did he combine the two passages of the 1552 edition, re-substituting *quatrieme* for *cinquieme*? I very much doubt whether he had intelligence enough for the latter operation. A third alternative remains, that he found them in Rabelais's rough draft.

The reading of the MS. is clearly original and not invented, for as a continuation of Book IV it is inappropriate, Pantagruel and his companions being at sea when that book closes. If, then, the text of the *Isle Sonante* is also original we must suppose that Rabelais at some time substituted the reading of the MS. for that of the *Isle Sonante* and transferred the latter to chapter ii of the Fourth Book of 1548. According to this view the *Isle Sonante* was written before the Fourth Book —but after the Third Book.

W. F. Smith, however, laying stress on the 2760 moons of chapter iii, thinks Rabelais wrote it at Turin between 1540 and 1542. The objection to this view is that the mention of a future voyage at the end of Book II is so casual that it is impossible to suppose that nearly ten years later he could have begun his account of it either with the reading of the *Isle Sonante* or with that of the MS.

My method of calculating the moons gives the year as 1551, and it is a fair supposition that the *Isle Sonante* was inspired by the Gallican crisis, but that Rabelais ultimately rejected it as containing too much dangerous matter and substituted for it the two episodes of the Papefigues and the Papimanes. This has something in its favour, but it is inconsistent with the idea that the editor of the *Isle Sonante* found the opening passage in Rabelais's draft.

The only way of reconciling these two conflicting views is to suppose that Rabelais wrote the episode in 1546, and that he then gave the number of moons as 2700; that five years later he again thought of using the episode and increased the number of moons to 2760; and that finally he rejected it altogether, at any rate for use in the Fourth Book.

It may be added that the date of 1546 does not conflict with the reference to the Capuchins in chapter iii or with that to the "two little Cardinjays" in chapter viii, so far as they furnish any indication of date. But the whole question of when the *Isle Sonante* was written is a very complicated one, and I have nothing but conjectures to offer for its solution.

Of one thing I am convinced, that it was written by Rabelais.

ISLE DES FERREMENS

Chapter IX

This short episode of the Island of Tools forms the subject of chapter ix. It is decidedly dull, but that is no reason for rejecting Rabelais's authorship. The germ of the idea is to be found in a few lines of chapter xxiv of *Le Disciple de Panta-*

gruel which correspond fairly closely to the sentence *Autres portans daguenets...cousteaux* of the *Isle Sonante*. This in itself is in favour of Rabelais's authorship, for he is indebted to this chap-book, the origin of which is still an unsolved problem, for certain ideas which furnish matter for the Fourth Book (*pays Lanternois, isle Farouche* and the *Andouilles*, death of Bringuenarilles). Marty-Laveaux takes exception to the phrase *sabouré l'estomac* as borrowed from an earlier book, but as Rabelais has used it not only once but twice, there is no reason why he should not have used it a third time. Smith refers to *Adagia*, III. 7. 57, where Erasmus cites Plaut. *Cistellaria*, I. 2. 2, as using *saburratus = cibo onustus*.

The three texts show certain differences in the lists of implements, and the *Isle Sonante* naturally makes nonsense of some of the words. But the most instructive difference is in the last word, which the *Isle Sonante* writes *braueté*, the MS. *bragguete*, and the 1564 text *manière*. The last reading is palpably wrong, as it misses the point completely, and there is no doubt that the true reading is *brayette*, an older form of *braguette*, which is correctly given by the *Isle Sonante* in chapter xi.

ISLE DE CASSADE

Chapter X

The first thing to be noticed is that at the beginning of the chapter the 1564 editor has introduced the words *Delaissans l'isle des Ferrements, continuasmes nostre chemin* in order to connect this episode with the preceding one. But neither in the MS., which begins with *Le jour ensuivant*, nor in the *Isle Sonante*, which has *Le tiers iour subsequent*, is there any trace of this connexion. The Island of Cheating is hardly more interesting or more productive of action than that of Tools. The account of it is at first a satire on the superstitious practices of gamblers, and then breaks off into ridicule of relics. A short passage is borrowed from Plutarch's treatise *On Isis and Osiris*, a favourite, as we have seen, with Rabelais, and there are references to the Florentine manuscript of the Pandects, and to the handkerchief of St Veronica in St Peter's at Rome, which point to the authorship of some one who had visited these places. From the same treatise of Plutarch comes also *Apollo par as, Diane par deux, Minerve par sept*. The following mistakes of the *Isle Sonante* are worth noticing: *Scyttes* for *Syrtes*, *pendettes* for *pandectes*.

LES CHATS FOURRÉS
Chapter XI

Here again the 1564 editor has introduced a phrase, *Voulut vendre à un serrargent des chapeaux de Cassade*, in order to connect this chapter with the preceding one, substituting it for *auoit bastu un* (*le* MS.) *chicanoux passant procuration* of the *Isle Sonante* and the MS. Again also we are puzzled by a difference between the three texts at the outset:

Isle Sonante: Ayant auttrefois eu procuration la laissames et passasmes condemnation;

MS.: *De là passasmes condemnation;*

1564: *Quelques iours après, ayant failly plusieurs fois à faire naufrage, nous passasmes*, etc.

Thus it appears that in the original text there is a reference to the beating of the Chiquanous by Brother John which is recounted in IV. xvi, and further that the travellers are represented as sailing for the second time by the Island of Procuration inhabited by the Chiquanous (see IV. xii). Leaving this difficulty for discussion till we reach the end of the episode, I note that in this chapter occurs the curious reading of the *Isle Sonante, Cytanes pro. et Ther.*, to which reference has already been made, and that in the next line *es coups endurciz* is clearly right as against *des corps endurcis* of 1564 and *ces coups advoués* of the MS. Further, it may be noticed that the description of Osiris, to whom Grippeminaud is compared, is borrowed either from Macrobius or from the *Hypneroto-machia*, but with the substitution of Osiris for Serapis.

Chapter XII

The *Isle Sonante* prints *frere Jehan des enlumineures* for *frere Jehan des Entommeures*, and it omits the words *y serez bien innocentés*, which are found in the MS. and the text of 1564.

Chapter XIII

Bourse monsieur is clearly wrong, but I doubt whether *de cuir* of the MS. and the 1564 text is the right correction. *Griphons* (last sentence but one), with which the MS. agrees, is of course right as against *garçons* (1564). In both this and the preceding chapter W. F. Smith has noted reminiscences of Erasmus's *Adagia*.

Chapter XIV

soixante et huict cohuz barguettes et fregates. Barguettes should of course be *barquettes* as in the MS., which gives *tabuz* for *cohuz*. The true reading is doubtless *cahutes*. The 1564 text gets out of the difficulty by reading *galeres* and omits *barquettes*. It may be noticed that the number of vessels is 68, which is perhaps a mistake for 78, Rabelais's favourite number. There is a reference to Xenophon's treatise *On Hunting* in *Xenophon escriuant estre de la vennerie comme du cheual de Troye yssus tous bons chefs de guerre,* a sentence remarkable for its bold inversion.

Chapter XV

A long chapter, chiefly composed of a conversation between Brother John and Panurge, which, though not particularly amusing, is on the whole characteristic of both these worthies. Note the inversion in *pour en cestuy voyage messe chanter* and the old form of *rien ne faire* (line 3), which is preserved in the *Isle Sonante* and MS. but not in the 1564 text. Note also the following mistakes: *mettre* for *mettoit* (perhaps due to a confusion in the manuscript); *Thidee* for *l'hidre*; *esse* for *est-ce*; *calabres oyes de panthile* for *celebres oyes de Pauthilé, Pauthilé* or *Potillé* being a village near Chinon. On the other hand, the *Isle Sonante* and MS. should be followed in *Feste de Saint Baletrou,* which the 1564 editor has heedlessly altered into *faictes. Et sainct hurlu burlu.* W. F. Smith pointed out to me that the reference to Semele and the two passages relating to the nether world and to Calpe and Abila are all suggested by the *Hypnerotomachia,* and with this I agree. The end of the chapter from *Si tost que frere Jehan* is omitted in the MS.

As regards the whole episode, its satire is bitter, even savage, to the entire exclusion of humour. This is not Rabelais's usual tone, but it is to be found in some passages of the Ringing Island. The portrait of Grippeminaud is decidedly powerful and has left a marked impress on French literature. La Fontaine, an enthusiastic admirer of Rabelais, borrows the name for *sa Majesté fourrée*, in the fable of *The cat, the weasel, and the little rabbit*. Vauquelin de La Fresnaye, who was seventeen when Rabelais died, refers to him as the creator of Grippeminaud, and so does Étienne Tabourot, who was born in 1549, quoting in his *Bigarrures* a passage from chapter xii.

The strongest evidence in favour of Rabelais's authorship is the use of the *Hypnerotomachia*. It is also to some extent in favour of it that the couplet in chapter xi is imitated from Marot, that the punning use of the word *griffon* for *greffier* (chapter xiii) also occurs in the same poet's *Enfer*, and that possibly the whole idea of the episode may have been suggested by that poem. It is curious that Grippeminaud's habit of interlarding all his remarks with the words *Or ça*, which becomes very wearisome, also figures in one of Des Periers's stories (xxi) as a characteristic of the speech of a Paris *curé*. These stories were not published till 1558, but Rabelais may have seen them in manuscript, or the same not very brilliant idea may have occurred to both writers.

ISLE DES APEDEFTES

This satire on the *Chambre des Comptes*, which forms the subject of chapter xvi of the *Isle Sonante*, is omitted both in the MS. and in the 1564 text, and was not reprinted till 1567, when it appeared as chapter vii, where it is manifestly out of place. The reason for the omission is to be found doubtless in its tediousness and technicality. That the omission was deliberate may be gathered from the peculiar numbering of the chapters which appears in the MS. in this place. For chapters xv and xvi are numbered respectively 38–15 and 39–16, which seems to denote a special indication that the chapter on the Apedeftes was to be omitted, and that chapter xvi—evidently a fragment, the contents of which do not fully correspond to the heading (*Comment nous passasmes outre, et comment Panurge faillit d'estre tué*), for there is not a word about Panurge nearly being killed—was to follow immediately after chapter xv. But this omission of chapter xvi of the *Isle Sonante* necessitated also the omission of part of chapter xv, which consequently ends in the MS. and the 1564 text with the words *moins de douze francs*. As the text stands in the *Isle Sonante*, the episode of the Apedeftes is closely connected with that of the Furred Cats and follows immediately after it. M. Boulenger and others seem to have found a difficulty in the words of Panurge, *nous venons du pays des savans*, regarding the term *savans* as inappropriate to the Furred Cats, but it surely denotes the contrast between the Criminal Judges who were "clerks," and the members of the *Chambre des Comptes* who were not, and who are therefore here termed Apedeftes (ἀπαίδευτοι). If M. Boulenger's supposition that this episode has been wrongly inserted here is right, we have to suppose that the "editor" of the *Isle Sonante* invented either the conclusion of chapter xv from *si tost que Frere Jehan*, or the opening of chapter xvi, down to *prins terre*. This is very unlikely. Moreover the reference to Grippeminaud at the close of chapter xvi points to a close connexion between the two episodes.

As regards the authenticity of the chapter, I quite agree with M. Boulenger that there is no serious reason for not attributing it to Rabelais. To find in it "contradictions, incoherences, and defects of style," as Des Marets and Rathery do, is to be blinded by prejudice, for, whatever its demerits, it contains neither contradictions nor incoherences, and the style, as M. Boulenger says, is very correct. Indeed, though it has little interest for modern readers, it must have seemed to Rabelais's contemporaries a powerful and vigorous piece of satire.

To come to details, a forger might have invented Brother John's exclamation of *Vertus d'Extravagantes* with its reminiscence of bishop Homenas, and Panurge's oath *Par la royne des Andouilles*, but the casual references to Panurge's spectacles and to Epistemon as one who "understood all languages" are touches almost beyond a forger's art. The mention of Lamballe, a town in the neighbourhood of Saint-Malo, which has already figured in IV. lii, also points to Rabelais, who evidently knew that part of Brittany.

On the whole the evidence in favour of Rabelais's authorship of this episode (apart from its inclusion in the text of the *Isle Sonante*) is decidedly strong, and, as it is difficult to separate it from the Furred Cats, it carries with it a similar presumption in favour of that episode.

It is a feature common to these two episodes that they read like finished work, without the hesitations, the incoherences, the rough places that we meet with in the three preceding episodes. It is true that in the account of the Furred Cats (chapter xi) we come upon that curious abbreviation in the *Isle Sonante* which is the strongest testimony to its having been printed from an unrevised draft, but no other similar indications occur in these chapters, and it is just worth noticing that in the very passage where this appears there are various discrepancies between the *Isle Sonante* and the other two texts, both of which have the following additions: *advenant*; *ne recordent*; *ne veulent*; *retournons*. *Retournons, dis-je, de par Dieu*. There is another difference between these episodes and the preceding ones. In the earlier books it is not Rabelais's practice to introduce his own personality into his narrative; throughout the Fourth Book there are not, I think, more than four instances of the use of the first person singular. But in the first ten chapters of the Fifth Book the narrator intervenes no less than nine times, four times in chapter x, twice in chapter ix, and once each in chapters ii, v and vi. In the 1564 text there is an additional instance in chapter vii. It may be said that this is an argument against the authenticity of these chapters. But Rabelais's rule is not so absolute as to warrant this inference. I rather infer that the intrusion of his own personality is a sign that these chapters had not been worked up into a final artistic shape. This is almost certainly the case with the episodes of the Island of Tools and the Island of Cheating (chapters ix and x), which have not received the impress of dramatic life charac-

teristic of most of Rabelais's finished work. Similar instances
are the episodes of the Island of Odes (chapter xxvi) and the
Island of Satin (chapters xxx, xxxi). The same cannot be said
of chapters ii, v and vi, but in v and vi occur two of the passages which M. Boulenger has adduced in support of his view
that the *Isle Sonante* was printed from a rough draft. On the
other hand, in chapters xi–xvi the narrator never intervenes
in his own person.

We are thus led to the conclusion that not only was Rabelais
the author of the episodes of the Furred Cats and the Apedeftes but that he had definitely intended to include them in
his narrative. We are met, however, with an apparent difficulty in the very first words of chapter xi, *Ayant autresfois eu
procuration la laissasmes et passasmes condemnation.* Why are
the travellers brought back to the country of Procuration,
inhabited by the Chiquanous, which they had already visited
in the early days of the voyage? Evidently this difficulty had
struck the editor of the 1564 text, who has omitted all mention of Procuration. The only explanation that I can suggest
is that the episodes were intended to form part of the account
of the homeward voyage. As M. Lefranc points out, the
travellers were evidently meant to return by the same route,
and, as he also points out, there is nothing to show that the
story is concluded with the Fifth Book. A more natural
conclusion would be the marriage of Panurge and perhaps also the marriage of Pantagruel. My suggested explanation is of course a mere conjecture, but it may serve
to accentuate the view that, if the Fifth Book is by Rabelais,
it is far from being in the state in which he intended it to
appear.

It remains to consider the date of the composition of these
two episodes. The only help that we get is from the mention
in the chapter on the Apedeftes of the *Extravagantes* and the
Queen of the Chitterlings, which shows that it must have
been written after the episodes of the *Papimanes* and the
Isle Farouche. But we have seen that the episode of the
Papimanes was suggested and inspired by the rupture
between Henri II and the Pope in the summer of 1551. The

chapter on the Apedeftes could not, therefore, have been written until after that date.

Though the episode of the Apedeftes is closely connected with that of the Furred Cats, it does not necessarily follow that it was written immediately after it. Rabelais may have written the episode of the Furred Cats at an earlier date, and then later on connected it with that of the Apedeftes, by the sentence, *Ainsi le vent......grands rochers*, which terminates chapter xv. Our only clue therefore to its date is the conjecture that it forms part of the narrative of the homeward, and not of the outward voyage. If it does, then like the episode of the Apedeftes it belongs to the last year or two of Rabelais's life. If it does not, then we are free to assign to it any date between 1546 and Rabelais's death, for Rabelais may have refrained from including it in the Fourth Book as likely to bring him into difficulties with one of the very bodies whose animosity he had to fear—the *Parlement* of Paris.

For this powerful and violent satire is obviously directed not merely against the general administration of criminal justice in France, but against the Criminal Court of the Paris *Parlement*, and the question has naturally been asked what had roused Rabelais to such anger and bitterness, so different from his ordinary tone of humorous and not ill-natured satire. Was it the temporary suspension by the *Parlement* of the sale of the Fourth Book? But Des Marets is doubtless right in saying that the vengeance is out of all proportion to the grievance. Or was it a later decree (which was evidently passed, though it has not been preserved) stopping the publication altogether?

Another suggestion presents itself. Towards the close of 1547 a second Criminal Court was formed for the trial of heretics. It sat from December 1547 to January 1549, and again for a time from March 1553, and so thoroughly did it do its work that it became known as *La Chambre Ardente*. Was it the proceedings of this court that stirred Rabelais, the lover of tolerance, the hater of persecution, to such unusual but justifiable wrath? In favour of this view I can only point to two passages in the narrative, one in which it is said that the spoliation committed by the Furred Cats "is found good by all human beings, except the heretics" (chapter xi), and the other in which Brother John, in answer to Grippeminaud's imprecation that he may be wedded to a quartan fever, replies, "Thou wouldst then marry monks? Ho! ho! I take thee for a heretic."

To sum up. The condition of the text of the *Isle Sonante* shows (*a*) that it was printed, at any rate as regards chapters i–x, from a rough draft, and that even in chapter xi, which forms part of the two last and closely connected episodes, there is a distinct proof of the lack of final revision; (*b*) that the proofs were never revised by the author; (*c*) that of the five episodes of which it is composed, the last two are continuous and may have been written at the same time, but the other three are quite distinct both from one another and from the last two and may have been written at different times with no idea of continuity.

On these grounds alone we are, I hold, justified in rejecting alike the hypothesis of an unscrupulous editor working upon Rabelais's authentic fragments and that of an out-and-out forger. And this view finds additional confirmation when we come to examine the chapters in detail. In every chapter we find passages which point strongly, though not inevitably, to Rabelais's authorship, while there is not a single passage in the text of the *Isle Sonante* which is demonstrably not by him. My explanation of the genesis of the work is that some person made a copy of certain of Rabelais's papers, and put it in the hands of a printer without attempting to edit them or taking any further trouble in the matter.

II

For the rest of the Fifth Book we are left to two texts, the MS. and the printed text of 1564.

Chapter XVI

As we have seen, the heading of this chapter, *Comment nous passasmes outre, et comment Panurge faillit d'estre tué*, does not correspond with its contents, for there is nothing about Panurge's narrow escape from death. Its style is like Rabelais's, and we may probably regard it as the fragment of a chapter which he intended should follow chapter xiii—Grippeminaud says *Passez outre*—but subsequently abandoned without finishing it.

LE ROYAUME DE LA QUINTE

Chapter XVII

Here we have the account of a second storm, although in IV. i it is said that the voyagers only encountered one storm during the outward voyage.

MS.: *Les Rats Saint Mahieu*. 1564: *sainct Maixent*. The MS. is certainly right; cp. IV. xxv, *Les Ratz de Sanmaieu*. The Cap Saint-Matthieu, of which Mahieu is the Breton form, is near Brest, and is the most western point of France. Saint-Maixent is a small town in Poitou, mentioned twice elsewhere by Rabelais, but it is not on the coast.

MS.: *Depuis Chinon jusques à San-Louan*. 1564: *jusques à Saulmur*. All editors seem to have accepted the latter reading, but Saumur is on the Loire, not on the Vienne. There is no such place as Saint-Louan, but I suggest that the true reading is Saint-Junien, which is at the confluence of the Glane and the Vienne. These two corrections, *sainct Maixent* and *Saulmur* are characteristic of the hasty corrections made by the 1564 editor whenever he comes to a word which is outside his limited field of knowledge.

MS.: *Hans Cotiral*. 1564: *Henry Cotiral*. So in chapter xxix the MS. has *Hans*, and the 1564 text *Henry*, and in both places the MS. is undoubtedly right (see below).

1564: *leurs tabourins de saucisses*. MS.: *de souisses de saulcisses*. Cp. IV. xxxviii, "Les Souisses, peuple maintenant hardy et belliqueux, que savons nous si jadis estoient saulcisses."

1564: *revoquez*. MS.: *remolquez*. The latter is right. *Remolquer* is another form of *remorquer*; cp. IV. xxi: "Notre nauf est encarée, comment la remolquerons-nous?" and note that the word *encarée* occurs in the heading of this chapter and that the MS. wrongly reads *encroé*.

There is another reminiscence of the storm in Book iv in the reference to St Elmo's fire, which, when double, was called Castor and Pollux and was held to be of good omen. Cp. iv. xxii, "O, s'écria Epistemon, je vous commande tous bien esperer. Je voy ça Castor a dextre."

1564: *Que laisissions d'orenavent la mer nous guider.* MS.: *Que là...la nauf nous guider.* The latter is probably right.

Note the inversions in *Autre propos ne nous fut loisible avec eux tenir* and *laquelle dit Platon avoir par quelques nuicts ouye dormant,* in both of which the order of the words is highly characteristic of Rabelais.

One cannot regard this chapter as the work of an imitator, but the storm seems to require explanation. It is possible that Rabelais wrote the whole episode of the kingdom of La Quinte before the Fourth Book, and that having laid it aside he wrote for the Fourth Book a much longer and fuller description of a storm. It should be observed that a new numbering of the chapters in the MS. begins here; 39–16 (= xvi) is followed by 50–17 (= xvii) and so on to 53–20.

Chapter XVIII

le nombre...recentement accreu par Scaliger. Scaliger only speaks of Entelechy in a book which was published in 1557, four years after Rabelais's death. Either the name of Scaliger or the whole passage from *le nombre* to *esmouchetez* is an interpolation.

1564: *Et n'y a homme, pour tous taire.* MS.: *Et n'y a prothonotaire.* In the chapter on the Apedeftes and in a letter of Rabelais to the Bishop of Maillezais we find the form *protenotaire.* The MS. text is probably the correct one.

In the last paragraph but one note that Pantagruel has become a giant again.

This chapter seems to have been tampered with in more than one place. Perhaps Rabelais only left it as a fragment.

Chapter XIX

Note the inversion at the beginning of the first sentence.

1564: *contrepointé d'allarmes.* MS.: *De al il vrior.* The correction of 1564 is generally accepted, but why should a little cabinet, in which dinner was served, be "lined with alarums," and how can a room be *lined* with alarums?

On dict que Jupiter...au monde. The source of this piece of learning is probably Erasmus, *Adag.* I. 8. 24 (W. F. S.).

1564: *Par ma foy.* MS.: *Par ma soif.* This is a Rabelaisian touch and no correction was needed.

In one particular the printed text of this chapter is clearly superior to the MS. and that is in the Hebrew terms for the officers of the Queen's household and for the strange foods upon which she dined. This is made clear by M. Sainéan in the first of his learned articles on Rabelais's vocabulary. Not only does the MS. omit eight words from the first list, but in the second list it gives *jarbots* in place of *jecabots*, which is nearer than *jarbots* to the Hebrew *sekhaloth* and to the form *secaboth* of two chapters later. It was suggested to M. Sainéan by the late distinguished Hebrew and Arabic scholar, Joseph Halévy, that the list of honourable titles in the first passage was furnished to the author of the Fifth Book by a rabbi. More important for my present inquiry is M. Sainéan's own observation that the Hebrew element is completely absent from the three first books, that in the Fourth Book Hebrew names are largely employed for the geography, and that "this tendency to allegory under a biblical dress is particularly marked in the Fifth Book." This proves that at any rate the episode of the kingdom of La Quinte was not written till after the completion of the Third Book.

Chapter XX

The printed text omits *alopex est nommé des Grecs.*

1564: *Fontaine de jeunesse.* MS.: *Jo[o]uvence*, which is of course right. This sentence and the remaining nine lines of the chapter, which contain references to Euripides, Lucian, the Homeric Hymns, Ovid, and two scholiasts, are characteristic of Rabelais. *Recuict* of the MS. is right; 1564: *reteint.* From *Cela estoit* to *Phenix d'Arabie* is perhaps an interpolation.

Chapter XXI

This and the next three chapters are not numbered in the MS.

Nous en vismes...Atlas. This passage is wanting in the MS. The expression *haulsoient le temps* also occurs in IV. lxv, but it seems pointless here and the whole passage is unlike Rabelais.

1564: *conduictes des guerres.* The MS. leaves a blank.

The chapter is probably by Rabelais but with some interpolations.

Chapter XXII

l'espreuve de vostre industrie...ce que faictes. This is an obscurely worded sentence both in the MS. and the printed text, but the MS. gives the better sense.

MS.: *plataine.* 1564: *platine.* The MS. is right; the gift of a golden plane to Darius is narrated by Herodotus and Pliny.

Chapters XXIII and XXIV

This description of living Chess is taken with considerable amplification from the *Hypnerotomachia.* The MS. omits it and puts the conclusion, *Durant lesquelles dances...brisans*, at the end of c. xxi, but the reference to the dances is unintelligible without it. Moreover it is careful and finished work, in fact an admirable example, so far as style goes, of Rabelais at his best.

The earlier chapters of the episode, on the other hand, are rough unfinished work, and xx and xxi in particular have clearly been tampered with. I have already suggested that this is an episode which Rabelais on second thoughts rejected —perhaps because he felt that the satire on scholastic philosophy was not highly entertaining. I have also suggested that he came to this decision before writing the account of the storm which figures in Book IV[1]. Probably he wrote the episode, not at Metz, but after his return to France in the summer of 1547. W. F. Smith thinks that he wrote it soon after *Gargantua,* on the ground that only in that book and the

[1] See above, p. 109.

Fifth Book are to be found long extracts from the *Hypnero-tomachia*. But this is not a good reason, for Rabelais may either have copied passages from the work in question into a notebook, or he may very easily have had opportunities of consulting it on more than one occasion. It is even possible that some one of his patrons may have presented him with a copy. Further, this argument for an early date is gainsaid both by the style, which shows the inversions and other characteristics of Rabelais's later style, *i.e.* from the Third Book onwards, and by the fact that when he wrote the episode the idea of the voyage must have been firmly established in his mind.

The Island of Odes

Chapter XXV

This interesting chapter, with its original and picturesque idea of roads which move and so enable travellers to find themselves at their destination without trouble or fatigue, is certainly by Rabelais.

There are several places in which the MS. and the printed text differ, and about ten times out of sixteen the MS. is almost certainly right. The following are some of the more striking instances:

MS.: *les voyagiers souvent ès habitans du païs demandaient.* 1564: *servans et*, which is nonsense.

MS.: *Ce chemin que voyez nasquit d'eau et en eau retournera.* 1564: *et s'y en retournera*, an inept correction.

MS.: *le Chemin ferré de Bourges et le veidz marcher au pas de Otarde.* 1564: *le grand chemin de Bourges et le vy marcher à pas d'Abbé. Chemin ferré* = paved road, is doubtless right, and so is *Otarde*. We have the identical phrase in *Pant.* II. xi. I do not know why all editors have accepted the 1564 reading of *Abbé*. But whether "bustard" or *Abbé* is right, the reason for the slow pace which these words imply is that Bourges was on the top of a hill. There was a pre-Roman road, afterwards used in Roman times, from Bourges to Limoges.

MS.: *le vert quemin.* 1564: *le vieux quemin. Quemin* is the

Picard form of *chemin*. Why should not the epithet *vert* denote a grass road?

MS.: *La Ferrière sus le Mont Cenis, creature du roy Artus, acompaigné d'un grand Ours.* 1564: *La Ferrare sus le mont d'un grand Ours.* Duchat says that *La Ferrate* (which is evidently the right reading) was the road from Limoges to Tours which crossed the mountain of the *Grand Ours*. But the picturesque comparison of the road to St Jerome which follows shows that *acompaigné* must be accepted. Secondly, the description is far more appropriate to a high Alpine road than to one between Limoges and Tours. Thirdly, *La Ferrate* (= *La Ferrata*) suggests a road leading to Italy.

In the first line, *avoir par deux jours navigé*, with its ellipse of *après*, is characteristic of Rabelais[1].

levées du Nil. This, as Smith points out, is from Coelius Rhodiginus, an author much used by Rabelais.

The printed text ends at *en Egypte*, but the MS. has two additional paragraphs, of which the first relates to King Panigon—I have already referred to this in paper III[2]—and the second is practically a repetition of the passage in IV. ii, relating to the painter Charles Carmoy.

Finally, it should be noted that there is nothing to connect this episode either with the chapter which precedes it or with that which follows it.

LES FRERES FREDONS

The canvas of this episode of the Quavering Friars is doubtless Rabelais's work, but one suspects—and hopes—that some of its embroidery is by another hand.

Chapter XXVI

The reference to La Quinte points to this chapter having been written after the episode of Queen Entelechy.

omoplates, os bregmatiques. These anatomical terms suggest Rabelais.

MS.: *la devise de Pontan*. 1564: *la devise Pontiale*. The MS. is right; the reference is to the Neapolitan humanist Pontanus,

---

[1] See above, pp. 93 f. [2] See above, p. 50.

who in his dialogue entitled *Charon* expresses his detestation of the sound of bells. Cp. *Garg.* XIX, and see n. 48 of Lefranc's edition.

Much of this chapter is dull and tiresome, but some of its passages are quite characteristic of Rabelais.

Chapter XXVII

The idea of the monosyllabic answers which the friar makes to Panurge appears in a versified dialogue printed in 1532 in an edition of Villon's poems, and it was probably a current joke in Rabelais's day. Desperiers (d. 1544) has a story (no. lviii) in which a monk answers in rhymed monosyllables, but his collection of stories did not see the light till 1558.

There was a great opportunity here for an irresponsible editor to try his hand, and he no doubt availed himself of it; but the two narrative passages, especially the one at the end of the chapter, read like Rabelais's work.

MS.: *freraille*. 1564: *ferraille*. The MS. is clearly right.

After *grands princes* the MS. has an additional passage, in which the unintelligible phrases *freres tenps* and *freres narjorie* occur.

Chapter XXVIII

This attack on Lent from the medical point of view is probably in the main by Rabelais.

MS.: *Le feu curé de Jouvert*. 1564: *le Curé de Jambet. Feu* is doubtless right, and if *Jambet* is the true reading we must suppose either that Rabelais is speaking of his predecessor or that he is following the precedent of the title-page of Book II, where he describes himself as *feu M. Alcofribas*.

PAYS DE SATIN

This episode is unquestionably by Rabelais; the interest shown in geographical discovery, the fact that the idea and name of the country of Satin is taken from the *Hypnerotomachia*, the frequent borrowings from Pliny, Aelian, and Coelius Rhodiginus, all point to his authorship. But the entire lack of action and the almost entire lack of conversation, together with the constant use of the first person, suggest that we have before us a rough draft which Rabelais had not worked up into an artistic form.

Chapter XXIX

MS.: *Hans Clebir.* 1564: *Henry Clerberg.* There was a rich German merchant named Hans Kleberger living at Lyons.

MS.: *Legugé.* 1564: *Limoges.* The true reading is *Ligugé*, where Rabelais once lived with his friend and patron the Bishop of Maillezais.

In the lists of animals, some real, some fabulous, our two texts show, as might be expected, certain differences[1]. In some cases the MS. is right, in others the printed text. Thus *Neades* (cp. IV. lxii) and *Ophions* (Plin. XXX. 52) of the MS. are right as against *Neares* and *Ophyres* of 1564. On the other hand the 1564 text rightly prints *Bytures* (Plin. XXX. 4) for *Bulures*, *Cepes* (Plin. VIII. 28) for *Cabes*, *Crocutes* (hyenas —see Plin. VIII. 30) for *Tronites*, and *Eales* (*ib.*) for *Dales*.

Lancercules (MS.) and *Cucocrutes* (1564) are both wrong; the true reading is probably *Leucrocotes*, a fabulous animal of India which was said to be a cross between a lion and a hyena (see Plin. VIII. 30). *Orophages* (MS.) and *Pephages* (1564) are also both wrong, but M. Sainéan's conjecture, *Pegases* (a bird with a horse's head mentioned in Plin. X. 70), does not carry conviction, for it does not account for the copyist's *Orophages*.

MS.: *Gebes.* 1564: *Steres.* The latter is supposed to be a truncated form of *Presteres* (Plin. XXXII. 67), a species of snake.

Finally, one animal which appears in the MS. is omitted altogether in the printed text; this is *Halces* = Elands (Plin. VIII. 16).

Rabelais's principal source for all these animals is Pliny, and chiefly his eighth book. But he has also made use of Aelian, from whom he borrowed the account of the trained elephants at Rome in the time of Germanicus (*De anim. nat.* II. 11), and one or two other particulars. I owe this information to W. F. Smith, who also suggested as a possible source

---

[1] See for what follows L. Sainéan in *Revue du seizième siècle*, III (1915), 210 ff. (*L'histoire naturelle dans l'œuvre de Rabelais*).

Ravisius Textor[1]. There is a list of birds and another of beasts in that writer which have a great many names in common with Rabelais.

Chapter XXX

For the list of travellers and historians see above, p. 36, where I have pointed out that the MS. in spite of some mistakes represents the original text more faithfully than the edition of 1564.

PAYS DE LANTERNOIS

Chapters XXXI and XXXII

Here again we have Rabelais beyond a doubt. The first chapter is very short and possibly unfinished, but the second is Rabelais at his best. The idea of Lantern-land comes from Lucian's *Vera historia* (I. 29), and some particulars are also taken from this source. But greater use is made of *Le Disciple de Pantagruel*, which had been beforehand in borrowing the idea and which devotes three chapters (xiv–xvi) to its execution.

There are two interesting differences to notice in our two texts.

Icosimixe (*i.e.* with twenty wicks), *jadis consacree par Canope fille de Tisias* is the reading of the 1564 text, but the MS. has *Critias* for *Tisias*. This is right, but an epigram of Callimachus shows that the words before *Critias* should run *à Canope par la fille de*, Canope being equivalent to the god of Canope, *i.e.* Serapis[2].

The Queen of the Lanterns is described in the 1564 text as *vestuë de Cristallin vierge, de Touchie, ouvrage damasquin.* MS. has *vergé par art de tauchie, et augeminée à ouvrage damasquin.*

M. Clouzot's learned and interesting article in the *Revue du seizième siècle* (IV. 31 ff.) makes it certain that the MS. is substantially right. *Tauchie* not *touchie* is the true spelling, but *augeminé(e)* should probably be written *azeminé* as in *Pant.* (III. 38, and IV. 1), where we have the form *azemine* = Persian

---

[1] In a letter dated September 7, 1907.
[2] W. F. Smith in *Rev. des études rab.* III. 304.

work (from Arabic *Adjem* = Persian). As to the precise difference between *tauchie, azemine* and damascened work I do not suppose that Rabelais had any very clear idea about it. M. Clouzot seems to accept *vierge* as preferable to *vergé*. But what is the difference between virgin crystal and ordinary crystal? And does not *vergé de touchie et azeminé à ouvrage damasquin* give a better sense than *de tauchie ouvrage damasquin*?

After chapter xxxiii the MS. has a third chapter on the same subject, entitled *Comment furent les dames lanternes servies à soupper*. It begins with a dull enumeration of dishes, largely consisting of repetitions from other parts of Rabelais. After supper there is a dance and there follows a long list of dances, which differs very little from the similar list in chapter xvi of *Le Disciple de Pantagruel*. The chapter ends with the queen offering the travellers the choice of a lantern for their guide to the Bottle. They choose the lantern of Pierre Amy, as "more learned, more wise, more eloquent, more kindly, more gracious" than any other, and this tribute to Rabelais's old friend can only be by the hand of Rabelais himself.

Oracle de la Bouteille

Chapters XXXIII–XLVII

We now come to the fifteen chapters which form the concluding episode of the Fifth Book, and I have no hesitation in recognising them not only as Rabelais's work, but as work to which, with the single exception of chapter xxxiv, he had given the final touches, and which he definitely intended to form part of his great romance.

Chapters xxxiii and xxxv, especially the latter chapter, have the lively dramatic form characteristic of Rabelais, and they read like finished work. Chapter xxxiv, on the other hand, seems to me to be still in the rough. It may be said that the glorification of Chinon might be a forger's attempt to give colour to his forgery, but would anyone except Rabelais have connected Chinon with Cain, and gravely spoken of it as the model after which more modern founders

—Athene, Alexander, Constantine, Hadrian—gave their names to the towns they founded or restored?

In chapter xxxiv there is an interesting variant; the MS. has *San Rame*, which the printed text corrects to *Suresnes*. The true reading is of course *San Reme*.

Chapters xxxvi, xxxvii and xl are for the most part translated from the *Hypnerotomachia*[1] and this is a strong argument in favour of Rabelais's authorship. It is true that one critic has taken a directly opposite view[2], but few who are well acquainted with Rabelais's methods will agree with him. Moreover, even more impressive than the borrowings from this favourite hunting-ground of Rabelais are the passages in which the author deserts it. For instance, at the close of chapter xxxvii he substitutes for Virgil's *Trahit sua quemque voluntas* a line which Seneca has translated from the Greek of Cleanthes:

Ducunt volentem fata volentem trahunt,

and for the Greek inscription Πᾶν δεῖ ποιεῖν κατὰ τὴν αὐτοῦ φύσιν the French sentence,

Toutes choses se meuvent à leur fin.

It may be noted that at the beginning of chapter xxxvii the printed text has *Sosistratus*, and the MS. *Sosus*. The latter reading is confirmed by Plin. XXXVI. 25, 60.

Chapter xxxviii and the first half of xxxix are mostly translated from Lucian's *Dionysus*, but some touches are borrowed from Jean Le Maire's account of the marriage of Peleus and Thetis[3].

In chapter xxxix the edition of 1564 has *vents, paroles, meurs et les esprits* and the MS. *vents, echo, les meurs et les esprits*. A reference to Pliny (XXXV. 10) shows that for *echo* we should read *ethe* (ἤθη).

In chapters xli and xlii there is a curious difference in the arrangement of the matter between the MS. and the 1564 text. In the latter, the former chapter consists only of a single

---

[1] See W. F. Smith, *The Modern Quarterly of Language and Literature* for April, 1899, pp. 286–288.

[2] H. K. Söltoft-Jenson in *Rev. d'hist. litt.* III. 608 ff.

[3] See my note in *Rev. du seizième siècle*, II. 30–33.

PLATE III

From the *Hypnerotomachia Poliphili* of Francesco Colonna, Venice, 1499

paragraph, stopping at *fontaine fantastique*. It then begins the next chapter with *Puis commanda estre hanaps...tres volontiers; car pour plainctive estoit une fontaine fantastique...dedans les limbes Pluto*. The MS. after *fontaine fantastique* has *d'estoffe ...ne songea* (as in 1564 text) *Dedalus. Les limbe* (*i.e.* the outer rim), *plinthe*, etc., and continues the chapter down to *la mer de vostre monde*. It then begins the next chapter with the paragraph *Puis commanda...tres volontiers* followed by *Car pleinement* (1564, *clerement*) *vous advertir*. The headings of the chapters make it evident that the arrangement of the MS. is the right one. Further, the words *pour plainctive* of 1564 are nonsense and the correction of *dedans les limbes Pluto* for *Dedalus. Les limbe, plinthe* shows more ingenuity than common sense.

In chapter xlii four variants are worth noticing.

(1) The MS. *par l'aide de l'art* (= Pliny's *artis opere*) is right as against the 1564 text's *l'art apprendre*, which is sheer nonsense.

(2) The MS. *Lullie Pauline*, with the change of one letter, is likewise confirmed by Pliny (IX. 35, 58). She was for a short time the wife of the Emperor Gaius. The 1564 text has *Pompeie Plautine*.

(3) 1564: *faits de marguerites fines en l'assiette de trois angles*. MS. *faits de murhine, confinez en l'acuité des troys angles*. The MS. is surely right; the channels could not have been made of pearls, but they might have been made of *murrha*, if, as some conjecture, that mysterious substance, so much prized by the ancients, was fluor-spar.

(4) 1564: *eau de Nonacris et Derce*. MS. *eau de Nome et Derce*. Here the MS. reproduces a passage in *Hypnerotomachia* which mentions the fountains of Derce and Nome as celebrated for their coldness (*che non sono Derce et Nome*). *Nome* may be wrong—there were hills called Nomia in Arcadia—but is probably what Rabelais wrote, and it is difficult to accept Nonacris, a town near the source of the Styx, as a correction.

In chapter xliii there is nothing that calls for notice, and as for the four noble and superbly written chapters which

conclude the book they seem to me to bear beyond the shadow
of a doubt the impress of Rabelais's genius.

The printed text of the final chapter ends differently from
that of the MS. It slightly abbreviates the reference to well-
known philosophers who had chosen friends for their guides,
and it substitutes two short sentences for two or three pages
of the MS., which are of considerable interest and are undoubtedly by Rabelais. A comparison with Coelius Rhodiginus (*Ant. Lect.* XXIII. 4) justifies the MS.'s account of the
philosophers and their friends.

Almost at the very end there is a passage—*irrigu et ver-
doyant...Mont Caspit*—which comes almost straight from the
Hypnerotomachia, and, as W. F. Smith has pointed out, a
reference to that work enables one to correct the blunders of
the copyist. We must substitute *Themiscyrie* for *Thermiscrie*,
Taure for *Thaure*, *Indicque* for *Judaique*, *Talge* for *Caliges*
and *Caspien* for *Caspit*[1].

There remains to be considered the Prologue. In the MS.
it comes to an abrupt end after the words *encloses entre*, while
in the printed text it is carried on for several pages farther.
My personal impression is that none of this additional matter
is by Rabelais, but as for the fragment I am inclined to regard
it as his work—work which he rejected as unsatisfactory.
Had the editor of the text, represented by the MS., written
it, he would not have stopped short in the middle of a sentence—unless, indeed, he was seized by a sudden illness
ending in his death. There is nothing to indicate at what date
it was written.

I must now briefly recapitulate the conclusions which seem
to result from this inquiry:

1. The whole of the *Ile Sonante* was written by Rabelais
and was handed over to the printer as he left it.

2. The rest of the Fifth Book (chapter xvi to the end) is in
the main Rabelais's work, but in several of the chapters there
are interpolations, notably in xviii, xx, xxi, xxvi–xxviii.

[1] Smith, *op. cit.* p. 285. For the form *Indicque* cp. the Prologue to Book III.

3. As, except for a few short sentences, all these inter-polations are found in the MS. as well as in the printed text of 1564 they must be due to the editor of the text which I have called C[1], that is to say, to some one who revised and added to Rabelais's genuine work.

4. But, though the Fifth Book is in the main by Rabelais, it clearly does not represent his final intentions.

5. Some of the chapters—xvi, xxxi, and possibly xviii—he left unfinished.

6. Other chapters he left in the form of a rough draft which he had not worked up into an artistic shape. Such are chapters xi, xxix and xxx (the Country of Satin), and xxxv.

7. The book is composed of eleven episodes: 4 and 5 (the Furred Cats and the Island of the Apedeftes) and 9, 10 and 11 (the Country of Satin, Lantern-land, and the Oracle of the Bottle) are continuous; 1, 2, 3 and 7—the Ringing Island, the Island of Tools, the Island of Cassade, and the Island of Odes—have no connexion either with what goes before or with what follows after[2]; 6 (the Kingdom of La Quinte) has no connexion with the episode which precedes it; 8 (the Quavering Friars) is loosely connected with 6 and even more loosely with 9, the connecting words in the latter case having very possibly been supplied by an editor.

8. Of these eleven episodes only the last three, forming chapters xxix–xlvii, were definitely intended by Rabelais to form part of a fifth book and of these, as we have seen, chapter xxxi was unfinished, and chapters xxix, xxx and xxxv had not been worked up into their final shape.

9. The important episodes of the Ringing Island, the Furred Cats, and the Apedeftes were rejected by Rabelais as containing heretical and dangerous matter; the Kingdom of La Quinte, the Island of Tools, and the Island of Cassade as dull and uninteresting. The Island of Odes I believe he meant to retain, but I cannot think that the Quavering Friars would have commended itself to his final judgment.

[1] See above, p. 88.
[2] The Island of Cassade was connected with the Island of Tools by the 1564 editor.

Though for convenience sake I have put the above conclusions in a categorical form, they of course only represent my personal opinions. The evidence upon which I have based them may have been incorrectly stated, and the inferences that I have drawn from it may be wrong ones. New facts, too, may come to light, or some acuter mind may hit upon a surer method of inquiry. One thing, however, is certain —it is only by patient investigation, chapter by chapter, of the Fifth Book that the question of its authenticity can be finally solved.

VI

HUMANISM UNDER FRANCIS I

In March 1515 Guillaume Budé published the *De Asse*, the work which established his reputation as one of the leading humanists of Europe; in the year 1547 Adrien Tournebus, known to scholars as Turnebus, was appointed a royal professor of Greek at Paris. These two dates, which exactly coincide with the beginning and the end of the reign of Francis I, serve to mark off that reign as a distinct epoch in the history of French humanism. Budé was a man of great learning; Turnèbe was a critical scholar. So were Henri Estienne, Lambin, and Dorat, while Vatable and Toussain, who both died on the same day of 1547, were of the same type as Budé. This difference of type distinguishes the reign of Francis I from the succeeding period, which is the golden age of French scholarship, and which may be said to have lasted from 1547 to 1572. The humanists of the later period were specialists; they were devoted to some single branch of humanistic study, history, or jurisprudence, or the critical construction of classical texts. The men of the reign of Francis I aspired to the whole domain of classical learning. Rabelais was a storehouse of erudition; Postel, Du Chastel, and many others were his equals, if not his superiors, in the extent and variety of their attainments. Fernel, the great medical writer, was at one time an ardent student of mathematics and astronomy; his colleague Sylvius (Dubois) was the first Frenchman to publish a grammar of his native language; Peletier was a physician, a mathematician, a spelling reformer, and a poet. But whatever the branches of learning in which these ardent spirits won distinction, they nearly all built upon the same foundation, the knowledge of Greek. It is this which makes Budé, the "restorer of Greek studies in France," the dominant figure of this period of humanism.

I have sketched elsewhere[1] Budé's career down to 1515, using as my chief guide the scholarly work of M. Delaruelle[2]. Throughout the reign of Louis XII Budé, though one of the royal secretaries, had, except for two missions to Italy, lived in the retirement of his library, translating into Latin four treatises of Plutarch and writing his *Annotations to the Pandects* and his *De Asse*. But in 1518 he began to hanker after employment at Court[3]. Accordingly, with the view of "making himself better known" to Francis I, he presented him with a collection of apophthegms, taken chiefly from Plutarch, which he had translated into French—for Francis knew neither Greek nor Latin—and had had copied in a fair manuscript[4]. In the course of a verbose preface he exhorts the King to give encouragement to the revived study of good literature (*bonnes lettres*)—in other words, of classical literature. Budé's offering, which was apparently made at the beginning of 1519, had the desired effect, and very soon afterwards he was summoned to Court. In the following year the publication by Josse Badius of a collection of Budé's letters, including several written in Greek, definitely established his reputation as a Greek scholar, and from this time he was recognised as sharing with Erasmus the primacy of European scholarship. A second collection of his letters, also published by Badius, followed in 1522, and in the same year he was appointed to the newly created office of Master of the King's library at Fontainebleau and made a Master of Requests. He now had to follow the Court in its many peregrinations

---

[1] *The Dawn of the French Renaissance*, pp. 269–278.

[2] *Guillaume Budé, les origines, les débuts, les idées maîtresses*, 1907. For Budé's later career see the Latin life by Louis Le Roy, 1541 (N.S.)—a panegyric rather than a biography—and the modern lives by Rebitté (1846) and E. de Budé (1884).

[3] See a letter to Pace of April 27, 1518 (*Opera*, 2 vols., Basle [1557], I. 242 D).

[4] Bib. de l'Arsenal, 5103, with a miniature which represents the author presenting his work to the King (a reproduction of this forms the frontispiece to M. Delaruelle's book). Seven years after Budé's death an unauthorised revision and expansion of this manuscript was printed under the title of *Le livre de l'institution du Prince*, Paris, 1547. See Delaruelle, *op. cit.* pp. 199–220, and 231–245.

and before long he was looking back with bitter regret to his former life of peaceful study[1]. In a letter to Christophe de Longueil (Longolius), written from Romorantin in January 1521, he complains that he is far from his home, without his books (*sine lare, sine libris*), and unable to resume his beloved studies[2]. Two months later, writing from the same place to the Italian humanist, Leonicus[3], he explains that he has not deserted philology, but that he considers it a duty to his brother humanists to show that a humanist is not unfitted for an active life[4]. At last, at the beginning of 1525, he was able to return to his home[5]. As a matter of fact, he had three homes —a hôtel in the rue Saint-Martin, and two country-houses in the neighbourhood of Paris, one at Saint-Maur and the other at Marly. From this time he ceased to travel with the Court and only put in an infrequent appearance, when the King was in Paris or its neighbourhood[6]. He had a good excuse, for he had suffered for more than twenty years from a chronic disease which inflicted on him severe bouts of pain.

As might be expected in a collection of letters the purpose of which was to establish Budé's reputation as a scholar, several are addressed to the leading humanists of other nations: to the Italians, Alciati, Egnatius (Giovanni Battista Cipelli), Leonicus, Sadoleto, and Bembo; to the Swiss, Zazius and Vadianus (Joachim von Watt); to the Englishmen, Linacre, Tunstall, More, Pace, Lupset, and Croke; to his old friend Janus Lascaris; and, above all, to Erasmus. The majority of those to Erasmus, twenty-two in number[7], belong to the years 1516–1519; after 1519 there are only seven, the

---

[1] See a letter to Vives written in August 1519 (*Op.* I. 253 A); L. Delaruelle, *Répertoire de la Correspondance de Guillaume Budé*, 1907, p. 76. This latter work contains an excellent summary of all Budé's extant letters (175 as against 160 in the Basle edition) arranged in chronological order.

[2] *Op.* I. 308; Delaruelle, p. 129.

[3] Niccolò Tomeo of Lonigo.

[4] *Op.* I. 333; Delaruelle, p. 137.

[5] *Op.* I. 438; Delaruelle, no. 157. In February 1531 (N.S.) Badius published a new edition of Budé's letters, comprising all those previously published, and 37 new ones. This edition is reproduced in the *Opera*.

[6] *Op.* I. 393; Delaruelle, p. 162.

[7] Eight of these will be found, not among Budé's letters, but among those of Erasmus. See P. S. Allen's monumental edition, 4 vols., Oxford, 1906–1921 (in progress).

latest bearing the date of April 22, 1527. The earliest ones, from February 1517 to October 1518, relate to the project, which Budé and the other French humanists had so much at heart, of bringing Erasmus to Paris as head of a college for the study of ancient languages. But Erasmus, though he coquetted for a time with the offer, which was made by the King himself, ended by declining it. Four years later (1522), and again in 1524, the idea of coming to France was broached by Erasmus himself, but nothing came of it.

As for the proposed college, the idea of which was suggested by the college founded in 1515 at Louvain by Jerome Busleiden for the study of the three ancient languages— Greek, Latin, and Hebrew—the project after the definite failure to secure Erasmus (October 1518) was for a time abandoned[1]. On the death of Maximilian (January 1519) Francis I at once began an active candidature for the Empire. Then, after the election of Charles V, came first preparation for war, then war, the disaster of Pavia, the King's captivity, and the renewal of the war, which was only ended by the Treaty of Cambrai in August 1529[2]. Moreover, since 1525, the opposition which the ultra-orthodox party in the University, headed by the Sorbonne and the College of Navarre, had from the first shown to the new studies, especially to Greek, was strengthened and embittered by the sympathy of the humanists with Reform. In 1525, when Francis I was in prison at Madrid, Louise of Savoy and the Chancellor, Du Prat, appointed a commission for the trial of Lutherans and instituted proceedings against the Meaux preachers. And, though the King on his return to France in 1526 showed favour to the Reformers, before long the excesses committed by their more fanatical wing, notably the mutilation of a favourite statue of the Virgin at Paris (1528), filled many of the humanists with apprehension, and the King with fury.

[1] The whole story is admirably told by M. Abel Lefranc in his *Histoire du Collège de France*, 1893. The Abbé Goujet's *Mémoire historique et littéraire sur le Collège royal de France*, 3 vols. 1758, is full of errors.

[2] In January 1521, a month before he began hostilities against the Emperor, Francis announced his intention of founding a college for the study of Greek. See Lefranc, *op. cit.* p. 76; and a letter of Budé to Toussain (Delaruelle, *Rép.* no. 84).

Budé, however, had never forgotten the proposed college. In September 1529, a month after the Treaty of Cambrai, he published through Badius his *Commentarii Linguae Graecae*[1], a species of Greek lexicon, which Erasmus had once or twice urged him to write. Like all Budé's writings, it is sadly lacking in method, but its appearance was a notable event in the history of French scholarship. In the preface, addressed to the King, he reminds him in very plain language of his promise to

found a school, a nursery, so to speak, of men of learning. You told us that you would adorn your capital with such an establishment, and that it should be a centre of learning ($\mu o \upsilon \sigma \hat{\epsilon} \iota o \nu$) for the whole of France. You promised that a magnificent building should be erected, in which the two languages should be taught....But now it is said that you have not kept your promises, and I, who was surety for their performance, am blamed for the delay. I am laughed at and treated as a perjurer.

Budé's bold words shortly bore fruit. It is true that there was no longer any question of a college, much less of a magnificent building which should provide a worthy home for learning; but before Lady-day 1530 four Royal Professors, each with a stipend of 200 crowns, were appointed—two for Hebrew and two for Greek. A fifth, for mathematics, was added a little later. In spite of the opposition of the obscurantist party, headed by Noël Bédier, the new professorships were a great success. Before the end of 1534 a Latin professorship, to which Bédier and his friends especially objected, was established. The next ten years saw the creation of a third chair for Greek, a third for Hebrew, a second for mathematics, one for philosophy and one for medicine, making eleven in all.

But, before this tale of professorships was completed, Budé, having seen the accomplishment (up to a certain point) of his heart's desire, had died on August 22, 1540, in his Paris hôtel. We know little or nothing of his life during its last decade; he apparently lived in comparative retirement, either at Paris or at one or other of his country-houses. The following words of Calvin express the verdict of his contemporaries:

[1] The best edition is that of Robert Estienne (1548), a magnificent specimen of typography.

"Gulielmus Budaeus primum rei literariae decus et columen, cuius beneficio palmam eruditionis hodie sibi vindicat Gallia[1]."

Of the leading humanists who were more or less Budé's contemporaries, of Deloynes, who died at an advanced age in 1525, Ruzé, Germain de Brie, Nicole Bérault, Jean Ruel, Jean de Pins and a rather younger man, Christophe de Longueil (Longolius), who died in 1522, I have spoken briefly in *The Dawn of the French Renaissance*, but Bérault demands further notice here. I shall also have occasion to mention Ruel and Jean de Pins.

At the opening of the reign of Francis I, Bérault, who was then about forty-five, was editing Greek texts for sundry publishers, and taking a few pupils[2]. In the year 1515 he married the widow of the printer and publisher Jean Barbier, whose business he carried on for two or three years. He was then fortunate enough to find a patron in Étienne Poncher, the Bishop of Paris[3], who took him to England in August 1518, and to Narbonne and Montpellier in 1519[4]. Between the two missions Bérault lectured in the University of Paris and continued to do so on his return from Montpellier. At the same time his few pupils had now developed into a small "pedagogy" or school, in which, a little later, Melchior Wolmar and Étienne Dolet were scholars. Bérault also served the cause of Greek by producing editions of Athanasius (1519) and the Latin-Greek dictionary of Giovanni Crastone (1521). In 1525 his patron died[5] and he found a new one in the person of Jean d'Orléans, Archbishop of Toulouse, who exacted from him constant personal service and left him no leisure for his own studies. His reputation for eloquence led to his being chosen to write an oration on the Treaty of Cambrai (1529). The oration was printed, and as on the title-

---

[1] Calvin, *Op.* v. 54.

[2] For Nicole Bérault see L. Delaruelle in *Musée Belge*, no. 8 (1909), pp. 253–312 (a recasting of an earlier article in the *Rev. des Bibliothèques*, 1902, pp. 420–445); Allen, *Erasmi Epist.* III. 503–4.

[3] See *The Dawn of the French Renaissance*, p. 198.

[4] The second mission was to arrange with the ambassadors of Charles V for the execution of the Treaty of Noyon. Poncher was now Archbishop of Sens. Budé also accompanied the mission.

[5] The traditional statement that he was tutor to the three Châtillon brothers seems to rest on no authority (Delaruelle, *op. cit.* p. 277, n. 3).

page he appears with the title of Royal Historian, it may be assumed that he succeeded Paolo Emilio, who died in May 1529. Then in 1533 Jean d'Orléans died, and Bérault entered the service of his successor, the sixteen-year-old Cardinal, Odet de Châtillon. It was even harder work than under his predecessor, for the young Cardinal was always moving about, and poor Bérault, who was now past sixty, groaned under the constant travelling. His literary work, which had greatly slackened since 1522, entirely ceased, but his name was held in high honour by the younger generation of humanists. In 1538 he was still in the Cardinal's service, and we learn from the *Bibliotheca* of Conrad Gesner that he was alive in 1545. By 1555 he was dead.

The first generation of French humanists, that is to say, the generation of Budé and his contemporaries, had to contend with many obstacles. In their own country there were no books, few manuscripts, and still fewer teachers; moreover, there was the constant opposition of the Paris University. It was by unshaken perseverance and untiring study that Budé and Bérault overcame these difficulties. The only alternative was that adopted by Germain de Brie and Jean de Pins, to spend several years in Italy.

The second generation of French scholars, men who had scarcely reached manhood at the time of the accession of Francis I, found on the whole a much easier task before them. In the first place they had better teaching; they could learn Greek in France, without going to Italy or trusting to the stray visits of foreign scholars. Secondly, thanks to the energy and liberality of Budé and one or two others, whose example was followed by the King, Greek manuscripts, though not as yet to any great extent, were being collected and multiplied; and, though few Greek books were as yet printed in France, they could be imported from beyond the Alps.

A letter written in 1519 by Budé to his son Dreux, then a boy of about twelve, puts very forcibly the difference in opportunity between the two generations. There were now, he said, abundance of books within the means even of a poor man, and there was a sufficiency of teachers, whereas in his youth books were rare and expensive and he had to fight his way to knowledge almost unaided[1]. M. Delaruelle aptly compares this with a similar passage in the famous letter of Gargantua to Pantagruel, and indeed the resemblance is so close that it is easy to accept his suggestion that Rabelais was inspired by the published letter of the great scholar whose encouragement of his own studies had been so precious to him.

Foremost among this younger generation were Danès and Toussain, the first Royal Professors of Greek. Pierre Danès[2] (1497–1577) was born to success. Of a good and well-to-do Parisian family, he entered the College of Navarre (*circ.* 1512), which possessed a competent classical teacher in Olivier of Lyons. Learning of all kinds came easily to him, and it was a sign of his high promise that Budé took him as a private pupil. He soon became proficient both in Latin and Greek, and he was marked out for one of the new professorships. He proved a brilliant and successful lecturer, attracting large and enthusiastic audiences. Among his pupils were Amyot, Dorat, Jean de Gaigny, and the jurist, Barnabé Brisson. But like Aleandro twenty years before he preferred a public life to one of cloistered learning. In 1534 he obtained leave of absence in order to join his friend Georges de Selve, the French ambassador at Venice, and in the following year he resigned his professorship. In 1543 he was sent to the Council of Trent as one of the French representatives, and in the following year he delivered a speech before the Council which was much applauded. Henry II made him tutor to the Dauphin, and conferred on him the see of Lavaur, in succession to Georges de Selve. After again representing his country at Trent, he spent the rest of his long life in his diocese, distinguishing himself by his disinterestedness and his charity. His published works were few and unimportant. He was succeeded

---

[1] Accedit librorum antiquorum recentiorumque copia vel inopi parabilis atque in triviis pene exposita, qui meo tempore rari grandi aere permutabantur (Budé, *Op.* I. 285–287; Delaruelle, *Rép.* no. 31).

[2] Launoy, *Hist. gymn. Nav.* pp. 720–726.

by Jean Strazel, a Fleming, who had acted as his substitute during his temporary absence.

Jacques Toussain[1] was a very different type of scholar from his colleague. Though he lacked his brilliance, he had a more whole-hearted devotion to learning, and as a teacher he was eminently thorough and helpful. We have an interesting testimony to his merits from Pierre Ramus, who expatiates on the precision, the clarity, and the completeness with which he expounded the subtleties of Greek grammar or commented on a Greek author[2]. He must have been a little older than Danès, for at the beginning of 1515, when Danès was still a student at Navarre, he was taking pupils and Badius dedicated to him the grammar of Raffaelle Maffei of Volterra[3]. At Paris, whither he migrated from the neighbourhood of Troyes, he lived for some years in the house of Louis Ruzé, that generous helper of promising students, receiving Greek lessons from the great Budé and doing work for Badius. In 1526 he began to correspond with Erasmus and in the following year to teach Greek in the University[4]. In 1529 he was living with Lodovico Canossa, the Bishop of Bayeux. He died in 1547 leaving the manuscript of a Greek-Latin dictionary, which was published in 1552. Among his pupils were Turnèbe and Louis Le Roy, and, later, Henri Estienne and Jean-Antoine de Baïf.

Another scholar, who had had the privilege of being Budé's pupil, was Guillaume Du Maine, who became his children's tutor, and then reader to Margaret of Navarre, and later tutor to the children of Francis I. Several of Budé's Greek letters are addressed to him. In 1523 he joined with Jean Cheradame in editing a new edition of Crastone's dictionary.

Cheradame is described in the *Histoire ecclésiastique des églises réformés* as "homme bien versé tant es lettres Hebraïques que Grecques: combien qu'il fust d'esprit fort leger et de petit sens[5]." He gave Greek lectures in the College of

---

[1] See Delaruelle, *Rép.* p. 33; Lefranc, *op. cit.* pp. 173–175; Allen, *op. cit.* III. 281; H. Omont, *Rev. des ét. grecs*, XVI (1903) 417 ff.

[2] A. Lefranc, *op. cit.* pp. 174 f.   [3] Renouard, *Badius*, III. 387.

[4] In the same year he published some notes on Budé's *Letters* (Badius, 1527 (N.S.); Basle, 1528).   [5] Ed. Baum and Cunitz, I. 6.

Lisieux and was in request as an editor of Greek books. His editions included the three Olynthiac orations of Demosthenes, Aristotle's *De virtutibus et vitiis*, and nine plays of Aristophanes (all except the *Lysistrata* and the *Thesmophoriazusae*), the printing of the last work being begun in November 1528 and finished on March 30, 1529 (N.S.). Each play has a separate title-page and a dedication in Greek, the individuals thus honoured being John Clerk, Thomas Winter, Pierre Danès, Jean Le Voyer, Jean de Tartas, Antoine Lapitheus, Nicole Bérault, Jean Ruel, and William Quin (?). Of these Danès, Bérault, and Ruel are already known to us; Jean Le Voyer gave Greek lectures in the College of Burgundy, and Jean de Tartas was the progressive head of the College of Lisieux, where Cheradame lectured. All I know of Antoine Lapitheus is that the preliminary matter to an edition of Seneca's *Tragedies*, published by Badius in 1514, comprises a Latin poem addressed by Gilles de Maizières, Rector of the University, to Stephanus and Antonius Lapitheus. John Clerk, Bishop of Bath and Wells, was Wolsey's chaplain and agent; he was in Paris in August 1528, and the printing of the *Plutus*, the play dedicated to him, was finished on November 19 of that year. Thomas Winter was Wolsey's natural son; he went to Paris about 1524 with Thomas Lupset as his tutor, and he held many preferments, including the Deanery of Wells, all of which he resigned, some in 1528 and the rest in 1529[1]. As for Κουίνος, I can only suggest that it represents the Irish name of Quin.

M. Abel Lefranc is clearly right in his contention that Cheradame became one of the Royal Professors, for, as he points out on the title-page of a Greek dictionary edited by him in 1543, he is described as "Eloquiorum sacrorum regium Lutetiae professorem[2]." The title of his professorship is an unfamiliar one, but from a discourse pronounced in 1595 by Monantheuil, a pupil of Ramus and the first historian of the Royal College, we learn that it was, as M. Lefranc contends,

---

[1] See Le Neve, *Fasti Ecclesiae Anglicanae*.
[2] Lefranc, *op. cit.* p. 353.

a Professorship of Greek[1]. Whether Cheradame was appointed as successor to Postel, who had to resign his professorship of Greek, Hebrew, and Arabic in 1543, is not so certain.

In an official list of the professors (in some cases with their names utterly misspelt) for March 1545 (N. S.) which is given in Pierre Galland's life of Pierre Du Chastel[2], Cheradame's name does not appear, so that he must have died or resigned before that date. The third Greek Professor in this list is Denis Coroné, who was attached for many years to the household of Cardinal de Tournon. In the dedicatory preface to the *Hieroglyphica* of Orus Apollo, printed in 1522 (N.S.), he is described as "vir utriusque linguae doctissimus[3]," so that he was probably born before 1500. The date of his death is not known.

The lectures of the Royal Professors were given either in the College of Cambrai, on the east side of the Rue Saint-Jacques and opposite to the Sorbonne, or in the College of Tréguier, which was separated from it by the narrow Ruelle de Cambrai, or in the College of Les Trois-Évêques[4]. For though the followers of Beda were in a majority in the University, they did not have it all their own way. There had always existed a feeling of considerable jealousy between the Faculty of Arts and that of Theology, and this doubtless helped to dispose those colleges which had few or no theological professors in favour of the new studies. The Greek lectures of Le Voyer in the College of Burgundy and of Cheradame in that of Lisieux have already been mentioned. The latter, a large college occupying a considerable area between the two southernmost gates of Paris, the Porte Saint-Jacques and the Porte Saint-Marcel, was, under the enlightened rule of Jean de Tartas (1525–1533), very favourable to the new studies. In the College of Cardinal Lemoine Jean Bonchamp (Evagrius) was the Greek lecturer and François Vatable the Hebrew lecturer.

---

[1] *Ib.* p. 232. Monantheuil says that his portrait should be in the classroom of the Greek Professors.
[2] *Vita Castellani*, p. 150, ed. with notes by Étienne Baluze 1674; Lefranc, *op. cit.* p. 163. There is no official list extant between 1538 and 1546.
[3] Herminjard, *op. cit.* I. 71, n.[10].   [4] Lefranc, *op. cit.* p. 113.

But the principal home of humanism in the University was the College of Sainte-Barbe, of which the Portuguese Jacques de Gouvéa and his nephew André were successively Principals[1]. Among the professors were the distinguished jurist and Latin poet, Antoine de Gouvéa, brother of André, Jacques de Teyva, another Portuguese, Jacques-Louis d'Estrebay (Strebaeus), George Buchanan (1529–1532), who has drawn in his first Elegy a harrowing picture of his experiences[2], Maturin Cordier, Jean Gélida, Jean Fernel, who, while he was pursuing his medical studies, supported himself by lecturing on philosophy, mathematics, and astronomy, and Barthélemy Masson, the future Royal Professor. Among the students at this time was another future Royal Professor, Guillaume Postel, who found the means for pursuing his studies by acting as servant to Gélida, and the ex-soldier Ignatius Loyola, who, having joined the University at the age of thirty-five and having, under similar difficulties to those of Postel, completed his "grammar" course at the College of Montaigu, was admitted to Sainte-Barbe as a pupil in philosophy (1529) and proceeded in due course to his degrees of Licentiate (1533) and Master of Arts (1534). In the latter year André de Gouvéa was succeeded as Principal by his cousin Jacques, under whose rule the staff was joined by the eminent Greek scholar, Adrien Turnèbe.

The services rendered by Maturin Cordier (1479–1564)[3] to the cause of Humanism have often been related, and only a word or two need be said about them here. For sixteen years (1514–1530) he taught in various colleges of the University, and during the last six of these, having given up the class of rhetoric to which he had lectured with great success, he devoted himself to the task of instilling pure Latinity into

---

[1] See J. Quicherat, *Histoire de Sainte-Barbe*, 3 vols. 1860. In 1526 the King of Portugal, John III, founded fifty bursaries in the college for Portuguese students (Quicherat, p. 127).

[2] Its title is "Quam misera sit conditio docentium literas humaniores Lutetiae."

[3] See Gaullieur, *op. cit.* pp. 96–99; Haag, *La France Protestante*, 2nd ed. 1884; E. Puech, *Maturin Cordier*, Montauban, 1896; W. H. Woodward, *Studies in Education*, Cambridge, 1906, pp. 154–166.

younger boys of the fourth class. He was at that time (1524) a lecturer in the College of La Marche, and among his pupils was Calvin[1]. From 1525 to 1528 he taught at Sainte-Barbe, and then for two years at Navarre. In 1530 he left Paris for Nevers, and in 1534 he joined the staff of the new college of Guienne. He was now a Protestant, having been converted by his friend Robert Estienne, and in 1535 after the affair of the Placards his name appeared on the list of those cited to appear before the Paris *Parlement*. In 1537 he accepted Calvin's pressing invitation to help him with the organisation of his new college at Geneva, but, after the temporary defeat of Calvin and his party, in the following year he migrated to Neuchâtel to become head of the college, and he did not return to Geneva till 1559. He died there in 1564. The two chief works in which he embodied his teaching are the *De corrupti sermonis emendatione libellus* (1530) and the famous *Colloquia*, published at Geneva in 1563, which retained their popularity till the last century.

In the foundation of the Royal Professorships Hebrew received equal attention with Greek; the first professors were François Vatable and Agatho Guidacerio. Vatable, whose real name was Wastebled or Wastabled, was a native of Picardy[2]. In 1508 he attended Aleandro's Greek lectures at Paris, and helped him to prepare, and eventually completed by himself, an edition of Chrysoloras's Greek grammar. He probably learnt Hebrew from Augustino Giustiniani, who came to Paris in 1516 on the King's invitation and lectured for five years[3]. They were the first Hebrew lectures given at Paris. In 1521 Vatable accompanied Lefèvre d'Étaples to Meaux, and remained there till 1524, helping to spread a knowledge of the Bible. But he belonged to the moderate group of reformers and in later years his orthodoxy was beyond suspicion. He had a great reputation as a lecturer, but his only published work was an edition of the Hebrew

---

[1] Calvin, *Opera*, ed. Baum, Cunitz, and Reuss, XIII. 525.

[2] For Vatable see Beza, *Icones*; Goujet, *ib.* 255–256; Teissier, *Éloges*, I. 1–4. For his residence at Meaux see Herminjard, *Correspondance des Réformateurs*, I. 71 n.[10], 110 n.[4], 181 n.[6].

[3] Echard, *Script. Ord. Praed.* II. 96.

Bible, the first printed in France, with the commentary of
the celebrated thirteenth-century rabbi, David Kimchi,
which he prepared for Robert Estienne[1]. Notes taken at his
lectures were printed in the margin of the same printer's
Latin Bible of 1545. He was abbot of Bellozane, a benefice
afterwards held by Amyot and by Ronsard. He died March
15, 1547, on the same day as his colleague Toussain.

Vatable's colleague, Guidacerio[2], was a Calabrian who had
been Professor of Hebrew at Rome. At the sack of that city
in May 1527 he lost his library, which contained a fine collection of oriental manuscripts, and very nearly his life. He
was a conscientious professor, and he published a good many
works, including a Hebrew grammar, but none of them were
of importance. He died in 1540 and was succeeded a year or
two later by Alain Restand de Caligny. In 1531 a third
Hebrew Professor was added in the person of Paolo Paradisi[3],
a converted Jew, whose real name was Canossa. Like his two
colleagues he was a Greek as well as a Hebrew scholar, and
he taught both languages to Margaret of Navarre. His agreeable and courtly manners brought him rapidly into favour
at Court, and he was a successful teacher and lecturer. He
was naturalised in 1536 and died in 1549.

Of greater distinction as a Hebrew scholar than either of
these Italians was their countryman, the Dominican Sanctes
Pagnini, who came to Lyons in 1525 and died there in 1536.
His Latin translation of the Old Testament, to which he had
given twenty-five years of labour, was published in 1528 and
his Hebrew-Latin dictionary—*Thesaurus Linguae Sacrae*—
in 1529, both at Lyons[4]. Another native Hebraist besides
Vatable was Pierre-Robert Olivetan, the translator of the
Protestant Bible, which was printed at Neuchâtel in 1535.
His translation, which was executed too rapidly to be
thorough or accurate, owed a good deal to Pagnini's Latin
version of the Old Testament.

---

[1] 4to, 1539–1544; 2nd ed. 16mo, 1544–1546.
[2] Lefranc, *op. cit.* p. 181.
[3] *Ib.* pp. 179–180.
[4] Echard, *op. cit.* II. 96.

The first Professor of Mathematics, Oronce Finé[1] (1494–1555), was a native of Briançon in Dauphiné. He entered the College of Navarre and, after completing his studies, lectured and resided there from 1516 to 1523, or possibly later. The story of his imprisonment is confirmed by a letter published by Herminjard in which, dated January 1, 1524, the writer, Joannes Angelus, says that he visited Finé in prison[2]. His offence arose out of his studies in astrology, and it is conjectured that he made some indiscreet prediction about the Queen-Mother. He did much to restore the study of mathematics, which had languished since the time of Lefèvre d'Étaples, but he was not a great mathematician. He believed that he had found a solution to the quadrature of the circle and to similar fantastic problems[3]. He is more interesting as a geographer. Three of his maps have come down to us: a map of France first published by Simon de Colines in 1525 and frequently reprinted, and two maps of the world, of which one was published in 1530 (by Chrestien Wechel) and the other, larger in size, in 1536[4]. The earlier of these is generally found in Galliot Du Pré's edition of the *Novus Orbis* of Simon Grynaeus (1532)[5]. In the later one the land explored by Verrazzano is indicated by the words *Terra Francesca, nuper lustrata*. Finé had a great reputation as a lecturer, but in spite of this and of his many attainments his whole life was a constant struggle with poverty.

At the beginning of 1534 the Faculty of Theology, under the leadership of Noël Bédier, made a determined attack on the new professors; it took the form of a complaint to the Paris *Parlement* against the delivery of public lectures on the Holy Scriptures by "simple grammarians or rhetoricians who had not studied in any faculty." The decision of the *Parlement* is not known, but it was doubtless in favour of the Royal Professors, for they continued to lecture, and before

[1] L. Gallois, *De Orontio Finaeo Gallico geographo*, 1890; there is a long article on him, with a full bibliography, in the *Nouv. Biog. Gén.*
[2] *Corr. des réformateurs*, I. 178.
[3] Montucla, *Hist. des mathématiques*, I. 574; M. Cantor, *Vorlesungen über Geschichte der Mathematik*, 2nd ed., 4 vols., Leipsic, 1894–1908, II. 375–378.
[4] See Gallois, *op. cit.*, where all these maps are reproduced.
[5] See above, p. 62.

the end of the year a Latin professorship, to which the orthodox party had especially objected as likely to lead to criticism
of the Vulgate, was established. The first professor was
Barthélemy Masson[1] (Latomaeus), a native of Luxembourg
and a friend of Erasmus. As the affair of the Placards had
recently occurred, he was looked on with suspicion as a
countryman of Luther, but he proved to be as zealous for
orthodoxy as Bédier himself. He lectured almost exclusively
on Cicero and published numerous commentaries on his works.
In 1542 he resigned his post, which after being vacant for
three years was filled up by the appointment of Pierre
Galland.

The next new chair was a professorship of Greek, Hebrew,
and Arabic literature, specially created by Francis I in
December 1538 for that remarkable man, Guillaume Postel,
whose early struggles in the pursuit of learning are highly
characteristic of the age[2]. He was born in 1510 in a village
near Barenton in Lower Normandy. At the age of thirteen,
having lost both his parents in childhood, he became a
teacher in a village school. As soon as he had saved a little
money he made his way to Paris, but his money and clothes
having been stolen during his sleep, he was reduced to such
misery that he contracted an illness which kept him in

[1] For Masson (1485–1566) see Lefranc, *op. cit.* 183; Erasmus, *Opera*, III.
1504 and 1508.

[2] The notices of Postel by Thevet (*Portraits et vies des hommes illustres*,
1584), and Du Verdier (*Bibliothèque française*; *Prosopographie*, III. 251–252),
both of whom knew him personally, are of little value. By far the best of
the older accounts are those of Chauffepié, *Nouveau Dictionnaire historique
et critique*, 1753, and Des Billons, *Nouveaux éclaircissements sur la vie et les
ouvrages de Guillaume Postel*, Liège, 1771. See also M. Marrier, *Monasterii
regalis S. Martini de campis historia* 1637, and Nicéron, VIII. 295–356. The
best modern life is G. Weill's Latin thesis, *De G. Postelli vita et indole*,
1892, for which the author consulted a manuscript life in the Dijon
Library written by the Abbé Joly. Lefranc has a good account in his
Histoire du Collège de France, pp. 284–291, and recently Sir G. Butler has
included a chapter on *William Postel, world peace through world power*
in his *Studies in Statecraft*, Cambridge, 1920, with an excellent bibliography
based on the very full one of Des Billons, to which he makes a few additions.
See also É. Picot, *Les français italianisants au XVIe siècle*, 2 vols., 1906, I.
313 ff. Some very curious and apparently little known letters from Postel
to Abraham Ortels, the geographer, are printed in the *Epistulae Ortelianae*,
ed. Hessels, Cambridge, 1887.

hospital for two years. On his recovery he earned some more money by harvesting, and then entered the College of Sainte-Barbe, where he supported himself by acting as servant to the professor Jean Gélida, and by priming him for his lectures on Aristotle with a translation of Themistius's paraphrases. He rapidly acquired several languages in addition to Greek and Latin—Hebrew, which he learnt from Vatable, Spanish and Portuguese—and his studies embraced physics, mathematics, and geography. Then early in 1535 he went to Constantinople in the suite of the ambassador La Forest[1], learnt various oriental languages, travelled for two years in Egypt and Asia, and returned to France in 1537[2]. In 1538 he published the alphabets of twelve languages (Hebrew, Chaldaic, Syriac, Samaritan, Arabic, Indian, *i.e.* Ethiopic, Greek, Coptic, Servian, Illyrian, *i.e.* Glagolithic, Armenian, and Latin), a little treatise on the Hebrew language, and an Arabic grammar[3]. In December of the same year he was appointed, as we have seen, Royal Professor of Greek, Hebrew and Arabic, and, when the Hebrew Professor, Agatho Guidacerio, died in 1540 and his estate escheated to the Crown by the *droit d'aubaine*, Francis I bestowed it on Postel[4]. His next publications were a *Descriptio Syriae* (1540)[5] and *De Magistratibus Atheniensium liber singularis* (1541), but at the end of 1543, having become involved in the disgrace of his benefactor, the Chancellor Guillaume Poyet, owing to a chivalrous but imprudent intercession with the King on his behalf, he resigned his chair and left France.

It was doubtless before he left France that he published at Paris a work entitled *Quatuor Librorum De Orbis Terrae Concordia, primus*[6]. The remaining three books were published

---

[1] Postellus...ad me venit salutandum cum profectus est Forestanus legatus regis ad Turcam (Delaruelle, *Guillaume Budé*, p. 275, from Budé's *Adversaria*). For the date see E. Charrière, *Négociations de la France dans le Levant (Doc. inéd.)*, I. 255 ff.

[2] Is xi° die octobris domum meam venit me salutatum post reditum suum, anno 1537 (*ib.*).

[3] University Library, Cambridge, Aa. 25. 16 (all bound together in a single volume).

[4] Lefranc, *op. cit.* p. 409.

[5] U.L.C., Z. 11. 9.

[6] U.L.C., C. 12. 42². Printed by Pierre Gromors, but without a date.

at Basle (?) soon afterwards[1]. This was the first of a series of works which Postel poured forth throughout the next ten years in order to expound his views as to the best method of promoting the unity of mankind. It was a noble dream, but Postel's exposition of it was rendered hazy by a strong vein of mysticism, which found expression in strange beliefs, including one that a certain Joanna, whom he had met in a Venice hospital, was a new Eve and an instrument of redemption. But this part of Postel's story has been so well and so sympathetically told by Sir Geoffrey Butler[2] that I need not dwell on it. It is sufficient to say here that he was absent from Paris for nine years, that in 1544 he was admitted at Rome to the Society of Jesus on probation, that in the following year Loyola dismissed him, that in 1547 he had a dangerous illness at Venice, and, as has been said, met in the hospital the "new Eve," that in 1549 we hear of him at Jerusalem, where the Seigneur d'Aramont, French Ambassador to Turkey, gave him a place on his staff, and that he returned to Italy in 1551 and to Paris in the following year. But at the end of 1553 he again set out on his travels, revisited Venice, was for six months a Royal Professor in the University of Vienna, spent three years and a half in prison, first at Ravenna and then at Rome (1556–1559), and finally, after three more years of wandering, came back to Paris in 1562. Tried before the *Parlement* for heresy, he was sentenced to confinement for three months in the Cluniac monastery of Saint-Martin-les-Champs. On his release he lectured to large audiences on geography, for in addition to his other attainments he was a scientific geographer. But, again showing symptoms of mental disturbance[3], he was removed from the lodgings of Joseph Scaliger, where he was living, and sent back to the monastery of St Martin (1563). Here he spent the remainder of his days in peace and honour, visited by princes and learned men; but, if he abandoned his theological errors, he still cherished some

---

[1] U.L.C., G. 9. 14. No place or date, but according to Des Billons printed at Basle by Oporinus.
[2] *Op. cit.* pp. 45–56.
[3] Fuit vere stultus, nam alioqui fuisset combustus: il couroit les rues (*Scaligerana altera*, p. 193). But *ana* are not very trustworthy evidence.

of his fantastic theories[1]. He died in 1581. In spite of the spirit of insanity, which was for ever lurking on his path, he was a remarkable man. His knowledge on no subject may have been as thorough as that of some of his contemporaries, but in his passion for learning of every kind, in his restless curiosity and his love of travel, he is a figure eminently characteristic of the Renaissance.

When Postel joined the staff of the Seigneur d'Aramont in 1549 he found as members of it André Thevet, Pierre Gilles, and Pierre Belon, all notable travellers, and the two latter of considerable distinction as naturalists. Pierre Gilles[2] (1490–1555), like the other men of science of that day, was a good Greek and Latin scholar, and founded his studies on Aristotle, Pliny, and Aelian. His chief work, *De vi et animalium natura* (1533), is a compilation chiefly from Aelian. His special subject was ichthyology, and as an investigator into the nature of fishes he figures in Rabelais's *Pays de Satin* (v. 31) in the company of Aristotle and other Greek writers on natural history. His great work included a book on Fishes, and before writing it he made many researches on the shores of the Mediterranean and the Adriatic. In about 1539 Francis I sent him on a mission to collect Greek manuscripts and to write descriptions of Constantinople and other places in the East[3]. But his funds ran short, and to obtain a livelihood he served as a soldier in the expedition of Solyman the Magnificent against the Persians[4]. At last money reached him from France, and falling in with D'Aramont at Constantinople he joined his staff and returned with him to France in 1550. Soon afterwards he went to Rome, and died there in 1555.

[1] See his letters to Ortelius written in 1567 and 1579 (*Epist. Ortel.* I. nos. 19, 20 and 81).

[2] According to L. Thuasne, *Rev. des bibliothèques*, XV (1905), 207, n.[2], the proper form of his name is Gylli.

[3] See his preface to his *De Topographia Constantinopoleos* and a letter of Cardinal d'Armagnac dated January 11, 1547 (N.S.), both cited by L. Delisle, *Cabinet des manuscrits*, I. 159. Delisle has only found one oriental MS. which appears to have been brought to France by Gilles, and he thinks that his services, as well as those of Postel, in the collection of manuscripts for the royal library have been greatly exaggerated.

[4] *Epist. Ortel.* I. no. 5 (from Gilles to Amyot, according to Ortelius's endorsement, see above, p. 138, n.[2]).

Pierre Belon[1] hardly falls within the limits of this sketch, being still a comparatively young and unknown man at the death of Francis I. He was born in Maine in 1517, and found a patron in the bishop of Le Mans, René du Bellay, who enabled him to study medicine at Paris. Another patron, Cardinal de Tournon, furnished him with money for a protracted tour in the East (1546–1549). The account of his travels, which he published in 1553, is said to be one of the best books of the kind written in the sixteenth century[2], and his book on birds, which appeared in 1555, shows considerable personal observation and some anatomical knowledge[3]. He was also a botanist and an ichthyologist, and he wrote a book on classical antiquities. Unfortunately, while still in the prime of life, he was assassinated in the Bois de Boulogne (1564).

To return to the Royal Professorships: in 1539 Francis I, urged thereto by Budé, Cardinal Du Bellay, and Pierre Du Chastel, who in 1539 had succeeded Jacques Colin as King's reader, reverted to his original intention of housing his professors in a magnificent college. Accordingly, he addressed a document to the treasurer of his exchequer calling upon him to provide ways and means for the building of a college on the site of the Hôtel de Nesle (December 19, 1539)[4]. But, like many of Francis's grand conceptions, it never bore fruit. The Royal Professors remained without a home till nearly a century later. However, an increase was made in the number of the professorships. A second chair of mathematics was created in 1540 and filled by Pasquier Duhamel. In 1542 chairs of Greek and Latin philosophy and medicine were added, both being given to Italians, the former to the Milanese Francesco Vicomercato, and the latter to the

---

[1] Nicéron, xxiv. 36; Hauréau, *Hist. Litt. du Maine*, ii. 64 ff.; *Ann. fléchoises*, July 1903.

[2] *Les observations de plusieurs singularitez et choses memorables trouvées en Grèce, Asie, Judée, Egypte, Arabie et autres pays estranges*, 1553. It was several times reprinted within the next few years.

[3] *Histoire de la Nature des Oyseaux*. See A. Newton, *A Dictionary of Birds* (1893–1896), p. 5.

[4] *Vita Castellani*, p. 154. Of Du Chastel's services to the cause of learning I have spoken in the *Literature of the French Renaissance*, i. 20–21.

Florentine Guido Guidi (Vidus Vidius), both of whom became high in favour with Francis and were liberally rewarded. Vidius contributed in some measure to the advance of anatomical study, but like all the physicians and surgeons of his days, with almost the single exception of Vesalius, he preferred to translate Hippocrates and Galen.

Even if I had the necessary knowledge, an account of humanist medicine would be beyond the scope of this sketch, but it may be well to point out here that in the work of "breaking Arabian domination and restoring to medicine the uncorrupted spirit of Greece[1]" France played a distinguished part. Cop and Ruel, among the older humanists, Günther of Andernach and Jacques Dubois (Sylvius) of the younger generation, were active translators of the Greek medical writers. Günther's versions of Galen were particularly numerous, and Jacques Dubois, whose fame as a lecturer on anatomy rivalled that of Günther, was a fervent admirer of both Galen and Hippocrates. Jean Fernel, equally distinguished as a physiologist and as an anatomist, though he did little or no translating, was Galen's faithful disciple. Rabelais edited translations of the *Aphorisms* and three other treatises of Hippocrates, and of Galen's *Ars medica*, while the frequent references to these two writers in his great romance testify to the care with which he had studied them[2]. Besides the translations made by Frenchmen or foreigners who lived and lectured in France, the presses of Paris and Lyons issued numerous Latin translations of Greek medical works by Germans, Italians, and Englishmen. Of the six works of Galen which Linacre translated, all except one appeared in Paris editions. The most important of them, the *De methodo medendi*, after being revised by Budé, was printed at Paris in 1519, Thomas Lupset seeing it through the press, and was reprinted there in 1526 and 1530.

A further step was taken towards restoring the knowledge of Greek medicine when Greek medical writings were trans-

---

[1] Sir W. Osler, *Thomas Linacre*, Cambridge, 1908.
[2] See W. F. Smith, *Rabelais in his Writings*, Cambridge, 1918, pp. 137–151.

lated into French. This work was carried out largely at Lyons, where, with the encouragement of Symphorien Champier, the physician Jean Tolet translated Aegineta and Galen (1540), and his colleague, Jean Canappe, various treatises of Galen and one of Hippocrates (1541–1542). All were published by Dolet[1].

In botany and zoology too humanism played an important part. Jean Ruel, who had become known by a translation of Dioscorides in 1516, published in 1536 his celebrated *De natura stirpium*, which is almost entirely a compilation from Greek and Latin writers on botany. It was published by Simon de Colines in a magnificent edition with a singularly beautiful title-page (Frontispiece). Of Pierre Gilles's *De vi et animalium natura*, which is largely compiled from Aelian, I have already spoken[2].

The advance of Greek studies at Paris naturally stimulated the activity of the Paris press. Two years before the foundation of the Royal Professorships the printing of Greek books began to show signs of continuous development. After the departure of Aleandro from France Gourmont's press had shown a marked diminution in activity and from 1514 to 1517 had only issued seven Greek volumes, while from 1517 to 1528 the average issue of Greek books in all Paris was only one a year. But in 1528 there was a marked improvement. Simon de Colines, who had married the widow of Henri Estienne the elder, published a translation into Greek by Theodore Gaza of Cicero's *De senectute*[3] and an edition of Sophocles which follows the text of the *princeps* (Aldus, 1502). Pierre Vidoue[4] published the three Olynthiac orations of Demosthenes with Cheradame for editor, and began the printing of the same editor's Aristophanes[5].

In 1529 there came from Simon de Colines an abridged

---

[1] See the bibliography of Dolet's impressions in Christie, *op. cit.*, traduit par C. Stryienski (1886), pp. 506–531; and for Canappe see Petit de Julleville, *Histoire de la langue et de la littérature française*, IV. 74–76.

[2] See above, p. 141.

[3] Ph. Renouard, *op. cit.* p. 113.   [4] *Ib.* p. 128.

[5] See above, p. 132.

Greek grammar, two orations of Isocrates, and Galen, *De pulsibus ad tirones*[1]; from Badius, Budé's *Greek Commentaries*, including his Greek letter to Francis I and a Greek epilogue, and three orations of Isocrates[2]; and from Chrestien Wechel an edition of Gaza's Greek grammar, printed for him by Simon Du Bois (Sylvius)[3]. Panzer also gives under this year an edition of Aristotle's *De virtutibus et vitiis* by Cheradame[4].

In 1530 the output of Greek books considerably increased. Badius published Demosthenes *Against Meidias*, the pseudo-Platonic *Axiochus*, and two more orations of Isocrates; Wechel a Greek alphabet; and Simon de Colines, Galen *De remediis facile parabilibus*[5]. But the list is swelled by no less than eleven works from the press of a German printer named Gérard Morrhe or Morrhy. He was a native of Kempen, in the diocese of Cologne, near the Netherlands border, famous as the birthplace of Thomas à Kempis. The works consisted of four dialogues of Lucian—the *Icaro-Menippus*, the *Sale of the Philosophers* and two others—the *Ajax* of Sophocles, Plutarch's *Apophthegmata*, Aristotle's *Rhetoric*, a Greek-Latin lexicon, the Commentaries of Didymus (the celebrated Alexandrian grammarian) on the Odyssey, the often-printed treatise of Gaza on *The Months*, and (in one volume) three short treatises of Galen, including the two books on *The elements of Hippocrates*, which according to the preface was the first work read by a candidate for a medical degree[6]. On the title-page of this last work the place of publication is given as *apud Sorbonam*, and at first sight it looks as if the Sorbonne had harboured a printer of that heretical language, Greek, within its orthodox precincts. But Morrhe's press was set up, not in the Sorbonne itself, but in a

[1] Renouard, *op. cit.* pp. 138–140.
[2] Renouard, *Josse Badius Ascensius*, II. 239 and 525.
[3] Wechel and Du Bois have the same device. The latter on account of his religious opinions fled to Alençon, where we find him in 1530.
[4] Panzer, VIII. 129.
[5] Three other volumes of Galen, published by S. de Colines without a date, probably belong to 1529 or 1530 (Renouard, p. 418).
[6] See Panzer; and H. Omont in *Mém. Soc. Hist. de Paris et de l'Ile-de-Fr.* XVIII (1891), 73–100, 133–144, and *Bull.* 1895, pp. 35–39.

house in the cloister of St Benedict which belonged to the college[1].

In the following year (1531) Morrhe issued only one Greek book, namely, seven speeches of Demosthenes including the *Philippics*. On the other hand, Wechel increased his output; he published Gregory Nazianzen's *Invective against the Emperor Julian*, a book by the second-century rhetorician Hermogenes, the *Table* of Cebes, the speeches from the First Book of Thucydides, and the rival orations of Demosthenes and Aeschines. He followed this up in 1532 with two volumes of Demosthenes (including the speech against Leptines) and with Plato's *Timaeus*. Badius, whose long and honourable career was drawing to a close—he died in 1535—published the Greek Anthology in 1531 and an oration of Demosthenes in 1532. In the latter year his son-in-law, Michel Vascosan, joined this honourable band of Greek printers; his contribution was the *Epitome of the doctrines of Plato*, a work of the otherwise unknown Platonic philosopher Alcinous[2]. No Greek work came from Morrhe's press in 1532.

From 1533 to 1536 the lead was taken by Wechel, who has to his credit editions of Pindar's Olympian and Pythian Odes, of the first five books of the *Odyssey*, of two dialogues of Lucian and of five speeches of Dio Chrysostom, besides some minor works. Other publishers contributed but sparingly: Simon de Colines a New Testament (1534); Vascosan two editions of Gaza's Greek grammar; Augereau, whose short career was ended at the stake in 1534, Hesiod's *Works and Days* (1533); and Jean Loys of Thiel in Guelderland (Lodoicus Tiletanus) the *Oeconomicus* of Xenophon (1535)[3].

But in 1539 encouragement was given to the work by the appointment of a King's printer for Greek. The man chosen

---

[1] Apud Sorbonam in coenobio D. Benedicti (see Renouard, *Imprimeurs Parisiens*, p. 277). In a letter of March 30, 1532, Morrhe says that he has friends in the Sorbonne who "quod sentiunt mussare coguntur verius quam proferre."

[2] It was first printed in a Latin translation in 1469, then in Greek by Aldus in 1521.

[3] He set up his press in 1535 and died in 1547 (Renouard, *Imprimeurs Parisiens*, p. 250). In 1536 he printed an edition of Quintilian for the heirs of Josse Badius.

for the post was Conrad Néobar, whose father came from the diocese of Cologne. "Distinguished men of letters," says the King in the letters-patent of the appointment, "have represented to us that art, history, morals, philosophy, and almost all other branches of learning, flow from Greek writers, like rivers from their source[1]." Néobar died less than two years after his appointment—killed, it is said, by hard work—and was succeeded by Robert Estienne, the second son of Henri I Estienne, and the son-in-law of Josse Badius, who already held the office of King's printer for Hebrew and Latin. In 1541 he was ordered by the King to procure from Claude Garamond, the typefounder and engraver, three sets of Greek types for the royal press[2]. The two larger sizes were modelled on the handwriting of Angelo Vergecio[3], and the smallest, it is said, on that of his pupil, Robert Estienne's son Henri, then a boy of ten. The exquisite beauty of these types together with the good quality of the paper and ink make the Greek books printed by Robert Estienne and his successors among the most finished specimens of typography that exist. Those printed by Robert included eight *editiones principes*, the most important being Eusebius, Justin Martyr, Dionysius of Halicarnassus, Appian, and Dio Cassius.

Robert Estienne was a scholar as well as a printer. His *Thesaurus linguae latinae*, which appeared in 1532, was, especially in the improved form of the third edition (1543), vastly superior to any Latin dictionary that had yet appeared, and may be considered as marking a distinct advance in Latin scholarship. It is, however, as an editor of the New Testament that he is best known to the world at large, particularly in this country, where until recently he was generally known as Stephens. His New Testament of 1550, either in its original form or in such a slightly modified form as it assumed in the Elzevir text of 1634, remains to this day the traditional text. Though this is due rather to typographical than to critical merit, it must be remembered that it was at any

---

[1] The document is printed by A. Bernard, *Geofroy Tory*, p. 379.
[2] A. Bernard, *Les Estienne et les types grecs de François I*, 1856.
[3] *Scaligerana altera*, p. 11.

rate the first edition of the New Testament which had any critical apparatus at all. Readings from fifteen MSS. are given in the margin. Its publication involved Robert Estienne in disputes with the Sorbonne, with the result that towards the close of 1550 he fled from France to Geneva. He had been among the earliest converts in France to the new religion. His brother Charles (1504 or 1505–1564) was a man of considerable learning as well as a distinguished physician and medical writer. He produced a *Dictionarium Historicum ac Poeticum*, which was a sort of encyclopaedia, and a *Thesaurus Ciceronianus*. His *Praedium Rusticum*, which continued to be a favourite book down to the end of the seventeenth century, was a collection of treatises on agriculture compiled from ancient sources and translated into French. His experimental work enabled him to correct certain views of Galen on the anatomy of the bones and muscles[1].

So far we have been concerned with the various forces of humanism which had their centre in Paris; but in the reign of Francis I, when the unity of the French kingdom was but of recent date, Paris was far from having the monopoly of learning and literature which she afterwards enjoyed. She had as rivals flourishing provincial towns, of which some until more or less recent times had been capitals of practically independent kingdoms. Moreover, the provincial universities were, on the whole, more favourably disposed towards the new studies than their Paris sister. At Bordeaux, where the university was at a very low ebb, an important step was taken by the transformation of the College of Arts into the College of Guienne (1533)[2]. The first principal was Jean de Tartas; but he very soon quarrelled hopelessly with his professors, and it was his successor, André de Gouvéa (1534), who made the College into one of the most enlightened and flourishing places of education in the kingdom. It had distinguished professors in his brother Antoine de Gouvéa, who attained great celebrity as a jurist, Jacques de Teyva,

---

[1] Ch. Daremberg, *Hist. des sciences médicales*, 2 vols., 1870, I. 329.
[2] Gaullieur, *Hist. du Collège de Guienne*, 1874; R. Dezeimeris, *De la Renaissance des lettres à Bordeaux au seizième siècle*, Bordeaux, 1864.

Robert Breton, André Zébédée, Guillaume Guérente and his friend Nicolas de Grouchy, Maturin Cordier and his friend Claude Budin, Arnold Fabrice, and Jean Gélida. All, except three, had been under him at Sainte-Barbe. Of these Breton (Britannus) and Fabrice had a great reputation as writers of pure Latin. Fabrice passed for one of the first orators of his day, and Britannus, who was a native of Arras, was, without being a "Ciceronian," a fervent admirer of Cicero. His letters, published in 1540, are one of our sources of information for the progress of humanism at Bordeaux and elsewhere. Grouchy and Guérente were both born at Rouen and, as they were inseparable, André de Gouvéa could not invite one to follow him to Bordeaux without the other. Grouchy filled the chair of logic; his lectures on Aristotle, which he delivered in Greek, became so celebrated that several students left the University of Paris to sit at his feet in Bordeaux[1]. He is, however, best known as the author of *De comitiis Romanorum*. Guérente like his friend was a commentator on Aristotle, and like George Buchanan and Marc-Antoine Muret, wrote Latin tragedies, in which Montaigne acted. Montaigne, who was a pupil of the College from 1539 to 1546, had for his *précepteurs domestiques*, or, as we should say, "tutors," as distinguished from class teachers, Guérente, Grouchy, Buchanan, and Muret; the latter, however, did not become a regular professor of the College till 1550. In Montaigne's opinion André de Gouvéa "was without comparison the greatest Principal in France[2]."

Humanism at Bordeaux was not confined to the College of Guienne. The *Parlement* and the Bar included several men of note: Aimar de Rançonnet, a native of Bordeaux, who had a high reputation for sound learning, both as a classical scholar and a jurist[3]; Briand de Vallée, Seigneur du Douhet,

---

[1] Gaullieur, *op. cit.* p. 102 (from De Thou's *Hist. univ.*).

[2] Cp. a letter of Britannus (fo. 46, v°) quoted by Gaullieur, *op. cit.* p. 132.

[3] In 1539 he was appointed a member of the Great Council, and in 1549 President of the second chamber of *enquêtes* in the Paris *Parlement*. He died mysteriously in the Bastille in 1559. See P. Tamizey de Larroque, *Un grand homme oublié, le Président de Ranconnet*; P. Bunel, *Epistolae*, 1581, pp. 66 and 82; Taisand, *Les Vies des jurisconsultes*, 1781.

the friend of Rabelais[1]; and Arnoul Le Ferron, who made his mark not only as a Greek scholar, but as a jurist and an historian. He continued Paolo Emilio's Latin history of France, which only went as far as the year 1488, down to the close of the reign of Francis I. Modern historians give high praise to his work[2].

The College of Guienne served as a model for a new University at Nismes, which was founded in 1539 with a single faculty, that of Arts. The first Rector was Claude Baduel[3], a native of Nismes, who had imbibed his religious opinions from Melanchthon at Wittenberg, and his educational views partly from Melanchthon and partly from Johann Sturm[4], whose fellow-student he had been at Louvain. In the preceding year (March 1538) Sturm had opened the celebrated gymnasium at Strasbourg which under his Rectorship was to exercise so lasting an influence on the education of Protestant Europe. In the same year he had published his famous *De litterarum ludis recte aperiendis*.

Sturm's method of education, which with its merits and defects—its insistence on the formation of character as an essential part of education and its excessive devotion to humanism, especially to the speaking and writing of Latin—has left so deep an impress upon our own public schools, lies outside my present subject, but it must be remembered that Sturm lived and taught in Paris for seven years and that it was in Paris that he established his reputation as a writer of pure Latin and a teacher of pure morals. Born in 1507 he received his first education at Liège in the school of the Brethren of the Common Life. From there he went to Louvain and from Louvain to Paris (1529), where he lectured on Cicero and logic and soon became known as a rising scholar.

---

[1] *Pant.* c. x; Book IV, c. xxxvii.

[2] It was published in 1550. See Ranke, *Zur Kritik neuern Geschichtschreiber* (*Werke*, XXXIV), pp. 140–142; R. C. Christie, *Étienne Dolet*, new ed. 1890, pp. 120–135; H. Hauser, *Les Sources de l'histoire de France, XVI⁶ siècle*, I. 26.

[3] M.-J. Gaufrès, *Claude Baduel et la réforme des études au XVI⁶ siècle*, 1880; Ménard, *Histoire de la ville de Nismes*, vols. 1750–1759, IV. 148 ff.

[4] For Sturm see C. Schmidt, *La vie et les travaux de Jean Sturm*, Strasbourg, 1855.

He also opened a school for young Germans and Swiss, which was so successful that it attracted the youth of other nations, including France. Rabelais knew Sturm and possibly borrowed something from his methods in his famous account of Gargantua's education.

The University of Nismes owed much to Margaret of Navarre, as did that of Bourges, the capital of her duchy of Berry. At her instigation the Italian jurist, Andrea Alciati, came to Bourges in the first half of 1528 and in the following year was appointed a professor with a regular salary[1]. He was the founder of the new jurisprudence in France. "Ainsi vint à Bourges, où estudia bien longtemps et profita beaucoup en la faculté des loix," says Rabelais of Pantagruel.

Among Alciati's pupils was François Duaren (1509–1559), who after lecturing on the Digest for three years at Paris became in his turn a professor at Bourges (1539). Though Alciati returned to Italy in 1532, the impulse which he gave to legal studies in Margaret of Navarre's University was a lasting one, and for the next forty years Bourges ranked as the chief law school in France, with the possible exception of Toulouse. Among its more distinguished professors, besides Duaren, were Éguinaire Baron (1495–1555) and François Baudoin of Arras (1520–1573). The latter was appointed in 1548 and was succeeded seven years later by "the pearl of jurists," Jacques Cujas. But the work of this great man, who was not born till 1522 and who did not begin to lecture till 1547, lies outside my subject.

While the fame of Bourges as a Law School increased, that of Orleans declined, especially after the death of Pierre de L'Estoile (1537). It had, however, a noteworthy professor in Anne Du Bourg, who suffered for his religious opinions in 1559, and a distinguished student in another Protestant, François Hotman.

Angers, which had been its rival in the fifteenth century as a school of practical law, surpassed it in the sixteenth as a school of scientific jurisprudence, numbering among its professors Baron, Coras, and, later, Baudoin. Poitiers was also

[1] For the dates see Mazzuchelli, *Gli scrittori d' Italia.*

a law school of some repute, but it never became eminent. It is true that it could boast of a distinguished student in Rabelais's friend, André Tiraqueau, but he studied there early in the sixteenth century, before the dawn of the new jurisprudence. The only jurist of distinction who held a professorship there seems to have been Baron.

Toulouse—Cujas's birthplace—as might be expected from the general orthodoxy of that University, was the sanctuary of medieval jurisprudence[1]. About 1530, however, the Renaissance began to make itself felt even there, and the new jurisprudence was represented by Jean de Boyssonné, one of the professors of law, and Jean de Caturce a licentiate. Unfortunately both these men also favoured the new religion, and in 1532 Caturce was burnt at the stake, while Boyssonné, who was first and foremost a humanist, recanted and soon afterwards went to Italy, where he remained for a year. He returned to Toulouse and to the duties of his chair in 1535, but in 1538 he was made a judge of the King's court at Chambéry and a member of the Council which administered the recently annexed province of Savoy[2].

His friend, Arnoul Du Ferrier (1508–1585), a native of Toulouse, was appointed to a professorship soon after Boyssonné's departure. He is on the whole the most illustrious French jurist of the reign of Francis I, and he had still more illustrious pupils in Cujas and Hugues Doneau.

Another friend of Boyssonné who held a law-professorship at Toulouse (1536–1541) was the Piedmontese, Matteo Gribaldi[3]. He had previously lectured with success at Pisa, Perugia, and Pavia. From Toulouse he went to Cahors, and soon afterwards to Valence, whence he was summoned in 1548 to Padua. Here his success was so marked that the great hall of the University could not hold all those who flocked to hear him.

---

[1] For an excellent account of Toulouse at this period see Christie, *op. cit.* cc. iv and v.

[2] For Boyssonné see Christie, *op. cit.* esp. pp. 86–88. Selections from his Latin correspondence have been printed by J. Buche in the *Rev. des langues romanes*, XXXVIII (1895), 176 ff., 269 ff.; XXXIX. 71 ff., 81 ff., 138 ff., 395 ff.; XL. 177 ff.

[3] *Nouv. Biog. Gén.*; Christie, *op. cit.* pp. 302–305 (where he is called Gripaldi); Tiraboschi, VII. pt. 2, 748.

A like success is attributed to Jean de Coras (1513–1572)[1] at Toulouse, his lectures being attended, it is said, by 4000 students[2]. But this was not till the reign of Henri II. Though he gave lectures at Toulouse before he was eighteen, he did not become a professor there till after he had held chairs at Angers, Orleans, Padua, Valence, and Ferrara.

One more law school remains to be mentioned, that of Valence, where in the reign of Louis XII the Milanese jurist, Filippo Decio, had lectured to large classes. He was followed by another Italian, Emilio Ferreti, whose career as a professor was divided between Italy and France. Coras was professor there for several years from 1544 onwards, and he had as successors, Duaren, Antoine de Gouvéa, Cujas, and Hotman. At Paris, where there was no Faculty of Civil Law, there were occasional courses of lectures on Roman law, but they encountered considerable opposition from the Canonists.

The work of these early French jurists, of Baron, Du Ferrier, Duaren, and Coras, chiefly consisted of lectures on selected titles of the Digest; their names are not associated, as those of Cujas and Doneau are, with any particular method of interpretation, or with any general conception of Roman Law as a whole. But they were admirable pioneers, stimulating interest in their subject and training pupils who could climb on their shoulders to higher things. Duaren, in particular, may be regarded as having paved the way for that synthesis of Roman Law which was the great achievement of Hugues Doneau[3]:

It was not only in its school of law that Bourges showed its humanist proclivities. At Bourges Melchior Wolmar was summoned from Orleans to fill the professorship of Greek, and Calvin, who was his pupil in 1531, testifies to the excellence of his teaching[4]. Besides the work of his professorship he still carried on the school which he had started at Orleans.

---

[1] Nicéron, XIII. 1 ff.; Moreri. He perished in the Toulouse massacre of 1572.

[2] The numbers, no doubt, are greatly exaggerated.

[3] See for a sketch of the whole subject E. Glasson, *Hist. du droit et des institutions de la France*, 8 vols. 1887–1903, VIII. 107–129.

[4] For Wolmar see Herminjard, *op. cit.* II. 280, n. 7. There is a portrait of him in Beza's *Icones*.

Among his pupils were Barthélemy Aneau and Théodore Beza. Beza, who had followed him from Orleans to Bourges, remained under him till 1535. In a letter addressed to him twenty-five years later, he says: "I can scarcely remember anyone that left your school, excepting me alone, who did not attain to notable learning[1]." Conrad Gesner taught in his school. Orleans had at least one distinguished professor in Gentien Hervet, who was appointed in 1534, after a brief experience at the new College of Guienne. But in 1540, or thereabouts, he was recalled to Rome by his patron, Cardinal Pole, to translate Greek authors, and from this time his energies were devoted partly to this work and partly to the championship by speech and pamphlet of the Catholic Church. His very numerous translations, chiefly of Christian writers, lie almost entirely outside our period.

At Toulouse humanism had to encounter serious obstacles, for its followers, all young men, were more or less in sympathy with religious reform. We have seen what befel Caturce and Boyssonné. Matthieu Pac, who was involved in the proceedings against them, saved himself by flight and Boyssonné's close friend, Étienne Dolet, who joined the University as a law-student in 1532, two years later similarly escaped arrest by a hurried migration to Lyons[2]. In 1529 Pierre Bunel, a native, had been expelled from the town on a charge of heresy. We shall encounter him later as a writer of Ciceronian prose. A better welcome was given to Adrien Turnèbe, who was appointed a professor in 1533.

The *Parlement* of Toulouse counted more than one humanist among its members, namely, the First President, Jacques de Minuti, a Milanese; his countryman and successor, Jean de Bertrandi, who became First President of the Paris *Parlement* and Keeper of the Seals and later Bishop, Archbishop, and Cardinal; and Arnoul Le Ferron, the historian, who was

[1] This letter is prefixed to Beza's *Confessio Christianae Fidei*; a translation of it is printed as an Appendix to H. M. Baird's *Theodore Beza*, New York, 1899.

[2] Rather earlier students at Toulouse were Michel de l'Hospital and the Spaniard, Michel Servet (1528), who was destined to the same fate as Caturce and Dolet.

also of Italian descent. But the chief patron of humanism in the capital of Languedoc was Jean de Pins, who after serving as ambassador at Venice (1516–1520) and Rome (1520–1523) was appointed to the see of Rieux, but who resided chiefly in his fine hôtel at Toulouse. Among those whom he helped and protected were Boyssonné, Dolet, and Visagier[1]. When Louis Le Roy, the future Regius Professor of Greek, came to Toulouse in 1535 to study law, he brought with him a letter of introduction to Jean de Pins from Budé[2].

More or less within the orbit of Toulouse and about half-way between that city and Bordeaux, lies Agen, where the humanist physician, Julius Caesar Scaliger (1484–1558)[3], the father of Joseph Scaliger, had been living since 1524. He was a man of very considerable learning, with a remarkable grasp of physical and metaphysical questions, but his egregious vanity and ill-conditioned temper brought him into perpetual collision with the other scholars of his day, especially with those who were connected with Toulouse. He quarrelled with his greatest friend, Arnoul Le Ferron, and *Atticus meus* became *Struma*. As a would-be Ciceronian, he attacked Erasmus in a virulent pamphlet, but when Dolet in his turn championed the same cause he turned upon the young scholar, hitherto his friend, for venturing to attack a foe whom he had routed. Rabelais knew him well, and it is possible that the Baryoenus against whom several of Scaliger's epigrams are directed is the author of *Pantagruel*. Dr de Santi's conjecture that the acquaintance was made at Agen is in accordance with the fact that Scaliger seems seldom to have left his home[4]. It is probable too that Rabelais was for a short time at Toulouse (though some of the reasons given by Dr de Santi[5] are not very convincing) for his references to that city suggest a knowledge of it from personal observation[6].

---

[1] For Jean de Pins (1470–1557) see Christie, *op. cit.* pp. 62–69; L. Thuasne, *Gaguini Epistolae*, 2 vols. 1904, I. 374; Allen, *op. cit.* III. 510 f.

[2] A.-H. Becker, *Loys Le Roy*, 1896, p. 4.

[3] See Christie's article in the *Encycl. Brit.* Thuanus, lib. XXI. c. 11, says: "Vir quo superiorem antiquitas vix habuit, parem certe haec aetas non vidit."

[4] *Rabelais et J. C. Scaliger* in *Rev. des études rab.* III. 12 ff.

[5] *Rabelais à Toulouse* in *Rev. du XVIe siècle*, VIII. 42 ff.

[6] In *Pant.* II. c. xxii, and v. c. xxx, he refers to the "moulins du Bazaele à

Montpellier, like Toulouse, had the advantage of a humanist bishop in its midst. This was Guillaume Pellicier (*circ.* 1490–1568), the friend and correspondent of Rabelais, a negligent bishop but a good humanist. He was a student of natural history and contemplated an edition of Pliny. He had a particularly fine library, his Greek manuscripts alone numbering 1104, and filling over 200 volumes[1]. The University of Montpellier was chiefly famous for its School of Medicine, but humanism went hand in hand with medical studies. Rabelais, who lectured there as a bachelor in 1530, possessed a "very ancient" Greek manuscript of Hippocrates, and made textual criticism a special feature of his lectures. Seven years later, when, after taking his doctor's degree, he again lectured there, he used a Greek text of the *Prognostic* of Hippocrates by the side of the Latin translation. Another distinguished *alumnus* of Montpellier was Guillaume Rondelet (1507–1566), who took his doctorate in the same year as Rabelais, and published his great work, *De piscibus marinis* in 1554.

Next to Paris the chief centre of humanism in France in the reign of Francis I was undoubtedly Lyons. Indeed in the number of scholars who either habitually or occasionally resided there, and in the books which issued from its presses, it almost rivalled the capital. But the names of its famous residents and the results of its intellectual activity at this period have been so often recounted that I need not repeat the story here[2]. Suffice it to say that the leading humanists

Toulouse." I cannot agree with Dr de Santi that Rabelais was at Toulouse in 1529; in this year he was almost certainly at Paris. I should place his visits to Agen and Toulouse conjecturally in 1526–1527, that is to say, between his leaving Poitiers and his going (as I believe) to Bourges. Pantagruel, it will be recollected, went from Poitiers by La Rochelle to Bordeaux and from there to Toulouse, Agen (where there was no University) being on the direct road between the two places.

[1] See J. Zeller, *La diplomatie française vers le milieu du XVIe siècle d'après la correspondance de Pellicier*, 1881; Tausserat-Radel, *Correspondance de G. Pellicier*, 1899; *Journal des Savants* (1900), pp. 78 ff.; Montfaucon, *Bibliotheca Bibliothecarum*, 1739, II. 1198 ff., who prints a catalogue of the Greek MSS.; H. Omont, *Cat. des manuscrits grecs de G. Pellicier*, 1886.

[2] See especially Christie, *op. cit.* c. ix; F. Buisson, *Sebastien Castellion*, 1892, c. ii; A. Baur, *Maurice Scève et la Renaissance Lyonnaise*, 1906, cc. i and iv; R. L. Hawkins, *Maistre Charles Fontaine*, Cambridge (Mass.), 1916, c. iv. For the older authorities see my *Literature of the French Renaissance*, I. 23, n.[2].

were Symphorien Champier, their *doyen*, who died about 1538[1]; Sanctes Pagnini, the great hebraist; Guillaume Du Choul, the archaeologist, whose works however—on the Roman army and religion respectively—were not published till 1555; the three brothers de Vauzelles, of whom Jean was an active collector of antiquities[2], and their friend, Jacques de Vintimille, the translator of the *Cyropaedia*; Guillaume Scève and his cousin Maurice; and the physicians Pierre Tolet and Jean de Canappe, who have been mentioned above as translators of Greek medical works.

Another illustrious native of Lyons was Jean Grolier de Servier, Seigneur d'Aguisi (near Verona). Budé's *De Asse* was dedicated to him, and it was at his expense that an edition of it was printed at the Aldine press (1522). His library, containing over 3000 volumes, must have been the finest private library in France[3]. Jean de Vauzelles and Guillaume Du Choul had also good libraries.

Lyons did not possess a University, but in 1527, partly through the exertions of Symphorien Champier, a college was founded of the same character as the college of Guienne at Bordeaux. It was called Trinity College, and from the first had a great influence on the development of humanist studies. The first principal of any note was Jean Raynier, a native of Angers; but Barthélemy Aneau[4], the professor of rhetoric, and the future author of *Le Quintil Horatian*, was its guiding spirit, though he did not become principal till 1540.

The chief printer and publisher of Lyons was Sebastian

---

[1] See my *Dawn of the French Renaissance*, pp. 315–316.

[2] See É. Picot, *Les français italianisants au XVIe siècle*, 2 vols. 1906, I. 117 ff., and notices by L. de Vauzelles of M. de Vauzelles (Lyons, 1870), J. de Vauzelles (Lyons, 1872), and J. de Vintimille (Orleans, 1865).

[3] For Grolier (1479–1565) see Thuanus, lib. XXXVIII. c. xiv; Le Roux de Lincy, *Recherches sur Jean Grolier*, 1866. His library was preserved in the Hôtel de Vic till 1676, when it was sold by auction. His copy of the Aldine *De Asse* is in the Rylands library.

[4] For the college and for B. Aneau see Buisson, *op. cit.* pp. 17–24; Breghot du Lut, *Biographie Lyonnaise*, pp. 189 ff.; A. Pericaud, *Notes et documents pour servir à l'histoire de Lyons*, Lyons, 1838; and C. Ruutz-Rees, *Charles de Sainte-Marthe*, New York, 1910, pp. 93–110. Aneau wrote Greek and Latin verses, and translated the third book of the *Metamorphoses*, the *Emblems* of Alciat, and More's *Utopia*. He was murdered by the populace in 1565 on the suspicion that he was a Protestant.

Gryphius, whose services to humanism were inferior to those of no other French printer. Himself a good Latin scholar, he especially devoted himself to the printing of Latin classics in pocket editions. He was the publisher of Pagnini's Hebrew lexicon (1529) and Dolet's *Commentaries on the Latin Tongue* (1536). Guillaume Scève, Dolet, and Rabelais were employed as correctors to his press[1]. Other Lyons printers of scholarly tastes were Guillaume Roville, who married Gryphius's daughter; Jean de Tournes, for many years his foreman[2]; and Jean Frellon. Above all there was Étienne Dolet, who set up his press in 1538. As I have said elsewhere, the life of this interesting man has been told by Christie[3] with such a rare combination of accurate learning, searching criticism, and generous sympathy, that there is no French humanist about whom we have such complete information. His high enthusiasm for learning makes him a typical figure of the Renaissance, and his *Commentaries on the Latin Tongue* (1536–1538) is, in the words of Christie, "one of the most important contributions to Latin scholarship which the sixteenth century produced[4]."

One of Dolet's most virulent and indecent attacks was made upon Erasmus in answer to the *Ciceronianus*, in which Erasmus had justly criticised the slavish admiration entertained by many Italian scholars for Cicero's style. His book took the form of a dialogue between Sir Thomas More and Simon Villanovanus in defence of Longolius. In fact, Villanovanus and Longolius were almost the only two scholars born this side of the Alps who had any reputation as Ciceronians, and whose letters were thought worthy of being printed with those of Sadoleto and Bembo. They were both Flemings, and both died young in the first half of Francis I's reign. Of Christophe de Longueil I have given a brief account in *The*

---

[1]   Inter tot nôrunt Libros qui cudere, tres sunt
         Insignes: languet caetera Turba fame.
         Castigat Stephanus, sculpit Colinaeus, utrumque
         Gryphius edocta mente manuque facit.

[2] For Roville and J. de Tournes see Picot, *op. cit.* I. 161 ff. and 183 ff.

[3] *Étienne Dolet*, 1880; new and revised edition, 1899. I know no single book which gives so graphic and so faithful a picture of French humanism; see pp. 175–178 for Gryphius.

[4] For a full account and estimate see *ib.* 242–288.

Dawn of the French Renaissance. When he died at Padua in 1522 he held an unofficial professorship of Latin, in which he was succeeded by Simon Villanovanus, a man of considerable reputation in his day, not only as a Ciceronian, but as a scholar generally. He died in 1530 at the age of thirty-five, to the great grief of Dolet, who had attended his lectures at Padua for three years and lived with him in the greatest intimacy[1].

At Padua Villanovanus had also as his pupil, Pierre Bunel (1499–1546)[2], whom we have seen expelled from his native Toulouse on a charge of heresy, and who was the only true Frenchman to attain fame as a Ciceronian. In November 1530 he left Padua for Venice to take up the post of secretary, first to Lazare de Baïf, the French ambassador, and then to his successor, Georges de Selve (from 1534). He returned with the latter to France and lived with him at his see of Lavaur till his death in 1541. Bunel himself died at Turin in 1546. A collection of his Latin letters was published by Charles Estienne in 1550, and these were included in a volume issued by Henri Estienne in 1581, which also contains letters by Manutius, who was Bunel's pupil, Bembo, Sadoleto, and Longueil.

Bunel's chief, Lazare de Baïf (1496–1547)[3], who represented the French King at Venice from 1529 to the beginning of 1534, ranked very high among the French humanists of his day, even to the point of being mentioned in the same breath with the great Budé. He was a good writer of Latin prose, but in Erasmus's treatise he is said to be an Atticus rather than a Cicero. He wrote three archaeological treatises, *De re vestiaria*, *De vasculis*, and *De re navali*, which went through numerous editions, the best being that of Robert

---

[1] See Christie, *op. cit.* pp. 27–31. From the fact that P. Bunel, in an epitaph which he wrote for him (*P. Bunelli et P. Manutii epistolae*, 1581, p. 10), calls him " Belga " Christie infers that he was a native of Neufville in Hainault, and he points out that this is no objection to his being with Rabelais's "le docte Villanovanus françois," who never dreamed.

[2] Bayle has an interesting article on Bunel. He was a friend of Montaigne's father.

[3] See Hauréau, *Hist. litt. du Maine*, 1852, III. 1–6; L. Pinvert, *L. de Baïf*, 1900.

Estienne, 1549, in which all three are included. He translated the *Electra* of Sophocles and the *Hecuba* of Euripides
into indifferent French verse, and the first two pairs of
Plutarch's *Lives*. The latter work, which was undertaken at
the request of Francis I, was continued by his successor at
Venice, Georges de Selve, who with the help of Danès translated two more pairs of *Lives*.

Two other men who had considerable reputation in France
as writers of Latin prose were Nicole Bérault, who is dismissed
in the *Ciceronianus* as a better speaker than writer, and
Robert Breton. Both have been already mentioned in this
sketch[1].

The first place among French writers of Latin verse—at
any rate, after the death of Brixius—was deservedly held by
Jean Salmon, a native of Loudun in Poitou, who, having been
nicknamed Maigret on account of his thinness, latinised his
name into Salmonius Macrinus. His admirers spoke of him
as the French Horace. He seems to have had less ambition
and greater modesty than most of his brother Latin poets,
and he was content to lead a quiet domestic life, writing his
best lyrics to his wife, who in return bore him twelve children.
In one of his odes he enumerates the chief Latin poets of
France as follows:

> Iam suo gaudet Genabum Doleto,
> Brixio fratres Hedui, Latinis
> Borboni salsis elegis tumescunt
> Vandoperani.
> Dampetro flavus Liger et iugosi
> Bloesii, Rhemi tuo honore, Vultei,
> Versibus tellus quoque gloriatur
> Julia nostris[2].

Jean Dampierre lived in the neighbourhood of Toulouse;
after practising for some years with success as an advocate,

---

[1] See above, pp. 128 f., for Bérault, and p. 149 for Breton.
[2] Another ode begins:

> Brixi, Dampetre, Borboni, Dolete,
> Vulteique operis recentis author.—*Del. poet. gall.* II. 478.

Joseph Scaliger said "Macrinus ᾠδῶν scriptor optimus," but "Doletus et
Borbonius poetae nullius nominis" (*Prima Scaligerana*). For Macrin see
Nicéron, XXXI. 264 ff.

PLATE IV

Nicholas Borbonius Poeta.

NICOLAS BOURBON

Photo. Braun & Co.

From a drawing by Holbein the younger in the Royal Collection, Windsor
Copyright of His Majesty the King

he entered a religious order and became director to a convent of nuns[1]. Nicolas Bourbon of Vandœuvre in Champagne is interesting to Englishmen as the tutor of Lord Hunsdon and the Dudleys, and as the friend of Bishop Latimer and Dean Boston[2]. When he was in England (1535), he made friends also with Holbein, who painted his portrait[3]. He was afterwards tutor to Jeanne d'Albret. Vulteius's real name was Jean Visagier; after studying at the College of Sainte-Barbe and holding for a short time a post as lecturer in the new College of Guienne at Bordeaux, he became, as we have seen, a law student at Toulouse and practised there as an advocate[4]. In 1535 and the following year he was living at Lyons, where he became intimate with Dolet and Bourbon. These three, with Gilbert Ducher of Aigueperse in Auvergne[5] and Hubert Susannée, formed a group of young humanists at Lyons, who were united not only by their cultivation of Latin poetry but also by their free criticism of Catholic doctrines and practices[6]. The harmony of their friendship was often broken by violent quarrels, in which Dolet was the most conspicuous, for he quarrelled with all in turn. Susannée was not much better, and there was a temporary breach of friendship between Visagier and Bourbon. All this furnished excellent material for stinging epigrams[7].

Outside this group was Claude Rousselet[8], a Lyons lawyer, whose *Epigrammata* were published posthumously in 1537,

[1] See Salm. Macrinus, *Hymnorum lib. sex*, 1537, p. 167; Vulteius, *Hendecasyllaborum lib. IV.* 1538, p. 22 v°; Nicéron, XXVI. 48 ff.

[2] See G. Carré, *De Vita et Scriptis N. Borbonii*, 1888.

[3] The picture has disappeared, but the drawing for it (Plate IV) is at Windsor. Holbein also made a smaller drawing for reproduction as a woodcut in the 1538 edition of Bourbon's *Nugae*. (See A. B. Chamberlain, *Hans Holbein the younger*, 2 vols. 1913, II. 72–75, and *Nugae*, 1538, VI. xii.)

[4] For Vulteius (*circ.* 1510–1542) see Bouillet, *Biographie ardennaise*, 2 vols. 1830. For his French name see *Revue d'hist. litt. de la France*, I. 530; Gaullieur had already suggested the possibility of this (*op. cit.* 119, n. [2]).

[5] See Buisson, *op. cit.* pp. 29–35.

[6] Susannée, however, was thoroughly orthodox. His French name is usually given as Susanneau, but I have adopted the form found by Miss Ruutz-Rees in the Grenoble archives (see *Some sixteenth century Schoolmasters at Grenoble*, Romanic Review, VIII. no. 1).

[7] See for these quarrels Christie, *op. cit.*

[8] See Breghot du Lut, *op. cit.* II. 349 ff.

and Antoine de Gouvéa, the distinguished jurist and editor
of Terence, who occasionally visited Lyons and who published
a volume of epigrams there in 1539. Poems by all these men,
and also by Simon Vallambert, a Burgundian doctor, find a
place in Gruter's collection. But the best Latin poetry written
in France at this time, except Macrin's and perhaps Visagier's,
was Theodore Beza's, whose *Poemata*, however, did not appear
till 1548, the year after the death of Francis I[1]. His tribute
to Rabelais is worth quoting:

> Qui sic nugatur, tractantem ut seria vincat,
> Seria quum faciet, dic, rogo, quantus erit.

Thus we see that in the reign of Francis I, not only in
Paris, but in every town of France that could claim to be an
intellectual centre, especially in the Universities, there was
a swift and vigorous development of humanist studies. Lyons,
Toulouse, and Bordeaux, the three chief towns of the south
—Marseilles, the importance of which dates only from the
time of Louis XI, was still mainly a commercial town—were
all active centres of humanism. Montpellier was first and
foremost a medical University, but several of its medical professors were also humanists. Valence provided chairs for
several distinguished professors of law. Rodez had a humanist

---

[1] Here is a list of the productions of these Latin poets:
Beza, *Poemata*, Paris, 1548.
Bourbon, *Nugae*, Paris, 1533; *ib.* 1535; *Opusculum puerile ad pueros de
   moribus sive Παιδαγωγεῖον*; *Nugarum libri octo*, Lyons, 1538.
Dolet, *Orationes duae in Tholosam...Eiusdem Carminum libri II*....[Lyons,
   1534.]
Ducher, *Epigrammaton libri duo*, Lyons, 1537.
Gouvéa, *Epigrammaton libri duo*, Lyons, 1539.
Macrin, *Carminum libellus*, Paris, 1528; *Carminum libri quatuor*, Paris, 1530;
   Lyricorum libri duo, Paris, 1531; *Hymnorum libri sex*, Paris, 1537; *Odarum
   libri sex*, Lyons, 1537; *Odarum libri tres*, Paris, 1546; *Epigrammaton libri
   duo*, Paris, 1548.
Rousselet, *Epigrammata*, Lyons, 1537.
Susannée, *Dictionarium Ciceronianum...Epigrammaton libri*, Paris, 1536;
   Ludorum libri, ib. 1538.
Vallambert, *Epigrammata*, 1545.
Visagier, *Epigrammatum libri duo*, Lyons, 1536; *Epigrammaton libri IIII.
   eiusdem Xenia*, Lyons, 1537; *Inscriptionum libri duo. Xeniorum libellus*,
   Paris, 1538; *Hendecasyllaborum Libri quatuor*, Paris, 1538.
   Dampierre's poems have been lost with the exception of a few printed in
Gruter's collection.

bishop in the person of Georges d'Armagnac, a friend
of Erasmus and Rabelais[1]. Further north were Nevers,
where Maturin Cordier for four years promoted the cultivation of pure Latin; Bourges with its flourishing law
school, where Alciati introduced humanist jurisprudence into
France; and Poitiers, in the neighbourhood of which, at his
priory of Ligugé, the young humanist bishop of Maillezais,
Geoffroy d'Estissac, the friend and host of Rabelais, was the
leader of a learned and literary society. Angers, like Poitiers,
was mainly a law school, but it was more progressive than
Poitiers, and during the last thirty years of the sixteenth
century it even rivalled Bourges. Orleans, which at the beginning of the century came next to Paris in its favourable
reception of the new studies, seems in spite of one or two
distinguished professors, to have declined from its high
promise alike in arts and law. It was probably too near Paris
to attract students in arts, and as a law school it was over-
shadowed by Bourges.

A good illustration of the high esteem in which a knowledge of Greek and Latin was held in France at this time is
afforded by Miss Ruutz-Rees's interesting account of the
Municipal School, or, as we should call it, the Grammar
School, of Grenoble[2]. Early in 1536 the post of Assistant-
Bachelor to the school became vacant, and the Town Council
appointed the Rector's nominee, who was no other than
Hubert Susannée, one of the Lyons group of humanists. He
was a good Latin scholar and had just published a dictionary
to Cicero, with a book of Epigrams by way of appendix; he
was fairly competent in Greek; and he had some experience
as a teacher. But alas! he had, as has been said, a highly
irascible temper, which expressed itself in deeds as well as
words, and four months after his appointment, "having proceeded to certain acts of violence," he fled from Grenoble.
But in 1540 a new Rector was wanted, and in spite of his
record, Susannée, now a doctor of law and medicine, was

[1] In 1536 he was appointed ambassador at Venice and from there passed
to Rome in 1539. He was created a Cardinal in 1544.
[2] *Op. cit.*

appointed—only to be dismissed two years later for more acts of violence.

Susannée was not a success, but his appointment by the Town Council of a small provincial capital to the Mastership of their Grammar School, especially after their first experience of him, is a sign of the rapid progress which humanism made in France during the decade which followed the creation of the Royal Professorships. It began in fact a little before 1530, namely, with the foundation of Trinity College at Lyons in 1527, the impulse given to the printing of Greek books at Paris in 1528, the publication of Budé's *Commentaries of the Greek language*, and the King's first important acquisition of Greek MSS. in 1529. Then comes the foundation of the Royal Professorships (1530), the publication of Robert Estienne's *Latin Thesaurus* (1532), the foundation of the College of Guienne (1533), the publication of Dolet's *Latin Commentaries* (1536–1538), the foundation of the University of Nismes and the appointment of Néobar as King's printer for Greek (both in 1539), and that of Robert Estienne as his successor (1540). The last of these years was the year of Budé's death; with a thankful heart he could sing his *Nunc Dimittis*, for he had lived to see the triumph of humanism in France.

We see from this retrospect how accurately Gargantua's letter to Pantagruel represents the condition of classical studies in France in the year 1532. "But now all methods of teaching are restored; the study of the languages renewed— Greek (without which it is a disgrace for a man to style himself a scholar), Hebrew, Chaldean, Latin; impressions of books most elegant and correct are in use through printing." We see too that the account of Gargantua's education, which was probably written in 1533, the year in which the College of Guienne was founded, is essentially a true picture—faithful in its general spirit, if exaggerated in its details.

There are certain features in this humanism which invite notice. First, the importance attached to the writing and speaking of Latin. Scholars hardly ever condescended to use the vernacular when they wrote. Good literature—*bonae litterae*—meant classical literature. All lectures were delivered in Latin; to speak Latin was obligatory on all students. Sturm and Cordier were equally insistent on this, though Cordier, at any rate, used the vernacular in the earliest stages of instruction. The difficulty was to carry out the practice in the home, but the well-known instances of Robert Estienne and of Montaigne's father, in whose households Latin was spoken even by the maidservants, were by no means isolated ones. But if Latin was universally employed by the learned, Greek, "without which it is a disgrace for a man to style himself a scholar," was the passport to fame and fortune. A knowledge of Greek was a sure road to the King's favour, and several of his bishops and diplomatists—Jean de Pins, Lazare de Baïf, Georges de Selve, Georges d'Armagnac, Geoffroy d'Estissac, La Forest—owed their appointments to their knowledge of that language, though in the case of some of them it was perhaps not very profound.

Another noticeable feature is the frequent migrations which took place from one University to another. We have seen how the law professors passed from one chair to another, sometimes with great rapidity, and sometimes even exchanging a French chair for an Italian one or *vice versa*. Rabelais's account of Pantagruel's wanderings from one University to another is only a characteristic exaggeration of a common practice, and Le Roy's statement that Rabelais is here relating his own experience has much to be said for it. A more indisputable example of a wandering scholar is Charles de Sainte-Marthe (1512–1555)[1], the son of the original of Rabelais's Picrochole. After completing his humanities— we do not know in what University—he became a law-student at Poitiers, whence he was invited in 1533 by Jean de Tartas to join the staff of the new College of Guienne. But he resigned his post towards the end of 1534 and after an interval returned to Poitiers, where he took his doctorate of law and also a degree in theology and was soon afterwards (probably in March or April 1537) appointed to the Regius Professorship

---

[1] His life has been fully and well told by Miss Ruutz-Rees in *Charles de Sainte-Marthe*, New York, 1910.

of theology. But the open sympathy which he expressed for the new religious doctrines in his lectures brought about his dismissal before the end of the year. There followed a period of wandering in the south of France, which ended with his appointment to a chair in Trinity College, Lyons (June 1540). But he did not remain there long; in February 1541 we hear of him at Geneva where he was invited by the Council to become head of the College. Unfortunately, a visit to France for the purpose of arranging his affairs resulted in his being imprisoned at Grenoble for two and a half years, and after his release he abandoned the teaching career.

Sainte-Marthe's migrations were almost entirely due to his religious opinions, but these opinions, like those of many of his brother humanists, were hardly more permanent than his tenure of his various posts. At first warmly sympathising with the new doctrines, to the extent of taking refuge in Geneva, he, as the result of his long imprisonment at Grenoble, with its opportunities for quiet meditation, returned to the fold of the Catholic Church. The only difference between his case and that of a good many others is that his Protestant phase came at a somewhat later period than theirs, that is to say, between 1535 or 1536 and 1543. On the other hand, the majority of those humanists who did not definitely end in Protestantism or, like Des Periers, and perhaps Dolet, in free thought, returned to orthodoxy either after the persecution which followed the affair of the Placards, or at the latest in 1538, when the Truce of Nice and the interview with the Emperor at Aigues-Mortes finally fixed the shifting policy of Francis I on the side of orthodoxy and persecution.

Before the end of Francis's reign the humanist type of education was permanent in nearly every university and college of France. It was the normal education not only for scholars and ecclesiastics, but for every gentleman who was destined to a civil career. Montaigne, born in 1533, the son of a country gentleman who had returned from the Italian wars strongly imbued with humanist ideas, was launched into a humanist training as soon as he could speak, first at home and then at the College of Guienne. At the same time the future magistrate and diplomatist, Henri de Mesmes, after writing Greek and Latin verses and spouting Greek and Latin declamations for a year and a half at the College of Burgundy at Paris, entered, in his fourteenth year, as a law-student at Toulouse where for three years (1545–1548) he attended law lectures, and read Greek and Latin authors for amusement, from five in the morning till seven or eight in the evening.

A reaction from this almost superstitious devotion to Greek and Latin was inevitable. In the same year (1545) in which Henri de Mesmes joined the University of Toulouse, Pierre Ramus, who was to lead the attack on the exclusive use of Latin for lectures and works of learning, was appointed to the headship of the College of Presles. Two years later, in Dorat's class-room at the College of Coqueret, Ronsard and his young friends were fired by a noble ambition to raise French poetry to be a rival to that of Greece and Rome.

VII

A PARIS BOOKSELLER—GALLIOT DU PRÉ

AMONG the sources of information available for the study of literary history, the annals of the press have a certain importance. They help us to realise for a given age what its literary tastes really were. They enable us to follow, year by year, the changes of fashion in literature. They recall the memories of books, now long fogotten, but which in their day enjoyed great popularity. It was doubtless the feeling that much may be learnt from a simple chronological record of the productions of the press that inspired Panzer, "the one true naturalist among general bibliographers," as Bradshaw calls him, to accomplish his great work, which covers the whole field of European literature from the invention of printing to the year 1536. The interest of Panzer's achievement, not only for the scientific bibliographer, but also for the student of literature, suggested to me that a record of the books of an individual publisher might serve to throw light on the literary history of his country during the period of his career. It might also, I hoped, furnish some material for the solution of one or two problems connected with the exercise of his profession.

With the object, then, of illustrating that interesting period in French literature when the Middle Ages were slowly and gradually dissolving into the light of the Renaissance, I selected the Paris bookseller and publisher, Galliot Du Pré, whose career extended from 1512 to 1560. He seemed to me to combine several advantages for my purpose. His career was a long one. He was not a printer, but a bookseller and publisher pure and simple, so that the inquiry would not involve me in the discussion of typographical problems, which are beyond my competence. Lastly, except for a decided bias in the direction of history, he was not a specialist. He did not confine himself to romances of chivalry, or books of Hours, or books with woodcuts. He did not, like the Estiennes and Simon de Colines, cater especially for scholars, nor, like Jean Trepperel, produce cheap and popular books for the lowest class of readers. His public was that of the better educated classes,—princes, nobles, and *bourgeois*—who were not humanists and whose reading was chiefly confined to the national literature. This public, at any rate for the first half of his career, he carefully studied, adapting himself to their needs, and changing when they changed. But he had enterprise as well as judgment, and the publisher of the first edition of Commines's *Memoirs* and the *Life of Bayard* by Le loyal Serviteur deserves the gratitude of posterity.

In one respect my choice proved to be a fortunate one, for soon after I had begun my investigations I learned that M. Paul Delalain had some years ago made Galliot Du Pré the subject of two notices, in which a considerable number of his publications were duly chronicled[1]. By consulting other means of information, I have been able to add to the books in M. Delalain's lists, and though my information, partly from the imperfection of my researches, partly because doubtless many of the less important works published by Galliot Du Pré have been entirely lost, does not pretend to be anything like complete, it is probably complete enough for my special purpose, that of throwing light on the literary tastes of the period.

Galliot Du Pré was, as I have said, a publisher and bookseller, and not a printer. In the Middle Ages the *libraire* (*librarius*) or bookseller was, as a rule, the mere commission agent of the *écrivain* (*stationarius*) or copyist. The term *libraire*, however, was used in common speech to denote the *écrivain*, as well as the *libraire* proper[2]. Both classes alike, together with the parchment-sellers (*parcheminiers*), illuminators (*enlumineurs*), and bookbinders (*relieurs*) were officers of the University, and as such were subject to its jurisdiction,

[1] *Notice sur Galliot Du Pré*, Paris, 1890, and *Notice complémentaire sur Galliot Du Pré, ib.* 1891.
[2] Stationarii qui vulgo librarii appellantur (University Statutes of December 6, 1275).

and enjoyed the same privileges as its masters and scholars. Before being appointed they had to give evidence of their qualification for the post, and to be sworn before the Rector of the University. Hence they were called *libraires jurés*. Out of their number four *grands libraires* were appointed, whose duty it was to fix the price of books and to exercise a general supervision over their brethren.

The introduction of printing does not seem to have made much difference at first in the position of booksellers. For the majority of the early printers, like the copyists before them, sold the books which they printed, either themselves or through the agency of some privileged bookseller. Nor were the copyists at once driven from the field. For some fifteen to twenty years after the introduction of the new art to Paris they continued to produce richly illuminated manuscripts for wealthy patrons. Antoine Verard, originally a calligrapher and miniaturist by profession, following the examples set by Fichet and Heynlin, was the first publisher to realise that the illuminator's art might be adapted on a large scale to the new conditions. His famous *éditions de luxe*, printed on vellum and illustrated with woodcuts, which were illuminated by hand with greater richness than taste, cut severely into the trade of the ordinary copyist. Henceforth only Hours and Greek texts were multiplied by hand.

The decline of the copyists and the growing importance of the booksellers is shown by the royal edict of March, 1489. For while the number of *libraires jurés* was fixed at twenty-four, only two copyists, together with two illuminators and two bookbinders, were allowed to enjoy the privileges of the University. Save that in 1533 the eminent printer and engraver, Geofroy Tory, was by special favour admitted as a twenty-fifth[1], the number of privileged booksellers remained at twenty-four. The non-privileged booksellers (*libraires non-jurés*) were, at the close of the fifteenth century, still subjected by the University to various restrictions. They might not sell books for more than a certain price, and they might only sell them at open stalls.

[1] A. Bernard, *Geofroy Tory*, 2nd ed. 1865, p. 372.

The majority of the early Parisian printers were, as we have seen, also booksellers, but as a natural result of the expansion of business, the two trades tended to become more and more distinct. There grew up an important class of men, who not being printers themselves, employed various presses in the production of books. In other words, they were publishers. Whether Verard was a printer at all is a question which experts have not decided, but in any case his main business was that of a bookseller and publisher. Of the brothers De Marnef, Simon Vostre, Guillaume Eustace, and Denys Roce, all of whom began to issue books before the close of the fifteenth century, it may be said with almost complete certainty that they were not printers. Jean Petit, who, during his long and useful career as a publisher (1495–1536), employed at least twenty-eight presses, never describes himself as a printer.

The rapid expansion of the book-trade in Paris, which followed the publication of the first French book, *Les grandes chroniques de France*, by Pasquier Bonhomme, brought a golden harvest to the more successful publishers. Simon Vostre became, like Caxton, a man of substance, owning at his death (*circ.* 1520) six houses. The chief printing and publishing establishments passed from father to son for several generations. Pasquier Bonhomme was succeeded by his son Jean I, his grandson Jean II, and his great-grandson Jean III, while his daughter Yolande, by her marriage with Thielman Kerver, became the ancestress of another line of distinguished printers and publishers. Jean Petit was the founder of a dynasty which flourished for more than a century. Of the two publishing houses which made a speciality of the more popular romances of chivalry and other favourite works in the vernacular, that of the *Écu de France*, in the Rue Neuve-Notre-Dame, was carried on by Jean Trepperel and his successors from the beginning till after the middle of the sixteenth century[1], while the rival establishment at the sign of St Nicholas, in the same street, after passing through the hands of Jean Saint-Denys (1525–1531), his widow Claude, and Pierre Sergent, with whom was associated Vincent Sertenas, became

[1] H. Harrisse, *Excerpta Colombiniana*, pp. xli ff.

the property of Sergent's son-in-law, Jean Bonfons, and remained in his family till well into the seventeenth century[1].

M. Harrisse, to whom we owe our knowledge of the chronological succession of these two houses, has pointed out that an important part was often played by widows in the transmission of a printing and bookselling business. It was a tradition, he says, down to the Revolution, that the widows of printers and booksellers should succeed to their husbands' business, even when their sons had already attained their majority, and he adds that "they acquitted themselves in their task with the zeal and intelligence which has always been characteristic of Parisian wives of men of business[2]." The most illustrious female printer of the sixteenth century was Charlotte Guillard, the wife, first of Berthold Rembolt, and then of Claude Chevallon. She exercised her trade for fifty-four years (1502–1556), during sixteen of which she was a widow. It was not uncommon for the widow of a printer or bookseller to take a second husband of the same profession. Thus Guyonne Viart, after the death of her first husband, Jean Higman, married successively Henri Estienne and Simon de Colines. She had no children by her third husband, but by her first she became the ancestress of three well-known families of booksellers and printers, Chaudière, Cavellat, and Macé, while by her second she became the mother of the most distinguished of French sixteenth-century printers, Robert Estienne[3]. Robert Estienne himself married Perrette, the daughter of the well-known scholar and printer, Josse Badius, two of whose other daughters were married to men of high distinction in the same profession, Jean de Roigny and Michel de Vascosan.

With these preliminary observations I will proceed to give an account in chronological order of Galliot Du Pré's publications. He began his career, so far as we know, in the year 1512[4], publishing in that year two Latin works. One of these

---

[1] H. Harrisse, *op. cit.* pp. lxi ff.
[2] *Ib.* p. 300.
[3] Ph. Renouard, *Documents sur les Imprimeurs*, 1901, pp. 128–130.
[4] He was no relation of Jean Du Pré, whose real name M. Renouard has discovered to be Larcher.

is a folio—an Eutropius, with the continuation by Paulus Diaconus[1]. There is a copy of the other in the University Library, Cambridge, and as, except for a reference in Panzer to a copy in the *Bibliotheca Telleriana*, this is the only mention of it that I have come across, I will give its title in full. It runs as follows: *Johannis Surgeti nationis Galli Suessionensis diocesis in legibus licentiati militaris discipline Enchiridion in quo varie iuris materie et peregrine questiones continentur, cuius finis est pacis persuasio inter principes christianos et belli exhortatio in saracenos et infideles hostes religionis catholice.* Below the title is the mark of Jean Petit, and his address alone appears on the title-page, but in the colophon we learn that Galliot Du Pré shared the expense of publication and that the work was for sale at the Golden Lily (the sign of Jean Petit) and "at the second pillar of the hall of the Palace, at the shop of the said Galliot Du Pré." The privilege is of April 6, 1511 (O.S.); it may therefore be presumed that the book, being a small one, appeared not long after this, especially as Jean de Ganay, the Chancellor of France, to whom it is dedicated, died before June 1512[2].

The author says in his dedication that he had served for six years under the late Juan de Cardona, presumably a relative of Ramón de Cardona, the Viceroy of Naples, but I know nothing further of him, nor do I know his French name. The plea for peace which fills the final fifteen pages of the little book was made at a time of general warfare. In October 1511 the "Holy League" between Julius II, Ferdinand, and Venice had been published in Rome, and a month later Henry VIII had signified his adhesion to it. The Swiss were employed by the Pope as mercenaries and he was endeavouring to draw the Emperor into the League. On Easter Sunday (April 11), 1512, was fought the battle of Ravenna, in which out of the 45,000 men between

---

[1] Delalain, *Notice Compl.* (from Cat. E. Piot). It is printed by Gilles de Gourmont.

[2] Finding that Archbishop Le Tellier bequeathed all his books to the abbey of Sainte-Geneviève, I thought that the copy of this work mentioned by Panzer might be in the library of Sainte-Geneviève. But the director, M. Kohler, informed me that, though it is mentioned in a manuscript catalogue of about 1752, it is not in the catalogue drawn up about 1800, and that he can find no trace of it.

10,000 and 15,000 lay dead upon the field, and the French victory was neutralised by the death of their brilliant young general, Gaston de Foix. On May 3 the Lateran council was opened, and the general of the Augustinians, Egidius of Viterbo, preached a profoundly impressive and eloquent sermon, in which, after referring amongst signs of the times to the slaughter on Easter Day, he prayed for the purification of Christendom, the expulsion of the Turks, and the revival of Christian love. It was a noble exhortation, but it had no effect on that most belligerent of Popes, Julius II[1]. The humble treatise of Surgetus was naturally no more efficacious; it was not till 1518 that a general peace was declared—a peace which lasted three years.

It was a common practice with the booksellers of this period to have, in addition to their regular places of business where they lived, an open stall or lean-to, either inside or outside the Palais de Justice. Those inside were placed either in one of the corridors or galleries leading from one part of the building to another, where they vied in attraction with the stalls of the mercers and the drapers[2], or on the steps which led up to the Great Hall, or in the Hall itself by the pillars which supported its two huge vaults[3]. There were eight of these pillars, but, as a rule, only the first three were occupied by book-stalls, two at each pillar. Sometimes the same bookseller had a stall at two pillars, and at the close of the sixteenth century we find Nicolas Bonfons, the head of the house "at the sign of St Nicholas," established not only at all the first three pillars but at the fourth as well[4].

I have found no publication of Galliot Du Pré for the year 1513, but in 1514 he issued, besides two short Latin treatises, four works of considerable size and importance; the *Grand Coustumier de France*, and *Les grandes chroniques*, both of these being first editions; *Les grandes chroniques de Bre-*

---

[1] See Creighton, *A history of the Papacy*, v. 171–172. The sermon is printed in Mansi, xiv.

[2] See Corneille's *La Galérie du Palais*, especially Act i, Scc. 4–7.

[3] See *Paris à travers les âges*, i. 16, with a contemporary illustration (p. 7).

[4] Renouard, *Imprimeurs parisiens*, pp. 401–402.

taigne, by Alain Bouchard[1], a work of considerable popularity and of some value for the later history; and Montjoye's *Le pas des armes*. This last is an account by the Chief Herald of the jousts held on the occasion of the marriage of Louis XII with Mary of England. The printing was finished on December 23, eight days before the King's death.

Les grandes chroniques is a translation, with additions, by Pierre Desrey of the well-known *Compendium super Francorum gestis* of Robert Gaguin. Founded, like the longer work of Nicole Gilles, on the great collection of chronicles at Saint-Denis, it shared its popularity throughout at least the first half of the sixteenth century. It was published by Du Pré in conjunction with Poncet Le Preux, one of the four "*grands libraires jurés*," whose device appears on the title-page. In the following year they issued a new edition.

It was doubtless the success of these publications which on May 16, 1515, led Galliot Du Pré to take the step of renting a house on the Pont Notre-Dame[2]. This new bridge, connecting the island of the *Cité* with the north bank of the Seine, had been completed in 1506, to take the place of the old one which had collapsed in 1499. At this period there were two districts of Paris to which the booksellers and printers were in practice, though not by law, confined,—the neighbourhood of Notre-Dame in the *Cité* and the quarter of the University. The latter district, the limits of which are roughly marked by the Church of St Séverin, the Place Maubert, the Pantheon, and the Place de la Sorbonne, was considerably the larger. The printers and booksellers were here conveniently situated under the eye of the University, whose colleges spread over the whole district. The principal street was the Rue Saint-Jacques, which extended from the Petit Pont to the Porte Saint-Jacques, a distance of rather more than half a mile. In its middle portion every house was occupied by booksellers and those of kindred professions. M. Renouard has counted over a hundred and sixty establishments occupy-

---

[1] See La Borderie, *Étude bibliographique sur les chroniques d'Alain Bouchart*, Rennes, 1889; *Les Sources de l'hist. de France*: Molinier, v 5424; Hauser, I. 28.

[2] Renouard, *Documents sur les Imprimeurs*, p. 81.

ing some eighty houses. They varied greatly in size, from that of Jean Petit, who occupied two whole houses, the Silver Lion and the Golden Fleur-de-Lys, to the small establishments in different stories of the same house. Other booksellers' streets in this quarter were the Rue des Carmes, the Rue du Mont Saint-Hilaire, the Rue Saint-Jean-de-Beauvais, and the Rue Saint-Jean-de-Latran.

The other booksellers' district consisted of a few streets in the immediate neighbourhood of Notre-Dame, the chief being the Rue du Marché-Palu (the continuation of the Rue Saint-Jacques across the Petit Pont) with its continuation the Rue de la Juiverie, and the Rue Neuve-Notre-Dame, which ran from the Marché-Palu to the Parvis Notre-Dame. This quarter was chiefly occupied by those who specialised in religious books, particularly books of Hours, in romances of chivalry, or in cheap popular works[1]. As we shall see, Galliot Du Pré did not belong to any of these classes, certainly not to the first.

As is well known, houses in those days were distinguished not by numbers, but by signs. On a change of occupation, the old sign was generally retained, but sometimes the new occupier introduced a new one. Thus Galliot Du Pré, by way of a play upon his name, took for his sign a galley. He does not appear to have used his new abode as a shop, for throughout his career his books are offered for sale only at one of the pillars in the hall of the Palais de Justice.

In 1516, the year after his instalment in the house on the Pont Notre-Dame, he published a new edition of the *Grand Coustumier*, the *editio princeps* of the Latin version of the *Songe du Verdier*, and, in association with two other booksellers, Jean Petit and Michel Le Noir, the first edition of the romance of the *Saint-Graal*.

To 1517 must be assigned a small work of considerable interest, namely the French translation by Mathurin Du Redouer, Licentiate of Law, of the *Paesi novamente retrovati e Novo Mondo da Alberico Vesputio Florentino intitulato*, that first collection of voyages, edited by Fracanzio da Montal-

---

[1] Renouard, *Imprimeurs parisiens*, p. xii.

boddo, which had been published at Vicenza in 1507. There is no date to the book, but as the privilege is dated January 10, 1516 (O.S.), and the book has only 132 leaves of text, the presumption is that it was published at any rate before the end of the year 1517. It is entitled *Le nouveau Monde et Navigations faites par Emeric de Vespuce Florentin,* and thus gives even greater prominence to the name of Vespucci than the original does[1].

In the same year, 1517, Galliot Du Pré began the most important work, from the point of view of size, that he had yet undertaken. This was the publication in four volumes of *La mer des histoires et croniques de France,* two books (I. pp. 1–270) being compiled from *La mer des histoires* and the rest from *Les grandes chroniques.* The first and second volumes appeared in 1517, and the other two in 1519.

From 1518 to 1520 Du Pré busied himself with the writings of Francesco Patrizi, Bishop of Gaeta, publishing his *De institutione reipublicae libri novem* in 1518 and 1520, his *Enneas de regno et regis institutione* in 1519, and a translation of the former work, *Livre tres fructueux et utile a toute personne de l'institution et administration de la chose publicque,* in 1520. Both works were in repute throughout the sixteenth century, and the *De regno* was edited in 1567 by the well-known scholar, Denys Lambin.

The copy of the 1520 edition of the *De institutione reipublicae* in the University Library, Cambridge, has the autograph of *Gulielmus Cæcellus, 1542* and W. C. on the stamped calf binding. It thus recalls the one romance in the staid life

[1] There was a copy in the Didot library (Catalogue of 1881, No. 472). See also *Raccolta di documenti e studi pubblicata dalla Commissione Colombiana,* VI. 154–155. In Quaritch's *General Catalogue,* VI. 3793, it is claimed that this is the first edition of the French translation on the ground first, that it has a privilege, and secondly, that it has in Vespucci's third voyage three diagrams of southern constellations which are wanting in the other early editions. This is, doubtless, a just claim. The only two editions that could possibly be earlier both bear the name and mark of the *Écu de France.* One of these has also the sign of Jehan Jehannot, and was printed by him. It therefore belongs to the period, 1512–1522, during which he was associated with his mother-in-law, the widow of Jean Trepperel. The other, which has no printer's name, but only the mark and name of the *Écu de France,* is in the same type, but the type is thicker and less clear, and the capitals are less elaborate. For an account of the original Italian work see above, pp. 27 f.

of William Cecil, the great Lord Burghley. In 1541, after spending six years at St John's College, Cambridge, he left the university without taking a degree; in July of that year he married Mary Cheke, the daughter of an Esquire Bedell's widow who had set up as a wine-merchant, and the sister of his tutor, John Cheke, who a year previously had been appointed Professor of Greek; on May 5, 1542, a son, the ancestor of the present Marquess of Exeter, was born at Cambridge; on February 22, 1544, the young wife died. The inference from the above facts is that the parents of William Cecil—his father was a rich Northamptonshire squire—removed him from Cambridge on hearing that he had fallen in love with a penniless girl, and that he, less obedient than Gibbon, then married her in secret. The Chekes, be it said, came of a good family, whose residence at Mottistone in the Isle of Wight is still standing, with the date of 1567 over the door[1]. John Cheke, as is well known, became tutor to the future Edward VI and Provost of King's College. He was knighted in 1552, the year after his brother-in-law.

In 1520, as we learn from the title-page of the *Livre tres fructueux*, the printing of which was finished on April 30, Du Pré transferred his stall from the second to the third pillar of the Great Hall of the Palais de Justice. Not long afterwards (before February 16, 1521) he was appointed one of the *libraires jurés*[2], and at Midsummer 1521 he renewed the lease of his house on the Pont Notre-Dame. In March 1521 he published a translation of the most popular of Petrarch's Latin treatises, the *De remediis utriusque fortunae*. In the dedicatory epistle addressed to Charles, Duc de Vendôme, he attributes the translation to Nicolas Oresme, the well-known translator, through Latin versions, of the *Ethics* and *Politics* of Aristotle. But Léopold Delisle has shown that it is really the work of Jean Daudin, a canon of the Sainte-Chapelle[3]. The preface, it may be noted, is written in the

[1] It belongs to General Seely, and oddly enough the tenant-farmer who was living there in 1919 married a Miss Cheke.

[2] See Du Pré's edition of *Suetone Tranquille*.

[3] *Notices et extraits des manuscrits de la bibliothèque nationale et autres bibliothèques*, XXXIII. pp. 273 ff.

latinised style, with its lumbering sentences and redundant vocabulary, of the average writer of the sixteenth century. It is the style of the *grand rhétoriqueurs* without their worst affectations. In another of Galliot Du Pré's prefaces, that to Meliadus (1528), the style is much simpler. It is very likely that he did not write his own prefaces.

In September of the next year (1522) Du Pré moved to the Rue des Marmouzets, a short street which ran from the Rue de la Juiverie (now the Rue de la Cité) to the archway leading into the cloister of Notre-Dame. His house is described as being near to the Church of La Madeleine, which was in the Rue de la Juiverie[1]. According to M. Renouard's list of addresses, he was the only bookseller in the street, for Gilles Corrozet did not go there till after Du Pré's death, and Jean de La Garde, who was burnt in April 1538 for having bought some heretical books from Jean Morin, the printer of the *Cymbalum Mundi*[2], had left it in 1512. Du Pré transferred his old sign of a galley to his new abode.

I have found only two publications for the year 1523, an Epitome in French of Budé's *De Asse*, and the *editio princeps* of *Ysaie le triste*, a late fifteenth century prose romance, which relates the fortunes of the son of Tristan and Yseult of Cornwall.

In 1524 Du Pré having changed his stall for the second time, moving to the first pillar, published the first edition of a very notable work, the *Cronique et histoire* of Philippe de Commines. The date of the privilege is February 3, 1523 (O.S.), and the printing was finished on April 26[3]. It was incorrectly printed and whole passages were suppressed. It was followed by a new edition in September, by a third in the following September (1525), and by a fourth and fifth in January and February, 1526. All these editions contain only six books, relating to the reign of Louis XI. The last two books, which Commines wrote in 1497 and 1498, and which

---

[1] See G. Corrozet, *La fleur des antiquités de Paris*, ed. P. Lacroix, 1874, pp. 103 and 105, and the map of Paris by Truschet and Hoyau (1552), part of which is reproduced by M. Delalain, *Notice Compl.* p. 9.

[2] See Herminjard, *Correspondance des réformateurs*, IV. 418–420.

[3] The date of the first edition is sometimes wrongly given as 1523.

deal with the Italian expedition of Charles VIII, were first printed for Enguilbert de Marnef in 1528. Du Pré published editions of the complete work in 1546 and 1552, both in association with Jean de Roigny. The edition of 1552 was edited by Denis Sauvage, who first introduced the division into books and chapters and gave the work the title of *Memoires*. Du Pré began another edition in 1560, but he did not live to see it completed, and it appeared, after his death, in 1561.

Two other interesting publications of Du Pré's belong to the year 1524: a greatly enlarged edition of Tiraqueau's *De legibus connubialibus*, in the preparation of which the author was in all likelihood assisted by his friend Rabelais, and Jacques Merlin's *Quatuor concilia generalia* in two volumes. Merlin, who died in 1541 and was buried in Notre-Dame at Paris, was a Canon of that church. He wrote a defence of Origen, for which he was pounced upon by the redoubtable Noël Bédier, and edited the works of the Scottish mystic Richard of St Victor. In 1527 he was imprisoned in the Louvre by the King's order for favouring the new doctrines, and was only released at the end of two years.

The chief publication of 1525 was *Les tres elegantes, tres veridiques et copieuses annales* of Nicole Gilles, which, as I have said, shared the popularity of Desrey's translation of Gaguin's *Compendium*. It was first published in 1492, but no copy of this edition is known. After the author's death (in 1503) numerous editions with continuations appeared—in 1510, 1520, 1525, 1527, 1531, 1538, 1544, 1547, 1549, 1551, 1552, all except the first two and those of 1544 and 1551 being published by Galliot Du Pré.

With the exception of a new edition—the fourth—of Commines none of Du Pré's publications for 1526 were of a historical character. They included the *editio princeps* of *Mabrian*, a fifteenth century continuation of *Maugis d'Aigremont*, Alain Chartier's *Les faicts et dictz*, and a volume entitled *Traictez singuliers*, which contained works by Chastelain, Molinet, and Cretin, the three successive chiefs of the *rhétoriqueur* school, and by Jean Lemaire de Belges, the

nephew and disciple of Molinet. They are all in verse except
Chastelain's *Epitaphes de Hector et Achilles,* which is partly
in prose and partly in verse[1]. The volume opens with *Trois
contes intitulés de Cupido et Atropos, traduits de l'italien de
Seraphin, le second et tiers de l'invention de Jean Lemaire.* As
a matter of fact, the first of these is not a translation from
Serafino but an original poem founded on one of his sonnets.
It is written in *terza rima.* The second *conte* is a continuation
of the same story, while the third is not by Jean Lemaire[2].
Serafino Ciminelli of Aquila, who died young in 1500, had a
great contemporary reputation, especially for his *strambotti,*
short poems full of conceits and extravagance, which he used
to sing to the accompaniment of the lute. His poetry was
much admired in France. There are traces of its influence in
Marot and Saint-Gelais's poems, but the poet whom it most
affected was Maurice Scève[3].

In the *Esperon de discipline* (1532) of Antoine du Saix, a
Canon of Notre-Dame de Bourg-en-Bresse and a friend of
Rabelais, there is an interesting list of the popular books of
the day. It includes

> La Maguelonne et Pierre de Prouvence,
> Le Peregrin pour fraische souvenance
> Ou Scelestine et le Perseforest,
> Roland, Maugis, Dardaine la Forest,
> Prison d'amours, addition et glose,
> Finablement le Roman de la Rose[4],

and it is interesting to find that five of these were published
by Galliot Du Pré from 1526 to 1528, the *Roman de la Rose,*
edited and rejuvenated by Clement Marot, and *La prison
d'amours,* a translation of Diego de San Pedro's sentimental
love-story, *Carcel de Amor,* in 1526; *La Celestine,* a translation through the Italian of the famous Spanish tragi-comedy
of *Calisto y Melibea,* and *Le Peregrin,* a translation by François
Dassy of Caviceo's *Libro del peregrino* (a prolix love-story,

---

[1] Picot, *Cat. Rothschild,* I. no. 487. The edition mentioned by Panzer
under the date of 1521 is clearly the same as this.
[2] A. Becker, *Jean Lemaire,* Strasbourg, 1893, pp. 254 ff.
[3] See Tilley, *Dawn of the French Renaissance,* pp. 141–142, and the references in n.[3] of p. 142.
[4] *Rev. des études rabelaisiennes,* IX. 246.

first printed at Parma in 1508) in 1527; and *Perceforest* in 1528.

For the six years, 1527–1532, Galliot Du Pré's publications apparently become more numerous; at any rate more have come down to us. One of the most notable is the well-known *Life of Bayard* by Le loyal Serviteur, who is probably to be identified with Bayard's secretary, Jacques de Mailles. Du Pré published it in 1527, but M. Roman, the modern editor of the work, thinks there was an earlier edition published in 1524 (not necessarily by Du Pré), the year of Bayard's death. The spirit of mediaeval chivalry is also represented—less nobly, but with greater variety—in the four folio volumes of Froissart, which Du Pré published in association with Jean Petit in 1530. Another considerable undertaking—this he shared with François Regnault—was the *Illustrations de la Gaule Belgique, antiquités du pays de Haynau et de la grand cite de Belges à present dicte Bavay*, 3 vols. fo. 1531–1532[1], an abridged translation of the Latin chronicle of Jacques de Guise, a Franciscan who died at Valenciennes in 1398—a few years before Froissart and possibly in the same place[2]. In 1531 Du Pré published the historical work of yet a third Hainaulter, Jean Lemaire de Belges, but to this I shall return presently.

The prose romances of chivalry appealed more or less to the same tastes as Froissart, and we find Du Pré publishing in 1528 not only *Perceforest* but also *La conqueste de Grèce*, and *Meliadus de Leonnoys*, and in 1530 *Perceval le Gallois*. All were first editions; two, *Perceforest* and *Meliadus*, by reason of the prominent part played in them by tournaments seemed particularly suited to an age which delighted in the outward shows of chivalry.

In the year 1531 Galliot Du Pré was particularly active. I have already mentioned the first volume of the *Illustrations de Belgique*, and of *Les Illustrations de Gaule* of Jean Lemaire; of *Le livre d'or* of Guevara I shall speak presently. To these must be added the *Speculum Principum ac Justitiae*, a work

---

[1] It was intended to be in four volumes, but it was completed in three.
[2] Froissart died soon after 1404, either at Chimay, where he was a Canon, or at Valenciennes, his birthplace. Jacques de Guise was born at Mons.

of the fifteenth century, and *Sidrach* a work of the four-teenth. The author of the *Speculum* was Pedro Belluga, a lawyer of Valencia, who entered the service of Alfonso I of Naples and Sicily, to whom the work is dedicated. He died in 1468, having been born about 1395 (he entered the University of Bologna in 1410)[1]. *Sidrach la fontaine de toutes sciences*, as it is usually called, was a highly popular work in the Middle Ages. In Du Pré's edition it is entitled *Mil et quatre vingtz et quatre demandes avec les solutions et responses a toutes propoz, œuvre curieux et moult recreatif selon le saige Sidrach*. M. Langlois believes it to have been written by an unknown writer during the last quarter of the fourteenth century, and he adds, "Quel qu'ait été l'auteur ou l'ar-rangeur...une chose est hors de doute: c'était un sot." The first printed edition, which contains 1073 questions, was published by Verard in 1486 (O.S.)[2]. Another publication of 1531 was *Les ditz moraulx des philosophes* translated from the Latin by Guillaume de Tignonville.

In Froissart and the romances it was not only the courtly spirit of chivalry but the underlying human element of adven-ture which stirred the imagination of sixteenth century readers. Du Pré early in his career had printed Vespucci's account of his voyages. Now in October 1532 he published a reprint of the most important collection of voyages which had yet appeared. This was the *Novus Orbis* of Simon Grynaeus (as it is always called, though Grynaeus only contributed a preface) first published at Basle in the preceding March. Du Pré sub-stituted for the map generally attributed to Sebastian Münster a far superior one by Oronce Finé[3].

Very different in appearance to this imposing Latin folio on the geography of the world was the little 16mo French book of 71 leaves on the geography of Paris which Du Pré published in the same year. Like the *Novus Orbis* it was a reprint, the original edition having been published by Denys

---

[1] For Belluga see Fustér, *Bib. Valenciania*, Valencia, 2 vols. 1827–1830, I. 27.
[2] Ch. V. Langlois, *La Connaissance de la Nature et du Monde au Moyen Age*, 1911, pp. 180 ff. And see Ward, *Catalogue of Romances*, I. 903 ff.
[3] For an account of this work see above, p. 137.

Janot in the previous March. Its author was Gilles Corrozet, poet, antiquary, and bookseller, and its title was *La Fleur des antiquités, singularités et excellences de la noble et triumphante cité de Paris*[1]. It was, in fact, the first guide-book to Paris.

Spanish literature seems to have attracted Du Pré; he published two French translations of famous Spanish works, one, already mentioned, of the *tragicomedia Calisto y Melibea*, better known as *La Celestina*, and the other of Guevara's *Libro aureo de Marco Aurelio*. The latter, by René Bertaut de la Grise (*Livre d'or de Marc Aurele*), appeared in 1531; two years before Du Pré had published the same work —it had been surreptitiously printed at Seville earlier in the year—in the original Spanish. It was not the only Spanish book published in France at this period. The *Celestina*, the poems of Boscan and Garcilaso de la Vega in a single volume, and other works were printed either at Paris or at Lyons in their original tongue. Probably they were intended for the Spanish market, rather than for home consumption.

The French books, other than those of an historical character, published by Galliot Du Pré during these six years have a special interest, in that they illustrate the change that was taking place in French literature—the decline of the *grand rhétoriqueur* school, the return to good sense and simplicity, and the "illustration" of the French language, after a long interval of dullness and imbecility, by works of real literary merit. Thus from 1527 to 1529 we find Du Pré still publishing works of the *rhétoriqueur* school: in 1527 *Chants royaulx, oraisons et autres petits traictez* by Guillaume Cretin, the last chief of the *rhétoriqueur* school, who had recently died, and a volume of 350 *rondeaux* of which the authorship has been attributed to Pierre Gringore; in 1528 the still highly popular poem, *Les lunettes des princes*, of Jean Meschinot (d. 1509), a translation of Ovid *Epistles* by Octovien de Saint-Gelais, and a new work by Gringore, *Notables enseignemens, adages et proverbes*, written in eight-lined stanzas; in 1529 Saint-Gelais's translation of the *Aeneid* and Guillaume Michel's translation

---

[1] There is a modern reprint (1874) by Paul Lacroix (Bibliophile Jacob).

of the *Eclogues* and *Georgics* in a single volume, and a new edition of Gringore's poem.

On the other hand during the years 1529–1531 he produces works of an earlier period; the ever-popular *Roman de la Rose*, in two editions, one in folio (1531), like the edition of 1526, and the other in small octavo with 31 new and pretty woodcuts[1]; the works of Alain Chartier; and Martin Le Franc's *Le Champion des Dames*. The last work, which was presented to Philip the Good, Duke of Burgundy, in 1442, had met with little success when it was first printed at Lyons in 1490. Du Pré was doubtless prompted to republish it by the fact that the time-honoured controversy on the subject of women was once more in full activity. He showed his impartiality by publishing in the same year the *Contredits de Songecreux*, a satirical poem of much vigour by Jehan du Pontalais, known as Songecreux, who took the other side to Le Franc.

It is true that Jean Lemaire de Belges, of whose *magnum opus* Du Pré published a new edition in 1531, was brought up in the *rhétoriqueur* school, being the relative and ward of Jean Molinet, but he had felt the breath of the Renaissance, as the true *rhétoriqueur* had never felt it, and he had, as none of them had, except Georges Chastellain, a real gift for writing both in verse and prose. In *Les Illustrations de Gaule* he meant to immortalise himself as a historian, but much of his history is fabulous, and his real talent is for narrative and picturesque description[2].

In 1532 Du Pré more definitely marked the coming change in literature by publishing in an uniform series Gringore's *Le Chasteau de Labour*—the most popular of his poems, first printed in 1499 and translated into English by Alexander Barclay[3]—*Pathelin*, Coquillart, and Villon, adding to each volume, except *Pathelin*, some new matter, either spurious or doubtful. Thus the edition of Villon includes *Le dialogue des*

[1] See F. W. Bourdillon, *The early editions of the Roman de la Rose*, 1906 (printed for the Bibliographical Society), pp. 57–62 and 88–91.
[2] I have discussed Lemaire at some length in *The Dawn of the French Renaissance*, pp. 333–352.
[3] The *Castell of Labour* was first printed in Paris for Verard *circ.* 1503.

seigneurs de Mallepane et Baillevent, and the excellent *Monologue du franc archier de Baillevent.* This year, 1532, was a memorable one in the history of French literature, for it saw the publication of the first works of real literary genius which had appeared in France for at least sixty years, the first since Villon's *Le grand testament* and *Pathelin*—Marot's *Poems* and Rabelais's *Pantagruel.*

In the following year Du Pré added a fifth volume to his series, namely a new edition of Villon, edited by Marot, in which all the spurious pieces were omitted and the old corrupt text was carefully purified. As *Pathelin,* Coquillart, and Villon were all well known to the author of *Pantagruel* we may regard Du Pré's latest publications as happily associating him not only with Marot but also with Rabelais.

After the year 1532 Galliot Du Pré's publications become less numerous, and their character less interesting and instructive. At this point, therefore, it will be convenient to consider the character of his publications as a whole.

In the first place it will be noticed that, as I said at the outset, he shows a decided predilection for history. He publishes not only popular and uncritical compilations like *La mer des histoires,* Desrey's translation of Gaguin's *Compendium,* and especially the *Chroniques* of Nicole Gilles, of which he issued altogether four editions, but he introduces the *Memoirs* of Commines to the world, and reprints them several times. Further, he shares in the publication of a new edition of Froissart, and he shows his interest in the cognate subject of political science, by publishing the works of Francesco Patrizi, the Latin version of the *Songe du Verdier,* and the *Speculum principum ac justitiae.* He publishes, too, if not the first, at any rate the oldest existing edition of that delightful work, the *Life of Bayard* by Le loyal Serviteur. The poetry published by him comprises the *Roman de la Rose, Le Champion des Dames,* Alain Chartier, works of the *rhétoriqueur* school (including several works by Jean Bouchet), Villon, Coquillart, and Gringore. The drama is well represented by *Pathelin.* He publishes seven romances of chivalry, five for the first time. All except two belong to the Arthurian cycle, the representations of which, with the possible exception of *Le petit Artus* (the connexion of which with the cycle is extremely slight), never descended in the form of popular chap-books to the lowest stratum of French readers. This choice of romances is, in itself, enough to show that Galliot Du Pré did not cater for the popular taste, but for the nobles and the better class of bourgeois.

Besides the romances, mediaeval prose is represented by such favourite works as *Sidrach*, *Le Mirouer historial*, and *Les ditz moraulx des philosophes*. The beginnings of Renaissance prose are marked by Jean Lemaire's *Illustrations de Gaule*, though its publication by Du Pré, as well as its general popularity, was probably due more to its historical character than to its real merits of style.

Of translations, which played so considerable a part in the revival of learning and literature, we have Caesar, Cicero, Virgil, Ovid, Quintus Curtius, Suetonius, Apuleius, Dionysius of Halicarnassus, and Josephus, both these last through Latin versions; a single work of Petrarch, an extract from Boccaccio's *Il Filocolo*, *Le Peregrin*, *Il libro aureo*, *Il carcel de amor*, and *Celestine*. But all these translations were more or less unskilful and inadequate, and were soon afterwards superseded.

Classical authors in their original tongue are conspicuously absent. There is not a single Greek book, and classical Latin is represented only by Eutropius (with Paulus Diaconus). Erasmus and Budé, the rivals for the primacy of European scholarship, appear respectively in a garbled translation of the *Encomium Moriae*, and an epitome in French of the *De Asse*.

Geographical discovery,—the discovery of the world, as humanism was the discovery of man,—is represented by two works, *Le Nouveau Monde* and the *Novus Orbis*. In this timid and tentative attitude towards the Renaissance, Galliot Du Pré accurately reflected the literary tastes of the ordinary educated Frenchman of his day. The study of the classics was still confined to a select circle of humanists; it was only in 1529 that the victory of Greek was assured, and it had not yet had time to bear fruit. Such translations from the Greek as had appeared hitherto were all made from Latin versions. Of translations from the Latin the only one of any literary merit was Marot's verse rendering of two books of the *Metamorphoses* (1532). The Italian works which most influenced the French Renaissance, the *Cortegiano*, the *Arcadia*, the *Principe*, Ariosto's *Comedies* and *Orlando Furioso*, were still untranslated. The *Decameron* was still represented by the mediaeval paraphrase—for it was little more—of Laurent Du Premierfait.

Thus Galliot Du Pré was influenced in his choice of works for publication by sound business instincts, by a legitimate desire to satisfy the demands of the "general reader" of his day. And within his field of operation he showed not only judgment but enterprise, publishing several new works which hit the public taste and put money into his pocket.

Another source of profit besides the ordinary sale of books, of which publishers availed themselves at this period, was the production of special copies, printed on vellum and adorned with illuminated woodcuts. In a few cases they were in the strict sense presentation copies, but as a rule they were destined for noble patrons who, judging by an extant bill sent in by Verard, paid for them pretty heavily. Du Pré adopted this practice almost at the outset of his career, by printing copies on vellum of the two editions of Desrey's *Chroniques*, which he published in 1514 and 1515. Van Praet mentions three copies of the former, one of which has twenty miniatures, and another sixteen[1]. Another early vellum copy of Du Pré's production is that of *Le temple de Jehan Boccace*, adorned with three miniatures, one of which represents the author (?) offering his book to Francis I[2]. Special mention must also be made of the vellum copies of the *Encomium trium Mariarum* (a work to be mentioned presently); they contain a full-page woodcut of the three Marys, which is absent from the paper copies[3].

To the year 1522 belongs the unique *Les coustumes du pays*

[1] 2nd part, III. no. 95.
[2] Van Praet (I), v. no. 91.
[3] Bernard, *Geofroy Tory*, pp. 359 ff.; Brunet; Bib. Nat. There is a vellum copy in the Bib. Mazarin.

et duche de Bourbonnoys, with illuminated initials, and an elaborate title-page, on which are the initials of Pierre de Beaujeu, his wife Anne, the able and ambitious daughter of Louis XI, and their son-in-law, Charles de Bourbon, Constable of France since 1515. The work is dedicated to Anne de Beaujeu by her Chancellor, Pierre Papillon, and this particular copy, the only one that is known—probably very few copies were printed—was evidently destined either for Anne or her son-in-law[1]. Other notable vellum copies produced by Galliot Du Pré are those of the French translation of Platina, with 228 portraits in the initial letters[2]; the *Roman de la Rose* of 1526, with ninety-five miniatures[3]; the Nicole Gilles of 1525, with fourteen miniatures, and with the arms of Charles, Duc de Vendôme, to whom the work is dedicated, on the first leaf of each volume[4]; the *Triumphante et glorieuse victoire* (1527)[5], with nine miniatures; the Virgil (1529), with thirty-one[6].

Du Pré's chief patron was Charles d'Urfé (grandfather of the author of *L'Astrée*), for whom five of his extant vellum copies were executed. Head of an ancient family of La Forez, he was squire in ordinary to Francis I, who in 1535 appointed him bailiff of his native province. It was not till the next reign that he became really prominent, being successively envoy to the Council of Trent (1548), ambassador to the Holy See (1549–1553), and governor to the Dauphin and his brothers. He had a fine library, part of which he had inherited from his mother-in-law, Mme d'Entragues[7]. Du Pré's connexion with him appears to date from 1531, when he produced for him a vellum copy of Bouchard's *Grandes chroniques de Bretaigne*[8]. The arms of the same patron are also found on vellum copies of the French Lactantius of 1543[9], of a Nicole Gilles of 1547

---

[1] I have taken this description from a note in the Monmerqué Catalogue (1851), which has been copied into both the Yemeniz and Didot (1879) Catalogues. The book is undated, but as it contains an extract from the registers of the *Parlement*, dated March 20, 1522 (N.S.) (Brunet), and as Anne died in November 1522, it certainly belongs to that year.

[2] Van Praet (1), v. no. 23.   [3] *Ib.* IV. no. 1623.
[4] *Ib.* v. no. 1525.   [5] *Ib.* v. no. 48.   [6] *Ib.* IV. no. 102.
[7] A. Bernard, *Les D'Urfé* (1839), pp. 45–51.
[8] Van Praet, v. no. 168.   [9] *Ib.* I. no. 375.

(with sixty-five miniatures)[1], of *Instructions sur le faict de la guerre* (1548), and of Jean Bouchet's *Les triumphes de la noble et amoureuse dame* (1535)[2]. Of two vellum copies of Josephus's *Jewish Antiquities*, which were in the Duc de la Vallière's library, one, which bore D'Urfé's arms, has disappeared, but the other, which has numbered among its possessors Francis I, Diane de Poitiers, and Count d'Hoym, is now in the Bibliothèque Nationale[3].

I need not enumerate all the other vellum copies produced by Du Pré. About a dozen more are recorded by Van Praet, and there were two, *Le Peregrin* and the French translation of Quintus Curtius, in the Harleian library[4]. They serve to show that Du Pré had numerous patrons among princes and nobles, and that consequently, in his choice of works of publication, he doubtless consulted their taste.

It will have been noticed that several of Du Pré's publications, more especially those of considerable size, were published by him in temporary partnership with other booksellers. We find him associated in this way with many of the leading men of his profession, with Jean Petit, with Josse Badius and his two sons-in-law, Michael de Vascosan and Jean de Roigny, with Poncet Le Preux, whose career extended to fifty-eight years, with Simon de Colines, with Jean Longis, and with Pierre Vidoue, and occasionally with provincial publishers. Sometimes in these joint publications each partner had a different title-page for the copies sold by him; thus in some of the cases referred to above Galliot Du Pré and his associate are both represented by the extant copies of the book[5]. Sometimes, if the book comprises several volumes, one publisher's mark or name appears in one or more volumes, and the other's in the remaining volumes. In other cases, chiefly with books published near the beginning of his career, Du Pré's name appears only in the colophon, and not on the title-page. The reason for this may either be

---

[1] Cat. MacCarthy, II. no. 4525.
[2] Cat. La Vallière, II. no. 3001.
[3] Cat. La Vallière, III. no. 4806; Van Praet, IV. no. 53.
[4] Bib. Harl. III. nos. 3201 and 3218.
[5] *E.g.* in *La mer des histoires et croniques de France* (1517).

that he occupied a subordinate position in the partnership, or that all the copies in which his name appears on the title-page have disappeared.

Numerous printers were employed by him in the course of his long career, but during that period of it which we are now considering, three especially enjoyed his favour. These were Pierre Vidoue, and the brothers Nicolas and Antoine Cousteau. Pierre Vidoue was a man of real distinction in his profession, whose work amply justified the qualification which he assumes of *Chalcographie artis peritissimus*. He began to exercise his art, according to M. Renouard, in 1510. It is in 1518 that we first find him working for Galliot Du Pré, and from that date down to 1524 he printed for him various works, including the *Coustumes de Bourbonnoys*, *Ysaie le triste*, the Epitome of Budé's *De Asse*, and Tiraqueau's *De legibus connubialibus*. In 1521 he made his first appearance as a Greek printer, with an impression of the curious and popular *Hieroglyphica* of Horapollo in Greek and Latin. But the most remarkable production of his Greek press is the complete series of Aristophanes's *Comedies*, edited by Jean Cheradame, which he printed for Gilles de Gourmont from November 1528 to March 1529. At this time he possessed some Hebrew type, for the verse of the 37th Psalm, "I have been young, and now am old: yet have I not seen the righteous forsaken, nor his seed begging bread," is printed in Hebrew as well as Greek on the title-page of each play[1]. In 1528 he also printed Demosthenes's *Olynthiac orations*. In 1538 he printed Guillaume Postel's first work, the alphabets of twelve languages. His connexion with Galliot Du Pré seems to have temporarily ceased after 1524, but from 1528 to 1531 he was again employed by him, printing for him in 1530 the long poem of Martin Le Franc and in 1531 the translation of Caesar.

During the years 1524 to 1527 Du Pré chiefly employed either Nicolas or Antoine Cousteau. They were sons of Gilles Cousteau, Nicolas, who succeeded to his father's stall in the Palais de Justice, being apparently the elder[2]. It was Antoine who printed for Du Pré the first three editions of Commines

---

[1] See above, p. 132.   [2] Renouard, *op. cit.* p. 85.

and the Nicole Gilles of 1525, while to Nicolas he entrusted the *Life of Bayard*, the *Celestina, Meliadus,* and *Perceforest.* In 1529 and 1530 Antoine was employed by him concurrently with Pierre Vidoue—he printed the Froissart of 1530—and at a later period we find Du Pré entrusting more work to Nicolas, the French Josephus and two other books in 1534, and *La mer des histoires* in 1536.

Among the printers whom he employed only occasionally was Jacques Nyverd, who, together with another bookseller, Jean André, acted as the spy and bloodhound of the terrible First President of the Paris *Parlement,* Pierre Lizet. He printed for Du Pré two romances, *Mabrian* and *La conqueste de grece,* the former, presumably, in 1526, and the latter in 1528. He lived in the Rue de la Juiverie, near the Pont Notre-Dame, and therefore not far from Du Pré in the Rue des Marmouzets. With such a neighbour it was lucky for our publisher that his faith was above suspicion, and that in the year 1529, when French Protestantism suffered a severe blow by the execution of Berquin, he published a work which was stamped with the seal of orthodoxy. This was a collection of three Latin theological treatises, *tria aurea opuscula,* by Jean Bertaud of Périgueux. The first is entitled *Encomium triarum Mariarum cum earundem cultus defensione adversus Lutheranos;* the second is an office for their worship; the third treats of their relationship with St John the Baptist. The three Maries are the Virgin Mary, Mary the wife of Cleopas, and Salome the wife of Zebedee, who, according to the orthodox belief of that time, was originally called Mary, and, together with the wife of Cleopas, was supposed to be half-sister to the Virgin. But Lefèvre d'Étaples, in the same treatise (1517) in which he denied the identity of Mary the sister of Lazarus with Mary Magdalene and "the woman who was a sinner," also questioned the received view about the three Maries. He was answered on both points by Noël Bédier, the well-known champion of the Sorbonne, whose second treatise, *Apologia pro filiabus et nepotibus beatae Annae,* appeared in February 1520, just after the writings of Luther had begun to circulate in Paris. Thus the cult of the three Marys came to be regarded as a sign of orthodoxy.

Two of the printers whom Galliot Du Pré employed suffered for their religious opinions, namely, Simon Du Bois and Antoine Augereau. The former printed for him the posthumous volume of Cretin (1527) and Gringore's *Notables enseigne-mens* (January 1527 (O.S.)). At the outset of his career he had been bold enough to print, in the dangerous year 1525, Lefèvre's translation of the New Testament, and in April 1529, when Berquin suffered at the stake, he was engaged in printing the *Livre de vraye et parfaite oraison*, a translation of one of Luther's writings, which is possibly from Berquin's pen. In the following year he fled to Alençon, the capital of Margaret's duchy, where he printed her *Miroir de l'âme pécheresse* in 1531. In 1533 he returned to Paris, but after the Affair of the Placards his name figured on the list of suspect Lutherans who had fled from Paris (January 25, 1535), and he disappears from our view[1]. About the fate of his fellow-Protestant, Antoine Augereau, the printer of Gringore's *Chasteau de Labour* (1532), the *Libri de re rustica* (1534), and the *Novus Orbis* (1534), there is no obscurity. On Christmas Eve, 1534, two months after the printing of this last book was finished, he was hanged and burnt in the Place Maubert. His offence was grave indeed; he had not only printed two editions of *Le Miroir*, but had included in the second of these Marot's translation of Psalm VI[2].

Such were the dangers to which booksellers and printers were exposed in France in the winter of 1534–1535. The Affair of the Placards had thoroughly frightened the king and had alienated the whole body of moderate reformers, and, though in the summer of 1536 Francis returned for a time to a milder mood, this was mainly due to the war with Charles V, which had broken out in the preceding April and left him no leisure to deal with heretics. But after the truce of Nice and the interview with the emperor at Aigues-Mortes, in July

[1] See N. Weiss in *Bulletin de la Soc. de l'hist. du protestantisme français*, XXXVI (1887), 669 ff., and XXXVII (1888), 152 ff., 432 ff., 500 ff.
[2] Harrisse, *Exc. Colomb.* p. 129.

1538, he adopted a policy of rigorous suppression, which he maintained with unwonted consistency till his death, and which was continued by his successor. Meanwhile, one of the immediate effects of the Placards was that on January 13, 1535, the Father of Letters issued letters-patent forbidding any book to be printed in France under the pain of death. Fortunately, the Parliament declined to register this extraordinary edict, and there was substituted for it another, in which it was enacted that "the Parliament should choose twenty-four persons duly qualified and provided with sureties, out of whom the king would select twelve, and that these, and no others, should print in Paris, but nowhere else, books approved and necessary for the public welfare, without printing any new composition, under pain of punishment" (February 23, 1535)[1]. This edict, however, which was hardly less absurd and arbitrary than its predecessor, remained a dead letter. A milder form of censorship was prescribed by an edict of December 28, 1537, by which it was enacted that no book should be offered for sale until a copy of it had been given to Mellin de Saint-Gelais, keeper of the royal library at Blois, "in order to prevent the propagation of erroneous doctrines[2]." In the face of these enactments it is amusing to find Francis I, in an edict issued from Villers-Cotterets on August 31, 1539, on the occasion of a threatened strike of the Paris journeymen printers, declaring that he had always "favoured and supported the art of printing good books and good literature." As a matter of fact, the censorship of the press became more and more severe. We have seen how the bookseller Jean de La Garde was burnt in April 1538 for his connexion with the *Cymbalum Mundi*. In 1539 both the printer and the bookseller were required to put their names in books[3]. In 1542 the University forbade the booksellers to expose any books for sale until they had been examined, and in the same year the Parliament ordered an inspection of all the bookshops and printing-houses with a view to the seizure of all heretical works.

---

[1] *Catalogue des Actes de François I*, III. 23.
[2] *Ib.* 426.
[3] H. Hauser, *Une grève d'imprimeurs parisiens au XVIe siècle*, 1895.

To return to Galliot Du Pré, with the exception of Marot's edition of Villon, I have found no publications of his which can be assigned with certainty to the year 1533. This is doubtless due to the incompleteness of my researches. There are, however, three works which have the date either of January or of February, 1533, in the colophon, and which may therefore possibly belong to that year according to the modern reckoning. Any one who has had to do with French books of the first half of the sixteenth century knows how difficult it often is to determine the date of a book published before Easter. For the new method of beginning the year on January 1, while it did not come into legal force till January 1, 1565, began to be used by printers and booksellers soon after the year 1500, at first only sparingly, but as the years went on with increasing frequency. The question becomes doubly difficult when we are dealing with books which, like Galliot Du Pré's, were printed by one man and sold by another. The only way of arriving at any light on the subject is to give the facts as they stand, classifying them as far as possible. In the first place, then, we have a group of cases in which the date is definitely stated to be before or after Easter, such as *Les grandes chroniques* (April 1514, after Easter), *La genealogie des rois de France* (March 20, 1520, before Easter), *Petrarcque, Des remedes* (March 15, 1523, before Easter), *Catalogue des Saints et des Saintes* (March 3, 1524, before Easter). In none of these instances is the printer's name given. Then we have the single case of the *De Regno* of F. Patrizi, in which it is stated in the colophon that the printing was finished on April 16, 1519, *ad Romanum calculum*, Easter-day in 1519 being on April 24. The printer was Pierre Vidoue, and we find him using the same formula in the *Hours of the Virgin*, which he printed for Guillaume Godard in 1523[1]. Yet in the Aristophanes, which he printed for Gilles de Gourmont in 1528 (O.S.), he begins his year at Easter. Other instances might easily be adduced to show that the printers and booksellers varied in their practice. Sometimes, indeed, the same man would use

---

[1] Cat. Didot, 1879, no. 140.

both methods in the same book. For instance, in *La prison d'amours* (No. 53) the year 1526 is on the title-page and the year 1525 in the colophon, while in the *Apologia pro filiabus et nepotibus beatae Annae* of Noël Bédier Josse Badius, who both printed and sold the book, puts the year 1519 on the title-page, and the year 1520 in the colophon.

Thus in the absence of any available criterion, we are compelled to deal with each case as a separate problem. Sometimes this is solved by the mention in the preface or body of the book of some historical event. Sometimes we are enlightened by some fact connected with the life of the bookseller or printer. For instance, the qualification of Galliot Du Pré as *libraire juré* on the title-page of the French translation of Suetonius, printed by Pierre Vidoue, shows that the date in the colophon, of February 16, 1520, must be referred to the year 1521 (N.S.), for on April 20, 1520, as we know from *Le livre tres fructueux*, he was not a *libraire juré*.

Another available help is the privilege, if there is one. It was the usual practice for publishers to apply for a privilege as soon as the book was ready for press, and to begin printing almost immediately after it was granted. But sometimes the printing was delayed. Thus, while *Perceval le Gallois* (No. 83), with 220 leaves, was printed in less than five and a half months from the date of the privilege, ten months elapsed before *La prison d'amours* (No. 53), which contains only eighty-seven leaves, was finished. It was not a universal practice to wait for the privilege before beginning to print a book, and I have found one or two instances in which the date of the privilege is only a few days earlier, and in one case even a few days later, than that of the completion of the book. Thus the privilege for *La conqueste de grece* is dated February 4, 1527 (O.S.), but the printing was finished on February 8, 1527 (O.S.). There was, however, a special reason for this, as Du Pré had already been granted a privilege for the work in November 1525, and this new privilege was in place of the old one[1]. A similar instance, without any obvious explana-

---

[1] The appearance of the six volumes of *Perceforest* within fifteen months of the privilege, is probably to be accounted for by the fact that the printing was begun before the privilege was granted.

tion, is the *Temple de bonne renommée* (No. 16), in which the book is dated eight days after the completion of the privilege.

Down to the year 1532 I have been able by means of the privilege to determine the year in most of the doubtful cases. But for three works with the imprint of January or February 1533 I have no such guide. In the descriptions of them—for I have not seen any of them—there is no mention of a privilege. Two of them relate to agriculture, one being an edition of the *Libri de re rustica*, published jointly with Jean Petit[1], and the other an edition of the French translation of the *Opus ruralium commodorum*, of Piero Crescenzi of Bologna. Made for Charles V, in 1373, the latter was first published by Verard under the title of *Livre des proufits champestres*. Du Pré's edition, which has on the title-page a woodcut of the publisher offering the work to Francis I, is entitled *Le bon Mesnager*[2]. Bearing almost the same date is a curious collection of miscellaneous treatises by Guillaume Telin, a gentleman of Auvergne, entitled *Bref sommaire des sept vertus, sept arts liberaux, etc.*[3] As up till now we have had only one instance of the new method of beginning the year being used in the colophon of Galliot Du Pré's books[4], there is a strong presumption in favour of all these three books belonging to the year 1534. It is, however, just possible that the *Libri de re rustica* may be dated according to the new method: firstly, because it is in Latin; secondly, because it was published in partnership with Jean Petit, whom I find using the Roman method in a preface as early as 1507[5]. These,

---

[1] February 4, 1533.

[2] January 15, 1533.

[3] February 12, 1533. The full title may be read in Brunet; his copy came later into the possession of the late Baron de Ruble (Catalogue No. 688).

[4] There is one other probable exception. In Bourdigné's *Histoire d'Anjou*, printed by Antoine Cousteau, the date in the colophon of the ordinary paper copies is January 1529, but in a vellum copy (Bib. Nat.) October 1529. Unless the latter was printed first, which is unlikely, the dating of the paper copies must be according to the new method.

[5] *Opus quadragesimale Oliverii Maillardi.* The date in the colophon is February 1, 1506.

however, are very slight reasons for abandoning the natural
presumption.

In any case, I can only find seven works, exclusive of
Marot's edition of Villon, for the two years 1533 and 1534. One
publication of the latter year calls for special mention, and
that is the *Ordonnance* of July 24 by which Francis I "ordered
the levy, after the example of the Romans, of a legion of 6000
foot-soldiers in each province of his kingdom[1]." Seven legions
—for Normandy, Brittany, Burgundy and Champagne,
Picardy, Dauphiné and Provence, Languedoc, and Guienne—
were ordered, but it appears that only six were actually
raised. This measure was part of the preparation for a new
war with Charles V, which began in February 1536 with the
invasion of Savoy and Piedmont by the French King.

This was not the only royal ordinance which was entrusted
to Galliot Du Pré for publication. In 1535 he published a collection of Ordinances made by successive kings from Charles
VII to Francis I, in 1536 the Latin text of the *Concordat* of
1516, and in 1539 in conjunction with two other booksellers
the very important Ordinances on the reform of justice which
Francis I issued from Villers-Cotterets in 1539.

Having these relations with the government, it was not surprising that our publisher, who was evidently a man of much
prudence and worldly wisdom, should have steered clear of
publications that had the least savour of heresy, and should
rather have been anxious to publish works which testified to
his strict orthodoxy. Thus from 1537 to 1541 we find him
issuing St Paul's Epistles and the Bible in Latin—both in
association with Simon de Colines—and two posthumous
works by Guillaume Petit, the King's late confessor.

He still continued his interest in history, publishing in 1535
the *Supplementum chronicorum* of Filippo Foresti of Bergamo,
in 1550 Jean Du Tillet's *Chronique des Roys de France*, in 1557
the *Gallica historia* of Robert Ceneau, in 1558 the so-called
Chronique Scandaleuse; and issuing new editions of Nicole
Gilles (1547, 1549, 1552) and, as we have seen, of Commines.

During the years 1535 to 1537 Du Pré specially favoured

---

[1] Du Bellay, *Mémoires*, Bk. IV, edd. Bourrilly and Vindry, II. 289.

Jean Bouchet. Thus he published in 1535 *Les triumphes de la noble et amoureuse dame*, a mystical work of great popularity, of which three editions had already appeared at Poitiers; in 1536 a new edition of *Les anciennes et modernes genealogies des Rois de France*[1]; and in 1537 a new edition of Bouchet's most important work, *Les Annales d'Aquitaine*. In 1536 he published a new edition, with continuations, of *La mer des histoires* in two volumes, saying in the preface that it was written in Latin in 1480 by Brocardus, and translated into French by a native of Beauvaisis. He is right as to the translator, who was a canon of Mello, near Beauvais, but Brocardus or Burchard (a German Dominican, who spent ten years in the monastery of Mount Sion) only wrote the description of the Holy Land in the original work[2], which was entitled *Rudimentum noviciorum*. At the very beginning of 1537, the printing having been finished on December 15, 1536, appeared the *Somme rurale* of Jean Boutillier, a summary of French customary law, completed in the early part of the fifteenth century, which enjoyed a high reputation even with the great jurists of the humanistic school. It was first printed at Bruges by Colard Mansion in 1479, and it was the first book printed at Abbeville (1486). In title and scope it closely resembles *Le grand Coustumier*, which Du Pré published in 1514, and La Caille, in a passage quoted by M. Delalain, has confused the two works. Like Froissart, Jacques de Guise, and Jean Lemaire, Boutillier was a native of Hainault, living at Tournai, where he was probably born.

In 1539 Du Pré published the *De rebus gestis Francorum libri x* by Paolo Emilio of Verona, originally published, in four books only, in 1517. This was the first history of France that was written after classical models. It was followed in 1541 by a reprint of *La Grande Monarchie de France*, the work of another Transalpine humanist—Claude de Seyssel, a native of Savoy—who had settled in France[3]. This little volume of 1541, which also contains a treatise on the Salic law by some

---

[1] First published at Poitiers in January 1527 (? O.S.).
[2] See *ante*, p. 30.
[3] See Tilley, *Dawn of the French Renaissance*, p. 366.

unknown author, has two features of interest apart from its contents. In the first place, the printer uses a barred "e," though by no means consistently, for "e" mute, and this nine years before Jacques Peletier (who is said to have invented it) published his *Dialogue de l'Ortografe e Prononciacion* (1550). Secondly, its title-page has a charming architectural border representing an arch supported by classical columns, between the bases of which are seated a pair of lovers, with a lute near them. The printer was Denys Janot, who, from 1539 to his death in 1545, issued books which are remarkable for the excellence of their woodcuts. One of these, also printed for Du Pré in 1539 and reprinted in 1541, is a volume containing the *De Officiis* and four other treatises of Cicero in French. Each part has a charming title-page.

Galliot Du Pré's title-pages, though inferior in beauty to those of many of his contemporaries, sometimes show much elegance and good taste. The title is often effectively printed in red and black. His favourite mark or device is a galley, which appears in two forms: a large one, in which the galley is rowed by monks, and a smaller one, in which the oarsmen are black. Both have the motto, *Vogue la guallée*. The larger device is rarely, if ever, placed on the title-page, but is printed on a separate page, usually at the end of the volume. Sometimes he employs a third mark, that of a horse, but always in conjunction with an architectural border composed of four separate pieces. This is a common form of title-page for his folios. In the Froissart of 1530, printed by Antoine Cousteau, the small galley is used as well as this border, and the whole title-page, which is printed in red and black, has a stately and dignified appearance. Other noteworthy title-pages are those of the *Roman de la Rose* of 1531, a small folio, which has a charming border, the *Roman de la Rose* of 1530, with a delightful woodcut of a man picking roses[1], and the Chartier of 1529[2].

A few publications still remain to be noticed. We have

---

[1] Library of Trinity College, Cambridge; reproduced in A. Lang's *The Library*.

[2] Reproduced in A. Lang's *Books and Bookmen*.

seen that in 1531 Du Pré published a French translation of the unauthorised version of Guevara's *Libro aureo*. In 1540 he issued under the title of *Lorloge des Princes*[1] a version made from the enlarged and first authentic edition, which bore the additional title of *El relox de principes*. In 1544 he published in a single volume *Du mepris de la Court*, a translation by Antoine Aleigre of Guevara's *Menosprecio de la Corte*, and several poems on the subject of love, which, mainly under the inspiration of Margaret of Navarre, was a favourite topic at this time. So too, *L'institution de la femme chrestienne*, a French translation by Pierre de Changy of the *De institutione christianae foeminae* of Louis Vives[2], which Du Pré published in the following year (1545), has a distinct bearing on the general question of the character of women. In the following year Rabelais published the Third Book of *Pantagruel*, in which this topic is handled with consummate wit and considerable impartiality[3].

In 1541 Du Pré published the *De magistratibus atheniensium liber* of Guillaume Postel, and in 1544 a translation by Jean Charrier of Cardinal Contarini's *De magistratibus et republica Venetorum*.

In 1548 he shared with Michel Vascosan in the publication of a remarkable little work entitled *Instructions sur le faict de la guerre*. On the authority of the preface the authorship has been generally attributed to Guillaume Du Bellay, amongst whose papers the manuscript was found; but the real author was Raimond de Rouer or de Pavie, Sieur de Fourquevaux (1511–1574)[4]. A second edition was issued by the same publishers in 1549, and a third in 1553. Its popularity continued, and it was translated into Latin, Italian, Spanish, and German.

[1] This volume has a large woodcut representing Francis I surrounded by his Court (Cat. Didot, 1879, no. 224).
[2] First published in 1524. The French translation was first printed in 1543. There is also a Lyons edition of 1545.
[3] See for the whole subject Abel Lefranc in *Revue des études rabelaisiennes*, II. 1 ff. and 78 ff.
[4] See V.-L. Bourrilly, *Guillaume Du Bellay*, 1905, pp. 324–326, and for a full account of the book and its author Abel Lefranc in the *Revue du Seizième Siècle*, III (1915), 109–154.

A book which Du Pré published in 1551 deserves a passing notice. Its title was *Tractatus duo de origine et usu jurisdictionum sive de duabus potestatibus*, and its author was Pierre Bertrand, a distinguished jurist, who, after holding chairs of law at Avignon, Montpellier, and Paris, took orders, and was made Bishop of Nevers and later of Autun. In 1331 he received a Cardinal's hat from Pope John XXII as a reward for his services at the Conference of Vincennes, summoned by Philip VI in 1329, where he had brilliantly defended the jurisdiction of the Church. He died at Avignon in 1349. He was the founder of the College of Autun in the University of Paris. One does not know what led our publisher to revive these old treatises, which were evidently the outcome of "the celebrated tournament of eloquence" at Vincennes. Was the publication suggested by the fact that at the beginning of 1551 the author's namesake, Jean Bertrand or Bertrandi of Toulouse[1], was appointed Keeper of the Seals in place of the disgraced Chancellor, Olivier? Or was its object to defend the jurisdiction of the ecclesiastical Courts in cases of heresy? For the sole right of trying such cases had been restored to them in November 1549, but, as they continued to show remissness, a new edict, issued from Châteaubriand on June 27, 1551, transferred to the Civil Courts the cognisance of those heretical acts which involved a public scandal or disturbance.

Two works of a historical character belong, as we have seen, to Du Pré's last years: the *Gallica historia* (1557) of Robert Ceneau, Bishop of Avranches—"homo ineptissimus et indoctissimus[2]"—and the so-called *Chronique Scandaleuse* of the reign of Louis XI, now revealed as the work of Jean de Roye, a public notary and secretary to Duc Jean II de Bourbon[3].

---

[1] Like his fourteenth century namesake he took orders, was made Bishop of Comminges, Archbishop of Sens, and finally Cardinal.

[2] Languet to Sidney, January 28, 1574.

[3] The first edition seems to have been published in the reign of Charles VIII, conjecturally at Lyons, about 1490. Galliot Du Pré printed it in the *Mer des histoires* of 1517–1519. His edition of 1558 is the second edition of the work printed separately. It bears the same title as the fifteenth century edition, but with his characteristic prudence Du Pré has suppressed about a

Finally, in 1559, Du Pré brought out the collected writings of Georges de Selve, Bishop of Lavaur, a diplomatist of some distinction, who with the help of his friend and *protégé* and successor in the bishopric, Pierre Danès, had translated eight of Plutarch's *Lives*, and who had died two years previously. The privilege for this publication is dated August 1, 1559, so that it presumably appeared before the end of the year, or at latest early in 1560[1]. In April of that year Galliot Du Pré died, and a perpetual mass was founded for the repose of his soul, facts which are recorded on a votive stone, now in the Musée de Cluny, but formerly placed in the church where the mass was to be said. The church nearest to Du Pré's house in the Rue des Marmouzets was La Madeleine, but the inscription as well as a carving on the stone seems to show that the church in question was Notre-Dame. He left several sons, of whom two, Pierre I and Galliot II, succeeded to their father's business, and for a time carried it on together. Then they separated, Pierre retaining the stall in the Palais de Justice, and Galliot taking a house in the Rue Saint-Jacques, with the sign of the Golden Galley. Pierre died in 1570 or 1571, and in 1572 his widow, after publishing in that year a book on her own account, transferred her affections and her business to Abel L'Angelier, the publisher of the 1588 edition of Montaigne's *Essays*. Galliot II, who was appointed a *libraire juré*, exercised his profession till 1580[1].

In the following list I have only attempted to describe each book with sufficient precision to permit of its identification. I have added either the name of some library which possesses a copy or the source from which I have taken the description. I have seen all the copies in Cambridge, as well as several in the British Museum and a few in the collection of Mr E. P. Goldschmidt. For those in the Bibliothèque Nationale I have depended on the printed catalogue, which has reached as far as HUN. Brunet, of course, has been of great help and so has Van Praet, *Catalogue des livres imprimés sur vélin de la bibliothèque du roi*, 5 tom. in 4 vols. 1822–1828, and *Cat. des livres...qui se trouvent dans les bibliothèques tant publiques que particulières*, 4 vols.

dozen passages which seemed prejudicial to certain families or to Louis XI. (See *Journal de Jean de Roye*, edited by B. de Mandrot for the Soc. de l'Hist. de France, 2 vols. 1894, pp. viii–xii.)
[1] See Renouard and Delalain.

1824–1828[1]. His descriptions are sometimes fuller than Brunet's, and the second part of his work is furnished with an index of printers and publishers. A good many titles I owe originally to Panzer. The following sale-catalogues have been helpful:

> La Vallière, 4 vols. 1783.
> Maccarthy, 2 vols. 1875.
> Yemeniz, 1867.
> A.-F. Didot, 1878 and 1879.
> Sunderland, 2 vols. 1881.
> Seillière, 1887 (London) and 1900 (Paris).
> Lakelands, 1891.
> Ruble, 1899.

Of these the descriptions in the Didot and Sunderland catalogues are particularly full and trustworthy.

Some titles have come from booksellers' catalogues: Morgand, Tross, Rosenthal, Voynich, and Quaritch's *General Catalogue*, vol. VI. Special mention must be made of the catalogue of the library formed by Baron James de Rothschild at Paris (3 vols. 1884–1893), the work of that accomplished scholar and bibliophile, Émile Picot, by whose name I have cited it. The fifty items recorded by M. Delalain in his *Notice complémentaire* are indicated by an asterisk, while for the twenty-two mentioned by him in his first *Notice* I have given a specific reference.

Finally I must record my grateful thanks to Mr E. Burrell of the Cambridge University Library, who has added some thirty or forty titles to my list and has given me most valuable assistance in the work of hunting out and verifying descriptions.

ABBREVIATIONS

> B.M.   = British Museum.
> B.N.   = Bibliothèque Nationale.
> Bod.   = Bodleian Library.
> U.L.C. = University Library, Cambridge.

1512

1. Eutropius...Paulus Diaconus*.
   B.M.; B.N.
2. Johannes Surgetus. *Militaris disciplinae Enchiridion.*
   With Jean Petit.
   U.L.C., Q*. 12. 53 (F).

1514

3. *Le grand Coustumier de France.*
   Brunet, I. 345.

[1] Cited as Van Praet (1) and Van Praet (2).

4. *Les grandes chroniques.* April 14, after Easter.
   Fitzwilliam Museum, Cambridge.
5. Alain Bouchard. *Les grandes croniques de Bretaigne.* November
   25. With numerous woodcuts.
   B.N.; Cat. Didot (1878), No. 705; Bib. Sund. I. No. 1854.
6. Montjoye*. *Le pas des armes.* December 23.
   Brunet, II. 993.
7. *Questiones fructuosissime ac practabiles per arresta supremi
   senatus Parisiensis curie...decise.* November 16.
   Brunet, V. 542.
8. Jean de Selve. *Tractatus beneficialis...legum ac principum
   palaciis...versatilis.* April 29.
   U.L.C., O*. 16. 16.

1515

9. *Les grandes chroniques* (a new edition of No. 4).
   For vellum copies of this and No. 4 see Van Praet, 2nd pt. III.
   Nos. 95 and 96.
10. *Le grant stille et prothocole de la chancellerie de France.* February
    18, 1514 (O.S.).
    Brunet, V. 539.
11. *Stilus supreme curie parlamenti.*
    Brunet, V. 242. As Brunet only gives the year, this might be
    1516 (N.S.).

1516

12. *Le grand Coustumier de France.* March 28 (after Easter).
    Brunet, I. 345.
13. *Aureus (de utraque potestate temporali et spirituali) libellus ad hunc
    usque diem non vivus. Somnium Viridarii vulgariter nuncupatus.*
    A Latin version of the *Songe du Verdier*, edited by Gilles
    d'Aurigny of Beauvais.
    B.M.
14. *Lhystoire du sainct-graal.* September 25.
    Quaritch, *General Catalogue*, VI. 3781; Brunet, V. 48.

1517

15. *Le Mirouer historial.* February 1516 (prob. O.S.).
    A compilation from various authors, including Gaguin.
    Brunet, II. 1439.
16. Jean Bouchet. *Le Temple de bonne renommée.* January 2, 1516
    (O.S.). The privilege is dated January 10, 1516 (O.S.).
    A panegyric in verse on Charles de La Trémoille, who had
    been mortally wounded at Marignano.
    Picot, I. No. 505.

17. George Chastelain. *Le Temple de Jehan Bocace.* Jean Bouchet.
(1) *L'instruction du jeune prince* (in prose); (2) *Le Chappelet des princes* (50 *rondeaux* +5 *ballades* addressed to Charles de La Trémoille); (3) *Lepistre de la royne Marie a son frere Henry roy Dangleterre.*
Picot, I. No. 506; Van Praet, v. No. 91.

18. *Le Nouveau Monde et Navigations faites par Emeric de Vespuce Florentin.* The privilege is dated January 10, 1516 (O.S.).
B.M.

19. *La mer des histoires et croniques de France**, vols. I (October 31, 1517) and II (October 29, 1517).
Harrisse, *Excerpta Colombiniana*, pp. xiii–xiv.

20. *Les ordonnances royaulx sur le faict des tailles aydes et gabelles.* Privilege of July 27.
Bod.; Brunet, IV. 217; Van Praet, VI. No. 57.

1518

21. *Lordre tenu et garde en la notable...assemblee des troys etatz...convoquez en la ville de Tours.* Privilege of this year.
Brunet, IV. 223. An official account of the Estates of 1484.

22. Francescus Patricius. *De institutione reipublicae libri novem.* November 22.
U.L.C., Sel. 3. 205.

23. Baptistus Fulgosus. *De dictis factisque memorabilibus collectanea.* B.M.

24. Apuleius. *L'Asne dore...translate par Guillaume Michel.*
Cat. La Vallière, II. No. 3842.

1519

25. F. Patricius. *Enneas de regno et regis constitutione.* April 16, ad Romanum calculum.
U.L.C., Sel. 3. 206.

26. *La mer des histoires et croniques de France*, vols. III and IV. March 10, 1518 (O.S.).
Van Praet (2), III. No. 16.

27. *Genealogies faits et gestes des saints peres Papes.*
B.M.; Van Praet, v. No. 23. A translation, ascribed by Du Verdier to Pierre Desrey, of Platina's *Vitae Pontificum.*

1520

28. F. Patricius. *De institutione reipublicae.* September 10, 1520.
U.L.C., O. 8. 20[1]. With autograph of William Cecil and with W. C. on the binding. A new edition of No. 21.

29. F. Patricius. *Livre tres fructueux et utile a toute personne et administration de la chose publicque.* April 30.
B.M.; Brunet, IV. 441. A translation of No. 28.

30. Erasmus. *De la declamation des louenges de folie*. August 2,
1520.
    B.N. This is perhaps the translation made by George Halewin,
    a great-nephew of Philippe de Commines, of which Erasmus
    complained that it was not very faithful (see P. S. Allen, *Opus
    Epist. Erasmi*, III. 62, and letter No. 660).
31. *La genealogie des tres chretiens roys de France*. October 27, 1520.
    Brunet, II. 1528.

1521

32. Suetonius*. *La tres illustre vie...des douze Cesars*. February 16,
1520 (O.S.).
    Brunet, v. 583; Cat. Didot (1878), No. 686.
33. *La genealogie des tres chretiens roys de France*. March 20, 1520
(O.S.).
    Van Praet (2), III. No. 93. A new edition of No. 31.
34. *Stille observe et garde par devant le Prevost de Paris*.
    Brunet, v. 541.
35. Petrarch*. *Des remedes de l'une et l'autre fortune*. March 15,
1520 (O.S.).

1522

36. *Les ordonnances royaulx sur le faict des tailles*, etc.
    Brunet, IV. 217. A new edition of No. 20.
37. *Les coustumes du pays et duche de Bourbonnoys*.
    Cat. Yemeniz, No. 449.
38. Lubin Dallier. *De Mandatis quae apostolica vocantur*. 1521 (O.S.).
    Printed by P. Vidoue.
    B.N.; L. Delaruelle, *Nicole Bérault* (*Musée Belge*, No. 8), p. 306.

1523

39. *Ysaie le triste*.
    Seillière Cat. 1147.
40. Budé. *Sommaire et epitome du livre de Asse fait par le com-
mandement du roi par maître Guillaume Budé*. February 20,
1522 (O.S.).
    B.N.

1524

41. Tiraqueau. *De legibus connubialibus*. November 30.
    U.L.C., Q*. II. 20 (D).
42. Commines. *Cronique et hystoire*. April 26.
    B.N.; Cat. Maccarthy, II. No. 4534.
43. —— *Cronique et hystoire*. September.
    B.M.; B.N.
44. Petrarch. *Des remedes de l'une et autre fortune*. March 15, 1523
(O.S.).
    Brunet, IV. 567. A new edition of No. 35.

45. Jacobus Merlinus. *Tomus primus (et secundus) quatuor concilio-rum generalium.* 2 vols.
     Brunet, III. 1658.

1525

46. Nicole Gilles. *Les tres elegantes, tres veridiques et copieuses annales.*
     December 6.
     B.N.; Van Praet, v. No. 1525.
47. Guy Breslay. *Le Catalogue des Saints et des Saintes traduit du Latin de Pierre des Natales.*
     Pietro de' Natali compiled from 1369 to 1372 a *Catalogus sanctorum*, which was printed at Venice in 1493. It includes personages of the Old and New Testaments, ecclesiastical writers, Emperors who favoured Christianity, legendary heroes like Roland and Oliver, etc.; it is wholly uncritical in character. The translator, Guy Breslay, studied the humanities under Simon Villanovanus at Padua and became a humanist and jurist of considerable distinction. In 1541 he was made President of the Great Council.
     Van Praet (2), III. No. 26.
48. Commines*. *Cronique et hystoire.* September. 3rd edition.

1526

49. Commines. *Cronique et histoire.* January 1525 (O.S.). 4th edition.
     B.N.
50. *Mabrian*.
     Cat. Didot (1878), No. 563 (the only known copy).
51. Alain Chartier*. *Les faicts et dictz.*
     Ib. No. 144.
52. *Le Roman de la Rose*. Fo. Privilege of April 19, 1526.
     Ib. No. 131; Van Praet, IV. No. 1623.
53. *La prison d'amours.* March 6, 1525 (O.S.). Privilege of May 8, 1525.
     Picot, II. No. 1747.
54. *Traictez singuliers.*
     Picot, I. No. 487.

1527

55. *Rondeaux au nombre de trois cent cinquante.*
     Attributed to Gringore.
     Picot, II. No. 1744.
56. Caviceo*. *Dialogue tres elegant intitule Le Peregrin...traduict par maistre François Dassy.* May 27.
     B.N.; Lakelands Cat., No. 651; Cat. Didot (1878), No. 549.
57. *Celestine.* August 1.
     Cat. Seillière, 1890, Nos. 597 and 598.

58. Le loyal serviteur*. *La tres joyeuse plaisante et recreative Hystoire ...des faitz gestes triumphes et prouesses du bon chevalier sans paour et sans reproche le gentil seigneur de Bayart.* September 18.
    Seillière Cat., No. 105; Crawford Cat., No. 272.

59. Guillaume Cretin*. *Chants royaulx oraisons et aultres petits traictez.*
    B.N.; Seillière Cat., No. 332.

60. *L'Histoire et Recueil de triumphante et glorieuse victoire obtenue contre les reduycts et abusez Lutheriens...par treshault et trespuissant prince...Anthoine duc de Lorraine*.*
    Van Praet, v. No. 48.
    By Nicolas de Volcyre. With seven woodcuts.

61. Nicole Gilles. *Croniques.*
    B.N.

62. *Le grand stille et prothocole de la chancellerie de France.*
    Brunet, v. 539. A new edition of No. 10.

1528

63. Pierre Gringore*. *Notables enseignemens adages et proverbes.* February 1, 1527 (O.S.). The privilege is of November 15, 1527.
    Cat. Didot (1878), No. 192; A. Bernard, *Geofroy Tory* (2nd ed. 1865), p. 255.

64. *La conqueste de grece.* February 8, 1527 (O.S.).
    B.M.

65. *Perceforest.* 6 vols. May 28.
    B.M.

66. Meschinot*. *Les lunettes des princes.* October 20.
    Cat. Didot (1878), No. 160.

67. *Meliadus de Leonnoys*.* November 30.
    B.M.

68. Ovide*. *Les XXI epistres Dovide, translatees...par monseigneur levesque Dangoulesme* [Octovien de Saint-Gelais].
    Cat. Yemeniz, No. 1495.

69. Caviceo. *Le Peregrin.*
    B.N. Dassy's translation revised by Jean Martin.

70. Gaguin. *De Francorum regum gestis.*
    B.M.; Eton College Library; Panzer, VIII. 116; Voynich, III. 1283.

71. *Compendium hystorial des polices des empires...translate de latin en françois.*
    Brunet, II. 195. By Henry Romain, Canon of Tournai. There is an edition of 1509 published by Verard.

1529

72. Guevara*. *Libro aureo de Marco Aurelio.*
    Panzer, VIII. 116.

73. Alain Chartier*. *Les Œuvres.*
    B.N.; Cat. Ruble, No. 128; Seillière Cat., No. 269.

74. Dionysius of Halicarnassus*. *Historiae in XI libros digestae.*
    Privilege of March 4, 1528 (O.S.).
    U.L.C., I*. 9. 32 (C).

75. Jean de Bourdigné. *Histoire aggrégative des annales et croniques d'Anjou.* January 1529 (N.S.).
    With two publishers of Angers. Since the vellum copies are dated October 1529, the date of the paper copies, which would naturally be printed first, must be N.S.
    B.N. (2 copies on vellum); Bib. Sund. 1. No. 1897.

76. Jean Bertaud. *Encomium trium Mariarum.*
    B.N. (3 copies); Bib. Mazarine (2 copies); Van Praet, v. No. 139; A. Bernard, *Geofroy Tory,* pp. 259 ff.

77. Virgil. *Les œuvres.*
    Van Praet, IV. No. 102. The *Eclogues* and *Georgics* are in the translation of Guillaume Michel and the *Aeneid* in that of Octovien de Saint-Gelais.

78. Cicero. *Les Offices.*
    Brunet, II. 52.

79. *Ordonnances nouvellement faictes par le Roy.* January 21, 1528 (O.S.).
    Brunet, IV. 215.

1530

80. *Le Roman de la Rose.* March, 1529, before Easter.
    Trin. Coll. Cambridge. With woodcuts.

81. Josephus*. *L'histoire escripte premierement en grec par* Josephus le Juif...*Et en apres mise en latin dont elle a este depuis faicte françoyse.*
    This translation has been attributed to Claude de Seyssel.
    Cat. Didot (1881), No. 483.

82. Estienne Daigue*. *Singulier Traicte, contenant la propriete des Tortues, Escargots, Grenoilles....*
    A French translation of an extract from the author's Latin commentary on Pliny. Estienne de l'Aigue (as his real name was) was often employed on diplomatic missions by Francis I. He died young at Avignon in 1538.
    Morgand, No. 42 (November 1897), No. 30136.

83. *Perceval le Gallois.*
    B.M. The only known edition.

84. Froissart.
    With Jean Petit.
    B.N.; Mr E. P. Goldschmidt.

85. Jehan du Pontalais*. *Contrediz de Songecreux.* May 2.
    Cat. Didot (1878), No. 193.

86. Martin Le Franc*. *Le Champion des Dames.*
    B.M.

87. *Stilus supremae curiae Parisiensis et Tolosani.* July.
    Delalain, p. 8; Brunet, v. 542.

88. Budé. *Sommaire et epitome du livre de Asse.* January 3, 1529 (O.S.).
    B.N.

1531

89. Nicole Gilles*. *Les tres elegantes et copieuses annales.* 2 vols. September 7.
    From Cat. Baillieu, No. 99.
90. Alain Bouchard. *Les Croniques Annales des pays dangleterre et Bretaigne.* September.
    With Jean Petit.
    U.L.C., Sel. 2. 58; Bib. Sund. 1. No. 1855; Van Praet, v. No. 168. A new edition of No. 5 with a new title and with additions by another hand than Bouchard's.
91. *Le Roman de la Rose.* Fo. June 9.
    With Jean Petit.
    B.M.; Fitzwilliam Museum, Cambridge; Mr E. P. Goldschmidt. This edition has the same small cuts as No. 80, with one new one, and with a large woodcut over the Prologue.
92. Jacques de Guise*. *Les Illustrations de la Gaule belgique.* Fo. Vol. 1.
    With F. Regnault.
    Mr E. P. Goldschmidt; Bib. Sund. 1. No. 5919.
93. Quinte Curce*. February 20, 1530 (O.S.).
    Translated for Charles the Rash by Vasco Fernandez, Conde de Lucena, a Portuguese gentleman who was as familiar with French as with his native tongue.
    Brunet, II. 451.
94. *Le Mirouer historial.*
    Brunet, II. 1439. A new edition of No. 15.
95. *Les ditz moraulx des philosophes.*
    Brunet, II. 766.
96. *Proverbiorum vulgarium libri tres.*
97. *Treize questions d'amour.*
    A rendering of the fourth book of Boccaccio's *Il Filocolo*, a complete translation of which did not appear till 1542.
    Brunet, I. 1015; Panzer, VIII. 137.
98. Guevara. *Livre dore.*
    B.N.
99. Franciscus Patricius. *Enneas de regno et regis institutione.* September 1.
    U.L.C., O. 8. 20² (sel.), bound in the same volume with No. 28.
100. Jean Lemaire. *Les Illustrations de Gaule.*
    Brunet, III. 964.
101. Pedro Belluga. *Speculum principum ac iustitiae.* January 29, 1530 (O.S.).
    B.N.; Panzer, VIII. 137.
102. *Sidrach.*
    Brunet, v. 606.

103. J. Caesar. *Les euvres et breves expositions*....with P. de Preux. Brunet, I. 1459. Gaguin's translation.

1532

104. Jacques de Guise*. *Les Illustrations de la Gaule belgique.* Vols. II and III.

Vol. III is dated 1532; there is no date to vol. II. The three volumes are generally found bound up together. Mr Goldschmidt's copy, formerly in the Sunderland library, has the autograph of *Chappuys* on the first title-page. This may be Claude Chappuy (*circ.* 1505–*circ.* 1572) who in 1523 was *sommelier de chapelle* in the royal household and later held a post in the royal library at Fontainebleau. (See Tilley, *Literature of the French Renaissance*, I. 90–91.)
See above, No. 92.

105. *Registre des ans passez et choses dignes de memoire advenues puis la creation du monde jusques en lan mil cinq cens XXXII**. April 6 (after Easter).

Cat. Yemeniz, No. 2655; Lakelands Cat., No. 725. A French abridgement of the *Cronica cronicarum.* With woodcuts.

106. *Les Coutumes anciennes de Lorris.*
Brunet, II. 372.

107. Gilles Corrozet*. *La Fleur des Antiquités.*
B.N.

108. *Novus Orbis Regionum ac Insularum veteribus incognitarum.*
Bib. Sund. I. No. 263.

109. Villon*. *Les Œuvres.* July 20.
B.M.; Cat. Ruble, No. 129.

110. Coquillart. *Les Œuvres.*
B.N. (2 copies); Cat. Ruble, No. 132.

111. *Pathelin.*
Brunet, IV. 434.

112. Gringore. *Le Chasteau de Labour.*
Picot, I. No. 493.

113. Plinius. *Historiae Naturalis libri XXVII.* October.
With Jean Petit.
U.L.C., L. 7. 21. Edited by Pierre Danès under the name of his servant "Bellocirius."

1533

114. Villon*. *Les Œuvres.* September 30.
B.M.; Cat. Didot (1881), No. 207.

115. *Libri de re rustica**. February 1533 (? O.S.).
With Jean Petit, who seems to have used the Roman method. (See above, p. 198.)
U.L.C., L. 8. 19.

1534

116. Piero Crescenzi. *Le bon Mesnager.* January 15, 1533 (? O.S.).
Brunet, II. 417. See A. Bernard, *Geofroy Tory*, pp. 264–265.

117. Guillaume Telin. *Bref sommaire des sept vertus, sept arts liberaux*
....February 12, 1533 (? O.S.).
See Brunet for the full title; Brunet's copy was later in the
Ruble collection (Cat. Ruble, No. 688).

118. Guevara. *Livre dore de Marc Aurele.*
Brunet, II. 1797.

119. Josephus. *De lantiquitez judaïques.* April 15 (after Easter).
Brunet, III. 571.

120. Pius II. *Asiae Europaeque elegantissima descriptio.*
With Claude Chevallon.
B.M. (2 copies, one with the name of Du Pré on the title
page, the other with that of Chevallon).

121. F. Patricius. *De institutione reipublicae.* January 1, 1534.
With Jean Petit.
Panzer, VIII. No. 3176.

122. *Ordonnances nouvelles faictes par le Roy...touchant les Legyons
des gens de pied par lui ordonnez et mis sus par les provinces pour
la tuition et deffence du Royaulme.*
Harrisse, *Exc. Colomb.*, No. 172.

123. Arnoul Ruzé. *Traités de droit canon.*
The author (*circ.* 1485–*circ.* 1550) was professor of civil and
canon law at Orleans and *scholasticus* (*i.e.* Chancellor) of the
University. Later he was appointed a Master of Requests and
a Councillor of the Paris *Parlement.*

1535

124. J. Filippo Foresti of Bergamo. *Supplementum Chronicarum.*
With Simon de Colines, but not printed by him. See Ph.
Renouard, *Bibliographie des éditions de S. de C.* p. 247.
This compilation was first printed at Brescia in 1485.

125. Jean Bouchet. *Les Triumphes de la noble et amoureuse dame.*
B.N.; Cat. La Vallière, II. No. 3001.

126. *Ordonnances et instruction faites par feu de bonne memoire les
roys Charles VII...François I.*
Tross, V (1872), 2785.

127. La Hogue. *Le Livre de Facet translate de latin en françoys et mys
en forme de rhetorique par Jacques de Lahogue.*
Brunet, III. 372.

128. *Le grand Coustumier.* October 20.
Brunet, I. 345. A new edition of No. 12.

1536

129. *Concordata inter...Papam Leonem X et...Franciscum primum.*
U.L.C., Acton 6. 9. 33. With a commentary and two treatises
by Pierre Rebuffy.

130. *Les Coustumes, Statuts particuliers de la plupart des bailliages et seneschaucees et prevostez royaulx du Royaulme de France*.*
     With Poncet Le Preux.
131. Jean Bouchet. *Les anciennes et modernes genealogies des Rois de France.*
     B.N.
132. *La Mer des histoires.* 2 vols. (I. April, after Easter; II. May 2).
     Brunet, III. 1642.

1537

133. Jean Bouchet*. *Les Annales d'Aquitaine.*
     Seillière Cat., No. 171.
134. Pedro Belluga. *Speculum Principum ac Justitiae.*
     Delalain, p. 8.
135. Jean Boutillier. *Le grand coustumier general de practique oultrement appelle Somme Rurale.* December 15, 1536.
     B.N.; Delalain, p. 8.
136. Guillaume Petit. *Hortus fidei apostolorum.*
     Delalain, p. 8.

1538

137. Nicole Gilles. *Les Annales et chronicques.* 2 vols.
     B.N.
138. Guillaume Petit. *La formation de l'homme.*
     Delalain, p. 9.

1539

139. *Divi Pauli Epistolae.* March 1538 (O.S.). 16mo.
     With S. de Colines (see Ph. Renouard, *op. cit.* p. 294).
     U.L.C., I. 35. 29. With a commentary by Jean de Gaigny.
140. *Recueil de divers histoires touchant les situations de toutes regions et pays contenuz es trois parties du monde...Nouvellement traduict de latin en françoys*.* December 15.
     Brunet, II. 747, and IV. 1164. From a Latin work by Johann Boem (Augsburg 1520; Lyons 1541), which had a considerable vogue in the sixteenth century. There is an English and an Italian translation.
141. P. Emilio. *De rebus gestis Francorum libri X.*
142. Cicero. *Les Offices. Le livre d'Amitie. Le livre de Vieillesse. Les Paradoxes. Le Songe de Scipio.* 2 vols.
     Brunet, II. 53.
143. *De doctrina moriendi.* March 19, 1538 (O.S.).
     U.L.C., K*. 13. 53 (G).
144. *Ordonnances royaulx sur le faict de la justice et abbreviation des proces*.* September 6.
     Brunet, IV. 215; Maccarthy, I. Nos. 1280 and 1282. Printed at Rouen and Paris. Du Pré published another edition in the same year (Maccarthy, I. 1281).

1540

145. *Les Coustumes des duchez contez et chastellenies du bailliage de Senlis*....*
     Seillière Cat., No. 328.
146. Guevara*. *Lorloge des Princes.*
     B.N.; Cat. Didot (1879), No. 224. With a large woodcut representing Francis I surrounded by his Court.
147. *Ordonnances royaulx*, etc.
     Brunet, IV. 216. A new edition of No. 144.

1541

148. Seyssel*. *La grande monarchie de France.* December 31.
     U.L.C., U*. 7. 41 (F).
149. *Historiae ecclesiasticae scriptores latini.*
     With F. Regnault.
     Delalain, p. 9.
150. *Biblia Sacra.*
     U.L.C., I. 23. 28. Printed by S. de Colines (see Renouard, *op. cit.* p. 337).
151. G. Postel. *De magistratibus Atheniensium.*
     With Michel Vascosan.
     U.L.C., Z. 11. 9; B.M.; Bod.
152. Nicolas de Mailly. *La diverse cognoissance.*
     Brunet, III. 1319.
153. Cicero. *Les Offices*, etc. 2 vols.
     B.N. A reprint of No. 142.

1542

154. *Ordonnances royaulx.*
     Brunet, IV. 216. A new edition of No. 144 with a supplement.
155. *Tractatus iuris regalium.*
     Delalain, p. 3. By Arnoul Ruzé (see above, No. 123).

1543

156. Lactantius. *Les divines institutions.* February 9, 1542 (O.S.).
     Bib. Sund. I. No. 7195; Van Praet, I. No. 375. Translated by Rene Famé.
157. *Novum Testamentum.*
     U.L.C., I. 33. 23. With Simon de Colines (see Renouard, *op. cit.* p. 381).
158. *Ordonnances royaulx...sur le faict de ladmirauté.* March 29 (after Easter).
     U.L.C., $\dfrac{\text{Syn}}{7}$ 54. 17 (2). Printed at Rouen.

1544

159. Guevara. *Du mepris de la court.*
     B.N.

160. Osiander. *Harmoniae Evangelicae...libri quatuor.*
     U.L.C., Td. 54. 37. With woodcuts.
161. Michel Amboise. *Le Guidon des gens de guerre.* March 15, 1543
     (O.S.).
     Brunet, *Supp.* 1. 36.
162. Contarini. *Des magistrats et republique de Venise.*

1545

163. *Antididagma seu Christianae et Catholicae religionis propugnatio.*
     U.L.C., B*. 6. 55 (F).
164. Jean Lemaire. *Le promptuaire des conciles de l'eglise catholique.*
     Brunet, III. 965.
165. Vives. *L'institution de la femme chrestienne.*
     Brunet, V. 1334.
166. *Tractatus de modo generalis Concilii celebrandi.*
     U.L.C., G. 2. 80. Written by a nephew of the great mediaeval
     jurist, Guillaume Durand, the author of the *Speculum judiciale.*
     He succeeded him in the see of Mende in 1296.
167. Carolus Degrassalius. *Regalium Franciae libri duo iura omnia
     et dignitates christianiss. Galliae regum continentes.*
     By Charles de Grassaille (1495–1582), a councillor of the
     presidential court at Carcassonne.
     Bib. Sund. I. No. 3776.
168. Antoine Demery. *Anthidote contre la Peste.*
     B.N. Demery was a physician, born at Abbeville.

1546

169. Commines. *Cronique et histoire.*
     B.N.
170. *Methodica iuris utriusque traditio...Conradi Lagi iurisconsulti*
     January 29, 1545 (O.S.).
     Delalain, p. 7.

1547

171. Nicole Gilles. *Croniques et Annales de France.* 2 vols.
     B.N.; Delalain, p. 9, reproduces the title-page.

1548

172. *Instructions sur le faict de la guerre*.
     With Vascosan, who printed it.
     Van Praet, III. No. 81.

1549

173. *Instructions sur le faict de la guerre.*
     Seillière Cat., No. 581. 2nd ed.
174. Nicole Gilles. *Croniques et Annales de France.*
     The first edition edited by Denys Sauvage.
     Bib. Sund. I. 5554.

1550

175. *Chronique des Roys de France puis Pharamond iusques au Roy Henry, second du nom**. Par J. T.

Seillière Cat., No. 280 (from the library of François II). By Jean Du Tillet (d. 1570), Bishop of Saint-Brieux and afterwards of Meaux. It was by his influence that his younger brother, the friend and correspondent of Calvin, was re-converted to Catholicism.

1551

176. *Stilus Parlamenti Parisiensis.*

Delalain, p. 10; Brunet, v. 242. A new edition of No. 11.

177. Pierre Bertrand. *Tractatus duo de origine et usu jurisdictionum, sive de duabus potestatibus.*

Delalain, p. 3.

1552

178. Commines*. *Les Memoires...Revues et corrigez par Denis Sauvage.*

B.N.; King's College, Cambridge.

179. Nicole Gilles. *Les tres elegantes et copieuses annales.* 2 vols.

Brunet, II. 1598.

1553

180. *Instructions sur le faict de la guerre.*

With M. de Vascosan.

Bib. Sund. II. No. 6698. 3rd edition of No. 171.

1555

181. *Pragmatica Sanctio...cum glossis Cosmae Guimieri Parisini.* 2 vols. Printing finished 1554.

U.L.C., Q*. 6. 21 (E).

1556

182. Jean de Neufville. *In septem Davidis Psalmos quos poenitentiales vocant commentarii.*

U.L.C., F. 5. 122 (2). Dedicated to the Cardinal of Lorraine.

183. —— *De pulchritudine animi libri V. In Epicureos et atheos homines hujus seculi.*

U.L.C., R*. 5. 62 (E).

1557

184. Robert Ceneau. *Gallica historia.* October.

U.L.C., I*. 8. 30 (B). Printed by Fezendat.

1558

185. *Stilus Parlamenti Parisiensis.*

Brunet, v. 242. A reprint of No. 175.

186. Seyssel. *La grande monarchie françoise.*
     Delalain, p. 105. A new edition of No. 148.
187. *La Legende des Flamens*.*
     Morgand, p. 51 (November 1900), No. 39419.
188. *La chronique du tres chretien et victorieux Louis XI.*
     Maccarthy, 11. No. 4533; Yemeniz, No. 3209; Morgand, p. 45
     (November 1898), No. 32919.

1559

189. Georges de Selve. *Œuvres.* Privilege of August 1.
     B.M.; Delalain, p. 10.

1561

190. Commines*. *Les Memoires.*
     B.N.

VIII

DORAT AND THE PLÉIADE

I

THAT the Pléiade had its origin in Dorat's lecture-room is no more than the literal truth. The affectionate gratitude with which he was regarded by his pupils finds expression in many poems by Ronsard, Du Bellay, and Baïf. Reference will be found to these in M. Chamard's excellent book[1] on Du Bellay, in which, after recording the enthusiasm which Dorat's teaching aroused, he proceeds to consider his merits as a philologist, or, as we should say, a classical scholar. First he cites Joseph Scaliger as saying that he knew no living critic except Cujas and Dorat who could satisfactorily emend good authors. "Non omnibus datum, etiam doctis, sed rarae cuiusdam felicitatis est, bonos auctores corrigere, et suae dignitati atque nitori restituere: nec quemquam hodie novi qui id praestare possit praeter Dom. Cuiacium et Dom. Auratum[2]." Next he cites Scévole de Sainte-Marthe, who in his *elogium* of Dorat says: "Summa eruditione et acerrima coniectura praestans optimi quoque critici laudem quotidie merebatur[3]."

M. Chamard then continues: "We are not, it is true, in a position to verify the correctness of these laudatory remarks; Dorat has not, like Turnèbe, Lambin, or Muret, left critical work which enables us to estimate his merits as a scholar." This is not altogether correct. It is true that Dorat has not left any edition of a Greek or Latin author, nor any volume of *Adversaria*; but a very considerable number of his emendations of one classical author, namely Aeschylus, have been preserved, and they have impressed at least two most distinguished editors of the same author with a very high idea of Dorat's scholarship. In a note on l. 1396 of his edition of the *Agamem-*

---

[1] *Joachim Du Bellay*, 1900, p. 51, nn. 1 and 2.
[2] *Prima Scaligerana*, Utrecht, 1670, p. 13.
[3] *Elogia*, 1602, p. 88.

non Gottfried Hermann boldly says that of all Aeschylean critics Dorat was the chief. "Omnium qui Aeschylum attigerunt princeps Auratus." And my friend Walter Headlam, whose early death robbed this country of a scholar who, thanks to his wide reading and acute intelligence, had an unrivalled knowledge of the Greek mind, once said to me in conversation that, though Turnèbe's emendations of Aeschylus were more numerous, Dorat's went deeper.

It is an interesting question how Dorat's emendations, seeing that he left no published work of criticism, became known. It appears that they may be traced to a copy of Victorius's Aeschylus (published by Henri Estienne in 1557) which belonged first to Scaliger, then to the Dutch scholar, Gerard Vos (1577–1649), and then to his son Isaac, who was born in 1618 and died in London in 1689, having been for sixteen years a canon of Windsor. After his death his valuable library was sold to the University of Leyden, but while it was still at Windsor, Ezekiel Spanheim, who was envoy of the Elector Palatine at the Court of St James, transcribed from the aforesaid copy of Aeschylus numerous manuscript emendations by Dorat, Scaliger, and the elder Vossius[1]. These were used by Hermann *ex libro Spanhemiano*, a volume—probably another copy of Victorius's Aeschylus—in the royal library at Berlin[2].

Hermann of course acknowledged his debts to his predecessors, but an earlier editor of Aeschylus, Thomas Stanley of Pembroke Hall, Cambridge, who drew from the same sources, acted differently. His edition of Aeschylus, which appeared in 1663, brought him great renown, but 150 years

[1] Spanheim was in London from soon after 1670 to 1680. In 1675 Evelyn met him and Isaac Vos at dinner. He was again in England from 1702 to 1710, as ambassador of the King of Prussia, but Vos's library by that time had gone to Leyden. Evelyn writing to Pepys in August 1689 regrets that it had not been bought by some noble Maecenas and presented to Trinity College, Cambridge. Hearne says, under September 21, 1710, that the University of Oxford had offered £2000 for it, but the writer in the *Dictionary of National Biography* is evidently mistaken in inferring from this that Hearne was referring to a recent event (see *Remarks and Collections of Thomas Hearne*, ed. C. E. Doble, for the Oxford Historical Society, Oxford, 1889, III. 51).

[2] See Moritz Haupt's preface to *Aeschyli tragoediae*, ed. G. Hermann, Leipsic, 1852, I. xvi.

later judgment overtook him. In 1812 Charles James Blomfield, afterwards Bishop of London, wrote an article in the *Edinburgh Review*, in which he pointed out that nearly all the striking conjectures proposed by Stanley in the single play of the *Agamemnon*, thirty-five in number, coincided with those of Casaubon; and in the *Museum Criticum* he followed up this exposure by enumerating ninety-eight emendations in the same play in which Stanley silently agrees with Scaliger or Dorat, without counting those in which he expressly mentions them. He further points out that the number of similar coincidences in the *Choephori* amounts to ninety-seven. One source of his information was a copy of Victorius's Aeschylus in the possession of the Rev. John Mitford, the editor of Milton and Gray, which formerly belonged to Samuel Musgrave (1732–1780), the well-known physician and Greek scholar. In the margin of this volume were written the conjectural emendations of Portus, Dorat, Casaubon, and of the person who noted them, whom Blomfield "suspects to be the elder Vossius." He also believes that the conjectures marked P. were not really those either of Franciscus Portus (1511–1581), a Greek who held a chair of his native language first in Italy and then at Geneva, or of his son Emilius, but rather of Casaubon, who was the elder Portus's successor at Geneva. As for the conjectures of Scaliger, they were, he says, "transcribed from a book formerly belonging to Joseph Scaliger, afterwards to J. G. Vossius, then to Is. Vossius, and now in the Leyden library[1]." This is evidently the volume referred to above, for which the links between Scaliger and Hermann are clearly established. I do not know how Scaliger came by Dorat's emendations, but probably at Dorat's lectures, for from 1558 to 1562 Scaliger was at Paris ardently studying Greek, and Dorat was appointed a Royal Professor of Greek in 1558.

[1] In a MS. volume in the University Library, Cambridge (Nn. IV. 6), the greater part of which is in the hand of the physician and scholar Anthony Askew (1722–1774), the following note is transcribed from the first page of a copy of the Aeschylus of 1557: "Gerardus Vossius emit me in auctione illustrissimi viri, Josephi Scaligeri, qui manu sua loca innumera restituit." Scaliger died at Leyden in 1609. Askew studied at Leyden between 1745 and 1750.

As for the Mitford volume it cannot be traced further back than Musgrave, for the person who noted the conjectures in it was not, as Blomfield supposes, the elder Vossius, for he says in one place, "Casaubonus me docuit," and Vossius was not a pupil of Casaubon's, nor indeed, so far as I know, ever met him.

Which was the volume that Stanley pillaged? Probably, says Blomfield, the Aeschylus of Isaac Vossius, lent to him by that scholar, for in his MS. notes Stanley refers expressly to a book which formerly belonged to Joseph Scaliger. It is amusing to note the various phrases in which Hermann records Stanley's thefts from Dorat, from the mild "suum fecit" and "Stanleius sive potius Auratus," to "tacens adscivit," "pro suo vendidit," and finally "suffuratus est Aurato."

In Hermann's notes the name of Auratus occurs most frequently in connexion with the *Agamemnon*. No conjectures of his are recorded for the *Persae* or *Prometheus Vinctus*, only one for the *Septem contra Thebas*, and only a few for the other plays. Blomfield gives rather more than Hermann does—about a dozen—for the *Choephori*. It is evident that Dorat was chiefly concerned with the *Agamemnon*. Here he had fewer editors before him, for the best MS. of Aeschylus, the Medicean or Laurentian, which was the only one used for the first three editions—the Aldine (1518), Turnèbe's (1552) and Robortelli's (1552)—has lost fourteen leaves of the *Agamemnon*, representing about 1250 lines, or three-quarters of the whole play. The first edition to give the complete text of the seven plays was that of Victorius (1557), who had the help of the codex Florentinus, a MS. of the fourteenth century. It was doubtless a copy of this work that Dorat used at his lectures. Pietro Vettori was the greatest Greek scholar that Italy ever produced, and his edition also had the advantage of some additional emendations by the publisher, Henri Estienne, who knew Greek as if it were his native language, and who says that he had consulted not less than fifteen MSS. (many of which, however, did not contain the *Agamemnon*). But even with these two great scholars before him Dorat had in so difficult a play as the *Agamemnon* a considerable field for conjecture, and a good many of his corrections have carried conviction to subsequent editors. Among the more striking are ἀνθαλοῖεν for αὖ θάνοιεν (l. 340), ἔδεθλα for ἐσθλά (l. 769), κληδόνας for ἡδονάς (l. 854), κλύζειν for κλύειν (l. 1181), and ὅρκου πῆγμα for ὅρκος πῆμα (l. 1197), a masterly correction suggested by the τοὺς κακῶς παγέντας ὅρκους of Euripides's *Iphigenia in Aulis*.

II

M. Chamard brings two reproaches against Dorat. The first is that he directed the special attention of his pupils to the most difficult Greek authors—Pindar, Aeschylus, Aristophanes. They are difficult, it is true, especially Pindar and Aeschylus; but more than any Greek author, except Homer, whom Dorat also expounded to his students, they combine high poetic imagination—Aristophanes, at any rate, in the *Birds*—with an unfailing sense of style, and this was just what French poetry needed in order to raise it to a higher plane than it had reached in the hands of Marot. M. Chamard's second reproach is that Dorat perverted the taste of his pupils by introducing them to Apollonius Rhodius and Callimachus, Aratus and Nicander, and even the obscure Lycophron, and by putting these Alexandrian poets of the third century B.C. on the same level as the great classics. In support of the second count of this charge M. Chamard adduces Ronsard's Ode to Michel de l'Hospital, in which he enumerates among the *poètes humains* Hesiod, Theocritus, Apollonius Rhodius, Lycophron, the Greek tragedians and comic poets[1]. As for the first count, we know from contemporary evidence that Dorat lectured on Callimachus and Lycophron[2], and that he amused himself by making anagrams in the manner of

[1] Laumonier adds a reference to the opening of the Hymn to Death (Bl. v. 240) in which Ronsard joins Aratus and Nicander with Hesiod and Homer. This hymn was published in the second half of 1555.

[2] For Lycophron see *Breve exposition du premier livre des Odes*, par I. M. P. (probably Jean Martin Parisien) printed at the end of the *Odes* of 1550 (*Œuvres*, ed. Laumonier, II. 203 f.). For Callimachus we have the evidence of Florent Chrestien, the Greek scholar and future tutor of Henry IV (*Seconde Response de F. de la Baronnie à Messire Pierre de Ronsard* [1563], cited by M. Augé-Chiquet, *J.-A. de Baïf*, 1909, p. 33, n.[3]).

Lycophron, as, for instance, Σῶς ὁ Τέρπανδρος, an anagram (neglecting one of the three ρ's) of Πέτρος Ῥώνσαρδος, which appears on the title-page of the *Odes* of 1550. As for Apollonius and the didactic poets Aratus and Nicander, the statement that Dorat introduced Ronsard to them is only an inference—I believe a correct one—from the fact that we find traces of their inspiration in some of Ronsard's poems.

It may be well therefore to consider at what date the poems in which Alexandrian influence can be detected were written. M. Laumonier's admirable edition of the *Odes* of 1550[1] and his equally admirable *Ronsard, poète lyrique*, where the sources of the poems are given, and their dates, so far as possible, are determined, will serve as a guide.

In the *épode* which concludes Ode III of Book I[2], written according to M. Laumonier in the second half of 1549 and therefore not long before the volume was published, Ronsard prides himself on having introduced to his countrymen, Callimachus, Pindar, and Horace. Now, as a matter of fact, Callimachus is the only Alexandrian poet besides Theocritus (admittedly a poet of the first rank) of whom undoubted reminiscences can be found in the *Odes* of 1550. They all occur in Book I—in the poem above referred to, in Ode II (written in 1547 or 1548)[3], and in Odes IX (to Joachim Du Bellay)[4] and XVIII[5], both of 1549, and they all come from the same poem, the *Hymn to Apollo*[6].

In 1553 and 1554 Ronsard, says M. Laumonier, made a careful study of the *Phaenomena* of Aratus, either in the original Greek or in the Latin verse translation by Avienus[7]. We have evidence of this study in the first line of the Ode to La Peruse (written in 1553), "Encore Dieu, dit Arate, n'a pas[8]," and in the opening of the *Ode à son laquais* from the *Bocage* of 1554:

---

[1] *Œuvres complètes*, I and II.
[2] *Œuvres*, ed. Blanchemain, II. 47.
[3] Bl. II. 43.
[4] Bl. II. 98.
[5] *Veu à Phebus Apollon, pour guarir la Valentine du Conte d'Alsinois* (Bl. II. 122).
[6] Ronsard used the edition of Callimachus printed by Vascosan in 1549.
[7] *Ronsard, poète lyrique*, p. 360, n.[2].   [8] Bl. VI. 43.

> J'ai l'esprit tout ennuyé
> D'avoir trop estudié
> Les Phenomenes d'Arate[1].

In the *Ode sur les misères des hommes*, first printed in the 1553 edition of the *Amours*, the last two stanzas are inspired by Nicander's *Theriaca*, and a *chanson* of the same volume begins with

> D'un gosier masche-laurier
> J'oy crier
> Dans Lycophron ma Cassandre[2],

the first line being a translation of Lycophron's δαφνηφάγων ...ἐκ λαιμῶν, from his poem of *Alexandra*, in which Cassandra prophesies the fall of Troy and the various adventures of the Greek and Trojan heroes. The same epithet of δαφνηφάγος caused Ronsard to alter the third and fourth lines of the fifth strophe of the Ode to Joachim Du Bellay to

> Sur tous ses enfans qui ont bien
> Masché le laurier Delphien.

But this alteration did not appear till the third edition of the *Quatre premiers livres des Odes*, published in January 1555. Among the new odes of this volume there is one addressed to Catherine de' Medici, and in this will be found an obscure reference to the birth and childhood of Zeus, which is evidently taken from Callimachus's hymn to that deity[3].

It must be remembered that in 1551, at the latest, Ronsard left the College of Coqueret and about this time, probably from 1551 to 1553, attended the lectures of Adrien Turnèbe, the Regius Professor of Greek, and that in 1553 Turnèbe edited a volume of selections from seventeen Greek poets[4].

In 1555 Ronsard began to substitute the Hymn for the Pindaric and other forms of the serious Ode; the First Book of Hymns appeared in the second half of that year, and the

---

[1] Bl. II. 162 (v. xviii). An edition of Aratus accompanied by the Latin verse translation of Avienus was published at Paris in 1540 by Jean-Loys of Thielt (Tiletanus).
[2] Bl. I. 130.
[3] Bl. II. 179; Laumonier, *R. poète lyrique*, p. 398.
[4] Laumonier, *R. poète lyrique*, p. 124; *Vie de R. par Binet*, p. 99.

Second Book in 1556 (after August). One of the hymns in the Second Book (Bl. I. ii) is inspired by Apollonius Rhodius, and another (Bl. I. iii) by the same poet and Theocritus, while two, one in the First Book (Bl. I. x), and the other in the Second Book (Bl. I. i), are modelled on the hymns of the neo-Latin poet Marullus—Greek by birth, Italian by adoption—who himself was largely inspired by Callimachus.

It will now appear that even during those years—1545 to 1556—in which Ronsard was most strongly influenced by his enthusiasm for Greek poetry he did not borrow much from the Alexandrians. His learning in fact is derived from very numerous sources, both Greek and Latin, especially from Ovid and Virgil, and, above all, Horace, and we have just seen what he owed to the neo-Latin poet, Marullus. But, when all due reservations have been made, the fact remains that Chamard, Laumonier, Vianey, and others are perfectly justified in pointing out that much of Ronsard's earlier poetry is over-burdened by learning to the point of pedantry; that in his noble passion for the poetry of Greece he did not sufficiently discriminate between sublime poets like Homer, Pindar, and Aeschylus, and third-rate writers like the prosaic Aratus, the harsh Nicander, and the obscure Lycophron; and that as the result of these errors his taste is not altogether sure. He had not that unfailing sense of style and of what is fitting in art which sustains Milton, with all his learning, in the empyrean of pure poetry.

But are these defects to be charged to Dorat's account? Was it Dorat's attitude towards literature which perverted the taste of his pupils? Listen to what Ronsard says in an ode addressed to his former teacher:

> Renommé parmi la France
> Ainsi qu'un oracle viens
> Pour denouer aux plus sages
> Les plus ennoués passages
> Des livres laborieux[1].

For it must be remembered that Dorat was not only an inspiring teacher who revealed to his pupils the glories of Homer

[1] A Jan D'Orat (*Odes*, I. xi).

and Pindar and the *Prometheus Vinctus*; he was primarily a scholar and a trainer of scholars; above all he was a textual critic, who had spent much time on the interpretation of a very difficult author, and one, moreover, who had a singularly wide range of poetic vocabulary. We read in Professor Pearson's preface to Headlam's *Agamemnon* that "Headlam had devoted himself for twenty years to the study of Aeschylus; he had ransacked the whole of the extant Greek literature in order to equip himself for the task of emending, explaining, and illustrating his favourite author." Now Headlam had a warm admiration for the work of Turnèbe and Dorat and Henri Estienne, and he admired it because the width of their reading enabled them to bring to the interpretation of Greek texts an intimate knowledge of Greek thought and Greek expression.

However, when all is said, it is very possible that Dorat spent too much time in his lectures over the discussion of "knotty passages" of "laborious" but third-rate authors, and that in his enthusiasm for everything Greek he was too lenient to the faults of pedantry and obscurity and a prosaic style. For when Dorat was appointed Principal of the College of Coqueret—sometime between 1545 and 1547—the appreciation of the great classical writers for their style was a new thing in France. Rabelais, who published his Third Book in 1546[1], certainly read his Greek and Latin authors more for their contents than for their style. He calls Homer "the paragon of all philologists," and he never mentions either Aeschylus or Sophocles. Dorat's attitude to the classical masterpieces, the enthusiasm for the beauty and elevation of their style which he kindled in his pupils, marks a great advance. But it was not till a generation later that Montaigne—no professional scholar, but a country gentleman who loved the classics with discrimination—could with unerring taste declare that the four greatest Latin poets were

[1] In a *huitain* addressed to Catherine de' Medici (*Poematia*, II. 102) Dorat says "quarante ans lisant publiquement." If this was written just before the publication of the *Poematia* (1586) we get 1546 for the beginning of his public lectures. This is the date suggested by M. Laumonier for his appointment to the Principalship. But *quarante ans* may be only a round number.

Virgil, Lucretius, Horace, and Catullus. Dorat and his fellow-professors were not pedants—Montaigne, who hated a pedant, says that Turnèbe "had nothing pedantic about him but the way in which he wore his gown"—they were too naive and sincere in their love of ancient literature for that, but they were professors and they had the faults of their class. They over-valued ancient learning and they under-valued modern literature, and though they communicated to their pupils a sense of style which was to have far-reaching effects, they led them to attach too much importance to mere learning, and to write for the learned few instead of for humanity at large. This is the fault of the Pléiade as a school; it is to Ronsard's infinite credit that he shook himself more or less free from his early teaching and became a great national poet.

III

Dorat was a first-rate Greek scholar and a prolific Latin poet[1], but he wrote little French verse and what he wrote was poor in quality. Yet, according to Binet, the biographer of Ronsard, he was one of the seven members of the Pléiade, and this statement of Binet's has been accepted without contradiction till the present day and has been consecrated by the inclusion of Dorat's poems in Marty-Lavaux's edition of the *Pléiade française*. Recently, however, M. Laumonier, in his edition of Binet's *Vie de Ronsard*, has re-opened the question. In the first place he agrees with M. Chamard that from 1549 the word *Brigade* was used as a distinctive term for Ronsard and his poetic school. But, as his followers became more and more numerous, he found it necessary to distinguish from the crowd a select band. This, thinks M. Laumonier, he first did in the well-known elegy addressed to Jean

[1] *Joannis Aurati Poematia*, 1586. Since writing the above I have read M. Foulet's remarks on Dorat and Ronsard in the *Revue d'histoire littéraire* for 1906 (XIII. 312–316). Perhaps he rather underrates the debt which the Pléiade owed to Dorat for inspiring them with enthusiasm for the beauties of Greek poetry, but he is quite right in saying that Ronsard wrote Pindaric odes in French before Dorat wrote them in Latin. The ode of Dorat's from which he largely quotes was first printed in 1550. A more elaborate ode, addressed to the Cardinal of Lorraine (*Poematia*, II. 209) is as late as 1557.

PLATE V

Tel fut Ronſard, autheur de ceſt ouurage,
Tel fut ſon œil, ſa bouche & ſon viſage,
Portrait au vif de deux crayons diuers:
Jcy le Corps, & l'Eſprit en ſes vers.

PORTRAIT OF RONSARD

Bastier de La Peruse, written in 1553 (*Œuvres*, ed. Blanche-main, VI. 43), in which he mentions the names of Du Bellay, Thiard, Baïf, Des Autels, Jodelle, and La Peruse. The last of these died in 1554, and his place, says M. Laumonier, was taken by Belleau. Then in 1555 after the publication of Peletier's *Art poëtique* (June) he thinks that the latter's name was substituted for that of Des Autels. With this part of M. Laumonier's argument I do not altogether agree. It seems to me that the mention of the six names in the elegy to La Peruse is accidental, and that Ronsard's object is merely to give in chronological order the chief productions of the new poetic school. Further, it is unlikely that Ronsard should have sacrificed Des Autels, "qu'il estimait," says M. Lau-monier, "d'une façon toute particulière," for Peletier. Lastly, the well-known lines addressed to Belleau in August, 1556,

> qui vins en la brigade
> Des bons pour accomplir la septiesme Pleïade[1];

surely imply that the Pléiade was not completed till the admission of Belleau. But I accept M. Laumonier's view that, when completed, it consisted of Ronsard, Du Bellay, Baïf, Thiard, Jodelle, Peletier, and Belleau. The evidence for this M. Laumonier finds in eight lines of the *Hymne de Henri II*[2], which Ronsard afterwards suppressed and which did not reappear till M. Laumonier reprinted them in the *Rev. d'hist. litt.* for April—June, 1905, p. 256:

> Non je ne suis tout seul, non, tout seul je ne suis,
> Non je ne le suis pas qui par mes œuvres puis
> Donner aux grands Seigneurs une gloire éternelle:
> Autres ce peuvent faire, un Bellay, un Jodelle,
> Un Baïf, Pelletier, un Belleau et Tiard,
> Qui des neuf Sœurs en don ont reçu le bel art
> De faire par les vers les grands Seigneurs revivre
> Mieux que leurs bastiments, ou leurs fontes de cuivre.

These lines were first published in the second half of 1555. At this date Belleau had not yet published a volume of poetry, for his translation of "Anacreon" did not appear till 1556, but some of his poems were already in print, an ode and a sonnet

---

[1] A Christophle de Choiseul, en la louange de Belleau (VI. 202).
[2] *Œuvres*, v. 64 ff.

in Denisot's *Cantiques* (1553), a sonnet in Magny's *Amours* (1553), and his *Papillon* in Ronsard's *Bocage* of 1554. Moreover in 1554 he had begun to translate "Anacreon" in friendly rivalry with Ronsard. He may have been admitted to the select band in that year, and possibly, as M. Laumonier suggests, in the place of La Peruse, but his admission brought the number up to seven, Peletier having been admitted before him—for I cannot accept the view that he was substituted for Des Autels. Peletier had strong claims to admission. On March 6, 1543, when he was secretary to the Bishop of Le Mans, René Du Bellay, he made the acquaintance of Ronsard, his junior by seven years, who had come to Le Mans to receive the tonsure. This interview, at which, if we may take a passage in Peletier's *Art poëtique* to refer to it, Ronsard confided to Peletier his intention of writing lyrics in imitation of Horace and Pindar, laid the foundation of a firm friendship between the two men[1]. In the following year (1544) Peletier, who had studied the humanities for many years at the College of Navarre, published a verse translation of Horace's *Ars Poetica*[2] with a dedication in which he anticipates many of the ideas expressed five years later by Joachim Du Bellay. In the year 1547 he was made Principal of the College of Bayeux at Paris and published a volume of poems, which comprised translations of the first two books of the *Odyssey* and the first book of the *Georgics*, twelve sonnets translated from Petrarch, and a small number of *vers lyriques*. Of these latter those on the four seasons are the most noteworthy, for though unequal they contain passages of real poetry written in an elevated and imaginative style which foreshadows the *Pléiade*. That Peletier was regarded as a precursor of the new school by his contemporaries is shown by the testimony of Estienne Pasquier, who says in one place that Peletier "began to clothe our poetry in the new fashion with great success[3]," and in another that "he was the first to raise our French poets

---

[1] See Laumonier, *op. cit.* pp. 23–26.
[2] La Croix du Maine, I. 426. The earliest known edition, "recongnu par l'auteur depuis la premiere impression," is of 1545 (see H. Chamard, *J. du Bellay*, 1900, p. 33, n. 3).
[3] *Recherches de la France*, III. 7.

to man's estate (le premier qui mit nos Poëtes François hors de page)[1]." Peletier, who was a physician, a mathematician, and a spelling reformer, and only a poet at his leisure, did not publish any more poetry till 1555, when he produced *L'Amour des Amours, Vers liriques*. In the same year appeared his *Art poëtique* (June). It is a question whether these latest publications earned him a place in Ronsard's select company, or whether he was admitted earlier on the strength of his previous services to the cause. The point is not important, but seeing that he resigned his Principalship after only a short tenure and that soon afterwards he left Paris, and successively resided at Poitiers, Bordeaux, and Lyons, and that his earlier volume of poems was remarkable rather for its promise than for its actual accomplishment, I am inclined to place, with M. Laumonier, his admission in 1555—but a little before that of Belleau.

To the piece of evidence as to the final composition of the Pléiade adduced by M. Laumonier I would add another from Du Bellay's *Regrets*. Sonnet CLII (written after his return to France in the autumn of 1557) is addressed to Ronsard, CLIII to Jodelle, CLIV to Baïf, CLV to Thiard, while in sonnet CLVI mention is made of Belleau, Baïf, Peletier, Ronsard, and Jodelle. Does not this confirm the view that the six poets named in sonnets CLV and CLVI, together with Du Bellay himself, formed the select band to which the term Pléiade was applied?

But the term was not in general use, nor did it originate with Ronsard, at least as a distinctive appellation. This is clear from a passage quoted both by Miss Evers in her edition of Binet's *Life*[2] and by M. Laumonier. To his attack on Ronsard (*Seconde Response*, 1563) Florent Chrestien had prefixed a sonnet in which he speaks of *la Plëiade enyvrée*. Commenting on this in the *Epistre au lecteur* at the head of his *Recueil des Nouvelles Poësies*, published in October 1563, Ronsard says, "Il me souvient d'avoir autrefois accomparé sept poëtes de mon temps à la splendeur des sept estoilles de

---

[1] *Lettres*, III. 4. I have taken these passages from M. Chamard
[2] *Critical Edition of the Discours de la vie de Pierre de Ronsard par Claude Binet*, Philadelphia, 1905.

la Pleïade, comme autrefois on avait fait des sept excellens poëtes grecs qui florissoient presque d'un mesme temps," evidently referring to the passage quoted above from the poem in praise of Belleau[1]. In 1566 and again in 1578 we find another Protestant, Henri Estienne—I am following M. Laumonier—using the word Pléiade as a distinctive and accepted term, and in the same year 1578 a poet named Imbert, who had been a fellow-student with Ronsard and Baïf at the Collège de Coqueret, says in a sonnet addressed to Dorat,

> Car je sçay que ne suis de ta docte brigade,
> Et qu'encor moins je suis de ceux de la Pleïade.

But the term did not become common, for it is not found, points out M. Laumonier, either in any of the funeral orations pronounced in honour of Ronsard, or in Brantôme, or in D'Aubigné, or in De Thou, or in Pasquier, or in the first two editions of Binet's *Life* (1586 and 1587). It is only in his third edition (1597) that Binet for the first time says that Ronsard gave the name of the Pléiade to Baïf, Du Bellay, Thiard, Jodelle, Belleau, Dorat, and himself. What was Binet's authority for including Dorat in the list? Evidently neither Dorat nor Ronsard. Otherwise, why did he not give the information in the earlier editions of the *Life*? For he was in fairly close relations with Dorat from 1570, and it was probably in that year that the latter introduced him to Ronsard. M. Laumonier suggests (*Vie*, p. xxxv) that he consulted Florent Chrestien, with whom he was on friendly terms, for the third edition. If this was the case, what is more likely than that he got from him his information about the Pléiade and its members? For, as we have seen, it was Chrestien who used the term in the sonnet prefixed to his *Seconde Response*. It is possible, therefore, as M. Laumonier says, that Dorat passed among the Huguenots for the seventh star of the Pléiade. But if the Pléiade was never a recognised term with Ronsard and his friends, there is no reason for supposing that the place in the select band of seven which became vacant by the death of Du Bellay was ever filled up.

[1] *Œuvres*, VII. 147.

IX

"FOLLOW NATURE"

I

In a powerful but prejudiced essay Brunetière has represented the philosophy of Molière as a philosophy of Nature, derived through the *libertins* of the first half of the seventeenth century from Rabelais and Montaigne[1]. How little truth there is in this theory so far as Molière is concerned has been clearly demonstrated by Faguet, who rightly maintains that the basis of Molière's philosophy is not nature but common sense[2]. In the following pages I propose to consider how far Brunetière's theory is true for Rabelais and Montaigne.

Both Rabelais and Montaigne were saturated with humanism, and much of their thought as well as their learning was drawn from the fountain-head of antiquity. It may be, therefore, well to consider at the outset what was the teaching of Greek and Latin philosophy on the subject of Nature as a guide to life, and to note how far this teaching was followed by humanists in Italy and elsewhere under the influence of the Renaissance.

The doctrine of "Life according to Nature," though by no means the exclusive possession of the Stoics, is chiefly associated with that sect, and it may be conveniently summarised by quoting a well-known passage from Diogenes Laertius's life of Zeno.

Thus the end [according to Zeno] is to live in conformity with Nature (whereby is meant both our own nature and the nature of the universe), and to do nothing that is forbidden by the universal law, which is right reason pervading all things and is identical with Zeus the guide and governor of the whole universe. And the virtue and even flow of life of the happy man consist in this, that his actions conform to his individual genius, working in harmony with the will of the governor of the universe....Now while Chrysippus understands by the nature in conformity with which we must live both universal

[1] *Études critiques*, IV. 179 ff., and see esp. pp. 183–195.
[2] *Rousseau contre Molière*, pp. 300 ff.

nature and the nature peculiar to each individual, Cleanthes, on the other hand, takes it to mean only universal nature and not that of the individual[1].

Cicero's interpretation of this Stoic doctrine is to be found chiefly in his eclectic treatise, the *De finibus*, especially in chapters five to seven of the Third Book. But there are also some passages bearing on the subject in his more distinctly Stoical work, the *De officiis*. For instance, he there explains that we have as it were two natures, one peculiar to each individual, the other common to all men and distinguishing them from animals by its rational character[2]. And a little further on he says, "We must act in such a way as in no wise to oppose universal nature; but, that being safeguarded, let us follow our individual nature[3]." And again, "That is most fitting to every man which is most in conformity with himself. Let everyone then know his own nature and constitute himself a clear-sighted judge of his own virtues and vices[4]." The same doctrine is preached by Seneca, who says in one of his Dialogues that "a happy life is the same thing as a life in accordance with nature[5]," and in the *Moral Epistles* dilates on the text "Omnia vitia contra naturam pugnant[6]."

From the very beginning of the Renaissance Cicero and Seneca played an important part in the development of humanism. Petrarch was steeped in them, and before his discovery of Cicero's letters his Latin style was mainly formed by Cicero's philosophical works and Seneca's *Moral Epistles*. The *Tusculans*, he says, were familiar to him from his youth[7], and he also possessed manuscripts of the *De officiis*, the *De natura deorum*, and the second book of the *Academica priora*[8]. He did not know the *De finibus*.

After Petrarch's death the study of Cicero was carried on at Florence by Coluccio Salutati, who was also a close student of Seneca, and at Padua by Giovanni Conversini, who had lived for three years with Petrarch as a copyist. Among

---

[1] Diog. Laert. VII. 88–89.
[2] *De off.* I. 30, 107.
[3] *Ib.* I. 31, 110.
[4] *Ib.* I. 31, 113–114.
[5] *De vita beata*, III. 8, 2.
[6] *Ep.* XX. 5.
[7] P. de Nolhac, *Pétrarque et l'Humanisme*, 2 vols. 1907, I. 221.
[8] *Op. cit.* I. 228.

Conversini's many pupils was the great schoolmaster, Vittorino da Feltre, who in his school of La Giocosa at Mantua
(1423–1446) taught the Stoic philosophy as part of his regular
curriculum. But in his hands, as in those of all the humanist
teachers, philosophy was confined to ethics, and "by ethics
was meant little more than the commonplaces of Roman Stoic
morality as expounded by Cicero and Seneca[1]." The writings
of Cicero that were chiefly used for this purpose were the
De officiis and the *Tusculans*. Battista Guarino, in his treatise
De ordine docendi et studendi, written in 1559, which claims to
represent the teaching of his distinguished father, Guarino da
Verona, says of Cicero that "none of his works are so attractive
to me personally as the *De officiis* and the *Tusculans*[2]."

The first critical treatment of Greek and Roman ethical
philosophy came appropriately from Lorenzo Valla, the
founder of modern criticism. In the year 1432 he published
his treatise *De voluptate*, in which under the form of a dialogue between Leonardo Bruni, Niccolò de' Niccoli, and
Antonio Beccadelli, he examines the ethical doctrines of the
Stoics and Epicureans and compares them with Christian
teaching. The first speaker is Leonardo Bruni, who defends the
Stoic position that virtue is the true good, but who at the
same time, oblivious of the Stoic precept of "Live according
to Nature," arraigns Nature as a maleficent agent and the
natural man as evil rather than good. He is followed by
Beccadelli, "Il Panormita," who appears not only as the
champion of the Epicureans and Nature—"quod natura
finxit atque formavit id nisi sanctum laudabileque esse non
posse"—but as the advocate of physical pleasure in its most
debased forms. The discussion is closed by Niccolò de' Niccoli,
who defends the Epicureans against the Stoics, but who
maintains the inferiority of both systems to Christianity.
Some modern critics—Voigt[3], for instance, and Symonds—
have chosen to regard Il Panormita as the mouthpiece of
Valla's own opinions, but there seems to be no justification

[1] W. H. Woodward, *Vittorino da Feltre and other humanist educators*,
Cambridge, 1905, p. 221.

[2] Woodward, *op. cit.* p. 172.

[3] *Die Widerbelebung des classischen Alterthums*, 3rd ed., 2 vols. Berlin, 1893.

for this. It is true that the Epicurean champion has the lion's share of the dialogue, but his unblushing hedonism is so greatly exaggerated and so thoroughly alien to the true doctrines of Epicurus that it is difficult to suppose that Valla can have chosen him to express his own views. Rather, the page or two in which he speaks in his own name lead one to the conclusion that he more or less agreed with Niccolò de' Niccoli in holding that there is more good than evil in human nature, that God is Love, and that the Christian religion is one of joyous freedom and not of gloomy asceticism[1].

The *De voluptate* was printed at Louvain by Rodolf Loeffs in 1483[2], but before this date a knowledge of the classical sources of ancient ethical theory had been diffused by the printing-press. The *De officiis* was printed at Mainz by Fust and Schoeffer in 1465, and Cicero's *Opera philosophica* at Rome by Sweynheym and Pannartz in 1471. The *editio principes* of Seneca's works appeared at Naples in 1475, and in the same year Ambrogio Traversari's Latin translation of Diogenes Laertius, which he made by order of Cosmo de' Medici about 1430, was printed at Venice by Nicolas Jenson[3]. The Greek text did not appear till 1533, printed by Froben at Basle. The *princeps* of Stobaeus is a Venice edition of 1535.

How familiar the phrase "Live according to Nature," as representing the ethical doctrine of the Stoics and the Epicureans, had become at the opening of the sixteenth century may be gathered from the famous letter of Amerigo di Vespucci to Lorenzo di Pierfrancesco de' Medici (1503) describing his third voyage, the Latin version of which by

[1] See G. Mancini, *Vita di Lorenzo Valla*, Florence, 1891, pp. 46–48. Had I seen this informing and sympathetic account of Valla before I wrote my *Dawn of the French Renaissance* I should not have described his attitude towards the Church as one "of cold and critical hostility," nor should I have made the blunder of attributing his translation of Homer to Niccolò Valla.

[2] The title of this edition is *Liber pangeticos de vero bono*. There is a copy at the Hague and there was one in the library at Louvain before it was burnt by the Germans. In the Paris edition of 1512 (Badius Ascensius) and in the Basle editions of 1519 and 1540 the title is *De voluptate ac de vero bono*. There is little difference between the two texts, except as regards the framework of the dialogue.

[3] There is another edition, without place or date, which may be a year or two earlier (Hain, 6196; Proctor, 7364).

Fra Giocondo, entitled *Mundus Novus,* obtained a wide circulation in Western Europe. Vespucci, though he had received a good education (which included Latin) from his uncle, a Dominican teacher at Florence, was far from learned, but he says that the natives "live according to Nature and may be called Epicureans rather than Stoics." In More's *Utopia,* the framework of which was suggested by Vespucci's accounts of his voyages and which was printed at Louvain in 1516, and at Paris in 1517, the doctrine of "Live according to Nature" makes a considerable figure. The Utopians, we are told, "define virtue thus, that it is living according to Nature, and think that we are made by God for that end"; "They imagine that Nature prompts all people to seek after pleasure, as the end of all they do...and they call every motion a state, either of body or mind, in which Nature teaches us to delight in pleasure."

Five years before the publication of the *Utopia* More's friend Erasmus printed at Paris the *Praise of Folly,* which he had written in More's house in England. It opens with an ironical defence of folly, which is based on the passions, as against the wisdom of the Stoics, which is based on reason.

Machiavelli's *Discourses on the first decade of Livy* and *Prince* were not printed till 1531 and 1532 respectively, but he began to write them both in 1513. His conception of human nature, upon which his whole theory of politics and government was based, was at the opposite pole to that of his fellow-countryman Pico della Mirandola's treatise *On the Dignity of Man*[1]. He not only believed in the essential depravity of man, but he held that he cannot alter his nature. "We cannot," he says in the *Discourses,* "run counter to the inclinations of Nature," and then he proceeds to give instances —Fabius Maximus from Roman history, Piero Soderini and Pope Julius II among his contemporaries—of men who could not alter their characters[2]. It follows from this that one of the chief functions of law and government is to prevent men from following nature.

---

[1] See L. A. Burd in *The Cambridge Modern History,* I. 203–211.
[2] *Discorsi,* III. 9.

II

All these sources of information as to the ethical theories current in the ancient world and revived at the Renaissance were accessible to Rabelais, but, though the great majority were certainly known to him, they do not appear to have much influenced him. His favourite work of Cicero was not the *De officiis* or the *Tusculans* or the *De finibus*, but the *De divinatione*. His borrowings from Seneca are few[1]. He mentions Diogenes Laertius once, but that great authority on Rabelais's sources, W. F. Smith, says in a letter to me that "there are very few passages that can with anything like certainty be referred to him." Rabelais makes no reference to Stobaeus, whose *Eclogae* were not printed, as we have seen, till 1535, but M. Plattard points out how useful this anthology might have been to him, and thinks it very probable that he actually made use of it[2], as Montaigne certainly did. As for the Renaissance writers, Rabelais had read the *Prince* but was strongly opposed to its theories, and only three passages are cited by Mr W. F. Smith in his exhaustive article on Rabelais's debt to Erasmus as borrowed direct from the *Praise of Folly*, whereas he enumerates about 320 possible borrowings from the *Adagia*[3]. It is different with More's *Utopia*. Rabelais evidently knew it well and he borrowed from it not a few suggestions and touches, but one need not look to this or any other particular source for such a commonplace of ancient philosophy as "Live according to Nature."

We may now consider how far Rabelais's conception of Nature corresponds to these classical theories of antiquity and the Renaissance, and first let us listen to what Brunetière has to say on the subject:

Pantagruel and Gargantua are personifications of physical force, of an unlimited capacity for eating and drinking, of health, of equilibrium and solidity of temperament. It follows that they are also "energies of nature"; and thus they represent at once what is most poetical and most philosophical in Rabelais's work....If paganism is nothing but the divinisation of the energies of nature, there has hardly ever been

[1] J. Plattard, *L'œuvre de Rabelais*, 1910, p. 251.
[2] *Op. cit.* pp. 252–253.
[3] *Rev. des études rabelaisiennes*, VI (1908), 215 ff.

a more fervent pagan than Rabelais, and neither the Renaissance nor even antiquity have produced anything more naturalistic than the poem of this monk and physician. Others besides Rabelais have no doubt loved nature, but one may say, one must say of him that he is literally drunk with it....Infiniment féconde et infiniment bonne, infiniment complaisante aux instincts qu'elle a mis en nous, c'est Nature, qui de son ample sein, comme d'une source intarissable, verse à flots pressés, dans toutes ses créatures, et y renouvelie incessamment le désir et la joie, l'orgueil et la volupté de vivre. Nature est tout en nous, et nous ne sommes rien qu'en elle. Tout vient d'elle, et tout y retourne[1].

Brunetière then proceeds to quote in support of his main contention two passages from Rabelais's book. The first is the well-known account of the manner of living of the Thelemites. I will give it in W. F. Smith's admirable translation:

All their Life was laid out, not by Laws, Statutes, or Rules, but according to their Will and free Pleasure. They rose from their Bed when it seemed good to them, they drank, ate, worked, slept, when the Desire came upon them. None did awake them, none did constrain them to drink or to eat, or to do anything else whatsoever; for so had Gargantua established it. In their Rule there was but this Clause:

DO WHAT THOU WILT.

Because that men who are free, well-born, well-educated[2], conversant in honest Company, have by nature an Instinct and Spur, which always prompteth them to virtuous Actions and withdraweth them from Vice; and this they style Honour. These same Men, when by vile Subjection and Constraint they are brought down and enslaved, do turn aside the noble Affection by which they are freely inclined unto Virtue, in order to lay aside and shake off this yoke of Slavery.

The above passage was written before the end of 1533[3], and appeared in print almost certainly before the end of 1534. In March 1536 Calvin published his *Christianae Religionis Institutio*. A second edition followed in August 1539, in which

---

[1] *Histoire de la littérature française classique*, I. 133.
[2] *Bien instruits*; Smith renders "well-bred."
[3] M. Hauser has suggested (*Études sur la Réforme française*, 1909, p. 51) that these chapters on the Abbey of Thelema were written at a certain interval after the rest, perhaps after the affair of the Placards (October 1534), on the ground that they are a refutation of the doctrine of grace, which he supports in cc. XXIX (Grandgousier's letter) and XL (Tous vrays Christians... prient Dieu; et Dieu les prend en grace). But the suggestion is untenable, for *Gargantua* must have been already published when the affair of the Placards took place.

the six original chapters were increased to seventeen and the whole work was more than trebled in matter. From this enlarged edition Calvin made a French translation in 1541, in which, says Brunetière, "Rabelais read the following words." He then proceeds to cite the passage (not quite correctly) from the French edition of 1560, which Rabelais could not have seen. But this is of no real moment, for the passage in question hardly differs at all in the two editions. It was as follows in the first edition:

Ceux qui ont definy le peché originel estre un défaut de justice originelle, combien qu'en ces parolles ils ayent comprises toute la substance, toutesfois ils n'ont suffisamment exprimé la force d'iceluy. Car nostre nature n'est pas seulement vuide et destituée de tous biens, mais elle est tellement fertile en toute espece de mal qu'elle ne peut estre oisive[1].

Six years later (1547) a similar account of original sin appeared in Budé's so-called *Institution du Prince*, the posthumous work evolved by an unscrupulous editor from the collection of Apophthegms which Budé had offered in manuscript to Francis I twenty-eight years before. Then, says Brunetière, Rabelais, unable to contain himself any longer, inserted at the end of his attack on Lent the well-known apologue, which he found in the Italian humanist Celio Calcagnini of Ferrara:

Physis, that is to say Nature, at her first Burthen brought forth Beauty and Harmony without carnal Intercourse, as being of herself very fruitful and prolific. Antiphysis, who from all time was the Party opposed to Nature, incontinently was envious of this beautiful and gracious Progeny and opposition brought forth Arnodunt and Discordance by Intercourse with Tellumon. They had Heads spherical and entirely round, like a Football, not gently flattened on the two sides like the shape common with Men....Antiphysis extolled her Offspring, and strove to prove that their Shape was handsomer and more engaging than that of the Children of Physis....Since then she brought forth the Apes, Hypocrites and Popemongers, the Maniac Pistols, the demoniac Calvins, Impostors of Geneva, the frantic Puy-Herbauts, Tearers and Renders, Church-vermin, False-zealots, Cannibals and other deformed Monsters, made awry in Nature's despite[2].

"We see then," comments Brunetière, "that Physis or Nature

---

[1] C. II (ed. Chatelain and Pannier, p. 37).
[2] *Pant.* IV. 32.

is Rabelais's divinity, and that this adoration of the energies of nature, invisible or present, circulates, so to speak, from one end of his book to the other." He has omitted to state that, whatever may be said for the apologue generally, the concluding paragraph is Rabelais's reply to two recent attacks, one by Gabriel de Puits-Herbault, a monk of Fontevrault, and the other by Calvin, who had spoken of him in his *De scandalis* (1550) as one "who after welcoming the preaching of the Gospel had been smitten with blindness." Probably it did not form part of the apologue as Rabelais originally wrote it, but was added later.

We may now consider how far Brunetière's interpretation of the two passages is justified. Taking first the account of the Thelemites, it may be pointed out that the abbey of Thelema is not the reasoned conception of a philosopher, but rather the passing dream of a poet, and of a poet who had been a monk and had felt to the full the irksomeness of monastic rules and regulations. The whole point of Rabelais's abbey is that it is the complete antithesis of the monastic system. In it there was to be no constraint, no regulations, no fixed hours, not even a clock. *Fay ce que vouldras* was its only rule, but in practice this led neither to an exaggerated individualism nor to an undue license. For in the first place the knights and ladies are in such perfect harmony with one another that the wish of one is the wish of all; and secondly they "have by nature an instinct and spur which always prompteth them to virtuous actions, and withdraweth them from vice; and this they style honour." But they are so prompted because they are *free, well-born, well-educated, conversant in honest company*. These are essential conditions: you must be well-born, that is to say, have inherited virtuous propensities; well-educated, that is to say, have been trained to virtuous endeavour; conversant in honest company, that is to say, live in a virtuous environment. Nothing is said about the grace of God; we have only the natural man—selected and cultivated, it is true, but still the natural man.

At first sight Rabelais, who in an earlier chapter has made

Grandgousier say in his letter to Gargantua that "the eternal
God had given Picrochole over to the guidance of his free
will and his own understanding, which cannot choose but be
wicked, if it be not continually guided by divine grace[1],"
appears to have veered round from Augustine to Pelagius. But
we must not forget that in his abbey of Thelema he is drawing the picture of a society which had inherited Christian
doctrines and ethics, and which, however much it may have
been imbued with pagan literature and thought, had had a
Christian education. Moreover, the Thelemites had each a
private chapel where we must suppose "they prayed to God,
and God gave them grace." The natural man of Thelema is
poles apart from the natural man of the New World whom
Montaigne glorified in his essay *On Cannibals*, or from the
natural man of Rousseau and the eighteenth-century philosophers.

Rabelais, in spite of his sympathy at this time with the
doctrines of the Reformers, in spite of Grandgousier's letter,
could never have been an Augustinian at heart. His view of
human nature was always an optimistic one. He agreed
cordially with the protest of the Renaissance against the
extreme view of the sinfulness of man which under the influence of St Augustine had prevailed in the Middle Ages.
Though the name of Pico della Mirandola is mentioned only
once in his pages, that noblest of humanists was too greatly
revered in France for Rabelais to have escaped his influence,
and Rabelais would have accorded his warm approval to the
treatise *On the Dignity of Man*. But from taking a hopeful
view of human nature to denying altogether the doctrine of
original sin is a long step, and there is nothing in Rabelais's
writings to show that he took it. His position, in fact, was
much the same as that of Niccolò de' Niccoli in Valla's dialogue, *De voluptate*, a position which after all does not differ
much from that of so orthodox a Christian teacher as Bossuet,
who says: "Nous naissons tout ensemble et bons par notre
nature et mauvais par notre péché[2]."

---

[1] C. xxix.
[2] *Correspondance*, iv. 322.

And here it may be noticed that in one of the chapters at the close of the Fifth Book (xxxvii) which every competent critic recognises as Rabelais's work, he deliberately substitutes for the Πᾶν δεῖ ποιεῖν κατὰ τὴν αὐτοῦ φύσιν of the *Hypnerotomachia* the French sentence:

Toutes choses se meuvent à leur fin[1].

In the second passage quoted by Brunetière in support of his argument, namely that from the apologue of Physis and Antiphysis, it will be noticed that Nature is used in a different sense to that in which it is used in the account of the Thelemites. There it means the nature of each individual; here it means Nature as a whole, Nature as a great creative spirit. In comparing Montaigne's conception of nature with Rabelais's Brunetière well brings this out:

Pour Rabelais, la croyance à la bonté de la nature était en quelque sorte le résultat d'une intuition et plus même d'une intuition, d'une révélation véritable. Il l'a en effet célébrée en poète ou en philosophe metaphysicien, comme s'il était enivré par elle; il la vénère et la chante; il chante la diversité de ses manifestations, la puissance et la fécondité de ses créations, la bienveillance quasi maternelle qu'elle montre envers ses créatures.

It was as a poet that Rabelais sang the praises of nature, and celebrated her beneficent activities. But it was also as a man of science who had held communion with nature neither as a sentimentalist nor as a moral teacher, but as a curious and careful observer of her productive forces and her orderly operations. Before beginning his lessons for the day and before retiring to rest Gargantua has to note the appearance of the sky and the position of the stars, and on fine days part of the afternoon is spent in botanising. Rabelais himself was a keen lover of plants and plant-lore and had a knowledge of botany which in a more scientific age might have been really scientific. In the third book he follows Pliny in admiring the care with which Nature has provided for the perpetuity of plants, by means of ingenious forms of protection, such as pods, husks, stones, etc., for their germs and seeds.

---

[1] See above, p. 118.

But Rabelais's studies were far from being confined to inanimate nature. He had a considerable knowledge of zoology, including comparative anatomy, while his knowledge of human anatomy and physiology was for his day really remarkable. The whole of the eloquent chapter in praise of creditors and debtors (III. 4) is inspired by his admiration for the works of nature, whether as manifested in the fruits of the earth —"O comment nature se y delectera en ses œuvres et productions"—or in the microcosm, man. Nature is essentially for him the mother of inventions, the wise nurse and guide who not only ministers to the physical wants of man but who spurs him on to continuous efforts for the furtherance of his well-being, and the general development of civilisation[1]. The herb Pantagruelion, or hemp, with which Pantagruel supplies his fleet in preparation for the great voyage, is chosen not only as a striking and beautiful plant in itself, but for its "admirable virtues" and the manifold uses to which it can be put. "Messere Gaster, the noble master of arts," is praised as the inventor first of agriculture, and then of all the arts necessary for the preservation of corn, such as the art of warfare, medicine, astronomy, the art of building cities and fortresses, and a thousand other useful inventions[2].

Finally, the priestess Bacbuc, when dismissing the travellers to their ships, cheers them with the assurance that nature has still greater treasures to reveal to them. "All that the earth has produced for you, all that the sea and the rivers contain, is not comparable to that which is concealed in the earth."

The word of the Bottle was simply "Drink," and in spite of the priestess's interpretation its full significance is far from clear. Just as when the priestess bade the travellers imagine before drinking a second time from the fountain, what at first had seemed to all to be pure water now tasted to one like Beaune, to another like Graves, and to a third like Mirevaux, so each commentator of Rabelais interprets the answer of the Bottle according to his own imagination. For Gebhart it means "Return to Nature...Man is not pure spirit...Live

[1] *Pant.* III. 8, from Plin. *N. H.* prologue to Book VII.
[2] Comment Gaster inventa les moyens d'avoir et conserver grain (IV. 61).

without constraint and let your senses attain the end which Nature has marked out for them; but let them stop there, and beware lest the intoxication of pleasure hinder the superior elements of the soul from accomplishing their destiny." M. Abel Lefranc finds in it an expression of the Dionysiac myth, in which the power of wine symbolises the hidden and primordial forces of Nature.

But however great was Rabelais's admiration for the forces of Nature, for her bountiful fertility and ingenious contrivances, he held firmly to a belief in an omnipotent God who not only created but who continued to guide and govern the universe. Nature was but the manifestation of God's energising power. "Do not believe," he says in the first chapter of the *Pantagrueline Prognostication*, "that in this year there will be any other governor of the Universe than God the creator, who by his divine word rules and moderates all things, by whom all things exist in their nature and property and condition, without whose maintenance and government all things would be in a moment reduced to nothing, just as from nothing they have been brought into being." Similarly, in the Almanac for the year 1533, he speaks of "the eternal King who disposes according to his free will and good pleasure everything that is and is done," and in the Almanac for the year 1535 he uses a similar phrase.

It is interesting to notice that one finds God and Nature spoken of in much the same terms by a pagan writer whom Rabelais knew well, namely Galen. In his chief work on physiology, the *De usu partium corporis humani*, with which Rabelais was especially conversant and from which he borrowed the greater part of his description of the anatomy of Lent, Galen expresses his reverent admiration for Nature and for the Creator in similar terms. The third book contains a "hymn," as Galen calls it, in praise of the wisdom and virtue and goodness of the Creator[1]. On the other hand, Galen constantly refers to the justice of Nature, and in a remarkable passage of the eleventh book he points out how she provides not only for the utility but also for the beauty of her works[2].

---

[1] *De usu partium*, III. 10, 237 f.   [2] XI. 13, 897 f.

We find an almost identical conception of the relations between Nature and God in our English poet, Cowper:

> Nature is but the name for an effect
> Whose cause is God.
>
> •   •   •   •   •   •   •   •
>
> There lives and works
> A soul in all things and that soul is God[1].

But Rabelais was not a Pantheist any more than Galen or Cowper were Pantheists. It may be true in a sense to say, with Brunetière, that he "divinises the energies of Nature," but he did not identify Nature with God. He believed in God's transcendence as well as in His immanence[2]. The word Pantheism is too loosely and too readily used in speaking of the creed of poets. Wordsworth, for instance, is often called a Pantheist, but Stopford Brooke is right in pointing out that Wordsworth's so-called Pantheism was a poetic and not a metaphysical thought. "As Wordsworth wanted a thought which he could use poetically, he transferred this idea of God realising His own personality in the whole of the universe to an actual person whom he creates, to a Being whom he terms Nature." Rabelais's conception of Nature, even as "a poetical thought," was less pantheistic even than Wordsworth's. He did not feel in the presence of nature

> A motion and a spirit, that impels
> All thinking things, all objects of all thought,
> And rolls through all things[3].

This poetical pantheism, which resembles that of Maurice de Guérin, as expressed in his beautiful allegory of the Centaur, and even more finely in the wonderful descriptions of the *Cahier vert*, is alien to Rabelais. He had not even that passionate sympathy with nature which we find in some Russian novelists, especially in Gogol and Turgenev, and in the *Years of Childhood*[4] of Serge Aksakoff.

[1] Quoted by Stopford Brooke, *Theology in the English poets*, pp. 48–49. Both passages are from the sixth book of *The Task*.

[2] See J. R. Illingworth, *Divine Immanence*, 1906.

[3] *Lines composed a few miles above Tintern Abbey.*

[4] Translated by J. D. Duff, 1916. See especially the chapter, *My first spring in the country*. See also in W. H. Hudson's recent *Far away and long ago* a chapter *On Animism*, in which he refers to Aksakoff and describes his own feelings for Nature—feelings for which "Animism" is a much better word than "Pantheism."

No; the basis of Rabelais's philosophy was not Nature-worship but Pantagruelism. If in the first two books of *Pantagruel* this signifies little more than a general love of good cheer, in the remaining books it acquires a well-defined meaning. "I recognise," he says in the prologue to the third book, "in all of them a specific form and individual property which our ancestors named Pantagruelism, by virtue of which they will never take in bad part whatever things they recognise as springing from a good, frank, and loyal courage." It was Pantagruel who invented the herb Pantagruelion. "For just as Pantagruel is the idea and pattern of all joyous perfection, so in Pantagruelion I recognise so many virtues, such energy, such perfection, such admirable effects, etc.[1]" In the Prologue to the fourth book Pantagruelism is defined as "a certain gaiety of mind made up in contempt of accidents of fortune." And of this spirit Pantagruel is the embodiment. "He took everything in good part, he put a good interpretation on everything, he never tormented himself and was never scandalised...for all the treasures that the heaven covereth and the earth containeth, in all their height, depth, length, and breadth, are not worthy to stir our affections or trouble our senses and spirits[2]."

III

According to Brunetière Montaigne resembles Rabelais in his pagan conception of nature and life[3]. "On the religion of Nature, and on the worship to which Nature was entitled, Montaigne expresses himself apparently in the same terms as Rabelais." There is, however, says the same critic, this important difference between them, that whereas Rabelais's belief in Nature is the result of intuition or even of a real revelation, Montaigne's is rather a deliberate conclusion, formed after a careful investigation.

Montaigne, like Rabelais, believes in the grandeur and

[1] III. 51.   [2] III. 2.
[3] *Hist. de la litt. franç.* I. 609–613.

infinity of Nature[1].   "Ce n'est pas raison que l'art gaigne le
poinct d'honneur sur nostre grande et puissante mère nature,"
he says in the essay On Cannibals (I. 30), from which Shakespeare borrowed through Florio the well-known lines in the
Tempest[2]. The whole essay is a glorification of the simple
children of nature who dwelt on the shores of Brazil with the
effete races of the Old World.

> Ils sont sauvages, de mesmes que nous appellons sauvages les
> fruicts, que nature de soy et de son progrez ordinaire a produicts : là
> où à la verité ce sont ceux que nous avons alterez par notre artifice,
> et destournez de l'ordre commun, que nous devrions appeller plustost
> sauvages.

But of course Montaigne is not altogether serious in his
defence of his cannibals. Nor does he really believe that the
civilisation of people who roast and eat their prisoners
"surpasses not only all the pictures with which poetry has
embellished the golden age, but even the imagination and
hopes of philosophers[3]." And it is humour, and not irony, as
Brunetière supposes, which prompts the concluding remark
of the essay: "Tout cela ne va pas mal: mais quoi! ils ne
portent point de hault de chausses." For he has just told us
that the only honour paid to a chief in times of peace was that
when he visited the villages which depended on him they cut
paths for him in their woods.

Eight years after Montaigne put the concluding touches to
the essay On Cannibals he wrote the essay On Experience,
which stands last in his book and which in all probability was
the last written[4]. In it he more or less sums up the results of

---

[1] In this conception he was no doubt largely influenced by Lucretius,
whom he ranked as a poet only a little below Virgil, and whom he cites in
his Essays, according to M. Villey, no less than 149 times, the great majority
of the citations being taken from the less technical books, the third, fourth,
and fifth (Les sources et l'évolution des Essais de Montaigne, I. 169–171).

[2] M. Chinard has discovered that Montaigne has borrowed a long passage,
almost textually, from the translation of Girolamo Benzoni's Historia del
Mondo nuovo (Venice, 1565), by Urbain Chauveton, which was published
in 1579. This part of the essay cannot therefore have been written before
that year (G. Chinard, L'exotisme Américain dans la littérature française au
xvie siècle, 1911, pp. 197–201). But the rest of the essay may be a good
deal earlier.   [3] M. Chinard recognises this.

[4] In two places in the essay he tells us that he was fifty-four years of
age. The essay was therefore written between March 1, 1587 and February
1588, when he set out for Paris to see about the publication of a new edition.

his personal experience, and no essay gives us a better idea of his attitude towards Nature at the close of his life. "The laws," he says, "that Nature makes for us are always happier than those that we make for ourselves." "Leave it to Nature" —he is inveighing against doctors—"she understands her business better than we do." "Everything which happens contrary to the course of Nature may be harmful, but that which happens in accordance with Nature must always be pleasant[1]." "Nature is a gentle guide, but not more gentle than prudent and just." "Nature has maternally observed this law that the actions which she has imposed upon us for our needs are also pleasurable[2]."

A great deal of this talk about Nature is mere sentimental rhetoric. There was never anyone less of an observer of nature, whether inanimate or animal, than Montaigne. His sole interest was in man. He had no eyes for the beautiful landscape which unfolded itself before the windows of his library. Trees and flowers play no part in his book. His comparison of his cannibals to the wild fruits of nature is singularly unfortunate, for everyone knows that nearly every kind of fruit under cultivation is far superior to the same fruit in its wild state. He extols nature as a "gentle guide," but if he had meditated on earthquakes and volcanic eruptions or the countless death-toll of the animal world, or even if he had observed his cat playing with a mouse or a bird, he might have written differently.

But when Montaigne sings the praises of Nature he is not thinking of Nature like a Wordsworth or a Tennyson or a Maurice de Guérin. The trend of his thought is clearly shown by an addition which he made in the last essay to the passage about nature being a gentle guide. After writing in 1588, "I search everywhere for her track; we have often obscured it by artificial paths," he added in the margin: "And that sovereign good of the Academics and Peripatetics, which is

[1] Added after 1588.
[2] Cp. Sir T. More in the *Utopia*: "With due gratitude they acknowledge the tenderness of the great Author of Nature, who has planted in us appetites by which those things that are necessary for our preservation are likewise made pleasurable to us."

'to live according to Nature' becomes on this account difficult to define and explain; as is the kindred one of the Stoics, which is 'To conform to Nature.'"

M. Villey's careful investigations have shown that among the authors whom Montaigne favoured during the last years of his life were Diogenes Laertius, Cicero, and Seneca, and that they furnished many of the additions which he made to his text. It was probably then, after reading one or the other of them, that he added the reference to the famous precept of so many ancient philosophies. But he had already quoted it with approval in the previous essay (III. 12) as it was printed in 1588, and it must have been familiar to him from the days when he studied philosophy at Bordeaux. But how did he interpret the word Nature? Did he, like Cleanthes, mean by it universal Nature, or did he, like Chrysippus, include in its meaning the particular nature of each individual man? Beyond a doubt he agreed with Chrysippus. Man must follow Nature, his wise and mighty mother, but he must also conform to his own nature[1]. This is well brought out by Professor Höffding in the few suggestive pages which he gives to Montaigne in his *History of Modern Philosophy*. "Montaigne's defence of the concept of Nature is classical in character. But he carries this concept beyond the limited form in which it appeared among the Greek thinkers. If Montaigne opposes Nature to the artificialities of man, he does so partly because the latter regard certain particular 'forms' as alone justified,

---

[1] Cp. Charron, *De la Sagesse*, bk. II. pref. 2: "La seconde [considération] est des fondemens de sagesse, qui sont aussi deux, vraye et essentielle preud'homie, et avoir un certain but et train de vie. Ces deux regardent nature, nous reglent et accommodent à elle le premier à l'universelle, qui est la nature, car preud'homie n'est autre chose, comme se dira: le second à la particulière d'un chascun de nous, car c'est le choix du genre de vie propre et commode au naturel d'un chascun."

"Nature, as Montaigne conceives it, is indeed Nature, the ruler's sovereign, it is also Isis the mother and instructress of all virtues, but it is also his individual nature, as observation of himself, contact with his fellow-men, and experience of life have revealed it to him; and this is a rather different thing" (Brunetière, *Études critiques*, VIII. 38). Brunetière's views on Montaigne were somewhat modified between his lectures (1900–1901), which are reproduced in the *History of French Literature*, and the article in his *Études critiques*, which first appeared in the *Revue des deux mondes* for September 1, 1906.

and thus overlook the fulness of Nature; and partly because they do violence to certain peculiar individualities, which possess the same right to develop themselves *sur son propre modèle* as do any others[1]."

But here another question arises. What did Montaigne mean by conforming to or following one's own nature? But to answer this we must go back a little and consider the development in his ethical views which took place during the time when he was engaged upon the *Essays*.

The first strong ethical influence that he encountered was that of the Stoic philosophy, and this Stoic phase, so far as precise dates are possible, finds its earliest expression in the essay *That philosophy consists in learning how to die* (I. 19), which he was writing on March 15, 1572. His favourite author at that time was Seneca; but not many months later he came under a new and more potent spell, that of Plutarch's *Lives*, and before the end of the year he also made acquaintance with Amyot's translation of the *Moralia*, which had been published in the previous August. The earliest essays in which we can trace the influence of the Moral works are II. 3 and 4, the latter of which opens with the well-known tribute to Amyot.

Under Plutarch's guidance Montaigne not only developed an increasing interest in moral questions, but he imported a new element into his essays. His earliest attempts had been strictly impersonal; even his opinions and judgments had shown little or no originality. Then, as he gained confidence, he began to exercise more independence of thought, and to give rein to his critical spirit. M. Villey points out the importance of the essay *That we must soberly meddle with judging of divine decrees* (I. 31) in this connexion, an essay which belongs to the early months of 1572. Another essay in which the critical faculty is displayed is that entitled *That it is folly to refer truth or falsehood to our sufficiency* (I. 26), but only part of it can be assigned with certainty to the early period; the rest may be as late as 1578.

Before this latter date his close intercourse with Plutarch

---

[1] E. T. (by B. E. Meyer), I. 33.

had been succeeded by a phase of scepticism, the acute stage
of which may be assigned, as we have seen, to the year 1576.
It was in that year in all probability that he wrote the last
and most important section of the long *Apology for Raimond
de Sebonde*, in which he expounds his Pyrrhonist creed. As
M. Villey has pointed out with admirable insight, it is practically a defence of relativity. "We have no communication
with Being; we cannot know the absolute; we only know
phenomena which are perpetually changing." And in support
of this view Montaigne could appeal to a great revolution in
scientific thought which had taken place in his own day. In
1543, when Montaigne was ten years old, Copernicus had
published, just before his death, his famous *De Revolutionibus
Orbium Celestium*, in which he gave the death-blow to the
Ptolemaic system. "What shall we reap from it," asks
Montaigne, "save only that we need not care which of the
two it be? And who knows whether a thousand years hence
a third opinion may not overthrow the two preceding ones?"
And as with the Ptolemaic astronomy so with the Ptolemaic
geography.

A thousand years ago it would have been heresy to avouch that
there were antipodes; yet see how in our own age there has been discovered an infinite extent of *terra firma*, not an island or a single
country, but a portion nearly equal in size to that which we already
knew. Our modern geographers do not fail to affirm that now all is
found, and all discovered. The question now is, if Ptolemy was formerly
deceived in the grounds of his reasoning, whether it were not folly in
me to trust now in what these latter say.

Even in mathematics there was no security that our knowledge was final. Jacques Peletier had told Montaigne that
"he had found two lines converging towards one another as
if they would meet; nevertheless he could prove that they
would never touch, even if prolonged to infinity[1]."

It is easy to imagine with what relish Montaigne would have
heard of Einstein's discoveries. "If Newton," we can hear
him saying, "was formerly deceived in the foundations of his

---

[1] All this is well brought out by Miss M. E. Lowndes in her *Michel de
Montaigne*, Cambridge, 1898, pp. 148–151.

reasoning, would it not be folly for me to trust now in what this fellow says?"

From the relativity of knowledge he passes on to what interests him still more, the relativity of morals. There is no such thing, he declares, either as sovereign good—that subject of so many violent and bitter disputes among philosophers —or as natural law. "Marriages between near relations are criminal with us; elsewhere they are held in honour."..."There is nothing so horrible to imagine as eating one's father; nevertheless the people who had in ancient times this custom regarded it as a sign of piety and affection." Montaigne would have agreed with Professor Sorley that "different conduct is appropriate to different circumstances or even to different persons in the same circumstances." But though Montaigne held that morality is relative to place and individual and circumstance, he would equally have agreed with Professor Sorley that "morality loses its meaning if the same thing may be both right and wrong" for the same person in the same circumstances[1]. Every man must determine for himself his own standard. "We who live a private life ought to establish a touchstone in our hearts by which to try our actions...I have my own laws and tribunal to judge of myself, and I resort to them rather than elsewhere," and "If Socrates were asked what he could do, he would say, 'Live in conformity with my natural condition[2].'"

The Stoic ideal was not for everybody. It was certainly not for him, Michel de Montaigne; he needed a more ordinary morality, a morality suited to his own temperament and capacity, shaped and moulded by his own experience. And what was true for himself was true for man in general. Man must follow his own nature.

Does this mean that man must follow his own instincts? This was the doctrine which the Italian Vanini preached at Paris from 1615 to 1617, and which one of his disciples, the poet Théophile de Viau, thus expressed in verse:

J'approuve qu'un chacun suive en tout sa nature,
Son empire est plaisant, et sa loi n'est pas dure.

[1] *Moral values and the idea of God*, Cambridge, 1918, pp. 93–96.
[2] *Essai*, III. 2 (*On Repentance*).

But it was certainly not Montaigne's doctrine. He had far too much good sense not to recognise that man is a social animal, and that a world in which every man followed his own instincts would be a world of anarchy.

But it is said that Montaigne was a lover of pleasure, "an Epicurean with an imagination not incapable of Stoicism[1]." True, but his conception of pleasure was not far different from that of Epicurus himself. "If he enjoyed life twice as much as other people," he was temperate and prudent in his pleasures and he preferred intellectual pleasures—books, society, conversation—to sensuous ones. In this spirit he boldly proclaimed pleasure as the end of life, "Toutes les opinions du monde en sont là, *que le plaisir est notre but*" (I. 19). The italicised words were added after 1588, and the edition of 1595 also contained the following new passage:

> Whatever the philosophers may say, the mark at which we all aim, even in virtue, is voluptuousness (*volupté*). I love to din into their ears this word, which they so much dislike; and if it denotes any supreme delight and excessive satisfaction, it is due more to the assistance of virtue than to any other aid.

The increasing licence in thought and language that we find in the manuscript additions which Montaigne made to his text after 1588 has led careless or unsympathetic readers to misjudge his character. He was something far more than a mere *jouisseur* or pleasure-seeker. He had a strong sense of moral obligation, he listened to the admonitions of conscience, he curbed his pleasures by reflexion and self-control. The charming essay *On Cruelty* (II. 11) which may belong to 1578 or 1579, is of great importance for the understanding of his ethical position.

> The gentle ascent, that soft and easy way, in which those take their steps, who are regulated by a natural inclination to goodness, is not the path of true virtue. This demands a rough and thorny road, and will either have difficulties from without to struggle with, or else internal difficulties that are introduced by the disorderly appetites and imperfections of our condition.

But then it occurs to him that by this rule the soul of Socrates, the most perfect that has ever come to his knowledge, would

[1] Guillaume Guizot.

have little to recommend it, for he cannot perceive in him any struggle with vicious desires. He concludes that there are three degrees of virtue, of which the first is to be so formed to virtue that the very seeds of vice are eradicated, the second is, after giving way to the first assaults of the passions, to take up arms and oppose their progress, and the third is to be endowed with an easy and *débonnaire* nature which is of itself disgusted with debauchery and vice. Montaigne then reviews his own character, and says that his hatred of cruelty, his love of truth, his compassion for the weak and the feeble, being all innate, his virtue is only of the third degree. But numerous passages in the *Essays*[1] may be adduced to show that his estimate of himself is too modest, and that his real place is in the second class. He had "given way to the first assaults of the passions," but he had "taken up arms and opposed their progress," and had mastered them in a certain measure. His Stoicism was not merely an intellectual phase; it had a permanent effect upon his character.

Thus in following his own nature Montaigne was not merely following his instincts; he was following a nature which had been strengthened and improved by conscious effort. This effort owed little or nothing to the immediate influence of the Christian religion, but was rather nourished on the precepts of pagan philosophers and fortified by the examples of pagan heroes. His great exemplar was not Jesus Christ, but Socrates. Not that he aspired to tread closely in his master's footsteps, for he made no claim to be "an heroic soul"; it was enough for him "to enjoy loyally his being."

It is interesting to notice how closely Montaigne's ethical creed corresponds with the teaching of so eminent a Christian as Bishop Butler. In the second sermon *Upon human nature* we read that "there is a superior principle of reflection or conscience in every man....It is by this faculty, natural to man, that he is a moral agent, that he is a law to himself." And in the third sermon we are told that "reasonable self-love and conscience are the chief or superior principles in the

---

[1] See especially *On Repentance* (III. 2), *On Diversion* (III. 4), and *On Experience* (III. 13).

nature of man."...These, "if we understand our true happiness, always lead us the same way."

Nothing can be more evident than that, exclusive of revelation, man cannot be considered as a creature left by his Maker to act at random, and live at large up to the extent of his natural power, as passion, humour, wilfulness happen to carry him, which is the condition brute creatures are in—but that *from his make, constitution, or nature,* he is in the strictest and most proper sense a law to himself.

Is not this what Montaigne means by "following Nature"? Man is a law to himself; let him follow his constitution or nature—not his mere animal instincts, or the dictates of passion, humour, or wilfulness, but his higher nature as purified and developed by reflection and conscience.

Montaigne's moral philosophy—though he himself would not have called it by so dignified a name—was founded upon a study of his own needs and character. It was primarily a philosophy for his own use, not for that of the world. "I am not writing as a teacher, but as a student; it is not a lesson for others, it is my own[1]." But all may read with profit in Montaigne's lesson-book. We may learn first to tolerate and then to respect what at the first approach seem to us defects in our neighbours. For men have the qualities of their defects as well as the defects of their qualities. Montaigne's indolence and egotism, for instance, may be reprehensible if judged by an absolute standard, but his indolence, as we call it, was inseparable from his love of meditation, and without his egotism the most valuable part of his book would never have been written. Whatever be our judgment on his doctrine of "Follow Nature," we at any rate owe to it the *Essays.*

Looking back on the results of this inquiry, we see that the attitudes of Rabelais and Montaigne towards Nature were widely different. Rabelais loved and admired Nature as a creative and ceaselessly working force, ministering to the wants of man, stimulating his activities, and holding in reserve for future discovery treasures infinitely surpassing those already revealed. And this wonder-working Nature was, he believed, the manifestation of an all-wise, all-loving and un-

---

[1] II. 6 (*On Practice*). The essay ends here in the edition of 1580.

resting God. He would have delighted in the theory of evolution, regarding it as a theory of growth and progress; and he would have welcomed the modern tendency to see in evolution not a struggle for life or "a gladiator's show" but a continuous effort towards reproduction—a process, not of hate, but of love.

Rabelais was no psychologist, no inquirer into the mainsprings of human character, but he shared to the full the belief of the early Renaissance in the essential goodness and high destiny of man. He believed in the effect of environment and education; but he also believed in the liberty of the individual. It is true that in "the company of man," by the help of his fellow-men and by helping his fellow-men, the individual best attains to true liberty[1]; but the individual must not be sacrificed to the society, he must not be constrained by a thousand petty regulations or be made virtuous by sheer compulsion. It was the rigid moral censorship of Geneva which made Rabelais denounce Calvin as one of the brood of Anti-Physis. Rabelais was no ascetic; indeed he did not sufficiently appreciate the bracing effect of moral effort on character; but, lenient though he was to the aberrations of human nature, especially to those which sprang from hard conditions of life or unsuitable training, he had too much common sense, too much interest in man as a social and political animal, to allow human nature a perfectly free rein, or to claim seriously for man the liberty "to do as he pleased."

Montaigne's praise of Nature is, as we have seen, in a large measure rhetorical, inspired by classical literature, especially by Lucretius, rather than founded on personal observation. He had read little in the book of Nature; his book was man, man in history, man in the contemporary world, above all man in Montaigne. And of man he had at one period of his life a very poor opinion. "The emptiness, the vanity, the miserable condition of man" is the theme of his longest essay, the *Apology for Raimond de Sebonde*, though with his habitual

---

[1] C'est donc en vivant pour la société...que l'homme peut, dans la pratique, déployer et accroître sa liberté (E. Boutroux, *De la contingence des lois de la nature*, p. 185).

and delightful inconsistency he was an ardent admirer of
certain individuals, of Socrates among the ancients, and of his
friend La Boétie in his own degenerate age. But the acute
scepticism of the *Apology* was not an enduring mood, and,
though in one of his latest essays (III. ix) he declared that
"the best man deserved hanging ten times in his life," his
opinion of human nature became higher with advancing years.
Looking back on his past life, he confessed that in spite of its
shortcomings he did not regret it; had he the chance, he would
live it over again. And as the result of his self-examination
he concluded that each man must work out his own moral
salvation. Once his character is formed, a process which calls
for serious effort and self-restraint, he must be a law unto himself; he must follow his own nature. Thus the precept "Follow
Nature" meant no more for Montaigne than for Rabelais
an invitation to licence. It was a recognition that there is
a certain relativity in morals, that we must not judge all men
by the same rigid and absolute standard, that we must make
allowances for differences of temperament and character and
environment.

PLATE VI

TOWER OF MONTAIGNE'S CHÂTEAU

X

MONTAIGNE'S INTERPRETERS

MONTAIGNE'S *Essays* reveal a rich and many-sided nature, and for this reason they have made many friends. Every reader can find in them something particular to himself, something that he can make his own and "incorporate with his own soul[1]." But the sympathy which Montaigne evokes may work in one of two ways. Either you may be drawn to Montaigne and interpret him with a quickened understanding, or you may draw him to yourself and claim him as the advocate of your own opinions or even invest him with your own personality. There is yet a third class, who, while they are powerfully attracted to Montaigne and are unable wholly to resist his spell, regard him with feelings of positive hostility. Such are Pascal and, in our own times, Guillaume Guizot.

Montaigne left two devoted disciples, Pierre Charron and his *fille d'alliance*, Mlle de Gournay. They honoured his memory in very different fashions: Charron by writing a book, *La Sagesse*, in which he arranged and tabulated his master's living ideas like dead flowers in a herbarium, Mlle de Gournay by publishing twelve editions of his *Essays*, beginning with the famous one of 1595 in which she incorporated with the printed text of 1588 all his marginal additions. But both alike were too enthusiastic and uncritical to be of any real value as interpreters.

The first critic of Montaigne who calls for notice here is Jean Guez de Balzac, who in two of his *Entretiens*, written a year or two before his death in 1654, and published in 1657[2],

---

[1] Il ne fault pas attacher le sçauoir à l'âme, il l'y fault incorporer (*Essais*, I. 24).
[2] I have a copy of this Paris edition which belonged to Saint-Amant and has his monogram on the binding. *Entretien* XXXVIII is preceded by a letter dated February 20, 1653, and *Entretien* II is followed by three letters dated July 1650.

discoursed on him, with no great insight indeed, but with average commonsense and a certain measure of sympathy. In the second of these *Entretiens* he occupies himself solely with Montaigne's style and language, but in the first he gives his views on the *Essais* in general. They are the views of a man who, though he had lived for many years a retired life either in his château near Angoulême or in Angoulême itself, had kept in touch, through his correspondents, with Paris thought and society as represented by the Hôtel de Rambouillet and the Académie française.

The influence of Montaigne on Pascal was admittedly great. Stapfer calls the *Essays* Pascal's "profane Bible," and says that it was "the only human book by which his whole being was affected." These words, however, require qualification. Pascal was, no doubt, profoundly impressed by certain portions of Montaigne's book, especially by the latter part of the *Apology for Raimond de Sebonde*; but, if we look a little closely into the matter, we shall see that his knowledge of the *Essays* was very far from being complete, and that for that reason his conception of Montaigne's intellectual outlook and of his design in writing his book goes considerably astray[1].

It has been shown that the edition of the *Essays* used by Pascal was one published at Paris in 1652, and, as his conversation with M. de Saci on the subject of Epictetus and Montaigne took place in 1654, this makes it practically certain that it was during one or other of his two visits to Paris, of which the first was from February to October 1652 and the second from May to December 1653[2], that he made acquaintance with Montaigne. Most probably it was at the time of his first visit; for at an earlier date he had made friends with the Duc de Roannez, and through him he now became acquainted with Mitton, the brilliant talker and incorrigible gambler, and the Chevalier de Méré, the accomplished man of the world, and

---

[1] When I wrote the above I had read but had not in mind the following words of M. Strowski: "Pascal's reading of the *Essays* was more profound than extensive: it was confined to the chapter *On custom*, the chapter *On the force of the Imagination* and the *Apology for Raimond de Sebonde*; the rest he only glanced at."

[2] F. Strowski, *Pascal et son temps*, II. 233–234.

through them, though we have no positive proof of this, he was doubtless introduced to the *salon* of Mme de Sablé in the Place Royale. Now in this circle Montaigne was held in the greatest admiration; Mme de Sablé even declared that the only writers in whom she found the art of "saying things," which was all that she valued, were Montaigne and Voiture. So Pascal, urged by his friends, read Montaigne and came under his spell, especially under the spell of his style. For him he was "the incomparable author of the *Art of conversation*[1]." On January 7, 1655, six weeks after the trance or vision of November 23, 1654 which confirmed him in his desire to separate himself from the world, he left Paris for Port-Royal, and there soon afterwards he had with M. de Saci (Isaac Le Maître), the nephew of Antoine Arnauld and the Mère Angélique, the well-known *entretien* on Epictetus and Montaigne, of which a full report has been preserved.

It is clear from this report that for Pascal Montaigne was chiefly the author of the *Apology for Raimond de Sebonde*. He gives a rapid summary of it to M. de Saci, and in answer to his Port-Royalist friend, who deprecated Montaigne's championship of an antiquated philosophy, he says: "I confess I am delighted to see this writer dealing such irresistible blows to proud reason with her own arms." How thoroughly he appreciated Montaigne's line of argument is shown by the fact that the long fragment of the *Pensées* which forms Article I of Havet's edition and fragment no. 72 of M. Brunschvicg's[2], is largely inspired by the last part of the *Apology*, in which Montaigne expounds his Pyrrhonist creed.

But Pascal was mistaken when he said to M. de Saci that all Montaigne's essays are based on the principle of doubt. He did not realise any better than his contemporaries that Montaigne's book covers a period of twenty years, during which its author's opinions were in a state of perpetual change and development. "My history is a record of divers and

---

[1] In the fragment, *De l'esprit géométrique*.

[2] It is composed of fragments 347–360 of the original manuscript =91 of the first copy. In the Port-Royal edition it appears (with some omissions) partly as *titre* XXII (*Connaissance de l'homme*), and partly among the *Pensées diverses* (no. 27).

variable accidents, and of unfulfilled and, when it so happens, contrary imaginations; whether it be that I myself am another or that I apprehend subjects by other circumstances and considerations....Could my soul find a firm footing, I would not merely make trial of myself but I would give a definite account of myself; but it is still a prentice and a probationer[1]."

Montaigne's scepticism, at least in the acute form which it assumed about 1576, was a passing phase. Though it left its imprint in the development which it gave to his critical faculty, it became considerably mitigated. During the two years which preceded the publication of the first edition of his *Essays* he was pre-occupied with a new design, that of painting his own portrait and making himself the central theme of his book. It was a design which found no favour with Pascal. "Le sot projet qu'il a de se peindre! et cela... par ses propres maximes, et par un dessein premier et principal." Had Montaigne been inspired merely by egotism, Pascal might have been justified in his condemnation. But between 1580, when the *Essays* were first published, and 1586, when he resumed the writing of them, his design underwent a change. At first he merely proposed to paint a portrait of himself for his friends, a portrait "for the corner of a library." But, supremely interested as he was in the study of man in general, he conceived that the most useful contribution that he could make to this study was this same portrait of himself. For in the first place it was a subject "in which he was the most learned man alive," and, secondly, "Every man bears the whole stamp of human nature." Thus while in the essays of his Second Book (8, 10, 17, 18) he dwells chiefly on his idiosyncrasies, on the qualities in which he differs from other men, in his Third Book, though by no means entirely, he lays stress rather on the qualities in which he resembles other men. "It is not in Montaigne," says Pascal, "but in myself that I find all that I read in his book." "Just so," Montaigne would have answered, "but that is because I propose myself as a type of humanity."

[1] III. 2.

Finally, in another *pensée*, Pascal calls attention to Montaigne's defects, his use of lascivious words, his credulity, his ignorance, his sentiments on suicide and death. "One cannot excuse his thoroughly pagan sentiments on death; for there is an end of all piety, if one does not wish to die as a Christian; but throughout his book his only idea is to die like a coward and a weakling." This latter remark is quite unjust. It is true that Montaigne's attitude towards death is inspired more by natural religion and pagan philosophy than by the mysteries of the Christian faith; but there is nothing cowardly about it. In his early essay, *That to be a philosopher is to learn how to die* (I. 17), which he wrote under the influence of Seneca and Stoicism, he urges that we should keep the idea of death always before our eyes, and that we should "combat her with a resolute mind." As for "the remedy of the vulgar sort[1]," which is "not to think on it," he stigmatises it as "gross blindness" arising from "brutal stupidity." But before he came to write his latest essays, he had completely changed his views. During the plague of 1585 he had seen the peasants dying like flies, and he had been profoundly struck by their resignation. There was as much, he now thought, to be said for their attitude as for the proud impassivity of the Stoic philosopher. But he himself adopted, as his habit was, a middle course. He was not tormented by the thought of death, but he did not refrain from thinking about it. He wished to die quietly and simply, without fuss or ceremony[1], and the account that we have of his last moments, though it is not by an eye-witness, shows that he had more or less his wish. In the presence of his wife and a few gentlemen, who were his neighbours, he heard Mass and received the Sacraments, and with his hands clasped and in perfect possession of his faculties "rendered up his spirit to God." There was nothing cowardly or pagan in Montaigne's death[2].

The year before the first appearance of the *Pensées* Bossuet preached before the Court on All Saints' day 1669 a sermon

[1] See *Essais*, III. 9 and 12, and for the whole question of Montaigne's attitude to death see P. Villey, *Les Sources et l'Évolution des Essais de Montaigne*, 2 vols. 1908, II. 390–398.

[2] Pasquier, *Lettres*, XVIII. I.

Sur les conditions nécessaires pour être heureux, in which he apostrophises Montaigne in a highly eloquent passage for putting animals above man without taking into account man's real greatness. "Do you really count it for nothing," he asks, "to know God? To know the source of Nature, to adore his eternity, to admire his omnipotence, to praise his wisdom, to abandon ourselves to his providence, to obey his will, is there nothing in this to distinguish us from beasts?" This is unfair to Montaigne, for it disregards not only many passages in his *Essays* but even the conclusion of the very essay which Bossuet is attacking; it serves however to show that for Bossuet, as for the majority of Montaigne's disciples and opponents in the seventeenth century, he was the sceptic *par excellence*, the author of the *Apologie de Raimond de Sebonde*. Bossuet, in fact, was anticipating Pascal's remark, "Il est dangereux de trop faire voir à l'homme combien il est égal aux bêtes, sans lui montrer sa grandeur."

Bossuet's friend La Bruyère, though he found Montaigne in some respects blameworthy, evidently read him with more than ordinary care and appreciation, for he has introduced into his chapter *On Society and Conversation* a *pastiche* not only of his style but also of his thought. In another chapter he says, "Two writers have blamed Montaigne. Both, it appears, held him in no sort of esteem. The one was not enough of a thinker to appreciate an author who thought much; the other was too subtle a thinker to be satisfied with thoughts which were natural[1]."

The keys to the *Characters* are unanimous in identifying the second of these two writers with Malebranche; but as regards the first they are divided in opinion, some saying that Balzac, and others that Nicole is meant. The objection to Balzac is that his criticisms on Montaigne are far from implying that he held him in no esteem. On the other hand, Sainte-Beuve has pointed out that the sixth book of Nicole's *Pensées sur divers sujets de morale*, which contains his unflattering estimate of the great essayist, was not printed till

---

[1] This *remarque* first appeared in the fifth edition of *Les Caractères* (1690).

after La Bruyère's death. But he thinks it possible that the reference may be to a passage in the *Logique de Port-Royal*[1], of which Antoine Arnauld and Nicole were the joint authors[2]. Here Pascal's strictures on Montaigne are reiterated in an exaggerated and acrimonious form. Montaigne's design of drawing his own portrait is represented not merely as a *sot projet*, but as unworthy of an *honnête homme*, and as springing from a faulty judgment as well as from an inordinate love of himself. The frankness with which he speaks of his defects is only an artifice which makes him all the more odious. But his worst fault is not vanity but libertinism, which is made all the worse by his avowal that he repents of nothing, and that had he to live over again, he would lead the same life. "Horrible words! which mark the complete extinction of all religious sentiment[3]."

I believe this to be the true solution, in spite of the double authorship of the *Logique de Port-Royal*, and that La Bruyère is thinking not of Arnauld, but only of Nicole[4].

No critic of Montaigne is more unjust than Malebranche. His only object in writing his book, says the idealist philosopher, was to portray himself. Now to be constantly speaking of yourself is a fault, but it is sheer effrontery or rather madness to be always praising yourself as Montaigne does. (This is a grossly unfair charge.) He is even more extravagant in his vanity when he describes his defects, for he only mentions those which owing to the corruption of the age passed for virtues. (This is still more unfair.) Moreover, he was mistaken in his opinion of himself; he had neither the good sense nor the penetrating judgment for which he takes credit. It is an error to suppose that he had a thorough knowledge of the human mind. He was a Pyrrhonist mainly because in his day you had to be a sceptic and an *esprit fort* in order to pass for a man of fashion. (This is quite untrue.) His admirers praise him for being wholly free from pedantry; but he was really a

---

[1] Published in 1662, the year of Pascal's death.
[2] *Port-Royal*, II. 460.
[3] Part III of VI (ed. Ch. Jourdain, 1854, pp. 242–244).
[4] M. Servois, the leading authority on La Bruyère, thinks that Balzac is meant.

pedant, for, firstly, he is always quoting and making a parade of his learning, and secondly, he cannot reason[1].

But in spite of all this prejudice and of the very imperfect knowledge of the *Essays* which it betrays, Malebranche is sensible of Montaigne's merits as a writer. He recognises the charm of his style, the natural liveliness with which he expresses his thoughts, and the beauty, vivacity, and range of his imagination. It is this victorious imagination which makes his book so original. *Tout copiste qu'il est, il ne sent point son copiste.* But his book, he adds, is not for edification. If readers merely sought in it diversion, there would be no harm done; but you cannot take pleasure in a book without becoming insensibly affected by its sentiments, and Montaigne's sentiments appeal dangerously to the natural corruption of our hearts[2].

It is not difficult to understand Malebranche's repugnance to Montaigne. Unlike Montaigne, he did not relish intercourse with those who differed from him, and from Montaigne he differed profoundly both in temperament and in intellect. There was nothing in common between the fervent admirer of Descartes and reason, who built up on a psychological basis a complete and orderly system of Christian philosophy, bridging over the chasm between rationalism and the Catholic faith with the bold and brilliant hypothesis of the vision of all things in God, and the unmethodical dreamer who recorded at haphazard the sallies of his imagination, who "added but did not correct," who gibed at reason and paid but a ceremonial allegiance to faith.

Among Montaigne's prominent admirers in the seventeenth century it would be surprising not to find Pierre Bayle, who though born in the middle of the seventeenth century—the exact date is 1647—belonged to the sixteenth by his erudition and to the eighteenth by his critical spirit. We know, in fact, that at the age of nineteen his favourite authors were

---

[1] The "futility" of Malebranche's criticism is exposed by the second Lord Lytton in an excellent appreciation of Montaigne in the *National Review* for April 1883.

[2] *Recherche de la Vérité*, Bk. II (*De l'imagination*), pt. III. c. 5. Malebranche's book was published 1674–1675.

Plutarch and Montaigne, and the name of Montaigne, with citations from his *Essays*, frequently occurs in his writings, especially in his *Nouvelles lettres critiques sur l'histoire du calvinisme de P. Maimbourg*. Montaigne, however, does not find a place in his *Dictionary*, which, considering how short an account of the essayist is given by Moreri, whom he designed to supplement, is highly disappointing.

It was no doubt Montaigne's scepticism and still more his critical and independent spirit, his habit of testing every opinion by his common sense, that attracted Bayle. On the other hand, Bayle's older contemporaries, Mme de Sévigné, and Mme de La Fayette, regarded him as a delightful companion, as a charming talker on men and books. With what joy does Mme de Sévigné take up a volume of the *Essays*, which she had unawares brought with her to Livry from Paris. "Ah! l'aimable homme! qu'il est de bonne compagnie! C'est mon ancien ami; mais à force d'être ancien, il m'est nouveau ...Mon Dieu, que ce livre est plein de bon sens!" Mme de La Fayette wished that she had him for a neighbour, and how welcome he would have been in that delightful garden in the Rue Vaugirard, where Mme de La Fayette sat in conclave with Mme de Sévigné and La Rochefoucauld! And how gladly would Montaigne, among whose chief pleasures in life was intercourse with well-bred and clever men and with fair and virtuous women, have made a fourth in that honourable company[1].

Bayle's familiarity with Montaigne, which is easily accounted for by the spiritual kinship between the two writers, must have been somewhat rare in his generation[2]. In the year 1659, the year in which Molière, having returned to

[1] See the essay, *De trois commerces* (III. 3).

[2] In the often-quoted passage of the *Huetiana*, Huet says that "You would hardly find a country-gentleman who wished to distinguish himself from the ordinary sportsman who had not a Montaigne on his chimney-piece." The *Huetiana* was edited by the Abbé Olivet in 1722, the year after Huet's death, from a manuscript consisting of "detached thoughts" put on paper during the years 1712–1721, which his friend had entrusted to him. It contains three pages on the *Essays* and the words above translated are preceded by "Bréviaire des honnêtes paresseux et des ignorants studieux qui brûlent s'enfariner de quelque connoissance du monde et quelque teinture de Lettres."

Paris from the provinces, may be said to have inaugurated the literature of the great age of Louis XIV with *Les Précieuses ridicules*, three editions of the *Essays* were published, one at Paris, one at Brussels, and one at Amsterdam. Ten years later, the year of Bossuet's sermon, those of Paris and Brussels were reprinted, but after that no edition of Montaigne appeared till 1724, when Pierre Coste, a Huguenot refugee, the friend of Locke and Shaftesbury, and the translator of Locke, published one in London[1]. It was reprinted four times before his death in 1747, twice in London[2], once at the Hague[3], and once at Paris[4]. Ten more editions of the *Essays* appeared before the close of the century.

Montaigne had many distinguished admirers in the eighteenth century, beginning with Montesquieu, whose two references to him, brief though they are, are indicative of his high appreciation. In the one he says that, in the majority of authors he sees the writer, but in Montaigne the thinker; in the other he ranks him with Plato, Malebranche, and Shaftesbury, as one of "the four great poets." It is a sign of the justice and candour of Vauvenargues's criticism that, although there must have been much in Montaigne's book to disquiet so serious and austere a moralist, he does not stint his admiration. He notes, indeed, his want of method, his inability to connect his thoughts or come to a conclusion; but he praises him for the bold and moderate tone of his thought, for his reflective spirit, his originality, his inexhaustible imagination[5].

Mme Du Deffand tried in vain to make Horace Walpole share her admiration for Montaigne. She declares to him that "he is more like Michel than he thinks; but Michel had a friend, and believed in friendship, and that is the difference between him and Horace[6]." On the other hand, she found

---

[1] 3 vols., 4to, Tonson.
[2] 1739; 1745.   [3] 1727.
[4] 1725; this is an improvement on the edition of 1724.
[5] *Sur Montaigne et Pascal.*
[6] *Lettres de Mons. Du Deffand à Horace Walpole* (1766–1780), ed. Mrs Paget Toynbee, 3 vols., 1912, I. 207 (written in 1767). Cp. also *ib.* 151 and 208.

a ready sympathiser in Voltaire. Unlike Pascal, he thought Montaigne's design of portraying himself a "charming one."

He has portrayed human nature. Had Nicole and Malebranche always talked about themselves, they would have been a failure. But a country gentleman of the time of Henry III, who is learned in an age of ignorance, who is a philosopher in an age of fanatics, and who depicts under his own name our weaknesses and our follies will always be loved[1].

Again, in a letter to the Comte de Tressan, written in 1746, he warmly praises Montaigne as "toujours originel, toujours plein d'imagination, toujours peintre, et, ce que j'aime, toujours sachant douter." And nearly twenty years later he speaks of him as "le plus sage et le plus aimable des philosophes," and recommends everyone who wishes to learn to doubt to read the eleventh essay of the Third Book (*Des Boiteux*[2]).

Diderot admired Montaigne as warmly as Voltaire, but he did not "learn from him to doubt," and he expresses his admiration with characteristic enthusiasm and dogmatism. "He will be read," he declares, "as long as there are men who love truth, strength, and simplicity. His book is the touchstone of a sound mind. If a man dislikes it, you may be sure that he has some defect of the heart or understanding[3]."

Jean-Jacques Rousseau's debt to Montaigne was considerable. It first appears in the *Projet d'éducation de M. de Sainte-Marie*, which he wrote in 1740 during his ill-starred tutorship to the two sons of M. de Mably at Lyons, and it re-appears in *Émile*, particularly in the attention paid to physical culture and to the study of history, and in the avoidance of regular lessons from books. The *Discours sur les arts* owes not a little to Montaigne, and he is three times referred to in the notes, but in the *Discours sur l'inégalité*, written five years later, Montaigne's influence is negligible[4]. In the first draft of the

---

[1] *Lettres philosophiques*, XXV (*Sur les Pensées de M. Pascal*). Voltaire originally wrote (after *la nature humaine*) *et le pauvre projet de Nicole, de Malebranche, de Pascal, de décrier Montaigne*, but in the 1748 edition of his works it is altered as above (see *Lettres philosophiques*, ed. G. Lanson, II. 216–217).

[2] *Doutes sur le testament attribué au Cardinal de Richelieu* (*Œuvres*, ed. Beuchot, XLII. 74).

[3] *Dict. Encycl.*, "Pyrrhonienne" (*Œuvres*, XVI. 485).

[4] See P. Villey, *L'influence de Montaigne sur les idées pédagogiques de Locke et de Rousseau*, 1911.

opening of the *Confessions* he says, "Je mets Montaigne à la tête de ces faux sincères qui veulent tromper en disant vrai[1]." The remark is a measure of Rousseau's growing inability to distinguish truth from falsehood.

Other eighteenth-century readers of Montaigne were Mirabeau, who cites him frequently in his *Essai sur le Despotisme*[2] (1776), Mme Roland who read him in prison[3], and André Chénier[4]. Finally, at the close of the century, La Harpe, who, though his criticism is often narrow and pedantic, had a natural taste for good literature, praises his good faith, says that he paints man as he is, and declares that "the *Essays* are the book of those who know how to read, and even of those who do not[5]."

In 1802 Jacques-André Naigeon, the disciple and admirer of Diderot, published an edition of the *Essays*, based on the Bordeaux copy, with its manuscript additions of the 1588 text; but he did his work so carelessly that it is of little or no value. Then in 1811 the Académie Française—or, as it then was called, the "Class of the Institute for the French language and literature"—proposed "Montaigne" as the subject for the prize of Eloquence. The successful *Éloge* was written by Villemain, while those of J.-B. Biot, the distinguished chemist and physicist, J.-M. Dutens, the economist, M.-J.-V. Fabre, F.-X.-J. Droz, and J.-V. Leclerc, were honourably mentioned and afterwards printed[6]. That by J.-V. Leclerc was prefixed to the edition of the *Essays* which he published in 1828.

The first interpreter of Montaigne in the nineteenth century who calls for special mention is Sainte-Beuve. In the lectures on Port-Royal which he delivered at Lausanne in 1837–1838 he relieved his weariness of his main subject with a digression

---

[1] Quoted by Sainte-Beuve, *Causeries du Lundi*, III. 80.
[2] Pp. 152, n. 1; 168, n. 1; 188; 229, n. 1; 261, n. 1.
[3] *Mémoires*, ed. Perroul, 2 vols., 1905, II. 190.
[4]   Le critique imprudent, qui se croit bien habile,
         Donnera sur ma joue un soufflet à Virgile.
         Et ceci (tu peux voir si j'observe ma loi)
         Montaigne, il t'en souvient, l'avait dit avant moi. *Épître*, III.
The reference is to a passage in *Essais*, II. 10.
[5] *Lycée*, V. 39–41 (*Introduction au siècle de Louis XIV*, 1797).
[6] Dutens's in 1818, the others, including Villemain's, in 1812.

on one whom, with Horace and Bayle, he claimed as a spiritual ancestor. The two chapters in *Port-Royal* which represent this digression are too well-known to need dwelling on here[1]. In the opening sentence, with its reminiscence of La Bruyère, Sainte-Beuve says with perfect truth that "Montaigne is not a philosophical system; he is not even in the first place a sceptic and a Pyrrhonist, but simply nature; civilised nature, but nature without Grace." That is why the Jansenists hated him, because he was *par excellence* the natural man. In his carefully drawn portrait every man finds something of himself. Critics, philosophers, moralists, La Bruyère, Huet, even St François de Sales—all are touched with the scepticism of Montaigne. This may or may not be true, but Sainte-Beuve is certainly wrong when he accuses Montaigne of perfidy, of attacking Christianity under the cloak of an orthodox Catholic. Sainte-Beuve is here, to use his own expression, "drawing Montaigne to himself"; he is seeing his own portrait in his ancestor.

Emerson, a man of clear-sighted and judicial sagacity, takes a very different view from Sainte-Beuve of Montaigne's good faith. He declares that "the opinion of an invincible probity grows into every reader's mind," and that "the sincerity and marrow of the man reach to his sentences." Except for this remark the rather famous essay in which these words occur is of little importance; of its twenty-nine pages only six relate specifically to Montaigne[2]. One of seven lectures on Representative Men delivered in 1845–1846, it is entitled *Montaigne; or the Sceptic*; but Sceptic is used in its original sense of a considerer, an inquirer, one who looks at all questions from every possible side.

Alexandre Vinet, the Protestant professor at Lausanne, who greatly influenced Sainte-Beuve and might have converted him to Protestantism had any real religious conversion been possible, included Montaigne in a course of lectures on the French moralists, treating the subject with insight and authority. He thoroughly appreciates the Essayist's good

---

[1] *Port-Royal*, t. II (1842), lib. III. cc. 2 and 3, pp. 395–453.
[2] *English Traits and Representative Men* (Macmillan), 1893.

qualities and recognises that he "talks about himself in order
to make known man in general." He finds that what is lacking in him as a moralist is a conception of man's relations
with the infinite. He further accuses him of substituting
conscience for the moral law and of setting up a purely sub-
jective standard of morals. Montaigne would have admitted
this, but he would have warmly defended his position. He
might have pointed out that the conscience of the individual
is itself moulded and shaped by the general moral law. But
he does not seem to have considered cases in which conscience
and the moral law come into collision. Would he have justified the burning of heretics by inquisitors who obeyed the
dictates of their own nature and their own conscience? Would
he have justified the assassination of Henry III by the
fanatical monk Jacques Clément?

Vinet, like Emerson, differs from Sainte-Beuve in finding
no perfidy in Montaigne's attitude towards Christianity. He
honestly believed, he says, that he was a good Catholic, but
his religion gave no colour either to his life or to his thoughts
of death. Scepticism pervades his whole book, but it is con-
centrated in the *Apologie de Raimond de Sebonde*. Its onslaught
on human reason is no service to religion, as Montaigne supposes,
for, as Montaigne himself says at the beginning of the essay,
it is the duty of the Christian to "embellish and amplify the
truth of his creed" by study and thought[1].

Much the same view of Montaigne's scepticism, of his attitude towards Christianity, and of his attack on human reason
is taken by Vinet's fellow-Protestant, Dean Church[2]. Like
Vinet he thoroughly appreciates the charm of his imaginative
style and rambling method, and he draws an admirable portrait of the man. But his charge of "deep-rooted selfishness"
is not borne out by the character which Montaigne bore with
his contemporaries, and "gross sensuality" is too strong a

---

[1] *Moralistes des seizième et des dix-septième siècles*, 1859, based on notes
of lectures given 1832 and 1833 and of another course given in 1847, a few
months before Vinet's death.

[2] *The Essays of Montaigne* (1857), reprinted in *Miscellaneous Essays*,
1888. W. L. Collins—*Montaigne*, 1879 (in Foreign Classics for English
Readers), an excellent little book—agrees closely with Dean Church.

term for the licence of speech and thought which disfigures some of the essays. It was an age of outspoken coarseness, and Montaigne's imagination and language were more licentious than his life. When the season of his hot youth had passed, he practised a self-control over his passions which he never afterwards abandoned.

Up to this time the knowledge of Montaigne's life was derived almost wholly from the *Essays*, but during the middle years of the nineteenth century, as the result of much quiet and persistent work some useful additions were made to his biography. Chief among the workers was Dr J.-F. Payen, a specialist on the subject of mineral waters, who published first a bibliography of Montaigne (1837) and then four series of unpublished documents relating to his life (1847–1856). In 1855 appeared *La vie publique de Michel Montaigne* by Alphonse Grün, which breaks new ground but is too conjectural to be of much value. Less ambitious, but more useful, is the little book by E. Galy and L. Lapeyre, *Montaigne chez lui* (1861), which gives, in the form of a letter to Dr Payen, an account of Montaigne's château[1]—it was burnt down, it will be recollected, in 1885—and particularly of his famous tower, happily still standing, with the library and study (Plate VI). Most important of all it gives a transcript of the Greek and Latin sentences which Montaigne had painted on the beams of the library. Another important contribution to Montaigne's biography was T. Malvézin's *Michel de Montaigne, son origine, sa famille* (1875). Before this, Bayle St John, who lived in Paris from 1848 to 1851 as the correspondent of the *Daily Telegraph*, had published in 1858, the year before his early death, the first English book on Montaigne and the first extended life of Montaigne in any language[2]. It includes what the author calls, with some justice, a "desultory chapter" on the *Essays*, but he pleads that intercourse with Montaigne has taught him to beware of dogmatism. "I feel an uncertainty about some of his doctrines which I should with regret see displaced by absolute conviction."

---

[1] It then belonged to Pierre Magne, the Finance Minister of Napoleon III, who was a native of Périgueux.

[2] *Montaigne, the Essayist, a biography*, 2 vols., 1858.

All these available materials were fully utilised by M. Paul Bonnefon, whose *Montaigne, l'homme et l'œuvre*, with numerous illustrations and facsimiles, appeared in 1893 and is now the authoritative life[1].

This notable work had the apparent effect of stimulating the interest in Montaigne. In 1894 Faguet published his *Seizième siècle*; in 1895 Stapfer and Lanusse contributed volumes on Montaigne to the *Grands Écrivains français* and the *Classiques populaires* respectively, while Mr Charles Whibley wrote an introduction for an edition of the *Essays* in the *Temple Classics*[2]. All these studies are marked by sympathy, good sense, and well-balanced appreciation. Faguet's chief points are that Montaigne "wrote exclusively on human nature," that "his scepticism is an invention of Pascal, revived by the French philosophers of 1840," and that it is his special merit that he has founded on the wisdom of the ancients "a morality which is healthy, manly, and brilliant." M. Bonnefon's book also led to Miss Lowndes's careful and scholarly study of Montaigne's life, framed in the setting of his age[3]. Her concise appreciation of the *Essays* is just on the whole, but she underrates the importance and interest of his self-portraiture[4].

Nine years earlier (1889) Walter Pater in his unfinished romance, *Gaston de Latour*, paid a charming and sympathetic tribute to the great Essayist. Gaston visits him at his château, and a chapter entitled *Suspended judgment* presents us with a skilfully constructed mosaic from the *Essays*, which is supposed to represent the substance of Montaigne's conversations during the nine months of Gaston's prolonged visit to his château in the year 1568. As a matter of fact at this time he had not even thought of writing his *Essays*[5].

As the nineteenth century merged into the twentieth there appeared two remarkable contributions to the study of Mon-

---

[1] Reprinted, with additions on Charron and Mlle de Gournay, under the title of *Montaigne et ses amis*, 2 vols., 1897.

[2] Reprinted in *Literary Portraits*, 1904.

[3] *Michel de Montaigne*, Cambridge, 1898.

[4] pp. 156–157.

[5] Montaigne's father did not die till June 1568. *Gaston de Latour* first appeared in *Macmillan's Magazine*.

taigne. Both were posthumous and incomplete works; both
were written by men of high character and refined intelligence
who for more than twenty years had communed with Montaigne in close intercourse; both were introduced by Faguet
in a commendatory and sagacious preface. The first to appear
was the work of Guillaume Guizot, the second son of the
statesman, who at the age of twenty had written a brilliant
book on Menander, which was crowned by the Academy and
published two years later (1855). Since 1874 he had held the
post of Professor of Germanic languages and literatures at
the Collège de France. He was an admirable conversationalist,
and was much beloved by his friends. Montaigne had been
the subject of his first public course of lectures, given in 1866,
and for more than twenty-five years he had devoted to him
every moment of his leisure, comparing texts, accumulating
notes and documents with a view to a definitive edition of
the *Essays* and a comprehensive study of his life, his philosophy, and his influence. But he never realised his dream,
and all that the piety of his friends was able to publish after
his death in 1892 was a collection of admirable fragments[1].
"Il y a, dans notre littérature, des écrivains qui ont plus
d'autorité, mais je n'y connais pas de plus grand séducteur."
Guizot felt to the full the charm of Montaigne's style, and he
realised that when Montaigne poses as an amateur who knew
nothing about the art of writing he is not to be taken seriously.
"As a writer and as an artist he is altogether of the first rank."
And Guizot notes among other gifts his rich imagination, his
power of choosing words and phrases which conjure up con-
crete images not only of facts but of ideas and sentiments.
Another cause of his charm is his "continual and familiar
presence" in his writings. "You seem to have him before
your eyes in his actual person; the movement of his style is
like the gestures of a man talking; you see him smile; you see
him shrug his shoulders; and you even hear his Gascon accent." And there is much in Montaigne's character, he says,
to attract, above all things his frankness, sincerity, and good
faith.

[1] *Montaigne, Études et Fragments*, 1899.

Guizot found it difficult to resist the spell, and for this very reason he has magnified Montaigne's defects and has judged him with austere severity. He admits that he abounds in intellectual gifts which are manifest on every page of his book and at every moment of his life. But he holds that his rare qualities were sterilised by two glaring faults, love of himself and lack of will-power. That Montaigne had a fair share of egoism in his character appears not only from the *Essays* but from the journal of his travels, which was written for his own eyes and those of his family. But it is untrue to say that egoism sums up his whole character. It may be admitted too, for he admits it himself, that he was indolent, and that he found it greatly difficult to decide on a course of action, because he always saw both sides of the question. But his retirement from public life, a retirement which, be it remembered, was neither complete nor continuous, was not due solely to indolence, still less to weakness of will. It was partly because he held that a man's first duty is to his own family and his own affairs, partly because he hated the cruelty and dissimulation which marked the course of the religious struggle. *La plus grande chose du monde, c'est de sçavoir estre a soy*[1]. "There are some men, and these not the worst, who look for no other profit but to watch how and why everything is done, and to be spectators of the lives of others, in order to judge of them, and by them to regulate their own."

Guizot is very emphatic on the subject of Montaigne's Christianity. He concedes that Montaigne believed himself to be a Christian, but he can hardly imagine anyone to be less of a Christian in reality. Saúl the persecutor and Paul the Apostle are not further apart than Montaigne and a true Christian. In a long fragment on the influence of Montaigne he attacks him in force, and with great eloquence. Here is a man, he says, who withdrew himself from public life, and even from the conduct of his own affairs and the care of his family, to dream in the secluded tower of his château and to pass his life in the observation and description of that self which he had made his universe. If this self-contemplation had led to

[1] *On Solitude* (I. 38).

that profound knowledge of his own soul which we find in the confessions of a St Augustine, there might be some excuse. But no, he presents to us man and this world and the other world, as enigmas to which there is no answer. Yet for three centuries he has been a general favourite, and he has exercised his seduction not only on those who, like Saint-Évremond and Bayle, resemble him in temperament, but on a man so wholly different from him as Pascal.

And to Pascal may be added Guillaume Guizot. For, as Faguet says at the end of his illuminating preface, "The fact that Guillaume Guizot wrote a book on Montaigne and to some extent against Montaigne is perhaps Montaigne's greatest victory." Indeed, the interest of the book does not lie in any novelty of interpretation, but in the force and skill with which the attack on Montaigne's character and opinions is delivered by one whose admiration for his opponent and consciousness of his seductive powers have endowed with peculiar penetration. We can enjoy with Faguet the "agreeable" and "salutary" spectacle of this clash between two men of radically opposite temperaments, between the man of action and the John-a-dreams, between the follower of the Christian code and the disciple of Epicurus.

It must have been a real pleasure to Faguet, with his well-balanced mind, to introduce Ruel's book after Guizot's, for, while Ruel was fully as sensitive as Guizot to Montaigne's charm, he interpreted him not as an opponent but as a warm admirer.

Édouard Ruel was a younger man than Guillaume Guizot, having been born in 1847, and, while Guizot was a Protestant, Ruel was a devout Catholic, the friend of Mgr d'Hulst, Charles Dejob, and the Catholic philosopher, Ollé-Laprune. A pupil of the École Normale and of the French School at Athens, he found a post especially suited to his combined love of art and literature, that of Professor of Literature at the École des Beaux Arts, a post which he held from 1876 till his death twenty years later. His book on Montaigne when completed would have consisted of two parts, Montaigne as artist, and Montaigne as philosopher. The first part, in ten chapters, is

more or less complete; the second is only represented by fragments, some of which, however, evidently belong to the first
part. The idea of considering Montaigne primarily as an artist
was a new one, and, though Ruel sometimes pushes his point
too far, he is always interesting and suggestive. After an
introductory chapter and a portrait of Montaigne which brings
into relief his artistic nature, he points out that the *Essays*
are a work of art (c. iii) and he goes on to demonstrate that
Montaigne is an artist, (i) in his faculty of observation, (ii) in
his love of truth, (iii) in his sense of personality, (iv) in his
sympathy for human weakness, (v) in his feeling for life,
(vi) in his love of measure and moderation, (vii) in his idealism.

The most novel feature in Ruel's argument is his insistence
on the artistic form of the *Essays*. He is very persuasive on
this point. "Do not be in a hurry to conclude that there is
no composition in the *Essays*; rather study nature and ac-
custom yourself to comprehend and admire the free and
varied harmony which reigns in her pictures." While Bacon's
essays are like a well-arranged botanic garden, and Addison's
like the park and gardens of a private house, Montaigne's
resemble Nature herself. They grow with the genius of the
author, they follow the undulations of the ground, now rising,
now falling, here making brusque transitions, there passing
by a gentle incline from one topic to another, but linked
together behind all their variations of level and line and colour
by the life which animates them at every point.

In one of the longest of his fragments Ruel gives an admirable analysis of the essay *On Coaches* (III. 6)[1], which is a good
example of Montaigne's method, with his love of digressions
and his habit of travelling to his goal by devious paths. Ruel
is full of admiration for the composition of this essay, the
close of which he compares to the *coda* of a symphony by
Beethoven. But is he right in his view that its main subject
is the question of progress as symbolised by the various ways
in which coaches have been employed in different ages and
in different countries? It seems to me that the central thought
is rather the question of pomp and magnificence, and of how

[1] pp. 374 ff.

far it may be carried without degenerating into extravagance[1].
It looks, too, as if the whole train of thought had been started
by the stories which Montaigne read in Crinitus's *De honesta
disciplina* of the strange teams which Mark Antony and
Elagabalus harnessed to their coaches[2].

It would no doubt have given intense satisfaction to Montaigne to find so much divergence of view among his interpreters, especially between two men like Guizot and Ruel,
who had held familiar intercourse with him for over twenty
years. Guizot, like Pascal, saw in him a complete sceptic, but
Ruel points out that Montaigne often speaks in the name of
the Pyrrhonists and not in his own, and that this is sometimes
overlooked by Pascal[3]. This is well worth bearing in mind. So
also is the caution given in the following note or *pensée*.
"Readers of Montaigne often take for scepticism what is
merely the observation of an artist, and Montaigne himself
is deceived by it[4]." We have seen what Guizot thought about
Montaigne's Christianity. Ruel admits that his morality is
not Christian; "but is that a reason," he asks, "for saying
that he was not a Christian[5]?" And in other fragments he
points out that Montaigne believes in revelation, that he is
constantly pre-occupied with the truth of Christianity, and
that the tone in which he speaks of God is that of a believer.
The last remark is perfectly true; any unprejudiced reader of
the *Essays* will be struck by the note of sincere reverence in
all the utterances about God and the unseen world. "There
is no end to our inquiries," says Montaigne; "our end is in
the other world." "The saying is profound," is Ruel's comment[6], and certainly Montaigne's theory of the relativity of
knowledge is a strong argument in favour of revelation as the
only alternative to complete scepticism. In an essay of the
First Book, which must have been begun as early as 1572,
though possibly part of it was added some years later[7], Mon-

---

[1] Quant à la pompe et magnificence, par où je suis entré en ce propos.
[2] Stapfer refers to this chapter as an example of the hidden art in the
composition of the *Essays* (*Montaigne*, p. 127), and Sir J. Stephen as an
example of their desultoriness (*Horae Sabbaticae*, I. 124 ff.).
[3] p. 393.   [4] p. 396.   [5] p. 426.   [6] p. 397.
[7] I. 26, *It is folly to refer truth or falsehood to our sufficiency.*

taigne exclaims against the presumption of concluding that miracles are impossible. "It is a foolish presumption to disdain and condemn as false that which does not seem probable to us." "Reason hath taught me that so resolutely to condemn a thing for false and impossible is to assume unto oneself the advantage of knowing the bounds and limits of God's will and of the capacity of our nature." It seems to Montaigne "singularly impudent" to condemn stories of miracles which are vouched for by men like St Augustine. He would have had no sympathy with the Modernists of to-day. "Either a man must submit himself wholly to the authority of our ecclesiastical policy or he must altogether reject it; it is not for us to determine what part of obedience we owe to it." This was written at any rate before 1580; it is interesting to compare with it a passage in another essay which first appeared in 1588:

> Simple minds, less curious, less well-instructed, are made good Christians, and through reverence and obedience hold their simple belief and abide by the laws. In intellects of moderate vigour and moderate capacity error of opinion is engendered....The great intellects, more settled and clear-sighted, form another sort of true believers; by a long and religious investigation they find a more profound and abstruse meaning in the Scriptures, and discover the mysterious and divine secret of our ecclesiastical polity.

A little further on Montaigne added after 1588 the following passage in the margin:

> The simple peasants are honest folk, and so are the philosophers.... The mongrels who have disdained the station of ignorance, but who have not been able to attain to the other station (sitting between two stools, as I and many others do) are dangerous, foolish, and importunate; it is they who trouble the world. Therefore I for my part retreat as much as I can to my first and natural station, from which I vainly attempted to advance[1].

Faguet speaks of Guillaume Guizot as playing Alceste to Montaigne's Philinte; it is therefore piquant to find Ruel in some excellent and suggestive pages[2] comparing Montaigne to Alceste and pointing out that his love of truth is more

---

[1] I. 54 (*On vain Subtleties*). Brunetière has called attention to the significance of this passage in an article on *Une nouvelle édition de Montaigne* (*Études critiques*, VIII. I ff.), which first appeared in the *Revue des deux mondes* for Sept. 15, 1906.

[2] pp. 106 ff.

active and practical than that of Molière's hero. Both hate lying and dissimulation in every form, but Montaigne makes truth the object and aim of his whole life.

Ruel is particularly instructive on Montaigne's retirement from active life[1], which he compares to Alceste's retirement to his "desert." He does not attempt to deny Montaigne's indolence, but he pleads that before condemning it we should investigate its cause and nature. Montaigne has done this largely for us in the essay *De mesnager sa volonté* (III. 10), and Ruel with this essay for a guide shows that Montaigne, in withdrawing from the heat and turmoil of the religious struggle, was preferring coolness and self-possession to action and personal feeling; modesty and simplicity to ambition and honours; liberty of judgment and impartiality to the spirit of party. Montaigne's egoism, he concludes, resolves itself into disinterestedness.

M. Edmé Champion, whose *Introduction aux Essais de Montaigne* appeared in 1900, the year before Ruel's book, is like Ruel reminded of Alceste by Montaigne's retirement, but he suggests a different reason for it. According to him, Montaigne loved action and the life of towns, and was horribly bored by solitude and the country. But he gave up being a magistrate because of the "vile traffic which covers itself under the honourable title of justice," and he held aloof from the Catholic cause with which he sympathised because of the perfidy and cruelty which stained its successes. The first reason will hardly hold good; the French magistracy in the second half of the century enjoyed a singularly high reputation, and there is no evidence that a profession which La Boétie had followed with honour had so far degenerated since his death that Montaigne could no longer remain in it. The simple fact is that judicial duties were distasteful to him, as to a man who habitually saw both sides of a question and disliked nothing more than coming to a decision on a disputed point. As for the second reason, it may readily be granted that, though a soldier's life sometimes strongly appealed to Montaigne, he was reluctant to take up arms in a cause

[1] pp. 207 ff.

which, however just it seemed to him, was conducted with a singular want of humanity. On the other hand, it must be remembered that when Montaigne retired to his "desert" or, as he quaintly expresses it in the famous inscription of his study, "to the bosom of the learned virgins," France had been at peace since the treaty of Saint-Germain (August 8, 1570). After St Bartholomew, Montaigne, like may of the more moderate Catholics, seems to have been for a time more favourably disposed to the Protestants, but less than two years later (May 1574) we find him in the Catholic camp, when he was entrusted by the Duc de Montpensier with a mission to the *Parlement* of Bordeaux[1].

At any rate M. Champion differs *toto coelo* from Ruel in regarding Montaigne as a man "to whom action seemed the true goal of existence, and the principal, if not the only, reason for life." According to him it was in a fit of temporary discouragement that Montaigne shut himself up in his château, and it was by way of distraction from ennui that he took to writing. At first his essays were mere cullings from the books in his library, with a word or two added by way of comment. Then as a "new amusement" he set to work to study and paint himself. But M. Champion insists that this was never an essential feature of the *Essays*, and that, when Montaigne says in his preface to the edition of 1580 that he is "the subject-matter of his book," he is far from exact. In support of this view M. Champion points out that, though Montaigne set special store by biographies and auto-biographies, he has not given us a biography of himself; he has told us nothing about his mother or his wife or his daughter; nothing about his life (except his education at the College of Guienne) before his retirement; nothing about his military career. He does not say what he thought of Erasmus and he has shrouded his religious opinions in such obscurity that it is very difficult to give an account of them. But Montaigne's design was not to write an auto-biography—far from it—but to give us a general picture of himself, and above all, to portray the shifting conditions of his inner life. Moreover, this design was only

[1] *Éphémérides*, no. 20 (Payen, *Documents inédits*, no. 3, p. 14).

PLATE VII

ESSAIS DE M. DE MONT.

à nous, qui n'y sommes pas instruicts par estude. Les grands
esprits plus rassis & clairuoians, font vn autre genre de bien
croyans : lesquels par longue & religieuse inuestigation, pe-
netrent vne plus profonde & abstruse lumiere, es escriptures,
& sentent le misterieux & diuin secret, de nostre police Ec-
clesiastique. Pourtant en voyons nous aucuns estre arriuez à
ce dernier estage, par le second, auec merueilleux fruict, &
confirmation : comme à l'extreme limite de la Chrestienne
intelligence : & iouyr de leur victoire auec consolation, a-
ction de graces, reformatiõ de meurs, & grande modestie. Et
en ce rang n'entens-ie pas loger, ces autres, qui pour se purger
du soubçon de leur erreur passé, & pour nous asseurer d'eux,
se rendent extremes, indiscrets, & iniustes, à là conduicte de
nostre cause, & là taschent, d'infinis reproches de violence. I
Mais parce que apres que le pas à esté ouuert à l'esprit, i'ay

chaufée, elle defcouure vn nôbre infiny de pareils exemples,
ie n'en adioufteray que cettuy-cy : que fi ces eflays eftoyent
dignes, qu'on en iugeat, il en pourroit aduenir à mon aduis,
qu'ils ne plairoient guiere aux efprits communs & vulgaires,
ny guiere aux finguliers & excellens ; ceux-là n'y entendroiêt
pas affez, ceux-cy y entendroient trop : ils pourroient viuoter
en la moyenne region.

Des Senteurs.   CHAP. LV.

L fe dict d'aucuns, comme d'Alexandre le grand, que
leur fueur efpandoit vn' odeur fouefue par quelque rare & extraordinaire côplexion : dequoy Plutarque &
autres recherchent la caufe. Mais la cômune façon des côrps

Facsimile of page 131 *recto* of the copy of the 1588 edition of Montaigne's *Essais* in
the Municipal Library of Bordeaux

of gradual development; it is not till the essay *On Presumption* (II. 17), which was written about 1578, that it is put forward as a definite conception[1].

According to M. Champion, Montaigne's main object, as soon as he began to take his *Essays* seriously, was to be of service to his fellow-creatures. With this intention, he made confession of his own faults and imperfections, partly as a warning but chiefly to enable him to criticise those of others. His whole book is an unmeasured attack on the society of his age, on its superstition, its pedantry, its education, its administration of justice, its fashions. He attacks all classes —nobles and peasants, doctors and lawyers, authors and professors, women as well as men. Finally, in the *Apologie de Raimond de Sebonde*, he includes the whole human race in one furious polemic. As for the Christian conclusion to the essay, M. Champion waves it aside. He admits that Montaigne remained till his last hour faithful to the practices of the Catholic Church, but he regards this as merely the survival of old habits, and he holds that in reality Montaigne became more and more anti-Christian. It is true that he never attacks Christian dogmas, and that he makes verbal concessions to Catholicism, but his later *Essays* reveal an indifference which is worse than doubt or negation.

M. Champion has taken the first part of the *Apology*, the comparison between men and animals, too seriously. It is evident that Montaigne in thus heaping paradox upon paradox to prove the vileness of man is more or less amusing himself, just as he does in the essay *On Cannibals* (I. 30), when he praises the civilisation of the savages of Brazil as superior to that of his own countrymen. Montaigne had a fund of quiet humour, and his interpreters have frequently gone astray by taking everything that he says as sober earnest. M. Champion forgets that the same Montaigne who declared that the best man deserves hanging ten times in his life was a fervent admirer of Socrates and Epaminondas, and that though he found much to criticise in his own age—and from the massacre

---

[1] See also II. 8 (*On the Affection of Fathers for Children*), 10 (*On Books*), 18 (*On giving the Lie*).

of St Bartholomew, which happened soon after he began to
write, to his death twenty years later, the condition of
France was indeed deplorable—he could admire men like
Michel de L'Hospital and François de La Noue. Moreover,
M. Champion himself points out that Montaigne's study of
man led him to an optimistic conclusion, and that the *Essays*
end on a note of almost lyrical rapture in praise of lives which
have been led in conformity to Nature, without miracle and
without extravagance.

It is one of the merits of M. Champion's book that he
realises that Montaigne's opinions changed with the years,
that he was not the same in 1580 as he was when he began
to write his *Essays*, nor the same in 1588 as he was in 1580.
The great majority of Montaigne's earlier interpreters had
failed to recognise this important fact. As Brunetière says,
they discussed the *Essays* as if, like the *Discours sur l'Histoire
universelle* or the *Recherche de la Vérité*, they had issued one
fine morning fully armed from their author's study. The first
step towards a truer conception of the *Essays* was taken when
M. Reinhold Dezeimeris, the *doyen* of Montaigne students,
and H. Barckhausen edited the original text of 1580[1]; the
next when MM. Motheau and Jouaust reproduced that of
1588[2].

Students could now distinguish between the text of the
Essays as it originally stood and the accretions of subsequent
editions, and could thus follow, if they were minded, the
changes and developments of Montaigne's thought. But it
was still rather a laborious process, and, unless a good library
was at hand, an expensive one; as we have seen, the
studies and appreciations which appeared in the nineties,
show little trace of it. But in 1904 Miss Grace Norton, sister
of the distinguished Dante scholar, Eliot Norton, published
a volume of *Studies in Montaigne*[3], in which she applied the
historical method to two of the Essays, the *Apologie de
Raimond de Sebonde* and the Essay *On Vanity* (III. 9). Her con-

[1] Bordeaux, 1870–1873.
[2] 7 vols., 1872–1875.
[3] New York (The Macmillan Company). Miss Norton has also published
The early writings of Montaigne and other studies (1904).

clusions—the division of the former essay into two parts,
written at different times, and that of the latter into two
originally distinct essays which Montaigne amused himself by
blending into one—have been very considerably modified by
M. Villey[1], but she was on the right path. In 1905 appeared,
also in America, the *Michel de Montaigne* of Edward Dowden[2],
charmingly written and thoroughly sympathetic, in which he
desiderates an edition of the *Essays* which should adequately
present the successive states of the text[3].

He had his wish in the following year when the first volume
was published of what has become known as the *Édition
Municipale*, which not only gives an accurate reproduction
of the Bordeaux copy of the *Essays* with all Montaigne's
manuscript additions and corrections, but enables the reader
easily to separate the successive texts of 1580 and 1588 from
the text as finally corrected by Montaigne. The second volume
appeared in 1909, the third in 1919, and the fourth in 1920.
The editor, M. Fortunat Strowski, who in 1906 was a
professor at the University of Bordeaux, took advantage
of his unique opportunities to publish later in the same year
what "he believed to be the first application of the historical
and genetic method to Montaigne's book[4]." It led him to
distinguish various stages in the development of Montaigne's thought—Stoicism from 1572 to 1574, Scepticism,
after a brief intermediary period, from about 1574 to 1578,
a return to a more positive phase as exhibited in the
essay *On the Education of Children* (1578–1580), a period of
travel and public life (1580–1585), a phase of practical and
mellow wisdom (the result of intercourse with his fellow-men),
embodied in the Third Book of the *Essays* and in the additions to the First and Second Books (1585–1588), and finally

[1] See *Rev. d'hist. litt.* 1905, pp. 520–522.
[2] Philadelphia, 1905 (French Men of Letters). The most important
chapter is that entitled "The Spirit of the Essays." The ample bibliography,
almost entirely composed of books in the author's own library, testifies to
his life-long interest in Montaigne.
[3] In 1906 appeared a slight but suggestive essay by R. Warwick Bond;
it takes no note of Montaigne's development.
[4] *Les grands Philosophes—Montaigne*, 1906. "Le conseil m'en a été donné,
il y a bien des jours, par mon maître M. Brunetière; il a été répété par
M. Lanson."

dilettantism, which finds expression in the manuscript additions made after 1588.

In pointing out that Montaigne's Stoicism and Scepticism were passing phases M. Strowski has done an inestimable service. But he is too rigid in his demarcation of these phases. They did not come to an end without leaving a considerable impression upon Montaigne's mind. If he no longer sat at the feet of his Stoic masters, their precepts could still at times fire his imagination. If the acute Scepticism of the year 1576, when he struck his Pyrrhonist medal, became greatly mitigated, it left his critical faculty permanently sharpened and invigorated, and his belief in the relativity of knowledge and morals in a large measure unimpaired. As for the charge of dilettantism, which M. Strowski rightly distinguishes from philosophic Scepticism, he points out that dilettantism has two main characteristics, an ardent curiosity and a desire to live in the imagination as many different lives as possible, and that both of these are present in Montaigne's latest additions to his book. Coming from a man whose attention had been specially directed to these additions by printing them in italic type, M. Strowski's opinion is not to be lightly rejected; but when he finds a complete resemblance between Montaigne and Renan as regards these characteristics, one wonders whether, if the word dilettantism had not been specially applied to Renan's mental attitude after the Franco-German war, we should have heard of it in connexion with Montaigne. The reason for this new development M. Strowski finds chiefly in the approach of old age, but partly in the discouragement and disillusion produced by the events of the last four years of Montaigne's life—the assassination of Guise, the murder of Henry III, the fanaticism of the Leaguers and the more stubborn Huguenots. But though he holds that Montaigne's writing during this period was "saturated with dilettantism," he does not believe that it affected him more than superficially, or that his life suffered any loss of dignity or self-control. M. Strowski quotes in support of this view Florimond de Raemond, Montaigne's successor in the *Parlement* of Bordeaux. "France," he says, writing in 1594, "has

recently suffered from the eclipse of that brilliant and incomparable light of learning, eloquence, and capacity for
public affairs," and then he goes on to speak of his "courageous
and almost stoical philosophy, his marvellous resolution in
the face of every kind of suffering and trouble.".…"This rare
personage seems by his death to have left virtue an
orphan."

But whatever there is that is too rigid and systematic in
M. Strowski's interpretation of the least rigid and systematic
of philosophers can be easily corrected by a careful study of
the two substantial volumes which M. Pierre Villey published in 1908 under the title of *Les Sources et l'Évolution des
Essais de Montaigne*. They are the fruit of six years' research,
carried on for at least half that time without the knowledge
of his fellow-worker. The first volume is devoted to an exhaustive investigation of the sources and chronology of the
Essays, or, in other words, to the three questions, (1) what
books Montaigne read, (2) when he read them, and (3) when
he wrote each essay. For the essays of the First and
Second Books were not printed in the order in which they
were written, and they contain very few direct indications of
date. The dates of the great majority can only be determined
by Montaigne's references to books. An investigation of this
sort depends for its success on the manner in which it is conducted, and it may be said without hesitation that M. Villey's
method is thoroughly sound, and that he is careful to distinguish between fact and hypothesis.

In his second volume M. Villey deals with "the evolution
of the *Essays*," or, in other words, with the development of
Montaigne's art and thought. He traces the form of the
Essays from the first modest attempts after the pattern of
the popular compilations of *Lectiones* or *Leçons* through the
type represented by essays 40 (originally 14), 19, 20, 22, 23,
42 of Book I, which, though more fully developed and far
more interesting than the first attempts, still contains little
of Montaigne except his imagination, through the still further
developed type, of which we have examples in II. 2–6, to the
essay *On the Education of Children* (I. 25) and essays 7–11 and

16–37 of Book II, all of which belong to the years 1578–1580, when Montaigne had become complete master of his instrument.

Montaigne's thought developed *pari passu* with the form of his Essays, and in his second volume M. Villey traces its evolution with remarkable insight. There is first the Stoical phase under the influence of La Boétie and Seneca, a phase which had nothing original in it and nothing Christian. From this Montaigne, gradually and without any violent rupture, emancipated himself under the influence of Plutarch, whose *Lives* and *Moral Works* he read in Amyot's translation. Plutarch, too, had an appreciable and important effect upon his whole mentality, widening and deepening his estimate of human nature, awakening his dormant critical faculty, and calling forth his latent originality. Then came the Sceptical phase, foreshadowed in essays I. 31 and 47, *On the Uncertainty of our Judgment*, both of which belong to 1572, but not reaching the acute stage till the year 1576, when he struck his Pyrrhonist medal, and when, as M. Villey conjectures, he wrote the last and most important part, with its numerous borrowings from Sextus Empiricus, of the *Apologie de Raimond de Sebonde*.

"The great novelty of the *Apology* and its governing thought," says M. Villey, "is that we have no communication with Being," *i.e.* that we have no knowledge of the absolute, but only of changing phenomena. Thus there emerges from the long diatribe against human reason the philosophic doctrine of relativism, the belief in the relativity of knowledge and the relativity of morals. When the phase of acute Scepticism had passed away, Montaigne continued to hold this belief, though with some modifications, and his relativism in morals, was, M. Villey suggests, the starting-point for his self-portraiture. But it was not, as we have seen, till the essay *On Presumption* (II. 17), written in 1578 or 1579, that he seriously put forward his design. The other essays of the First and Second Books (I. 25, II. 8 and 10), in which he gives effect to it, are among the very latest of those Books.

Between the completion of these books and the time when

Montaigne again settled down to more or less continuous writing there was an interval of six years, during which he garnered much experience of the world and public affairs. The essays of the Third Book appear to have been written in the order in which they are printed, and roughly speaking it may be said that essays 1–9 belong to the year 1586 and 10–13, together with the additions to the earlier books, to the year 1587. It is to these essays, the richest and most original of all, that we must look for the final expression —so far as the word final can be applied to so Protean a mind—of Montaigne's opinions. Thus in the first essay, *On Expediency and Honesty*, he expounds his political principles, and in the second, *On Repentance*, his views on morality; essay 11, *On the Lame*, is a warning against dogmatism and credulity; while the last, *On Experience*, is a sort of general profession of his whole philosophy of life.

M. Villey points out that in the Third Book Montaigne's self-portraiture has assumed a different character. He is no longer drawing a portrait for his friends, but, believing that "Chaque homme porte la forme entière de l'humaine condition," he regards it as a contribution to the general study of man, and the fact that he was (as he modestly thought) an ordinary individual made it all the more valuable.

M. Villey does not agree with M. Strowski in thinking that the additions which he made to the *Essays* after 1588, with their often indiscreet frankness and their excessive licence of expression, are a sign of dilettantism. It is certainly against M. Strowski's view that during these final years of his life Montaigne read more assiduously and more methodically than before, and that his reading included such solid authors and works as Plato, Aristotle's *Ethics*, Diogenes Laertius, Xenophon's *Anabasis*, Herodotus, Livy, Quintilian, Cicero's philosophical treatises, his old friend Seneca, and St Augustine[1].

That Montaigne was a dilettante in its ordinary sense of an

---

[1] M. Villey has counted no less than 270 citations from Cicero, over a hundred from Seneca, Diogenes Laertius, and Plato, sixty-six from Livy, fifty from Herodotus, and forty from St Augustine.

amateur, that he was not a professional either in philosophy, or in morals, or in education, is a truth sometimes forgotten by over-censorious critics. But he was not a dilettante in M. Strowski's sense, that is to say, the sense in which the term was applied to Renan after the Franco-German war, to denote one who, as a diversion from disillusion and *ennui*, amuses himself with moral and philosophical speculations in which he does not really believe. This is not the character of Montaigne's latest additions. They show rather, notes M. Villey, an increased predilection for citation, for stories, and for personal details and confidences, which are often trivial and indiscreet. They are characteristic of a man whom age has made garrulous, and whom literary success has made secure of his public and indifferent to criticism. Yet the graver side is not wanting. Many of the new meditations have an eminently serious character, and this is to be found even in several of the new stories.

M. Villey rightly points out that the additions have one inconvenience; they often injure the form and obscure the sense of the essays. Ruel would be hard put to it to justify some of them on artistic grounds. Yet along with this disregard for the form of his essays Montaigne shows an increasing pre-occupation with his style. One word is replaced by another; sentences are reinforced or scratched out or altogether re-written. The majority of these changes are made in the interest of his thought, but often it is a pure question of style. Repetitions and negligences are pruned away or corrected; grammar and punctuation are carefully attended to, and there are minute typographical directions to the printer[1]. "Je suis moins faiseur de livres que de nulle autre besogne," he had said in the address to Mme de Duras which forms the *envoi* of the first edition of the *Essays*, and now at the close of his life we find him sparing no pains to make his book as perfect as possible.

From the clash of these diverse interpretations, and from the

---

[1] M. Villey has counted more than three thousand small corrections of details in the manuscript additions. See II. 535–545, for the general question of Montaigne's pre-occupation with matters of style.

renewed and more penetrating examination of Montaigne's own testimony which they invite, certain points of agreement seem to emerge. In the first place it is all-important to bear in mind that Montaigne's opinions were in a continual state of flux and development, and that in the First and Second Books of the *Essays* as many as three different strata of thought are represented. Secondly, we must remember not only that Montaigne was not a professional philosopher, but that he was constitutionally averse to anything that savoured of system or dogmatism. His one aim was to record his impressions as they occurred to him, without any thought of consistency or finality. And his record was made in good faith. Sainte-Beuve is almost alone in accusing him of perfidy. The rest of his interpreters, whatever their attitude in other respects to his character or opinions, are unanimous in recognising his honesty and candour. But the opposite mistake must not be made of taking everything that he says exactly according to the letter. He was a Gascon, he was a man of humour and rich imagination, and he loved to give rein to the fancies of his active brain.

Myself, who make it a point of conscience to lie and who care not greatly to give credit or authority to what I say, perceive nevertheless that in the discourses I have in hand, when I am heated either by another's opposition or by the warmth of my narration, I swell and amplify my subject by voice, gesture, vigour and force of words, and even by extension and amplification, not without prejudice to the simple truth.

And a little further on he added in the margin, "An unaffected and lively speech, as mine ordinarily is, is easily betrayed into hyperbola[1]."

From the first moment when Montaigne begins to write his essays his interest in human nature appears. His earliest experiments are nearly all anecdotes in illustration of some moral trait. Thus in his amateur fashion he became a moralist and a psychologist. To draw his own portrait was certainly not part of his original design, but being interested in himself rather beyond the ordinary it occurred to him that here he had a subject upon which he was really competent to speak. Then

[1] III. II, *On the Lame.*

in the interval between the first publication of his *Essays* and that of the enlarged edition with the addition of the Third Book he realised that self-portraiture might be made something more than the mere amusement of a man who liked to communicate himself to his friends, that every man, however obscure and humble, had in him the impress of the human race, and that to draw a faithful portrait of yourself was a valuable contribution to the study of man in general.

This highly important side of Montaigne's book was largely ignored in the seventeenth century. On the other hand, friends and foes alike greatly exaggerated its scepticism. The excessive scepticism of the *Apology for Raimond de Sebonde* was in part due to its writer's love of paradox; in part it was a passing phase, which did not preclude a good many positive beliefs, especially in certain moral virtues. But it left Montaigne with a very modest opinion of human reason. "Un instrument libre et vague" he terms it in the essay *On the Lame*, the whole trend of which is to caution us against credulity and dogmatism. And in dogmatism he includes religious dogmatism. "After all, it is putting a very high price on one's conjectures to roast a man alive for them."

This brings us to the question of Montaigne's Christianity. That the Christian religion had no influence on his ethical conduct, that it taught him neither how to live nor how to die, all his interpreters are agreed. But it is an open question how far he accepted it as a matter of faith. Did he merely conform to the outward observances of religion from habit and for the sake of appearances? Or did he, holding that knowledge of the Absolute is unattainable to human reason, render unquestioning obedience to the teaching of the Catholic Church? His actions no less than his utterances make it impossible to reconcile the former alternative with the honesty which nearly all recognise in him. On the other hand, the plain construction of more than one passage in the *Essays*[1] points to the latter alternative, and if it seems inconsistent with Montaigne's ethical attitude, and especially with the essay *On Repentance*, we must bear in mind that in Montaigne's

[1] See above, pp. 279–280.

day the divorce between religion and morality was almost complete. It was one thing to accept Christianity as a creed; it was another to take it as a guide to moral conduct.

So far, with certain notable exceptions, there is a fairly general consensus of opinion among Montaigne's interpreters. At any rate it is ground which has been thoroughly explored. But there remains a further field of inquiry. Montaigne, it is now generally recognised, was not an out and out sceptic; in spite of his *Que sais-je?* he held and expressed some very definite opinions, in particular on education. What were these opinions? What was his message to those who came after him? M. Villey has made a highly important contribution to the subject by pointing out that relativity is the governing idea of the last part of the *Apology for Raimond de Sebonde*. But this essay was written twelve years before the publication of the 1588 edition of the *Essays* and sixteen years before Montaigne's death, and Montaigne was not the man to hold fast without change or modification to any one idea. Certainly his views as to the relativity of morals underwent considerable change, and it is in morals and conduct, or in other words, in the art of life, that Montaigne was most interested. Individualism—Nature—Conscience—what parts did these play in Montaigne's mature philosophy of life? Here is a rich subject upon which we may look for further light from his future interpreters. They will find an admirable point of departure in the thoughtful pages of M. Villey and also in some suggestive notes which M. Lanson has printed in *La Civilisation française*[1].

---

[1] *L'Idéal français dans la Littérature de la Renaissance à la Révolution*, IVme *leçon, Montaigne* (*La Civilisation française* for July-August 1919).

SOME PAMPHLETS OF THE FRENCH WARS
OF RELIGION

THE period of the French wars of religion was emphatically an age of pamphlets. From the *Tigre* of François Hotman, that remarkable pamphlet which was published in the year of the Tumult of Amboise, to the *Satire Ménippée*, that still more remarkable pamphlet which heralded the entry of Henry IV into Paris, they were produced in long succession. At first, indeed, the production was somewhat sparse, but the massacre of St Bartholomew gave it additional impetus, and, if it slackened somewhat during the earlier years of Henry III, towards the close of his reign it became enormous. The revival of the League, the question of the succession, the murder of the Guises, and finally the murder of the King himself, were each an occasion for a fresh fusillade. After his death the firing became less furious, but it was more effective; a share in the final victory of Henry IV was rightly attributed by a contemporary historian to the *plumes bien taillées* of the pamphleteers of his party[1].

Some of the pamphlets were, originally at least, written in Latin. Dealing for the most part with questions of constitutional law or political philosophy, they appealed from the passions of contending Frenchmen to the judgment of educated Europe. But, though they rise above the dust of party warfare to the clear atmosphere of philosophy, and though they wear an air of candid inquiry, they are none the less inspired by contemporary events; the fighting man's harness peeps out under the philosopher's cloak, and in the heat of the

---

[1] The fullest bibliographical lists of the pamphlets will be found in Lelong, *Bibliothèque historique*, II. 233–354, nos. 17,757–19,557, and in the sale catalogue of the Coste library (Lyons, 1854), nos. 1575–2066. A great many are noticed by G. Weill, *Les théories sur le pouvoir royal en France pendant les guerres de religion*, 1892.

scuffle the combatants often interchange weapons. Of the
two most important of these learned pamphlets, the *Franco-
Gallia* and the *Vindiciae contra tyrannos*, an admirable account
has been given by Mr Armstrong[1]. My own interest lies more
with those written in the vernacular, and especially with those
that have any literary merit. The *Tigre* and the *Satire Ménippée*, the *Livre des Marchands* of Regnier de la Planche, the
two *Discours* of Michel Hurault, the *Anti-Espagnol* of Antoine
Arnauld, are all more or less remarkable specimens of French
prose, which the student of literature must take into account.
But they have an historical interest as well, and in saying
something about these as well as about some others less
remarkable for literary merit, I hope I may be of some service
to the historical student. I shall concern myself more especially with bibliographical questions, though I cannot claim to
have solved them all. But it is, at any rate, of importance to
the historian to know when a pamphlet was first published.

From 1560 to 1565 the favourite mark of the pamphleteers
was the house of Guise. Already in the reign of Henry II the
Guises had disputed with their rival, the Constable de Montmorency, the first place in the royal council chamber; the
accession of Francis II, the sickly husband of their niece,
Mary Stewart, brought the whole power of the crown into
their hands. The conspiracy of La Renaudie, which came to
an untimely birth in the so-called Tumult of Amboise, was
engendered rather by the discontent of the nobles at the
power of the Lorrainers than by zeal for the reformed religion.
The feeling of the malcontents found expression in an often-
quoted quatrain:

> Le feu roi[2] divina ce point,
> Que ceux de la maison de Guise
> Mettraient ses enfants en pourpoint,
> Et son pauvre peuple en chemise.

---

[1] *The English Historical Review*, IV. 1889, 13 ff. See also Weill, *op. cit.*
pp. 98 ff.; A. Elkan, *Die Publizistik der Bartholomäusnacht*, Heidelberg,
1905; K. Glaser, *Beiträge zur Geschichte der politischen Literatur Frankreichs
in der zweiten Hälfte des 16 Jahrhunderts* in *Zeitschr. für franz. Sprache und
Litteratur*, XXXIX. 240 ff.

[2] Francis I.

It was more especially against the Cardinal of Lorraine, the guiding mind of the Guise family, that the wrath of their opponents was directed. It overflowed at boiling point in a tiny pamphlet, containing ten small pages of text, which appeared in 1560, the year of the Tumult, under the title of *Epistre envoiée au Tigre de la France*[1]. It was naturally anonymous, but we know from tolerably conclusive evidence that it was written by the well-known jurist and publicist, François Hotman, the author of the *Franco-Gallia*. Modelled on Cicero's Catiline orations, it reads like a succession of pistol-shots fired point-blank at the cardinal. Rarely had the French language been used with such nervous and concise energy. But, as a full account of the pamphlet will be found in Baird's *History of the Huguenots*[2], I need say no more about it here.

The next pamphlet that I shall notice belongs to the year 1565. The first civil war had, after a year's duration, been terminated by the Edict of Amboise in March 1563. In December the council of Trent had concluded its labours; the Counter-Reformation had begun. In January 1564 the cardinal of Lorraine returned to France and tried in vain to procure the recognition of the council's decrees in that country. In the following March Catherine de' Medici and Charles IX began that "progress" through France which was to culminate in the celebrated interview at Bayonne with the Queen of Spain and the Duke of Alva (June 1565). Meanwhile the Huguenots were complaining that the Edict of Amboise was not being observed. It must have been a little before the interview at Bayonne that the new pamphlet appeared[3]. The title-page contains nothing but the date—1565—and the title *Du grand et loyal devoir, fidelité et obéissance de messieurs de Paris envers le Roy et Couronne de France, addressée à*, etc. Here follow the names of the Provost of the Merchants and the four

---

[1] Edited by C. Read for the Académie des Bibliophiles (1875) from the copy then supposed to be unique, which escaped the destruction of the Hôtel de Ville library by the Commune. Since then a copy was sold in the Sunderland sale (no. 4918) for £42.

[2] 2 vols., 1880, I. 445 ff.; see also K. Glaser, *op. cit.* in *Zeitschr. für franz. Spr. und Lit.* XXXII (1907), pp. 250 ff.

[3] The printing had been finished for three months, says the publisher.

sheriffs of Paris[1]. The pamphlet was commonly known as *Le Livre des Marchands*, and its author was undoubtedly Louis Regnier de La Planche, the son of a magistrate of Poitiers, who was attached to the household of the Constable of Montmorency[2]. He was a Protestant, but, as he says of himself in his admirable *Histoire de l'Estat de France sous François II*, he was *homme politique plutost que religieux*[3], and in this pamphlet he wears the mask of a moderate Catholic. Its occasion was the entry of the cardinal of Lorraine into Paris on January 8, 1565, when, contrary to the royal prohibition, he was attended by an armed escort. Accordingly, François de Montmorency, the Constable's son, in his capacity of governor of the Ile de France, having in vain warned him, while still on the road, that he would not permit such an infringement of the king's orders, dispersed the escort by force as soon as it had entered the gate of Saint-Denis, and forced the cardinal and his friends to take refuge in some neighbouring houses. The pamphlet opens with a description of this event, of which the writer represents himself as an eyewitness. He then describes how he engaged in conversation with several shopkeepers on the state of public affairs and in particular on the merits of the house of Guise. A representative of each trade is brought forward in turn, and made to express his opinion, the author professing merely to record these opinions without adding anything of his own. With great skill the Guises are represented in the light most calculated to make them unpopular with the Paris *bourgeoisie*. Their foreign descent, their greed of power and office, their offences against the clergy, the nobles, and the Tiers État, are all dwelt on in turn; while generally their selfish and antinational policy is contrasted with the patriotism of the house of Montmorency. But the pamphlet is not merely an attack on the Guises; it is an appeal in favour of moderation and

---

[1] I possess a copy. It will be found in the *Panthéon Littéraire* under *Chroniques et Mémoires*, and in the edition of the *Histoire de l'Estat de France*, published by Techener in 1836.

[2] *Réveille-matin*, dialogue I, p. 104.

[3] I cannot agree with Baird's reasons (*History of the Huguenots*, I. 410, note) for doubting the authorship of La Planche.

tolerance, of that policy which Michel de L'Hospital, now chancellor, was in vain endeavouring to carry out. Speaking by the mouth of a Catholic draper (pp. 27 ff.), La Planche, while regretting the errors of the Protestants, extols them as honest men and good citizens; and he likens the ultra-Catholics to a man who would scuttle a ship because he had a quarrel with someone on board.

The style of the pamphlet is strongly latinised as regards the syntax and the order of the words, but it is distinguished by admirable management of both clause and sentence, at that date a rare quality in French prose, and by a lively and vigorous use of metaphor. These qualities enable one to assign with confidence to the same writer a later attack on the cardinal, entitled *La Légende de Charles, cardinal de Lorraine*[1], which appeared in 1576, two years after the cardinal's death. It was intended to be in three books, but only the first book, which deals with events down to the year 1570, ever appeared. On the other hand, the *Response à l'espistre de Charles de Lorraine*, etc., published in 1565, which is generally attributed to Regnier de la Planche, though, as far as I know, on no satisfactory evidence, is, judging by the style, certainly not by him.

From 1572 to 1576 the pamphlets are all more or less inspired by the massacre. Even a grave philosophical treatise like the *Vindiciae contra tyrannos* is a cry for vengeance against the tyrant; and the tyrant is Catherine de' Medici: it is she, and not the house of Guise, who is now the main object of attack. The *Discours merveilleux* is the pendant to the *Légende du cardinal de Lorraine*.

The first of these pamphlets that calls for notice is the well-known *Réveille-matin*, which was published early in the year

---

[1] *La Légende de Charles, cardinal de Lorraine, et de ses frères de la maison de Guise, descrite en trois livres*, par François de l'Isle. A Reims, de l'imprimerie de Jacques Martin, 1576. A second edition was published in 1579 (Reims: Pierre Martin). The place of publication and the publisher's name are doubtless spurious in both cases, for Reims was devoted to the Guises. The pamphlet will also be found in the *Mémoires de Condé*, VI. M. Hauser in *Les Sources de l'hist. de France, XVIe siècle*, III. 82, thinks the attribution to La Planche improbable; he notes the writer's use of his recognised works.

1573 in both Latin and French, the French version being issued at Basle and entitled *Dialogue auquel sont traitées plusieurs choses avenues aux Luthériens et huguenots de la France*[1]. It was republished in both languages at the beginning of 1574, with the addition of a second part. The French version now received the title of *Le Réveille-matin des François*[2], and was dedicated to the queen of England in a letter dated November 20, 1573. This is followed, in both versions, first by another dedicatory letter addressed to the estates and princes of Poland, and secondly by a letter purporting to be written to the duke of Guise by a follower of the house of Lorraine, and sent to him with a copy of the pamphlet[3]. The duke is assured that his accession to the throne would find favour with a large majority of the nation, including the Huguenots, and he is urged to come forward at once as the liberator of his country. A similar expression of the Huguenot views occurs in the body of the work[4].

The *Réveille-matin* has been attributed to at least three authors, but two of these attributions may be dismissed at once; that to Beza, as resting only on the unsupported statement of Adrien Baillet, who was born between seventy and eighty years after its publication; that to Hugues Doneau, the well-known jurist, as based on the sole authority of Cujas, who was his bitter opponent. The claims of Nicolas Barnaud, a gentleman of Crest in Dauphiné, are more deserving of consideration. They depend on the statement of J. J. Frisius, a native of Zürich, who, in his edition of the *Bibliotheca* of Conrad Gesner, published at Zürich in 1583, says that Barnaud was reputed to be the author, and that seven or eight years

---

[1] Cat. Coste, 1684. The printing was finished on the twelfth day of the sixth month *d'après la journée de la trahison, i.e.* on February 12, 1573.

[2] *Le Réveille-matin des François et de leurs voisins. Composé par Eusèbe Philadelphe cosmopolite, en forme de Dialogues*, à Edimbourg, de l'imprimerie de Jacques James, 1574*. (The asterisk indicates that I have a copy.) The real place of printing is evidently either Basle or Geneva or Lausanne. The Latin version, though it bears the same fictitious names of printer and place of printing, is from a different press.

[3] The letter is dated from Reims; in the Latin version the date is January 1, 1574, in the French version December 10, 1573.

[4] pp. 104–105. The whole passage is quoted by Mr Armstrong in the *English Historical Review*, IV. 26.

previously one M. de Lafin had given him a tremendous box
on the ear for it in a street of Basle without his making any
resistance[1]. But, supposing this story to be true, it hardly
proves that Barnaud was the author of the *Réveille-matin*;
and probably Lenient is right in his conjecture that, like the
Satire Ménippée, it is the work of several hands[2]. There is
certainly considerable difference in the style of the different
speakers, which, judging from other pamphlets of this time,
is not to be accounted for by an attempt at dramatisation.
As regards the subject-matter of the pamphlet, it is too well-
known to require any reference to it here. I will only point
out that the tone of the second part, though more calm and
serious, is much more republican and revolutionary than that
of the first part, and that one of the questions discussed by the
two speakers—the historian and the politician—is whether
it is lawful to resist an unjust magistrate. This question
forms the third and most important of the four *quaestiones* of
the *Vindiciae contra tyrannos*, and was at this time the chief
topic of discussion among the political writers on the Protestant side. It forms the staple subject of Beza's tract *Du
Droit des magistrats sur leurs subjects*[3] and of *Le Politique du
temps*, both published in 1574, while similar in character is
La France-Turquie, published in 1575[4]. Mr Armstrong has
called attention to the close connexion that exists between
the whole of this group of pamphlets, and there is a good deal
of plausibility in his suggestion that they were the work of
"a kind of syndicate." It is also worth noticing that for the

---

[1] p. 833; the passage is correctly cited by P. Marchand in his *Dictionnaire
Historique* (1758), I. 86 (F), and is referred to by Placcius, *Theatrum
Anonymorum*, II. 497. The same story is told in B. G. Struvius's *Bibl. Hist.*
(ed. Meusel), VII. pt. II. p. 316. See Haag, 2nd ed., *s.v.* Barnaud, and Loise-
leur, *Trois énigmes historiques*, pp. 113–116, both of whom have failed to
find the passage in Gesner's *Bibliotheca*.

[2] A passage in the *Mémoires de Nevers* (I. 343) implies that the authorship
was unknown in Court circles in May 1575.

[3] Beza's authorship is established by A. Cartier, *Les idées politiques de
Th. de Bèze, Bull. Soc. de l'hist. et arch.*, Geneva, vol. II. bk. IV. 1900. See
for the tract itself Weill, *op. cit.* pp. 88–90.

[4] With another pamphlet entitled *Lunettes de cristal de roche*; but there
must have been an earlier edition, for it was written in answer to a pamphlet
supposed to be written by the Chevalier Poncet, the *Lunettes de cristal* being
a rejoinder to his reply. See D'Aubigné, *Hist. Univ.* ed. A. de Ruble, IV. 191.

most part they were published both in Latin and in French, the Latin version in several cases being the original one.

Among the borrowings of the *Réveille-matin* (second part) is a long extract from the famous *Discours de la Servitude voluntaire* or *Contr'un* of La Boétie, which, though it was written as far back as 1548, was printed for the first time in entirety in Goulart's *Mémoires de l'estat sous Charles IX* (1576). Remarkable for its literary merit and promise of future excellence, it is to be regarded rather as a schoolboy declamation than as a serious contribution to political thought. The fact, however, that it was first published at this time is significant.

Another noteworthy pamphlet, which appeared in 1574, is the *Discours merveilleux de la vie et actions et déportemens de Catherine de Medicis*[1], or the *Vie Sainte Catherine*, as it was often called by contemporaries[2]. It has been attributed to Henri Estienne and to Jean de Serres. The authorship of Henri Estienne has been clearly disproved by Mark Pattison[3]. It is equally impossible that it could have been written by Jean de Serres, who aspired to be a grave and impartial historian and who advocated a policy of conciliation. Moreover, he would hardly have made a mistake in the age of Charles IX. Though the writer, whoever he is, poses as a Catholic, we may accept the statements of Pierre de l'Estoile and Louis Dorleans (in the *Catholique anglois*) that he was a Huguenot. He is not unfriendly to the house of Guise, but Catherine is painted in the blackest colours; her policy is represented as having for its sole object the concentration of the government in her own hands; personal charges of the gravest character, especially of poisoning, are brought against her. It is here that the story of her having poisoned Jeanne d'Albret first appears.

Another violent attack on Catherine is *Le Tocsain contre les*

---

[1] This is the title of the earliest known edition, 8vo, pp. 164, 1575 (*Bib. Sund.* I. no. 4877). Several other editions as well as a Latin and an English translation appeared in 1575. In the original edition the title was *Deportemens de Catherine de Medicis*. I have an edition of 1576: *Seconde edition plus correcte, mieux disposee que la premiere et augmentee de quelques particularitez*.

[2] For the date see *Registre Journal de P. de L'Estoile, notice et extraits d'un nouveau manuscrit*, ed. H. Omont, 1900, pp. 5, 6. The Cardinal of Lorraine, who died December 29, 1574, read it.

[3] *Essays*, I. 120 ff.

massacreurs[1], which, though not published till the summer of 1577, was written soon after the massacre, of which it contains a full account, differing in some important particulars from that of the *Réveille-matin*. For instance, it expressly says that Charles IX did not fire at the Huguenots—*non pas qu'il y mit les mains*—and it gives the number of those killed at Paris as 2000 instead of 10,000. It differs, too, from most of the Protestant pamphlets of this period in its respect for constituted authority, and in being printed in France and not at Basle or Geneva. Nor, so far as I know, is there a Latin version of it. The Duke of Alençon, although at the time of publication he had deserted the *Politique* and Huguenot cause, and was in nominal command of the Catholic forces, is treated with great consideration as the one member of his family whose hands were not stained with Huguenot blood. It is to Catherine's door that the sins of her two other surviving sons are laid. She is charged with having purposely educated them in vice, and especially with having instructed them in the precepts of "that atheist Machiavelli[2]." *Et de fait, on peut bien appeller ce livre-là l'evangile de la Roine mere.*

This representation of Catherine, to whose father *the Prince* was dedicated, as an ardent student of Machiavelli, was a favourite topic with the Protestant writers. It is therefore noticeable that just about this time, namely in 1576, Gentillet published his *Anti-Machiavel*[3], a book which, like the *Franco-Gallia* and the *Vindiciae contra tyrannos*, is none the less a *livre de circonstance*, because it is in form a philosophical treatise. It may be noticed, too, that he dedicated it to Alençon, then the nominal head of the *Politique* party. In fact all the pamphlets of this period—1572 to 1576— show traces of the *rapprochement* between the two parties, which resulted in a regular alliance being declared between the Protestants of Languedoc and the *Politiques*. Moreover,

---

[1] *Le Tocsain contre les massacreurs et auteurs des confusions en France... adressé à tous les princes Chrestiens.* Reims: Jean Martin, 1577*. Here, again, the place and printer's name are no doubt a blind. It was reprinted in 1579. Printed in Cimber and Danjou, *Archives curieuses*, VII. 3–76.

[2] f. 33 rº.

[3] The proper title is *Discours sur les moyens de bien gouverner et maintenir en bonne paix un royaume ou autre principauté, contre N. Machiavel Florentin.*

we find in some of them, notably in the second dialogue of the *Réveille-matin*, signs of that tendency to decentralisation, federalism, and even separatism which the royalist party regarded as one of the most dangerous features of Protestantism[1].

The death of Alençon (1584) was, in Ranke's caustic phrase, of more importance than his life had ever been. It left a heretic next in succession to the throne, and, just as the coalition between the *Politiques* and the Huguenots had led to the formation of the original League, so this new turn of the wheel of politics produced a revival of it with a new and more effective organisation, the heart of which was Paris. "The League has two main principles," says a pamphlet of 1586, "one, that no religion save that of the Catholic, Apostolic, and Roman Church shall have a place in this kingdom; the other, that no one shall be admitted to the throne unless he is a Catholic." The anonymous pamphlet in which these words occur, the *Apologie des catholiques unis*[2], was written by Louis Dorleans, a Paris lawyer, who became the chief pamphleteer of the League, and was certainly their best writer. This first production of his controversial pen, which only numbers 32 pages, has at any rate two merits which the later ones lack—moderation in tone and concision in statement. He was not, however, the first in the field. Already in 1585 Pierre Du Belloy, a native of Montauban and advocate-general of the parliament of Toulouse, had published the well-known *Apologie Catholique*[3]. Like the rest of his writings it is

---

[1] See Weill, *op. cit.* p. 96, and the whole of the excellent chapter (VI) on the Protestants and the *Politiques*.

[2] *Apologie ou defence des Catholiques unis les uns avec les autres, contre les impostures des Catholiques associez à ceux de la pretendue Religion*, 1586*.

[3] *Apologie Catholique contre les libelles, declarations, advis et consultations faictes, escrites et publiees par les Liguez perturbateurs du repos du Royaume de France: qui se sont eslevez despuis le decez du feu Monseigneur, frere unique du Roy, par* E. D. L. I. C., 1585*. The initials have been interpreted as standing for Edmond de l'Alouette *Jurisconsulte*, but there can be no doubt that the real author was P. Du Belloy, to whom it is ascribed by P. de Mornay (*Mémoires*, I. 657); De Thou (LXXXII. 5), and P. Cayet, *Nov.* I. f. 20 v⁰, though the latter does not actually mention Du Belloy's name. Several reprints of the work appeared during 1585 and 1586, as well as a Latin version. Indeed, Bayle, whose account of P. Du Belloy is full and good, says that he had seen two Latin versions.

distinguished by good arrangement, considerable learning, and a vigorous and lively style, and it deserves the careful attention of those who are interested in the history of political theory. The second part, which deals with the heresy attributed to Henry of Navarre by the League, is the more instructive. After stating in no ambiguous terms the divine right of kings, Du Belloy argues at some length that even supposing Henry were a heretic he could not be excluded from the throne. "But," he continues, "he is not a heretic, for the Council of Trent, which claims to have defined the teaching of the Catholic Church, is devoid of all authority." Coming from a Catholic this bold statement of the Gallican point of view is noteworthy.

In September of the same year the Pope, Sixtus V, gave expression to the ultramontane point of view by excommunicating both Henry of Navarre and the prince of Condé. This act called forth a pamphlet entitled *Moyens d'abus, entreprises et nullitez du rescrit et bulle de Pape Sixte V*[1], in which the absolutist claims of the papacy are subjected to a searching attack. It is attributed to Du Belloy, and its character and style point to the attribution being correct.

The *Apologie* of Louis Dorleans was written more or less in answer to Du Belloy's two pamphlets, to which he alludes several times without, however, directly mentioning them. In the same year 1586 he published another pamphlet entitled *Advertissement des Catholiques anglois aux François catholiques* but commonly called *Le Catholique anglois*[2]. It is written in a clear and good style, though with an occasional abuse of declamation and the rhetorical artifice of interrogation, but the tone of the writer may be gauged from the

---

[1] The rest of the title is too long to reproduce here, but is noteworthy in that it is said to be *par un Catholique, Apostolique, Romain: mais bon François, et tresfidele subjet de la Couronne de France.* There are two editions, both of 1586, one with Cologne as the place of printing (probably fictitious)*, and the other with Embrun. According to M. Hauser it was printed at La Rochelle.

[2] *Advertissement des Catholiques anglois aux François catholiques du danger où ils sont de perdre leur religion, et d'experimenter, comme en Angleterre, la cruauté des ministres s'ils reçoyvent à la couronne un Roy qui soit Heretique,* 1586 (*Bibl. Sund.* no. 4703); 1587. Reprinted with some omissions in Cimber and Danjou, *Archives curieuses,* XI. III ff.

fact that he speaks of the massacre as a *saignée très-salutaire* and of heretics as being worse than Jews or infidels. The most important thing to notice is that here for the first time we find the theories of the Protestant writers being turned against them.

> En leur *Françoise Gaule*, qui est l'un des plus détestables livres qui ait veu le jour, et que l'on a composé pour mettre toute la France en combustion, ils chantent qu'il est loisible de choisir un Roy à son appetit. Dites doncques aux hérétiques que le Roy de Navarre n'est à vostre appetit, et partant qu'il se tienne en son Béarn jusques à ce que le goust vous en soit revenu. Ainsi les faut-il fouetter des verges qu'ils ont cueillies.

The pamphlet provoked an answer from Duplessis-Mornay under the title of *Lettre d'un gentilhomme catholique françois contenant breve Response aux calomnies d'un certain pretendu Anglois*, 1586[1], and another entitled *Response à un ligueur masque du nom de catholique anglois, Par un vrai Catholique bon François*, 1587*. To these Dorleans replied with the *Replique pour le catholique anglois contre le catholique associé des huguenots*, 1588.

Two other pamphlets deserving notice belong to the year 1587; one of them, entitled *De l'authorité du Roy*[2], is certainly by Pierre Du Belloy, for in a later edition, of 1594, it was published under his name. The other, *Examen du discours public contre la maison royalle de France*[3], may be ascribed to him with equal certainty. Like the *Moyens d'abus*, it is said to be *par un Catholique, Apostolique, Romain*, etc., while on its title-page is a curious allegorical woodcut which had already adorned that of the *Apologie Catholique*. But the author's active championship of the royalist cause was now brought to a sudden close. He had said in the *Apologie* and he repeats in the *Examen*, that the League was due, not to any zeal on

---

[1] Printed, according to Claudin, at La Rochelle or Montauban; according to E. Picot (*Cat. Rothschild*) at La Rochelle. I have an edition of 1587, which was printed apparently in Belgium. Reprinted in Duplessis-Mornay's *Mémoires*, 2 vols., 1624, I. 619–673; *Mémoires de la Ligue*, I. 454; *Archives curieuses*, XI. 205 ff.

[2] *De l'authorité du Roy et crimes de leze majesté qui se commettent par ligues, designation de successeur, et libelles contre la personne et dignité du prince*, 1587.

[3] The title continues, *et particulierement contre la branche de Bourbon, seule reste d'icelle, sur la Loy Salique, et succession du Royaume*, 1587*.

behalf of the Catholic religion, but to the ambition of the house of Guise[1]. The Guises recognised him as a formidable opponent, and Henry III, yielding to their persuasions, ungratefully threw him into prison, where he remained for four years, till he escaped on May 18, 1591[2].

The success of the League was greatly helped by the character of Henry III. No king of France was ever more hated by his subjects. He was by no means altogether bad; indeed, he had at times fits of well-directed energy; but the most devout believer in the divine right of kings might be pardoned for asking himself whether a man who masqueraded by night as a woman and by day as a barefooted friar, and who oscillated from the wildest debauchery to the most abject superstition, could in truth be "the Lord's anointed[3]." A more particular cause of his unpopularity was the existence of his *mignons* or favourites. Had he chosen to make common cause with the *Politique* party and with those of the great Catholic nobles who were opposed to the Guise domination, he might easily have put himself at the head of a central or King's party which would have been stronger than either the Protestants or the ultra-Catholics. But the great nobles, indignant at seeing high offices of state, which they regarded as hereditary in their own families, heaped upon dissolute youths like Joyeuse and Épernon, rallied to the Guises, while the *Politiques*, though too loyal to the principle of hereditary monarchy to break with the King, were too much alienated by his outrages on common sense and decency to be very active in his cause.

Pamphlets and pasquinades against Henry and his *mignons* began to appear quite early in his reign, but the only one of any importance or interest, so far as I know, is the *Isle des hermaphrodites**, which though not published till about 1605 evidently relates to this time. It is worth looking into for the

[1] II. 10.

[2] P. de l'Estoile, in mentioning this, says he had been in prison nearly three years; but see Bayle. Belloy died in 1611, and L'Estoile regretted him as a good Frenchman and a good friend (*Journal*, XI. 108). See, for all these pamphlets of 1585–1587, Weill, *op. cit.* pp. 207–215.

[3] For Henry's character, as drawn by a violent Leaguer, see the *Second avertissement* of Dorleans, fo. 44 ff.

picture it gives of the ridiculous, not to say scandalous, vagaries of a court which its enemies compared, not unfairly, to that of Elagabalus. A special attack was directed against the most hated of the *mignons* by the one-eyed preacher of the League, Jean Boucher, whose *Histoire tragique et mémorable de Pierre de Gaverston**, published in July 1588, two months after the day of the Barricades, veiled under the story of the rise and fall of the favourite of Edward II a transparent allusion to Épernon, the favourite of Henry III. It is, however, neither interesting nor important. As usual, it produced a reply *L'antigaverston*, and a counter-reply *Replique à l'anti-gaverston*[1]*, both of the same year.

About the same time was published on the other side, in answer to Guise's letters to the King of May 17, the *Libre discours sur l'estat présent de la France*[2]. Its author was Michel Hurault, Sieur Du Fay, a grandson of the Chancellor de L'Hospital[3]. He was a Huguenot and secretary to the King of Navarre. His pamphlet, which is well written, well reasoned, and temperate in tone, begins with a sketch of the course of events from 1585; it then reviews with much insight the existing political situation; and concludes with a sharp attack on Guise. We learn from Palma Cayet that Guise read it on December 21, while he was in attendance on the King at Vespers in the chapel of Blois. Forty hours later he was assassinated[4]. His death caused the League to break definitely with the King, and Boucher in his *De justa Henrici III abdicatione* (1589) proclaimed with arguments borrowed from the Protestant writers of the preceding period the divine right of revolution[5]. Under April 1589 Pierre de l'Estoile, who made it his business to collect every pamphlet

[1] See p. 4 of the *Replique* for an interesting list of pamphlets, beginning with the *Apologie catholique*, which had appeared on the royalist side during the last three years, and which Épernon is accused of having had printed at his expense.

[2] Printed in the *Mémoires de la Ligue*, III. 2 ff.

[3] D'Aubigné, *Hist. Univ.* VIII. 327; *Perroniana* under Fay.

[4] P. Cayet, *Chron. nov.* I. p. 103 r⁰ (ed. of 1608).

[5] Written and partly printed, though not published, before the death of Henry III. Another edition was published at Lyons in 1591. For Boucher and his pamphlets see Glaser, *op. cit.* in *Zeitschr. für franz. Spr. und Lit.* XIV (1917–1919), 299 ff.

and broadside that appeared, tells us that he had collected over three hundred which were published at this time against the King, and he gives the names of fifteen[1], the first of which, by André de Rossant, a Lyons lawyer and poet[2], *Les meurs, humeurs et comportemens de Henry de Valois*, 1589, I possess. It is very violent, ill-arranged, and ill-written. Its concluding appeal to all good Catholics to unite in deposing the King was responded to by his assassination, and this called forth a fresh salvo of pamphlets, in which the monk Jacques Clément was hailed as the saviour of society.

Pope Sixtus V spoke of the event as a sign that God still had the kingdom of France in His keeping[3]. But this seemed to the more ardent leaguers hardly strong enough for the occasion. There was accordingly published at Paris what purported to be a true version of the papal allocution, three doctors of theology, of whom one was Boucher, certifying that they had compared it with a copy which had been sent from Rome[4]. The blasphemous exaggeration of the language leads one to suppose that the real author of the document was Boucher himself. It was, however, widely accepted as genuine[5], and provoked two answers which find particular mention in a well-known passage of D'Aubigné where he speaks of "those delicate and learned treatises which opened men's eyes and brought them to the King's service[6]." One of these was in Latin and entitled *Anti-Sixtus* (1590)[7]. The other, *La Fulminante* (1589)[8], a coarse and abusive little pamphlet, far from deserving D'Aubigné's praise, was, accord-

[1] *Journal*, III. 280; and see D'Aubigné, *Hist. Univ.* VI. 238.

[2] Hauser, *op. cit.* IV. 125.

[3] Ranke, *The Popes*, II. 121, and cf. Tempesti, *Vita di Sisto V*, II. 221.

[4] It was reprinted at London in 1678, the year of the popish plot.

[5] *E.g.* by De Thou, XCVI. 10, and in modern times by Macaulay and by Prof. Baird. The Comte de l'Épinois in his *La ligue et les papes* (p. 347), which is largely based on the Vatican archives, speaks of it as apocryphal. It is treated as such in a contemporary pamphlet, *Harangue pretendue par ceux de la Ligue avoir esté prononcee par N. S. Pere en plein consistoire et assemblée de Cardinaux le 11 Septembre*, 1589 (1589).

[6] *Hist. Univ.* VIII. 327.

[7] Ascribed by Brunet to Hurault, but, so far as I know, without authority.

[8] *La Fulminante pour feu tres grand et tres Chrestien Prince Henry III Roy de France et de Polongne. Contre Sixte V soy disant Pape de Rome et les rebelles de la France.*

ing to L'Estoile, the work of André Maillard, a master of requests, who died in 1592, having loved his King, says the diarist, better than his God[1].

The death of Henry III reduced, for a time at least, the number of parties to two, the party of the League and the party of Henry IV. At first, indeed, a large body of Catholic nobles and gentlemen held aloof from either camp. But the King's rapid successes during the first three months of his reign, the victory of Arques, the capture of the southern faubourgs of Paris, the submission of Maine with the greater part of Brittany and Normandy, brought them trooping to his standard. Accordingly, Louis Dorleans sat down to write a second *Warning from the English Catholics*, which was published with a reprint of his former pamphlet at the end of February 1590[2]. It is even more intemperate in tone than the first. The writer compares Henry III to Nero, and Henry IV to Herod, and he dwells on the latter's cruelty to the Catholics in Navarre, with other instances of his wickedness equally improbable and devoid of foundation. He attempts to set the *Politique* Catholics against the Huguenots by pointing out the hatred which the latter bore them, and the certainty that if they ever had the chance they would take vengeance for the massacre of St Bartholomew. The whole pamphlet, in its violence and narrowness, in its exaltation of sectarian religion above national feeling, reflects closely the spirit of the more fanatical portion of the League; but however strongly it may have appealed to the preachers and populace of Paris, it can only have disgusted those, if they ever read it, to whom it was addressed[3].

But while Dorleans was trying to sow dissension in the enemy's camp, his own party presented anything but a united front. It was divided into three factions, known respectively as the Spanish, French, and Lorraine leaguers, who were agreed in little else beyond opposition to Henry IV. The

---

[1] *Journal*, III. 317; V. 199.
[2] *Premier et second advertissements des Catholiques Anglois aux François Catholiques, et à la Noblesse qui suit à present le Roy de Navarre*, 1590*.
[3] D'Aubigné, *Hist. Univ.* VIII. 181.

Spanish faction, thanks chiefly to the able diplomacy of the Spanish ambassador Mendoza, seemed at present likely to predominate, and it was this danger which called forth at about the same time as Dorleans's pamphlet one of the most famous pamphlets of the period, the *Anti-Espagnol*[1].

Its author was Antoine Arnauld, a Paris lawyer (the father of Arnauld d'Andilly the eldest, and *le grand* Arnauld, the youngest of his twenty children), who soon afterwards became famous by his speech against the Jesuits[2]. His pamphlet is a piece of pure declamation, but the declamation is often very effective, and it is expressed in well-balanced musical periods, and in language which, though sometimes not in perfect taste, is always energetic and forcible. It became very popular, and was often reprinted. Its author had to fly from Paris disguised as a mason.

From the fact that the *Anti-Espagnol* makes mention of several reverses suffered by the League towards the close of 1589, but says nothing about the battle of Ivry, it may be inferred that it was written, at any rate, if not published, early in 1590. The events of the rest of the year tended strongly

---

[1] *Copie de l'Anti-Espagnol faict a Paris*, 48 pp. 1590 (*Bib. Sund.* I. 4806); an English translation of this appeared in the same year, entitled, *The Coppie of the Anti-Spaniard made at Paris by a Frenchman, a Catholique*. Later editions are *L'Anti-Espagnol et l'exhortation de ceux de Paris qui se veulent faire Espagnols*, 1591*; *Anti-Espagnol autrement les philippiques d'un Demosthenes François touchant les menees et ruses de Philippe Roy d'Espagne pour envahir la Couronne de France, Ensemble l'Infidelité, Rebellion et Fureur des Ligueurs Parisiens et Jesuistes en faveur de l'Espagnol*, 1592* (printed almost certainly at Chartres); *L'Anti-Espagnol et exhortation &c.; à tous les François de leur party, de se remettre en obeissance du Roy Henry IV et se delivrer de la tyrannie de Castille*, 1593 (*Bibl. Sund.* I. no. 5140).

[2] The express statement of Arnauld d'Andilly in his Memoirs that his father was the author of the *Anti-Espagnol* is confirmed not only by a sonnet which was written for his epitaph, and which contains the following lines—

> Contre un second Philippe usurpateur des lys
> Le second Démosthène anima ses écrits—

but by the internal evidence. The general style of the pamphlet is similar to that of Arnauld's speech against the Jesuits, and we even find the same metaphors and turns of phrase (see Froment, *Essai sur l'histoire de l'éloquence en France avant le XVIIe siècle*, 1874, pp. 151 ff.). The only reason for attributing it to Hurault, as is done by Lenient on the authority of Adrien Baillet, is its appearance in the *Quatre excellens discours*. M. de Ruble's note to D'Aubigné, *Hist. Univ.* VIII. 328, in which he says that there were two pamphlets with the same title, is clearly wrong.

to confirm the view that the only alternative to Spain was Henry IV. The battle of Ivry increased immensely the King's prestige. The siege of Paris taught its inhabitants by the most cruel of lessons the danger of resisting him; while its relief by the duke of Parma made it more and more clear that it was only Spain that could enable them to resist him successfully. Meanwhile the death of the old Cardinal de Bourbon, the King of the League, in whose election the three factions had concurred as a temporary expedient, helped to disintegrate the party more thoroughly. The more violent of the French leaguers began to enter into closer relations with Spain, while the more moderate were prepared to accept Henry IV, provided he became a Catholic. A movement was also made in the same direction chiefly in the interests and at the instigation of the two younger sons of the Prince of Condé, the Cardinal Charles de Bourbon and the Comte de Soissons. The appearance of two bulls of Gregory XIV, dated March 1, 1591, in which Henry was again declared excommunicate, and the clergy, nobles, and third estate of France were threatened with various penalties unless they renounced obedience to him, seemed a suitable occasion for starting a *Tiers parti*, as they called themselves. They accordingly issued, by way of manifesto, a paper addressed to the King, in which they called upon him to become a Catholic[1]. It became known from the place of its printing as the *Remonstrance d'Angers*, and immediately provoked various answers, notably a second *Discours* by Michel Hurault and the *Francophile* by André Maillard.

The author of the latter[2], after regretting the presence of men *plus parés d'hypocrisie que de foi, et plus patenostriers qu'hermites* in the party, proceeds to examine and refute their arguments in detail. He contends that it would be contrary to religion to advise the King to become a Catholic; that at

---

[1] P. Cayet, *Nov.* II. 458 v⁰.

[2] *Le Francophile pour tres-grand, tres-chrestien, tres-magnanime et tres-belliqueux Prince, Henry Auguste 4ᵉ, Roy de France et de Navarre. Contre les conspirations du Roy d'Espagne, du Pape, et des rebelles de France.* [Chartres], 85 pp. 1591*. The dedicatory epistle to the King is dated August 6.

most they should pray for his conversion and urge him to submit to instruction; that even if he remained a heretic it was God's command that they should recognise him as their King, and that if the Pope commanded the contrary they must disobey the Pope rather than disobey God[1]. Here we have a clear statement from the mouth of a Catholic of the doctrine of divine right. It is a direct negation of the two doctrines of the supremacy of the Pope and the sovereignty of the people, the compound of which, as prepared by Bellarmin and the Jesuits, had been found so serviceable by the League as a weapon against Henry IV[2].

The second *Discours*[3] of Michel Hurault is as temperate and well-reasoned as the first. It is, however, only the latter part of it—about a third of the whole—which is a direct answer to the *Remonstrance*[4]. The discourse begins with a sketch of events from the beginning of 1588 to the close of 1590, followed by an admirable discussion of the situation as it was in 1591. After examining the condition and prospects of the two parties, the writer proceeds to sketch Mayenne's character. Though studiously moderate in tone, he artfully brings out the two features of it most calculated to excite mistrust in his followers—his irresolution and his ambition to secure the crown for himself. A little later on we have the companion picture of Henry IV, in which with the same seeming show of impartiality all the King's most attractive qualities as a leader are thrown into high relief[5].

I do not know of any remarkable pamphlets that belong to the year 1592, but mention may be made of *Philippiques contre les bulles et autres pratiques de la faction d'Espagne*, Tours, 1592*, with a dedicatory letter to the King, dated April 10. The author, who signs himself F. D. C., was François

---

[1] See his summary of his argument, p. 82; it is quoted by P. Cayet, *Nov.* I. 459 r⁰.

[2] Bellarmin's *De summo pontefice* was published in 1586.

[3] *Suite du discours sur l'estat de la France*, 128 pp. 1592, printed in the same volume with a reprint of the first *Discours*, pp. 88—*Premier discours sur l'estat de la France. Suyvi d'un Second, sur le mesme subjet*.

[4] This part is printed in the *Mém. de la Ligue*, IV. 659 ff. without the name of the author being given.

[5] See Weill, *op. cit.* pp. 257–259.

de Clary, a member of the Great Council and the King's Advocate-General, who had published in the previous year (1591) *Remonstrance faicte au grand Conseil du Roy sur le retablissement requis par les officiers qui ont suyvi la Ligue**. The pamphlet of 1592 consists of two *Philippiques*, the first having been published separately earlier in the year, without place of publication. A third and fourth *Philippique* followed, the four being reprinted together at Tours in 1594. They are in substance an attack on the Pope, Gregory XIV, from the point of view of a Gallican and a Parliamentarian[1].

During the year 1592 the royalist cause made little progress in the field, but this was more than compensated for by the death of Parma, which took place in December. Meanwhile in Paris events had been working for Henry. The summary chastisement which Mayenne had inflicted on the leaders of the Sixteen for their murder of President Brisson had encouraged the *Politiques* to hold up their heads. They held meetings at the house of their leader, the Sieur Daubray, and set on foot a rival organisation to that of their opponents. Mayenne as usual played for his own hand. Though he had not abandoned his hopes of the crown, he judged it prudent to negotiate terms of submission with both Henry and the King of Spain. At last he was forced by the agents of Spain to summon a meeting of the states for January 17, 1593, and on January 5 he published a declaration calling upon the Catholics of the royalist party to rejoin the union and to send deputies to the meeting. This declaration provoked various answers, notably one from Antoine Arnauld entitled *La Fleur de Lys*[2]. Inferior to the *Anti-Espagnol* from a literary point of view, it is on the whole more effective as a pamphlet. Mayenne, the Duke of Savoy, the Jesuits, the Paris preachers, and the "old tyrant of Spain," are all in turn marks for the writer's brilliant and cutting invective. It is noteworthy that he points out the effect of Parma's death on the conduct of the war, returning to it again in his fine peroration which

---

[1] Hauser, *op. cit.* IV. no. 3038.

[2] *La Fleur de Lys; qui est un Discours d'un François retenu dans Paris, sur les impietez et deguisements contenus au Manifeste d'Espagne publié au moys de Janvier dernier*, 32 pp. 1593 (*Bib. Sund.* I. no. 4730).

begins: *Courage donc, François, la victoire est vostre, Parme est mort.*

La Fleur de Lys was republished twice in this year; first with the two *Discours* of Hurault in a volume entitled *Trois Excellens Discours sur l'estat present de la France*[1], and secondly in a volume entitled *Quatre Excellens Discours*, which also contains the *Anti-Espagnol*, but with considerable omissions and additions[2]. One of these additions is a defence of the Salic law, *vrai Palladium de la France*; another is a sharp attack on Louis Dorleans, and must have been added after July at the earliest, for it refers to a pamphlet of his which was called forth by the King's abjuration.

Dorleans had marked his disapproval of the murder of President Brisson by withdrawing from the Sixteen, and in October 1592 we hear of him inveighing against his former associates. But by December he had turned round again under the persuasion, according to L'Estoile, of Spanish gold; "for," says that amusing diarist, "he resembled the great Epaminondas in having to stay in bed to mend his breeches." His new pamphlet, though it was not printed till the end of February 1594, was no doubt circulated in manuscript long before this. It is entitled *Le Banquet du Comte d'Arete*[3], and professes to be an account of a conversation held after a dinner given by the count at the end of July. The attempt to give a dramatic setting to the work is a complete failure; the bad wit is as tedious as the ponderous learning, and the attack on Henry IV is even more outrageously scurrilous than anything that had yet come from Dorleans's pen. The following passage gives a good idea of the writer's sentiments, whether professed or real: "May God pardon that noble, royal, and generous soul Charles IX, but the clemency of St Bartholomew's day has been a rigorous and cruel clemency for France; for the sparing of a little blood has caused the death of a

---

[1] There is no name of place or publisher.

[2] I have not seen this edition of the *Quatre Discours*. I have one of 1594, which is clearly not from the same press as the *Trois Discours*; the *Anti-Espagnol* has the same title as in the separate edition of 1593.

[3] *Le Banquet et après-dinée du Comte d'Arete, où il se traicte de la dissimulation du Roy de Navarre, et des mœurs de ses partisans*, Paris, 1594*.

thousand millions, and is in danger of bringing to destruction France and the Christian religion." The only feature of interest in the pamphlet is the verse, some of which is not devoid of merit, especially the sonnet with which the pamphlet concludes, and which begins thus:

> Vous nous pensez perdus, ô monstres Politiques,
> Vous nous pensez perdus par l'infidelité.
> Vos Chastres, vos Vitris, pleins de rapacité,
> Ont vendu nos citez au roi des Heretiques[1].

There is also a well-known portrait in verse of the Chancellor de L'Hospital with his pale face, bald head, and long beard down to his breast.

The *Banquet d'Arete* is the scream of passion of a beaten cause. The King's conversion had cut the ground from under the League. If, on the one hand, it may be said to have justified the existence of the League, on the other it made that existence no longer possible. Had not Louis Dorleans himself said in his first pamphlet that if Henry abjured his religion in order to be king, every leaguer must rejoice, as the angels rejoice at the conversion of a sinner?[2] And now, almost on the very day when the printing of his latest pamphlet was completed, Henry was crowned at Chartres with the full ritual and ceremonial of the Catholic church[3]. As for Dorleans himself, he lived to write a glowing and apparently sincere panegyric on Henry IV after his death, and died himself in 1629, aged eighty-seven years.

The only remaining pamphlet which I propose to notice is the well-known *Dialogue d'entre le Maheustre et le Manant*. It is often cited by historians, being the principal authority for the formation of the Paris League, but the circumstances of its publication make it desirable to say a few words about it here. It appeared early in December 1593 without name of publisher or place of publication[4]. The attack on Mayenne

---

[1] This sonnet must have been written just before the publication of the pamphlet. The news of the surrender of Orleans by La Chastre reached Paris on February 20 (L'Estoile, VI. 127).

[2] *Apologie des Catholiques*, p. 15.

[3] February 27, 1594, the first Sunday in Lent.

[4] So far as I know, there are only two copies of this first edition; one (which I have consulted) is in the Bib. Nationale, and the other was formerly in the collection of the late Baron de Ruble (*Cat. Ruble*, 1899, no. 624).

which it contained made him very angry; he had a search made for the unknown printer, and two printers to the League, Rolin Thierry and Lyon Cavellat, were imprisoned on the charge of having printed it[1]. The pamphlet itself was suppressed and became exceedingly rare. On December 30 a summary of its chief points which had been made by Pierre de l'Estoile was read to Henry IV, who was much pleased, and said he would give any sum for a copy of the pamphlet. He had to pay ten crowns for one[2]. The authorship of the work has been variously assigned to Crucé, to Louis Morin, surnamed Cromé, and to Nicolas Rolland, all members of the Sixteen, and the two former among its most prominent leaders. There is nothing to connect Rolland with the authorship. Crucé, according to L'Estoile, was privy to the publication, but contemporary gossip pointed to Cromé as the author. "If you had hanged Cromé when you had him in your hands," said a member of Mayenne's council to him, "the book would never have seen the light[3]." For Cromé had escaped by flight from the death to which Mayenne had sentenced him as one of the principal agents in the murder of Brisson and his companions. He had afterwards returned to Paris, and had been discovered and denounced to Mayenne, but by his orders had been left in peace. There was no more thorough-going leaguer. When the Sixteen proposed the establishment of a *Chambre ardente* for the trial of heretics and traitors to the League, his name was fitly suggested for the office of president.

In spite of the suppression of *Le Maheustre et le Manant*, it was republished early in the following year (1594) under the same title[4], but with considerable additions to the part of the *Maheustre*, which have the effect of greatly strengthening his case. For instance, he is made to insist on the sincerity

---

[1] L'Estoile, VI. 110–113. Thierry's partner in general business was Nicolas Nivelle.

[2] L'Estoile, VI. 123.   [3] *Ib.* 115.

[4] The edition (of which I have a copy) to which my references are made has 158 leaves; on the back of the title-page there is a woodcut representing the two interlocutors. There is another edition of 1594 with 123 pages, badly printed in small type, which according to Brunet is later. This revised version is also printed in the Ratisbon edition of the *Satire Ménippée* (1726), III. 367 ff.

of the King's conversion, and to argue at some length that the Pope's absolution was unnecessary to make it complete[1]. He inculcates more than once the duty of obedience to lawful authority—*je vous ay monstré que sur peine de damnation eternelle Dieu nous commande d'obeir à noz superieurs tels qu'ils soient*[2]—and he points out that the action of the Sixteen in putting to death Brisson and his companions was contrary to the teaching of the Scriptures[3]. Again a long continuous narrative by the *Manant* in justification of the League's course of action since its formation is in the revised version constantly interrupted by the *Maheustre* with abuse of the Sixteen[4]. In another new passage they are charged with being one and all in the pay of Spain[5].

Such being the character of the additions, we are justified, I think, in accepting as correct a manuscript note on the titlepage of the copy of the original edition in the Bibliothèque Nationale, which states that the revised edition was printed by the King's party. In fact, if one reads the pamphlet in the revised edition, the case for the League appears so weak that it seems incredible that a leaguer should have written it. But read in the original edition, it appears in its true light as the apology of the League made in its last agony. "I would rather be the subject of a foreigner who is a Catholic than of a Frenchman who is a heretic." These words faithfully represent the state of feeling which the League leaders and the Jesuits had so skilfully fostered among the populace of Paris; and while they show how utterly the King's conversion had cut the ground from under them, they serve to remind us that in a sense the League's existence was justified by the issue. It had been instituted to prevent the succession of a heretic to the throne of France, and in this at any rate it had succeeded.

NOTE. When this paper appeared in the *English Historical Review* for July 1899, it was followed by a note in which I discussed the meaning of the term "the Sixteen." Since then

---

[1] 24 r⁰–28 r⁰.   [2] 21 r⁰.   [3] 71 r⁰.
[4] 61 v⁰–66 r⁰.   [5] 132 v⁰.

the origin of the League and its early organisation have been
recounted with great clearness and precision by M. Mariéjol
in vol. VI. part I. of the *History of France*, edited by M. Lavisse.
His account follows that of our principal source, *Le Maheustre
et le Manant*, so closely that it leaves little or no room for
criticism.

The League then, as at first organised, consisted of a
Council of nine or ten members, and of five persons, not
members of the Council, whose duty it was to obtain new
adherents, dividing between them for that purpose the sixteen quarters of the town. These five with the addition of
Charles Hotteman, Sieur de La Rocheblond, the originator
of the League, were known as "the Six." In their work of
recruiting they had the help of twelve assistants, whose names
as well as those of the Six are given in *Le Maheustre et le
Manant*.

As the League grew in numbers the organisation became
more elaborate. The Council of nine or ten seems to have disappeared and its place was taken by the General Council of
the Union, a body of forty who represented and were elected
by the three Estates. *Le Maheustre et le Manant* gives their
names; among the most prominent are Rose, Bishop of Senlis
and Rector of the University, Prevost, Boucher, Aubry, and
Launoy for the clergy; Acarie, La Bruyère, Auroux, Drouart,
Crucé, and Senault for the Third Estate. We also learn that
after the death of the old Cardinal de Bourbon the League
set up councils of nine in each of the sixteen quarters of the
city, and M. Mariéjol adds, as an inference, that the heads of
these councils or committees formed the directing Council of
the League. Now there was a Council which was commonly
called the "Council of the Sixteen," but the full title of which
was the "Council of the sixteen quarters of Paris." Did it
consist of sixteen members, neither more nor less? It is true
that such a Council is mentioned in an account of the Religious Wars by one Nicolas Lefèvre de Lezeau, which treats
of the years from 1585 to 1594 in some detail, and that the
names of the first sixteen members are duly set forth. They
consist of Crucé, Bussy-Leclerc, Louchart, Senault, La

Morlière, La Bruyère, Drouart, Alvequin, Aimonnot, Oudineau, Morin, Debart, Letellier, Jabliet, Messier, and Passart[1]. This is clear enough, but we must add to Lezeau's statement two other pieces of evidence. On February 24, 1591, the "Council" of the sixteen quarters of the city, sent a letter to the Pope which was signed for the whole body (*toute la compagnie*) by eight of their number—Genebrard, Boucher, Aubry, Launoy, Bussy-Leclerc, La Bruyère, Crucé, and Senault. Eight signatories, it may be noted, is rather a large number, if the whole number was only sixteen[2]. Again, a letter of November 20, 1591, addressed to the King of Spain was signed by sixteen signatories who describe themselves as *les gens tenans le Conseil*. The names include Genebrard, Ameline, Louchart, Cromé (who is described as *Conseiller au grand Conseil*), Crucé, Acarie, Launoy (*un des Presidens au Conseil*), and La Bruyère, but they do not include Aubry, Bussy-Leclerc, or Senault. Nor, in the copy of the document given by Pierre de L'Estoile[3], do they include Boucher. Ranke, however, who had seen the original document in the Simancas archives at Paris, draws attention to the signature of Boucher, which makes seventeen signatories. Of course Bussy, Aubry, and Senault may have gone off the Council between the dates of the two letters, but Senault, according to L'Estoile, was the *Seize* of his quarter.

On the whole the right conclusion would seem to be that, if we may trust Lezeau, who was born hardly before 1580, the Council consisted originally of only sixteen members, one for each quarter, but it was afterwards enlarged by the addition of other members. At any rate one thing is certain: in current speech the "Sixteen" denoted the whole body of the more violent leaguers, or *catholiques zélés* as they called themselves—some 30,000 in number.

---

[1] Cimber and Danjou, XIV. 9 ff.
[2] Palma Cayet, *Nov.* II. 412 r⁰.
[3] *Mémoires—Journaux*, v. 136.

NOTE ON DORAT

IT was not till after my paper on *Dorat and the Pléiade* was in type that I had an opportunity of consulting M. Pierre de Nolhac's *Ronsard et l'Humanisme*[1], and as about the same time Professor Pearson kindly directed my attention to an article bearing on Dorat by John Masson in the *Journal of Philology*, XVI (1888), 114 ff., it seemed convenient to incorporate this additional information in a supplementary note. M. de Nolhac's contribution is particularly valuable because he formerly had the intention of dealing with Dorat as a philologist and collected materials for that purpose. To the witnesses to Dorat's merits as a scholar and teacher of scholars that I have cited above he adds Marc-Antoine Muret and the Dutchmen Jan van der Does (Janus Dousa) and William Canter, both of whom were Dorat's pupils. The latter, whose industrious career was cut short at the early age of thirty-two[2], records with approval in his *Novae lectiones*[3] emendations by Dorat in Theocritus, Athenaeus, Propertius, Statius, and Ausonius. And in the little pocket editions of Aeschylus (1580) and Sophocles (1579) which he edited for Plantin he signifies his assent to certain emendations of Dorat's in the *Agamemnon* and the *Philoctetes*.

It is with the *Philoctetes* that Masson's paper is concerned, for he discovered in the British Museum a copy of Turnèbe's edition of Sophocles (1553) which had belonged to Denys Lambin, and in which that scholar has recorded in the margin various emendations suggested by himself or Dorat. Those credited to Dorat number between twenty and thirty, besides some explanatory notes. Jebb, referring to them in his preface to the play, says that they are more or less obvious, but he singles out four for special mention.

In Masson's article reference is made to Lambin's preface to his edition of Lucretius, in which he speaks of having consulted his colleagues Turnèbe and Dorat with regard to his proposed corrections of the text. The passage is quoted by M. de Nolhac (p. 76, n. 1), who also notes that the second book of the *De natura deorum* is dedicated to Ronsard, the fifth to Turnèbe, and the sixth to Dorat (p. 80).

Finally, let me record that M. de Nolhac reproduces a beautiful drawing of Dorat, which he discovered in the Cabinet des Estampes.

---

[1] *Bibl. des Hautes Études*, fasc. 227 (1921).
[2] 1542–1575.
[3] *Novarum lectionum libri quatuor*, Basle, 1564; *libri sex*, Basle, 1566; *libri octo*, Antwerp, 1571.

INDEX